Forensic Testimony

Forensic Testimony
Science, Law and Expert Evidence

C. Michael Bowers

AMSTERDAM • BOSTON • HEIDELBERG • LONDON
NEW YORK • OXFORD • PARIS • SAN DIEGO
SAN FRANCISCO • SINGAPORE • SYDNEY • TOKYO

Academic Press is an imprint of Elsevier

ELSEVIER

Academic Press is an imprint of Elsevier
The Boulevard, Langford Lane, Kidlington, Oxford, OX5 1GB
525 B Street, Suite 1800, San Diego, CA 92101-4495, USA

First published 2014

British Library Cataloguing in Publication Data
A catalogue record for this book is available from the British Library

Library of Congress Cataloging-in-Publication Data
A catalog record for this book is available from the Library of Congress

ISBN: 978-0-12-397005-3

For information on all Academic Press publications
visit our website at store.elsevier.com

Printed and bound in Singapore

14 15 16 17   10 9 8 7 6 5 4 3 2 1

Working together
to grow libraries in
developing countries

www.elsevier.com • www.bookaid.org

*To my dear wife Cynthia. Words are insufficient to explain
how important you are to me.
Thank you.*

Contents

Preface

The use of forensic expert testimony in criminal investigations and judicial proceedings has increased tremendously in the United States over the last 30 years. Approximately 10% of criminal cases in the United States use some form of forensic expertise for either the prosecution or defense litigators. The specialized expertise possessed by a wide spectrum of scientists, forensic examiners, profilers, psychologists, social workers, and medico-legal experts is in demand. How these people work within the judicial and investigatory systems, both for good and bad, is the subject of this book.

There is no "science" regarding how an expert witness can effectively testify in court. All the various types of courtroom participants, including the forensic people, play their roles within the parameters of the judicial system. Forensic experts must realize that the courtroom environment is the antithesis of a scientific forum due to its adversarial nature (within the United States, at least). Legal rules abound for experts to know, and their presentations are primarily based on communication skills and good personal habits. Detailed scientific narrations in the courtroom are generally poorly understood by both the jury and the judge.

This book is a hybrid of forensic expert witnessing information. The first portion is a concise illustration of the legal and organizational information necessary to conduct a forensic investigation and analysis of the evidence for later courtroom presentation. It contains details of the scientific and legal processes in action in the forensic arena and describes methods for providing clear and fair testimony. Multiple authors' points of view of certain subjects are presented to create a broad discussion of topics. Rules of evidence, proper guidelines, and ethical tenets for any forensic expert are described, with a focus on the knowledge base necessary for judicial use.

The second portion is particularly unique to the literature regarding forensic experts as it exposes the damage that experts and their testimony have contributed to wrongful convictions and incarcerations. It also narrates where expert mistakes and conclusions in criminal courts have destroyed the lives of an unacceptable number of criminal defendants. Whether any actual "acceptable number" of allowable mistakes exists in any judicial system depends on one's tolerance for injustice.

The beginning and ending chapters of this book are exemplary. In the Introduction, the Hon. Harry T. Edwards, the co-chairman of the 2009 National Academy of Sciences report "Strengthening Forensic Science in the United States: A Path Forward," speaks to the resistance to graded and open denials of problems by certain forensic experts after the report was published. The final chapter by Wendy Koen showcases the personal fight individuals in the United States have had in repudiating biased and unscientific evidence and the resulting wrongful convictions. She acted as both investigator and appellate litigator in *People of California vs. William Richards*. Her chapter goes beyond a mere litany of scientific inadequacies by expert witnesses and vividly focuses on the U.S. appellate courts' reliance on procedural minutiae and their hackneyed legalistic opinion to support their construct of "justice." Scientific acumen and understanding the application of forensic advances and failures were ignored in favor of the "stare decisis" tradition (e.g., the reliance on previous cases for their decision making).

There is no use sugar-coating the fact that poor performance and faulty forensic methods and interpretations contributed to nearly 50% of wrongful convictions, resulting in personal tragedies for the criminal defendants. This book is meant to educate and prepare anyone performing expert services in the forensic arena for how to avoid joining this fiasco playing out in the legal system of the United States today.

The intended audiences for FT are those men and women currently training for forensic careers and those already practicing and admitted as court experts. The staid stereotype of bookish, soft-science experts occasionally testifying is a vanished breed. They have been supplanted by the media and the courts with professionals specifically educated in the scientifically based analysis of forensic evidence AND in the communication of their scientifically established techniques and conclusions. Their audiences are investigators, lawyers of the prosecution and defense bars, the judge presiding in court proceedings, and the nation's appellate court systems. Juries given the responsibility to determine civil liability and guilt or innocence of a criminal defendant must be honestly informed by expert witnesses and protected from junk science advocates who masquerade as scientists. Forensic testimony is a field that impacts constitutional freedoms and has life and death implications. Forensic experts should consider themselves members of a professional occupation that requires significant and continuing preparation, training, and a high degree of professional and moral integrity to meet these responsibilities.

> *These things ... have been communicated for the serious reader. Many other things could have been brought forth and many other things have already been well described, which I thought I should not repeat...Goodbye reader*

Athanasius Kircher S.J., *China Illustrated* (1667)

C. Michael Bowers, DDS, JD
June 6, 2013
Associate Professor of Clinical Dentistry, Ostrow School of Dentistry, University of Southern California, Ventura, CA USA

Foreword

A few forensic science specialties that have previously and routinely presented scientific testimony to the courts appear to be on the verge of imminent extinction. Judges and juries have been incapable of filtering the forensic science disciplines that are based in reliable objective science versus those that are composed of pseudoscience, or purely junk science. The admission of bad science to the courts has resulted in many wrongful convictions. *Forensic Testimony,* edited by Dr. C. Michael Bowers, is essential reading for those that are associated with forensic scientific testimony in the courts. Judges, litigators, forensic experts, and leaders of forensic disciplines will all find this book to be valuable in the quest for understanding the composition of reliable and valid scientific evidence that is necessary for the justice system. In his book Dr. Bowers and the accompanying authors examine the root cause for some forensic specialties to resist science. Unfortunately, and too often, proponents of a debunked invalid model have perpetuated acceptance of junk science into the courtroom. Dr. Bowers explains the origins of how flawed scientific evidence has led to wrongful convictions.

I met Dr. Bowers over 25 years ago while in Kentucky as we both were challenging our board certification in forensic odontology. Dr. Bowers was an early skeptic of bite mark analysis as it was being used to establish a connection between a defendant and a crime based on pattern analysis. In the 1990s Dr. Bowers published papers calling for scientific evidence to support the claims of those testifying in court in his own specialty of forensic odontology. Dr. Bowers has been a strong advocate and respected by all for the use of scientifically based forensic science testimony in the courts. He personally has been instrumental in many of the dozens of exonerations to date of the wrongfully convicted that were based on bite mark evidence. Dr. Bowers, myself and a few others were instrumental in a 1999 study of board certified bite mark experts that demonstrated a false positive rate of 63.5% when attempting to identify a biter among a lineup of four unknowns. Although the courts and law enforcement authorities knew this information, bite mark experts were still called on and allowed to testify.

Today, the public and governmental agencies are calling for forensic science reform for those forensic techniques that are not supported by science. This national action blossomed in 2009 when the National Academy of Science was mandated by Congress to review the forensic sciences. The report delivered a scathing review of many of the forensic science disciplines that lack science to support their opinions. Dr. Bowers's academic publications are the most cited of any forensic dentist in the National Academy of Science publication titled "Strengthening Forensic Science in the United States." His new book will be required reading for those interested in how some pseudoscience corrupted the courts and the requirements of forensic disciplines and experts that are necessary to provide scientific testimony in the courthouse.

David C. Averill, DDS, DABFO
Past President, American Board of Forensic Odontology
Past President, American Society of Forensic Odontology

Acknowledgements

The process of writing a book on forensic testimony is a daunting task. A major difficulty is the general lack of information written by the forensic community itself. The forensic profession seems to rely on the lawyers and judges to create what is available for reference on the subject. To remedy this disconnect, *Forensic Testimony: Science, Law and Expert Evidence* has sought out individuals who contributed their wisdom in science and law to present information that is both related to legal practice and scientific standards and ethics. Because of them, this book reflects the reality of forensic expert activities involving both scientific analysis and the US court criminal court.

I would like to thank the following individuals who, although not directly contributing to this book, are responsible for laying the ground work for the ongoing discussions on the legal and empirical studies necessary to improve forensic science testimony and criminal law outcomes in the US. These standouts are:

Michael J. Saks, Regents Professor of Law and Psychology, Sandra Day O'Connor College of Law, Arizona State University.

James E. Starrs, Professor of Law and Forensic Science, The George Washington University Law School.

Peter Neufeld, co-founder, with Barry Scheck, of the New York-based Innocence Project; IP Senior Staff attorney Vanessa Potkin and Chris Fabricant, Director of the IP's Strategic Litigation Unit; the IP staff and in particular IP Forensic Policy Advocate Sarah Chu who has been invaluable in providing me litigation data and current events about forensic reform proposals in the courts and the US Congress. Finally, Paul Cates, director of the IP's communication department for his generous reprint permissions.

Vanzetta Williams, staff attorney, Mississippi Office of Capital Post Conviction Counsel, Jackson, MS.

Justin Brooks, Director of the California Innocence Project (CIP), and CIP staff attorneys and Case Western Law School faculty Jan Stiglitz, Allisa Bjerkhoel, Michael Semanchik, Alex Simpson, and Mario Conte.

Tucker Carrington, Director of the Mississippi Innocence Project, staff attorney Will McIntosh and Program Director Carol Mockbee.

Criminal defense counsel and law school faculty from around the country with whom I have collaborated in casework over the years: Sandra Babcock (Northwestern Law School); Cary Clennon (DC); Craig Cooley (North Carolina Center on Actual Innocence); Joseph Flood (VA) and Lauren Kaeseberg (ILL). There are unnamed others who are examples of unrelenting determination to protect all of us from wrongful convictions and incarceration by misapplied and bad forensic science.

The last group:

The investigative reporters and their staff, who have taken true forensic facts from cases and empirical research, ignored the forensic blusterings of a desperate few and published numerous articles showing the failures of forensic sciences and in particular, bitemark identification.

Radley Balko (HuffPost), Steve Mills (Chicago Tribune), Pulitzer Prize recipient Maurice Possley (Senior Researcher for the National Registry of Exonerations), Amanda Myers (Associated Press, OH) and Mark Hansen (American Bar Association). Honorable Harry T. Edwards, Court of Appeals for DC and Professor Jay Koehler, Northwestern School of Law, for their generous reprint permissions.

Introduction

Jurimetrics Journal
Fall, 2010

Reflection

THE NATIONAL ACADEMY OF SCIENCES REPORT ON FORENSIC SCIENCES: WHAT IT MEANS FOR THE BENCH AND BAR

Harry T. Edwards[1a]

Editor's Introduction

On May 6, 2010, the Honorable Harry T. Edwards delivered a presentation to the Conference on *The Role of the Court in an Age of Developing Science & Technology.* Sponsored by the Superior Court of the District of Columbia, the conference was held in Washington, D.C. on May 6-7, 2010. *Jurimetrics* is pleased to present the text of Judge Edwards's lecture.

CITATION: Harry T. Edwards, The National Academy of Sciences Report on Forensic Sciences: What it Means for the Bench and Bar, 51 Jurimetrics J. 1-15 (2010).

On February 18, 2009, after more than two years of work, the Committee on Identifying the Needs of the Forensic Science Community at the National Academy of Sciences (NAS) issued a report entitled, "Strengthening Forensic Science in the United States: A Path Forward."[1] The committee was composed of a diverse and accomplished group of professionals. Seven of the 17 committee members are prominent professionals in the forensic science community, with extensive experience in forensic analysis and practice; 11 members of the committee are trained scientists (with expertise in physics, chemistry, biology, engineering, biostatistics, statistics, and medicine); 10 members of the committee have Ph.D.'s, 2 have M.D.'s, 5 have J.D.'s, and one has an M.S. in chemistry.

Because of our extensive research and countless interviews, the committee's project involved an extraordinary amount of time. In addition, there were many hours of committee meetings, which involved deliberations between forensic analysts and

---

[1a]The Honorable Harry T. Edwards is Senior Circuit Judge and Chief Judge Emeritus for the United States Court of Appeals for the D.C. Circuit. Currently Judge Edwards is a Visiting Professor of Law at New York University School of Law. He also served as co-chair for the Committee on Identifying the Needs of the Forensic Science Community, The National Academy of Sciences.

[1]COMM. ON IDENTIFYING THE NEEDS OF THE FORENSIC SCI. CMTY. ET AL., NAT'L RESEARCH COUNCIL OF THE NAT'L ACADS., STRENGTHENING FORENSIC SCIENCE IN THE UNITED STATES: A PATH FORWARD (2009) [hereinafter NRC Report].

practitioners, experts in the physical and life sciences, a former federal prosecutor, a defense attorney, a crime lab director, a medical examiner, an engineer, statisticians, educators, and a judge. Our interactions were challenging and fruitful; in the end, despite our differing professional perspectives, the committee was unanimous in its findings and recommendations.

With the benefit of hindsight, I can now say that the substance of the committee's report was not difficult to write. The problems that plague the forensic science community have been well understood for quite some time by thoughtful and skilled forensic professionals, and their views and concerns were well known to us. For example, in 2003, when he was President of the American Academy of Forensic Sciences (AAFS), Kenneth Melson, a former prosecutor and now Director of the Bureau of Alcohol, Tobacco, Firearms and Explosives, wrote:

> *[M]ore research is needed in the techniques and science already in use. With the importance of forensic science to truth and justice, the science employed and relied upon by judges and juries must be valid. It does not matter how well forensic scientists abide by testing protocols or how reliable the techniques are, if the underlying science does not actually reveal what the expert says it does. Method validation studies and new research must be ongoing even in the areas of traditional forensic science disciplines. Justice demands good science and we have an obligation to provide it. We can no longer expect the courts or public to accept the truth of our science merely because we say it is good. In order to maintain the integrity of both the science and the justice system, we must prove that it is so. Moreover, we cannot overlook the fact that scientific evidence was presented at many of the trials where innocent people were convicted and later exonerated by DNA. The evidence in many of the trials showed associations between the defendants and the victims or crime scenes. While modern day science is exonerating the innocent, it is also showing us that some inferences drawn from scientific associations in the past were wrong. The use of DNA to exonerate wrongly convicted persons has certainly taught us lessons about forensic science in general and underscores the importance of continuing research.[2]*

Thomas Bohan, the most recent Past President of the American Academy of Forensic Sciences, published a similar statement earlier this year.[3]

When Congress passed legislation in 2005 directing the NAS to create an independent committee to study the forensic science community, it did so at the urging of the Consortium of Forensic Science Organizations.[4] The legislation establishing our committee was, in effect, a response to a *call for help* from forensic science professionals.

---

[2]Kenneth E. Melson, *President's Editorial–The Journey to Justice*, 48 J. FORENSIC SCI. 705, 707 (2003).

[3]*See* Thomas L. Bohan, *President's Editorial: Strengthening Forensic Science: A Way Station on the Journey to Justice*, 55 J. FORENSIC SCI. 5, 5-7 (2010).

[4]Science, Justice, Commerce and Related Agencies Appropriations Act of 2006, Pub. L. No. 109-108, 119 Stat. 2290 (2005).

The committee spent an enormous amount of time listening to testimony from and reviewing materials published by numerous experts, including forensic practitioners, heads of public and private laboratories, directors of medical examiner and coroner offices, scientists, scholars, educators, government officials, members of the legal profession, and law enforcement officials. Not only did we examine how the forensic disciplines operate, we also carefully considered any peer-reviewed, scientific research purporting to support the validity and reliability of existing forensic disciplines. Additionally, we invited experts in each discipline to refer us to any pertinent research. Committee members and staff spent countless hours reviewing these materials. And before the report's release, it was peer reviewed by outside experts in the fields of science, law, and forensic practice.

I started the NAS project with no skepticism regarding the forensic science community. Rather, I assumed, as I suspect many of my judicial colleagues do, that the forensic disciplines are well grounded in scientific methodology and that crime laboratories and forensic practitioners follow proven practices that ensure the validity and reliability of forensic evidence offered in court. I was surprisingly mistaken in what I assumed.

Our committee found that although there are many dedicated and skilled forensic professionals, the quality of practice in the forensic disciplines varies widely, and the conclusions reached by forensic practitioners are not always reliable. The reasons for this include:

- the paucity of scientific research to confirm the validity and reliability of forensic disciplines and establish quantifiable measures of uncertainty in the conclusions of forensic analyses;
- the paucity of research programs on human observer bias and sources of human error in forensic examinations;
- the absence of scientific and applied research focused on new technology and innovation;
- the lack of autonomy of crime laboratories;
- the absence of rigorous, *mandatory* certification requirements for practitioners;
- the absence of uniform, *mandatory* accreditation programs for laboratories;
- the failure to adhere to robust performance standards;
- the failure of forensic experts to use standard terminology in reporting on and testifying about the results of forensic science investigations;
- the lack of effective oversight; and
- a gross shortage of adequate training and continuing education for practitioners.

These findings[5] and the committee's accompanying recommendations[6] have been taken very seriously by those with an understanding and interest in forensic science.

---

[5]*See* NRC REPORT, *supra* note 1, at 14-19.
[6]*Id*. at 19-33.

Just after our report issued, Carol Henderson, who preceded Dr. Bohan as President of the American Academy of Forensic Sciences, said:

> *We have been presented with an opportunity to make forensic science serve justice even more reliably and effectively. This is the time to build better "forensic science" ....*
>
> *The report identified shortcomings in research, education, and standards of practice in the Nation's crime labs. In-depth research and analysis of options leading to strategic policy and implementation plans is needed.[7]*

The overall reaction to the report really has been extraordinary. Moreover, interest in the report's findings and recommendations has not waned during the 14 months since the date of issuance. Why is that? Perhaps it is because no one has meaningfully refuted the committee's finding that "[w]ith the exception of nuclear DNA analysis, ... no forensic method has been rigorously shown to have the capacity to consistently, and with a high degree of certainty, demonstrate a connection between evidence and a specific individual or source."[8]

The good news is that important developments are now underway to help the forensic science community get its house in order:

- The Senate Judiciary Committee is pursuing hearings aimed at corrective legislation.
- The White House National Science and Technology Council has chartered a Subcommittee on Forensic Science to address problems identified in the report.
- The National Institute of Justice (NIJ), the research arm of the Department of Justice, has launched an effort to promote new research on forensic sciences, including a recent grant of $866,764 to UCLA to conduct a comprehensive study of error rates in latent fingerprint evidence.[9]
- In September 2009, the American Academy of Forensic Sciences issued a press release saying: "[a]fter extensive consideration, discussion, and drafting, the Board [of AAFS] unanimously voted to support the recommendations of the NAS Report ...."[10]
- In March of this year, *Nature*, the prestigious international journal of science, endorsed the committee's report.[11]

---

[7]*Strengthening Forensic Science in the United States: The Role of the National Institute of Standards and Technology: Hearing Before the Subcomm. on Tech. and Innovation of the H. Comm. on Sci. and Tech.*, 111th Cong. 17-18 (2009) (statement of Carol E. Henderson, Immediate Past President, American Academy of Forensic Sciences).

[8]NRC REPORT, *supra* note 1, at 7.

[9]News Release, Lauri Gavel, UCLA Newsroom, UCLA Professors Awarded Major Federal Grant to Study Error Rates in Fingerprint Evidence (Feb. 11, 2010), http://newsroom.ucla.eduportal/ucla/two-ucla-professors-awarded-national-153642.aspx.

[10]Press Release, Am. Acad. of Forensic Sci., The Am. Acad. of Forensic Sci. Approves Position Statement in Response to the Nat'l Acad. of Sciences' "Forensic Needs" Report (Sept. 4, 2009) (on file with author).

[11]*Science in Court*, 464 NATURE 325, 325 (2010).

- The Board of Directors of the American Statistical Association recently voted to endorse the recommendations of the report, "recogniz[ing] the pivotal role of forensic science in our judicial system and cit[ing] the value of statistical methods and research to improve forensic methods."[12]
- And there also have been countless media reports, articles, and conferences describing the problems that plague the forensic science community.

These developments are encouraging.

From my vantage point, the response to the report has been very positive and I have seen a ground swell of support in favor of major reforms to correct the ills of the forensic science community. I have encountered a few pockets of resistance, however, to what I believe are the rather obvious implications of the committee's findings. Recently, I had an opportunity to read several briefs filed by various U.S. Attorneys' offices in which my name has been invoked in support of the Government's assertion that the committee's findings should not be taken into account in judicial assessments of the admissibility of certain forensic evidence. One brief, for example, asserts:

> [T]he NRC Forensic Science Report does not support the conclusion that finger-print evidence is inadmissible under the Frye calculus. In fact, the Honorable Harry T. Edwards, Co-Chair for the NRC Forensic Science Report, has stated on the public record that the report is not intended to affect the admissibility of any forensic evidence.[13]

This is a blatant misstatement of the truth. I have never said that the committee's report is "not intended to affect the admissibility of forensic evidence," and I have never publicly addressed the "*Frye* calculus." To the degree that I have commented on the effect of the report on admissibility determinations, I have said something quite close to the opposite of what these briefs assert.

What is true is that, in February 2009, when the committee report was released. I said that judges would continue to follow established law. The committee's charge was not law reform and, to be circumspect, I did not offer my own views on that subject. But there is a critical difference between saying that judges will continue to apply existing legal standards, like the *Frye*[14] analysis, and saying that the report should have no effect on how judges apply those standards. I most certainly never said, or even suggested, that judges should not take into account the new information provided by the report in assessing the validity and reliability of forensic evidence while making admissibility determinations. Claims to the contrary are without basis in fact and utterly absurd.

---

[12]Press Release, Am. Statistical Ass'n, Am. Statistical Ass'n Supports Major Reforms of the Nation's Forensic Sci. Sys. (May 3, 2010) (on file with author), *available at* http:// www.amstat.org/about/pressreleases/ASASupportsMajorReformsofForensicScience.

[13]Government's Opposition to Defendant's Motion to Exclude Expert Testimony Concerning Latent Fingerprint Evidence at 3, United States v. Faison, No. 2008-CF2-16636 (D.C. Super. Ct. Feb. 19, 2010).

[14]Frye v. United States, 293 F. 1013 (D.C. Cir. 1923).

In the public statement that I made when the report was issued, I said,

> *[T]he committee's report does not mean to offer any judgments on any cases in the judicial system. The report does not assess past criminal convictions, nor does it speculate about pending or future cases. And the report offers no proposals for law reform. That was beyond our charge. Each case in the criminal justice system must be decided on the record before the court pursuant to the applicable law, controlling precedent, and governing rules of evidence. The question whether forensic evidence in a particular case is admissible under applicable law is not coterminous with the question whether there are studies confirming the scientific validity and reliability of a forensic science discipline.[15]*

During the question and answer session that followed. I clarified that law reform was not part of the committee's charge, saying:

> *I think judges will continue to follow the law as it is. We're not proposing law reform. Will there be law reform? We don't know. Might some people propose it. I don't know. Maybe. But there is no law reform proposal here; so judges will continue to do what they have been doing.[16]*

In my testimony before the Senate Judiciary Committee in March 2009, I suggested–contrary to the mischaracterization of my position in the Government's briefs–that "courts [will] take the findings of the committee regarding the scientific foundation of particular types of forensic science evidence into account when considering the admissibility of such evidence in a particular case."[17] As I explained to the Senate committee, because the report presents "findings about the current status of the scientific foundation of particular ***7** areas of forensic science," it would be "no surprise if the report is cited authoritatively" by the courts in their assessment of particular cases.[18]

Why was that my prediction? Because it seemed quite obvious, at least to me, that if a particular forensic methodology or practice, once thought to be scientifically valid, has been revealed to lack validation or reliability, no prosecutor would offer evidence derived from that discipline without taking the new information into account, and no judge would continue to admit such evidence without considering the new information regarding the scientific validity and reliability of its source. Nothing in *Frye*[19] or *Daubert*[20] commands unyielding adherence to past methodologies or

---

[15]Honorable Harry T. Edwards, Co-Chair, Forensic Sci. Comm., Opening Statement, 4 (Feb. 18, 2009). http:// www.nationalacademies.org/includes/OSEdwards.pdf.

[16]The Nat'l Acads., *'Badly Fragmented' Forensic Science System Needs Overhaul*, (Feb. 18, 2009), http://nationalacademies.org/morenews/20090218.html.

[17]*The Need to Strengthen Forensic Science in the United States: The National Academy of Science's Report on a Path Forward: Hearing Before the S. Comm. on the Judiciary*, 111th Cong. 10 (2009) (statement of Hon. Harry T. Edwards, C.J. Emeritus, D.C. Circuit, and Co-Chair, Comm. on Identifying the Needs of the Forensic Science Community).

[18]*Id.*

[19]*Frye*, 293 F. at 1013-14.

[20]Daubert v. Merrell Dow Pharm, Inc., 509 U.S. 579 (1993).

practices once they are found wanting. As one state court in a *Frye* jurisdiction aptly observed, "Science moves inexorably forward and hypotheses or methodologies once considered sacrosanct are modified or discarded. The judicial system, with its search for the closest approximation to the 'truth,' must accommodate this ever-changing scientific landscape."[21] The Supreme Court made the same point in *Daubert* when it reminded us that "[s]cientific conclusions are subject to perpetual revision."[22] I really do not understand how any jurist could reasonably think otherwise.

If courts blindly follow precedent that rests on unfounded scientific premises, this will lead to unjust results. Nothing in established law compels this course. Therefore, when the report was released and I said that judges must continue to follow the law, I did not mean to suggest that judges would apply existing law without taking into account the findings in the report that raise serious doubts about the validity and reliability of certain forensic disciplines and practices. Our system of justice demands more than this. What I expected is that judges would, within the existing evidentiary regimes, consider the report's findings and recommendations.

A judgment recently issued by Judge Nancy Gertner in the United States District Court for the District of Massachusetts provides what I believe is a reasonable and balanced account of the committee's 2009 report:

> *While the [NRC] report does not speak to admissibility or inadmissibility in a given case, it raised profound questions that need to be carefully examined in every case prior to trial: "(1) the extent to which a particular forensic discipline is founded on a reliable scientific methodology that gives it the capacity to accurately analyze evidence and report findings and (2) the extent to which practitioners in a particular forensic discipline rely on human interpretation that could be tainted by error, the threat of bias, or the absence of sound operational procedures and robust performance standards."*
>
> *The Report noted that these fundamental questions have not been "satisfactorily dealt with in judicial decisions pertaining to the admissibility" of evidence ....*
>
> **8 In the past, the admissibility of this kind of evidence was effectively presumed, largely because of its pedigree—the fact that it had been admitted for decades. As such, counsel rarely challenged it, and if it were challenged, it was rarely excluded or limited.*
>
> *The [NRC] report suggests a different calculus—that admissibility of such evidence ought not to be presumed; that it has to be carefully examined in each case, and tested in the light of the NAS concerns, the concerns of Daubert/Kumho case law, and Rule 702 of the Federal Rules of Evidence.*[23]

---

[21]State v. Behn, 868 A.2d 329, 343 (N.J. Super. Ct. App. Div. 2005).

[22]*Daubert*, 509 U.S. at 597.

[23]Procedural Order: Trace Evidence at 2-3, United States v. Oliveira, Crim. No. 08-10104 (D. Mass. Mar. 8, 2010) (quoting COMM. ON IDENTIFYING THE NEEDS OF THE FORENSIC SCI. CMTY. ET AL., STRENGTHENING FORENSIC SCIENCE IN THE UNITED STATES: A PATH FORWARD S-7 (2009) (Prepublication Copy Feb. 2009) [hereinafter NRC REPORT Prepublication Copy]).

As Judge Gertner recognizes, new and better scientific data helps judges assess the reliability of forensic evidence to ensure that it serves, rather than defeats, the ends of justice. The information amassed by the committee regarding hair comparison provides a noteworthy example of such new data. The committee's report states that "testimony linking microscopic hair analysis with particular defendants is highly unreliable."[24] We now know that hair comparisons without mitochondrial DNA are highly questionable. A number of people whose convictions were based in part on faulty hair comparisons have been exonerated by DNA testing. A Federal Bureau of Investigation (FBI) publication reviewed by the committee stated that subsequent DNA testing proved that hairs did not match in 11 percent of the cases in which hair examiners had previously declared two hairs to be "similar."[25] Surely this new data on hair comparisons would be highly relevant under existing law in any judge's assessment of the admissibility of such evidence.

Bullet lead comparisons offer another example. Comparative bullet lead analysis, or CBLA, "compares trace chemicals found in bullets at crime scenes with ammunition found in the possession of a suspect."[26] This forensic technique was used for many years, until a retired FBI examiner began questioning the procedure.[27] The FBI consequently asked the NAS to review the technique. The NRC report, published in 2004, severely undercut CBLA.[28] The report found that the available data did not support any expert claim that a crime bullet came from a particular box of ammunition. In the wake of the National Academy's report, several state courts excluded CBLA evidence, finding that because the forensic technique was based on erroneous scientific foundations, ***9** CBLA no longer satisfied the requirements of *Frye* for the admissibility of scientific expert testimony.[29]

The point here is simple: *When scientific methodologies once considered sacrosanct are modified or discredited, the judicial system must accommodate the changed scientific landscape.*

Let me turn now to the report itself and highlight a few points made there to underscore the problems to which I have alluded.

---

[24]NRC REPORT, *supra* note 1, at 161 (footnote omitted).

[25]*Id.* at 47 (citing M. Houck & B. Budowle, *Correlation of Microscopic and Mitochondrial DNA Hair Comparisons*, 47 J. FORENSIC SCI. 964, 964-67 (2002)).

[26]Paul C. Giannelli, *Daubert and Forensic Science: The Pitfalls of Law Enforcement Control of Scientific Research* 35 (Case Research Paper Series in Legal Studies, Working Paper No. 2010-6, 2010), *available at* http:// ssrn.com/abstract=1568904.

[27]*Id.* (describing retired FBI examiner William Tobin).

[28]COMM. ON SCIENTIFIC ASSESSMENT OF BULLET LEAD ELEMENTAL COMPOSITION COMPARISON, NAT'L RESEARCH COUNCIL OF THE NAT'L ACADS., FORENSIC ANALYSIS: WEIGHING BULLET LEAD EVIDENCE 109 (2004).

[29]*See* Clemons v. State, 896 A.2d 1059, 1078 (Md. 2006); State v. Behn, 868 A.2d 329, 344 (N.J. Super. Ct. App. Div. 2005); *see also* Blackwell v. Wyeth, 971 A.2d 235, 243 (Md. 2009) (describing *Clemons* as a case where the court "consider[ed] whether a theory, which had been accepted in the scientific and legal communities, continue[d] to meet the [*Frye*] standard"). CBLA evidence has also been excluded in *Daubert* jurisdictions in the wake of the 2004 report and other new studies criticizing CBLA. *See* Ragland v. Commonwealth, 191 S.W.3d 569, 578-80 (Ky. 2006).

1. *Science*

I think that the most important part of our committee's report is its call for real science to support the forensic disciplines. Simply increasing the number of staff within existing crime laboratories will not solve the principal problems of the forensic science community. What is needed is interdisciplinary, peer-reviewed, scientific research to determine the validity and reliability of existing disciplines and to achieve technological advancements. What we are talking about is adding a culture of "science" to the forensic science community. From what I have seen, we have a long way to go.

2. *Subjective Interpretations, Exaggerated Testimony, and a Paucity of Research*

Often in criminal prosecutions and civil litigation, forensic evidence is offered to support a claim that an evidentiary specimen is a "match" to a particular individual or other source. But, as I have already said, with the exception of nuclear DNA analysis, no forensic method has been rigorously shown to have the capacity to consistently, and with a high degree of certainty, demonstrate a connection between evidence and a specific individual or source. Yet, for years, the courts have been led to believe that disciplines such as fingerprinting stand on par with nuclear DNA analysis. Indeed, a noted FBI fingerprint expert testified in federal court that "the error rate for fingerprint comparison is essentially zero," and his testimony was credited with approval in later cases.[30]

*10 The committee's report rejects as scientifically implausible any claims that fingerprint analyses have "zero error rates."[31] We also found a dearth of scientific research to establish limits of performance, to ascertain quantifiable measures of uncertainty, and to address the impact of the sources of variability and potential bias in fingerprint examinations and in other forensic disciplines that rely on subjective assessments of matching characteristics.

One of the most telling moments for me during the committee's hearings occurred when I heard the testimony of an expert fingerprint analyst who is a member of the Scientific Working Group on Friction Ridge Analysis, Study, and Technology. At one point in his testimony, he was asked what the scientific basis was for determining a "match" in prints when the examiner has only a partial or smudged print. The expert did not hesitate in conceding that the "research has yet to be done." In April 2009, at a major conference on forensic science at the Sandra Day O'Connor College of Law at Arizona State University,[32] the Director of the National Institute of Justice (NIJ) was asked why NIJ had not funded any serious studies to determine the validity of fingerprint analyses. He acknowledged the dearth of research and urged everyone to be patient as NIJ tried to develop some "foundational studies." Eight months later,

---

[30]United States v. Havvard, 260 F.3d 597, 599 (7th Cir. 2001). In overstating the expert's testimony in *Havvard*, subsequent cases give rise to the misconception that the forensic discipline of fingerprinting is infallible. *See* NRC REPORT, *supra* note 1, at 103-04. *See, e.g.*, United States v. John, 597 F.3d 263, 275 (5th Cir. 2010); United States v. Crisp, 324 F.3d 261, 269 (4th Cir. 2003); State v. Escobido-Ortiz, 126 P.3d 402, 412 (Haw. Ct. App. 2005).

[31]NRC REPORT, *supra* note 1, at 142.

[32]Michael J. Saks, *Symposium: Forensic Science for the 21st Century, Foreword*, 50 JURIMETRICS J. 1, 3 (2009).

UCLA was awarded almost $900,000 to conduct a comprehensive study of error rates in latent fingerprint evidence.[33]

The committee found that, as is too often the case, when there is no good scientific basis to support a forensic discipline and experts cannot quantify certainty and uncertainty, the testimony that they offer is not infrequently exaggerated, and sometimes even fabricated. Not too long ago, a story in the *San Jose Mercury* reported that for years, San Jose police never told anyone when fingerprint technicians could not agree on whether a suspect's prints matched those taken from the crime scene.[34] Instead, the police department's Central Identification Unit generated a report indicating that two technicians agreed that the suspect's prints had been positively identified, while omitting that a third technician dissented. Stories like this are appalling and disheartening, to say the least.

Another serious concern is contextual bias. In one study, for example, fingerprint examiners were asked to analyze fingerprints that, unknown to them, they had analyzed previously in their careers. Contextual biasing was introduced–that is, examiners were told that the "suspect confessed to the crime" or the "suspect was in police custody at the time of the crime." In 25 percent of the examinations that included contextual manipulation, the examiners reached conclusions that were different from the results they had previously reached.[35]

*11 3. Inconsistent Practices in Crime Laboratories

In recent years, the integrity of crime laboratories has been called into question, with some heavily publicized cases highlighting (1) unqualified practitioners, (2) sometimes lax standards that have generated questionable or fraudulent evidence, and (3) the absence of quality control measures to detect questionable evidence. In one notorious case, the Texas Department of Public Safety confirmed serious inadequacies in the procedures used by the Houston Police Department Crime Laboratory, including routine failure to run essential scientific controls, to take adequate measures to prevent contamination of samples, to adequately document work performed and results obtained, and to follow correct procedures for computing statistical frequencies.[36] There have been a number of other dismaying reports about crime labs–most recently, the San Francisco drug lab[37]–that suffer from problems like those uncovered in Houston.

4. Scientific Working Groups or SWGs

There are a number of scientific working groups, or SWGs, for forensic disciplines. For example, the Scientific Working Group for the Analysis of Seized Drugs

---

[33]Gavel, *supra* note 9.

[34]Tracey Kaplan, *Fingerprint-Match Doubts: S.J. Police Reverse Policy Cops Had Withheld Dissenting Views*, SAN JOSE MERCURY NEWS, Mar. 8, 2009, at 1A.

[35]NRC REPORT, *supra* note 1, at 123 (citing Itiel E. Dror & David Charlton, *Why Experts Make Errors*, 56 J. FORENSIC IDENTIFICATION 600, 600-14 (2006)).

[36]NRC REPORT, *supra* note 1, at 44-45, 193 (footnotes omitted).

[37]*See, e.g.*, Jaxon Van Derbeken. *Lab Tech's Behavior Worried Prosecutor: Assistant D.A. Complained about Her Months Before Drug Scandal Broke*, S.F. CHRON., Apr. 15, 2010, at A1.

(SWGDRUG) recommends minimum standards for the forensic examination of seized drugs. The chair of SWGDRUG testified before the committee and explained how his SWG operates. His answers to my questions indicated that, as a general matter, SWGs are of questionable value. Why? Because:

- SWG committees meet irregularly and have no clear or regular sources of funding.
- There are no clear standards in place to determine who gains membership on SWG committees.
- Neither SWGs, nor their recommendations, are mandated by any federal or state law or regulation.
- SWG recommendations are not enforceable.
- A number of SWG guidelines are too general and vague to be of any great practical use.
- SWG committees have no way of knowing whether state or local agencies even endorse the standards.
- Complaints are not filed when a practitioner violates an SWG standard.
- SWG committees do not attempt to measure the impact of their standards by formal study or survey.

In other words, there is nothing to indicate that the standards are routinely followed and enforced in a way to ensure best practices in the forensic science community. Problems such as these merely highlight some glaring weaknesses in the forensic science community. The report illuminates many more problems.

*12 The work of the forensic science community is critically important in our system of criminal justice. Forensic science experts and evidence are routinely used in the service of the criminal justice system. Therefore, it matters a great deal whether an expert is qualified to testify about forensic evidence and whether the evidence is sufficiently reliable to merit a fact finder's reliance on the truth that it purports to support.

In June 2009, the Supreme Court issued a judgment in *Melendez-Diaz v. Massachusetts*, a case involving a drug conviction in a Massachusetts state court.[38] The prosecutor in *Melendez-Diaz* introduced written certificates prepared by state laboratory analysts confirming that material seized by police and connected to the defendant was cocaine of a certain quantity.[39] The crime lab analysts were not called to testify.[40] The defendant claimed that the admission of the lab certificates violated his Sixth Amendment right to confront the analysts who prepared the certificates.[41] The Supreme Court held that because the laboratory certificates were testimonial statements against the defendant, the defendant was entitled to confront the persons giving this testimony at trial.[42]

---

[38]Melendez-Diaz v. Massachusetts, 129 S. Ct. 2527 (2009).
[39]*Id.* at 2530-31.
[40]*Id.* at 2531.
[41]*Id.*
[42]*Id.* at 2532.

This holding would have been enough to decide the case; however, in one of the prosecution's briefs, the state had urged that laboratory analysts should not be made to testify, because forensic science evidence is the product "of neutral, scientific testing."[43] The Court went out of its way to reject this claim. First, the Court noted that "[s]erious deficiencies have been found in the forensic evidence used in criminal trials."[44]

The Court then pointed out, by way of example, that:

> *The affidavits submitted by the [forensic] analysts [in the Melendez-Diaz case] contained only the bare-bones statement that "[t]he substance was found to contain: Cocaine." At the time of trial, [the defendant] did not know what tests the analysts performed, whether those tests were routine, and whether interpreting their results required the exercise of judgment or the use of skills that the analysts may not have possessed.[45]*

Finally, the Court cited the finding from our committee's report that "[t]he forensic science system, encompassing both research and practice, has serious problems that can only be addressed by a national commitment to overhaul the current structure that supports the forensic science community in this country."[46]

*13 The Court's statements in *Melendez-Diaz* are hardly laudatory of our existing forensic science system. It is also particularly noteworthy that the Supreme Court did not say that the availability of cross-examination in criminal trials will cure the ills of the forensic science community. Rather, the Court said that "*[c]onfrontation is one means of assuring accurate forensic analysis.*"[47] In other words, cross-examination is a minimal constitutional safeguard that helps to test the reliability of forensic evidence that is offered in criminal trials. But, it is far from adequate.

There is an inherent dilemma in the committee's report–one that it really does not address–better science to determine the validity and reliability of forensic disciplines will take time. So there is a question as to how we can ensure better practices before we know whether a particular forensic discipline is founded on good science. For example, if we cannot quantify measures of uncertainty and we do not know sources of variability, how can we establish best practices? The UCLA study on fingerprint error rates hopefully will address some of these issues, at least with respect to that discipline. To my knowledge, no one seriously doubts that we should require mandatory certification of practitioners and mandatory accreditation of labs, but we have yet to decide by whom and on what terms.

As scientific studies are being conducted, there are three recommendations relating to forensic *practice* that I am sure will have salutary effects, even in the short term. The first is the committee's recommendation requiring forensic experts to use standardized, honest, and clear terminology in reporting on and testifying about the

---

[43]*Id.* at 2536 (quoting Brief for Respondent at 29, Melendez-Diaz v. Massachusetts, 129 S. Ct. 2527 (2009) (No. 07-591)).

[44]*Id.* at 2537.

[45]*Id.* (internal citation omitted) (quoting App. to Pet. for Cert. 24a, 26a, 28a).

[46]*Id.* (citing NRC REPORT Prepublication Copy, *supra* note 23, at P-1) (emphasis omitted).

[47]*Id.* at 2536 (emphasis added).

results of forensic science investigations.[48] When their testimony is admitted in court, forensic experts should offer nothing more than what they actually know, leaving it to the jury or judge to weigh the evidence offered against the other evidence that is presented in a case. My concern is that some forensic practitioners may not know what they do not know about the limits of their discipline. They will have to be taught this so that they can be appropriately circumspect in their testimony.

Relatedly, the committee also recommended the adoption of model laboratory reports with specifications regarding the minimum information that should be included in a lab report.[49] This recommendation is intended to facilitate the ability of lawyers, judges, and jurors to better comprehend the limits of forensic evidence that is offered in a case. Obviously, this is crucially important.

Lastly, the committee recommended the removal of all public forensic laboratories and facilities from the administrative control of law enforcement agencies or prosecutors' offices.[50] As the report makes clear, forensic scientists*14 should function independently of law enforcement administrators. The Supreme Court commented on this in its *Melendez-Diaz* decision, stating:

> *According to a recent study conducted under the auspices of the National Academy of Sciences. "[t]he majority of [laboratories producing forensic evidence] are administered by law enforcement agencies ... where the laboratory administrator reports to the head of the agency." ... And "[b]ecause forensic scientists often are driven in their work by a need to answer a particular question related to the issues of a particular case, they sometimes face pressure to sacrifice appropriate methodology for the sake of expediency." A forensic analyst responding to a request from a law enforcement official may feel pressure–or have an incentive–to alter the evidence in a manner favorable to the prosecution.[51]*

The committee believed that this is not as it ought to be.

As we continue to face terrorist threats–like the recent attempted bombing in Times Square, New York–we are reminded of our need for reliable forensic methods and practices, and also skilled forensic practitioners. Every forensic laboratory in the United States–not just the FBI Laboratory–should use appropriate protocols and employ highly skilled practitioners. Right now, however, this is merely an aspiration, not a reality. We have every incentive to do all that we can to help the forensic science community get its house in order.

Let me be very clear in what I am saying. I do not mean to suggest that no forensic discipline has value. Rather, as the committee's report makes clear, because of a dearth of scientific data, we do not know how to assess the value of many forensic disciplines because we cannot measure their limits. For example, all fingerprint

---

[48]NRC REPORT, *supra* note 1, at 21-22 (discussing Recommendation 1).

[49]*Id.* at 22.

[50]*Id.* at 24 (discussing Recommendation 4).

[51]*Melendez-Diaz*, 129 S. Ct. at 2536 (quoting NRC REPORT Prepublication Copy, *supra* note 23, at 6-1, S-17).

samples are not equally good, and not every forensic practitioner is equally good in understanding and explaining the differences. Hopefully, better scientific research, mandatory accreditation and certification, uniform standards, better practices, and national oversight will cure issues of this sort. For now, however, it is the responsibility of the legal profession to protect the integrity of the criminal justice system.

Professor Jennifer L. Mnookin, who will head the study on error rates in latent fingerprint evidence, wrote a telling piece for the *Los Angeles Times* just after the NRC report was released. Her words are worthy of our consideration:

> *Science deals in probabilities, not certainty. The only forensic science that makes regular use of formal probabilities is DNA profiling, in which experts testify to the probability of a match. None of the rest of the traditional pattern-identification sciences–such as fingerprinting, ballistics, fiber and handwriting analysis– currently has the necessary statistical foundation to establish accurate probabilities. Yet, instead of acknowledging their imperfect knowledge, fingerprint experts, for example, routinely testify that they *15 can identify a specific person's prints to the exclusion of all other people in the world with 100% certainty.*
>
> ....
>
> *The courts have almost entirely turned a deaf ear to these [problems], essentially giving forensic science and its practices a free pass, simply because they've been part of the judicial system for so long. Meanwhile, scandals continue to come to light across the nation involving error and even fraud in labs.*
>
> *The findings in the National Academy of Sciences report should spur judges to require higher standards. At a bare minimum, judges should immediately prohibit experts from testifying to impossibilities such as "an error rate of zero" or asserting that they are capable of making 100% certain identifications.*
>
> ....
>
> *We want and need forensic science in our legal system, but we have to be able to trust it.*
>
> *... [W]hen forensic science rests on an appropriate scientific foundation, it will be far more deserving of our confidence. Our system of justice demands no less.[52]*

I hope that the members of the bench and bar heed the concerns raised by Professor Mnookin. She does not subscribe to the view that all forensic science disciplines and practitioners are unworthy or bad; nor do I. Moreover, we agree that the adversarial process relating to the admission and exclusion of scientific evidence is not always well suited to the task of finding "scientific truth." However, we also agree that there is still much more that can be done by members of the legal profession, bench and bar, within the existing legal framework, to ensure that forensic evidence is properly assessed and admitted only when it will serve the ends of justice. If we insist on valid and reliable forensic methodologies and practices, and qualified practitioners, change will happen. And our systems of law enforcement and criminal justice will be the better for it.

---

[52]Jennifer L. Mnookin, Op-Ed., *Clueless 'Science,'* L.A. TIMES, Feb. 19, 2009, at A21.

The History of Experts in English Common Law, with Practice Advice for Beginning Experts

C. Michael Bowers

Associate Professor of Clinical Dentistry, Ostrow School of Dentistry, University of Southern California, Los Angeles, CA USA

…all the responsibility of medicine, the intricacy of the law and the universality of science. In as much as it carries higher penalties for error than other professions, it is not a matter to take lightly, nor to trust to luck.
Paul L. Kirk

1.1 A brief history of the expert witness in English common law and the relationship to current expert witness practices

The origin of the U.S. legal system is based in the English legal tradition born in the early Middle Ages. The King's Court of those times determined legal remedies for problems involving crimes, property disputes, and taxation. Experts were also summoned as witnesses but were not considered expert witnesses, as the legal codes did not exist for experts until the end of the 18th century. "Juries of the town" were used in earlier courts as a panel of knowledgeable citizens in matters specific to merchandise and other disputes germane to court proceedings (Golan, 1999). Generally this process was used in large municipalities. Physicians testified in criminal, insurance, and estate cases; surveyors in property cases; merchants in cases concerning the particular practices of their trade; tradesmen in cases concerning the standards of goods; ship builders about the operation and construction of vessels; other artisans based on their respective skillsets; and so on (Rix, 1999). Still, despite a growing presence in the court, the expert witness was not regarded as a distinct legal entity. Another method of the times used witnesses equivalent to an "expert" as "assessors" to the courts.

Unlike court appointed experts or those serving in expert juries, there was no legal procedure to define experts attending court as individual witnesses. A "professional man" who had inspected the facts of the case but not observed events related to a contentious event and who testified to his conclusions was not distinguished from other lay witnesses who often were permitted to testify to their opinion based on direct personal knowledge and observations (Hand, 1901). Thus, in the absence of a particular legal procedure or theory that would define them, experts testifying in court were regarded merely as witnesses. Expert procedure and legal theory on the subject evolved only late in the 18th century as part of a larger transformation of the English legal system that legal historians call the Adversarial Revolution (Golan, 1999). The adversarial system (or adversary system) is a legal system where two advocates represent their parties' positions before an impartial person (judge or magistrate) or group of people who attempt to determine the truth of the case. The judge rules on allowing or disallowing evidence and witnesses offered by both sides and administers the law and instructions for the juries both during the trial and after (during jury deliberations on the verdict).

The King's Court, in its later transformation into geographical judicial entities, does show the use of expert testimony in the later 18th century. You can be assured that "science" or "forensics" were unknown at the time for use as a foundation for opinion. However, expert testimony was a significant departure from the courts only admitting a witness who had personal knowledge of facts, events, or personal opinions. It was the seed which led to future change. Much later, in the 20th century, expert opportunities mushroomed into common occurrences in civil and criminal proceedings in the U.S. and abroad. The "expert witness" is allowed to expound and deliberate on probabilities and causation of events and analyses of the physical world that is deemed "outside the ken" of members of the jury *and* the judge. It is now a powerful tool that can change the scope of and issues present in forensic cases involving financial gain and loss, the breach of contractual obligations and damages, criminal convictions, and dismissal or exoneration of charges for serious offenses and crimes. However, the effects of experts in the U.S. are two-sided, as the adversarial system in its courts commonly presents opposing experts who present opinions based on "science" regarding physical evidence. One should understand that "science" is human-based knowledge subject to human foibles and attitudes. It is the responsibility of those presenting themselves as knowledgeable in certain fields to present proof of their opinions that follow the scientific method rather than only being based on assumptive opinion.

Looking back at the earlier days of this form of "legal expertism" in courts, it is enlightening to trace the thread of the court's expectations of obtaining a balanced representation of reliable facts via the use of expert opinion. The courts regarded (and still do regard) this type of testimony as a privilege that carries a responsibility for experts in their relationship to the courts.

Prior to the end of the 18th century, courts were ruled completely by the judge in regards to evidence review, presentation of witnesses, and direct and cross-examination. Lawyers were limited in their actions and their objections to decisions and the course of the proceedings. The birth of the English adversarial system, as mentioned above, changed this course to one much more familiar in the present day. The courts began to recognize specific courtroom controls for expert opinion being introduced as evidence. The lawyers embraced this opportunity by addressing their objections and limits to the content and form of witness evidence through the *hearsay rule*, proofs of reliability, and relevancy of *opinion evidence*.

The *hearsay rule* attempts to limit testimony to information based solely on personal observation. The *opinion doctrine* seeks to control the form in which witnesses communicate their observations and conclusions to the jury, requiring them not to use inferences (opinions derived from their experiences) where the subject matter relates to factual statements (i.e., "the car ran the red light"). The courts, already practiced in admitting a form of expert knowledge in legal proceedings, sought to carve exceptions to continue allowing experts to assist in the questions presented in cases.

These new rules to restrict testimony eventually fit expert witnesses into their own special role. Some call this an expert "exception" to the general rules, but the inherent purpose of the courts is clear. The expert who did not have to personally observe events was needed to explain events in clear language and enlighten the courts in numerous inquiries into areas of special knowledge. This outcome took the experts away from "court helpers" and into the realm of the lawyers representing both sides of courtroom disputes. The era of an "impartial expert" evolved (or devolved) into experts battling each other in court. Today's judicial "thresholding" or "gatekeeping" of the court testimony of opposing experts was seen back in 1782 in the following classic English law case, which is the cornerstone of the role of the solo expert as an adversarial "entity" (Hand, 1901).

Lord Mansfield ruled in the case of Folkes v. Chadd (1782). A harbour had decayed, and the question was whether it had anything to do with the demolition of a sea-bank erected to prevent the sea overflowing into some meadows. The defendants (owners of the sea-bank) brought in an expert named Smeaton. The plantiffs (the harbor owners) objected and focused on not expecting this strategy and being "surprised at his doctrine and reasoning." The trial judge excluded the defendant's expert who then appealed to the "Royal Judges of the King's Bench" about the booting of their engineer. The appellate court granted a new trial. Lord Mansfield (Chief Justice of the Royal Bench) determined the ruling on the trial court's excluding Smeaton. The Chief Judge admitted that Smeaton was giving opinion evidence, but he reasoned, the entire case was based on opinion.

> "It is objected that Mr Smeaton is going to speak, not to facts, but as to opinion. That opinion, however, is deduced from facts which are not disputed; the situation of banks, the course of tides and of winds, and the shifting of sands. His opinion, deduced from all these facts is that, mathematically speaking, the bank may contribute to the mischief, but not sensibly. Mr Smeaton understands the construction of harbours, the causes of their destruction and how remedied ... I have myself received the opinion of Mr Smeaton respecting mills, as a matter of science. The cause of the decay of the harbour is also a matter of science, and still more so, whether the removal of the bank can be beneficial. Of this, such men as Mr Smeaton alone can judge. Therefore, we are of the opinion that his judgment, formed on facts, was proper evidence."

These statements from Lord Mansfield indicate what he considered the value of Mr. Smeaton's participation in the court proceedings. This value superseded the opposing counsel's objection to Mr. Smeaton's testimony. Lord Mansfield's statements can be summarized:

1. Mr. Smeaton had scientifically studied the subject.
2. Mathematics assisted Mr. Smeaton's testimony.

3. The expert was known to the judge from previous cases.
4. His certainty of the causal connection with the effects of the bank and its potential removal from the harbor was couched in the relative term "may have."
5. His testimonial evidence was derived from facts, not assumptions.

1.2 Other legal concepts about experts derived from English case law

Additional cases from early English cases provide emphasis to the necessities of being an expert witness in court.

The witness must have adequate knowledge of and skills relating directly to the evidence.

An early case tested the abilities of a lawyer who had previously determined handwriting characteristics of wills and other legal documents. A policeman's determination about the effects of alcohol is another example. The Court of Appeal ruled that:

The test of expertness, so far as the law of evidence is concerned, is skill, and skill alone, in the field of which it is sought to have the witness's opinion. I adopt, as a working definition of the term 'skilled person', one who has by dint of training and practice, acquired a good knowledge of the science or art concerning which his opinion is sought. It is not necessary, for a person to give opinion evidence of a question of human physiology, that he be a doctor of medicine (Rix, 1999).

This rings true for some but not all aspects of expert opinion. Sadly, the line is blurry regarding where the threshold might really exist for admissibility of opinion simply based on experience with some aspects of criminal investigation or knowledge of a related science. The judicial answer commonly is to accept the testimony over opposing counsel's objection but somehow limit the "weight" or influence it can have on the jury's interpretation of events or decisions . A common objection to more aggressive (according to the defense, of course) opinions (i.e., a policeman stating he saw a bite mark on a crime victim) is that the testimony is only derived from a short course on pattern injuries rather than from, for example, a dentist expounding on the characteristics of human teeth marks in skin. The policeman is definitely not "trained" in any formal sense. The judge, however, probably would admit it into court.

The expert does not provide answers to the trial's ultimate question, i.e., "Is the defendant guilty?"

This is the province of the prosecution's theory and the jury's final verdict. The defense will counter with their opposing view, i.e., "The DNA is not a match to my client because it was planted by the police and, therefore, she is not guilty of murder."

The court (meaning the jury or a judge sitting as a jury) has to reach its own conclusion based on the facts of the case as presented at trial. It will not be swayed if the expert states the ultimate opinion as if he were better than the jury.

> *Expert witnesses, however skilled or eminent, can give no more than evidence.*
> *They cannot usurp the function of the jury or judge sitting as a jury, any more*
> *than a technical assessor can substitute his advice for the judgment of the court.*
> *Their duty is to furnish the judge or jury with the necessary scientific criteria for*
> *testing the accuracy of their conclusions so as to enable the application of their*
> *criteria to the facts proved in evidence. The scientific opinion, if convincing and*
> *tested, becomes a factor (and often an important factor) for consideration along*
> *with the whole other evidence in the case, but the decision is for the judge and*
> *jury (Rix, 1999).*

A recent case in a southern U.S. state that is noted for its cowboys illustrates this topic. The Federal Court judge was holding a post-conviction hearing (no jury was present) to consider an appeal to a sentence of murder. All the original trial evidence was critically reviewed and presented at the hearing to show, in part, that the defendant was not convicted beyond a "reasonable doubt." Doubts existed as to the validity of bite mark evidence presented at the trial six years prior and whether it had undergone a sufficient amount of scientific study to scientifically validate the prosecution's bite mark experts. Defense counsel presented facts and opinions stating that using bite marks in the skin to identify a specific person was dangerous and did not satisfy the threshold for admission at the original trial. Numerous cases where DNA had ultimately overturned faulty bite mark opinions after erroneous convictions were offered as proof of this reasoning. The judge was not happy with this strategy; she considered it stepping on her toes regarding the ultimate issue of scientific decisions. She clearly stated the bite mark evidence was proper due to prior judgements made by previous courts. The idea of scientific review using new empirical studies was irrelevant in her decision-making process.

"BEST PRACTICE" SUGGESTIONS FOR EXPERTS IN COURT

1. Talk only within your field of expertise. If questions from a lawyer travel beyond your training, be ready to say, "I am sorry counselor, but that is beyond my level of expertise. If I answer your question, it is merely my own personal opinion."
2. Beware of offering an opinion on the ultimate issue. "The defendant pulled the trigger and shot the victim" is an example of a statement to avoid.
3. Do not offer an unnecessary opinion such as, "My first cases began 35 years ago; let me tell you about a few of them."
4. State the facts or assumptions on which your opinion is based. Do not muddle opinion evidence with statements about how "accurate" your findings are unless there is testing available to prove it. Your assumption of total accuracy in your methods and opinions is nothing more than your own opinion on the subject. Your certainty of opinion is not proof of scientific reliability.
5. Show the reasoning behind your opinion. It should rely on facts, not on the courts' prior use of similar opinions over the years or decades.

Continued

"BEST PRACTICE" SUGGESTIONS FOR EXPERTS IN COURT—Cont'd

6. Be objective and unbiased of this book.
7. Include and identify points which detract from your opinion. This is the home ground of experts who refuse to discuss weaknesses of their assumptions and the evidence. It is the prime territory of the adversarial expert witness.
8. If you change your opinion, say so. Science evolves as the influence of research and testing also evolves. This is called progress. Forensic science should not be immune to changes and different interpretations due to these processes. Prior testimony and opinions should be allowed to evolve as well. The law does not progress as rapidly in regards to what is "best science," but it does change. When there are conflicts between the two, be prepared to explain your reasoning based on factual evidence.

1.3 What is forensic science? A coat of many colors with serious problems regarding poor oversight and inconsistency of opinions within certain disciplines

To be exact, both terms—*forensic* and *science*—must be considered. The "foren" is universally defined as "in the forum" from Roman history. In other words, it is used in legal systems throughout the world. These are places where decisions of great importance are made. "Science" derives from the Greek word meaning "knowledge." In combination, the words give rise to thoughts of Sherlock Holmes, *CSI: NY*, and the OJ Simpson trial in the United States. Some consider forensics a proper blend of applied science and the courts. This is a gross overstatement of the term "applied science" because of its inconsistent presence in certain forensic disciplines created solely for court use. Sherlock never accused the wrong perpetrator of a serious crime. In his later life as an activist for legal reform, the author of the Sherlock Holmes mysteries, Sir Arthur Conan Doyle, became more interested in wrongful convictions in courts of law around the world.

"Applied science" is a well-described list of university-based academic disciplines (human pathology, anthropology, and other physical sciences adopted for forensic applications). A gap or disconnect between some of forensics and the applied sciences has revealed that the police science "forum" (not the research centers) has established use of methods for "forensics" that have not been borne in the crucible of laboratory science, research, and the scientific environment. The courtroom has been the environment of these "poor cousins" of the multidisciplinary "soup" of forensic science. So what subjects are in this forensic category? Their historical name was "police sciences" in Great Britain. They are criminal investigation (suspect interrogation and witness interviewing), firearms and ballistics identification, questioned documents (the non-chemical analysis aspect), photography, fingerprint classification and identification, trace evidence investigation, arson and explosion investigation, and blood spatter, footprints, and other pattern investigations including bite mark identification (non-DNA matching of teeth to human skin injuries). Each of these police-developed or associated areas of investigation is the offspring of prosecutorial and judicial inquires into causes and perpetrators of criminal acts. Their geographical activities are in the crime lab and the courtroom with little to no influence from the scientific communities in the "applied science" world. Herein lies the rub and the challenge to forensic experts in the 21st century.

1.4 **What are the expectations of parties using forensic science?**

Each of the participants in the criminal justice system has differing expectations of what the scientist or forensic examiner can deliver for them. The natural thought of all groups (be it prosecution, defense, or judicial) is "what can Dr. Brown or Ms. Jones provide that will further our arguments?" In fact, these queries can produce conflicts in the lawyer's case strategy which later may meet in the cauldron of the court proceedings. Prosecutorial investigations many times may be dependent on forensic opinion to produce direct proof of guilt (rarely) or at least strong circumstantial evidence supporting the case against the defendant(s). Direct proof might be videotaping of the actual crime with the perpetrators and victim clearly recorded. Circumstantial evidence leads to the arguments that the defendant was at the crime scene at the time of the crime, left DNA or fingerprint evidence at the scene, or was later found in possession of objects that had originated at the crime scene (again, it could be DNA, jewelry, or guns or other weapons). The forensic testing outcomes of the evidence usually determine their use or disuse at trial. When results come in conflict with the prosecution theories, they may be retested, ignored, used to redirect the investigation, or reduced in importance if used in court. All the same applies for defense experts, with the exception that these experts by law are not mandated to divulge evidence incriminating the defendant. The prosecution, however, must provide to the defense counsel evidence results that tend to lead to or could prove the innocence of the defendant or enable impeachment of a government witness. Failure to provide substantial proof of innocence is deemed a *Brady* violation and is used to argue prosecutorial misconduct and constitutional rights abuse (abuse of due process) in post-conviction appeals.

One additional conflict between the science and forensic groups is the collision between scientific truth and the social concept of justice. Justice is rule-based and determined by state and federal criminal law statutes, the U.S. Constitution, interpretations of the U.S. Supreme Court, and the case law of other judicial opinions. Adherence to these dicta concerning rights and privileges of the accused is the aegis of the court system. The track of justice on this road is where collisions occur in that the truth of science may not wholly exist in matters concerning forensic testimony in certain instances. Poor police science may be allowed into court; the police science expert can overstate findings of absolute certainty in tests results, but at the same time, be considered an upholder of justice for all. The forensic examiner may do this due to an honest belief in training and methods, but it is still poor science providing the "legal truth." The law of the adversarial process "cherry picks" the forensic physical evidence that assists it. This is not necessarily a scientific determination using scientific logic, but is the customary practice in the legal community.

1.5 Disagreement between lay witnesses, science, and forensic examiners

The two forensic groups do not always agree in their individual results. False identifications of a suspect by witnesses, the overstatement of opinions from prosecution forensic experts, and faulty police science are now colliding with trace evidence available for DNA profiling. You can be sure that pretrial DNA profiling redirects investigations in many instances. However, cases of wrongful convictions in the last 20 years show irrefutable proof of this conflict of the results of some court approved "sciences." In fact, there is a double standard in their being allowed into the courtroom. The police methods have been used for nearly the entire 20th century in courtrooms. This has created a nearly immutable body of court opinions throughout the modern criminal justice system. The weight of new DNA methods has vacated convictions in hundreds of cases since their judicial inception in the 1980s, but the courts have rarely, if at all, extended their exoneration opinions to addressing why the mis-convictions occurred. Judicial appellate rulings actually don't consider the seriousness of the forensic misconduct or partisan interpretations by experts. A case's reversal only occurs if the exclusion of the forensic misadventure would have led to a different outcome at trial (a not guilty finding by the jury). Until very recently, it has been left to legal commentaries critical of erroneous forensic and defense litigation groups to delve into the facts leading to wrongful convictions. The fact is that over 50% of the time, erroneous forensic testimony has contributed to the wrong person going to prison in the U.S. cases. This empirical evidence comes from exoneration litigation by the Innocence Project Network and recorded by The National Registry of Exonerations.[1] The IP Network involves the NYC IP with affiliated law schools and legal centers around the U.S. See www.innocencenetwork.org for more information. The prosecutors in these exonerations seldom admit making mistakes during trial and commonly, when faced with new facts of innocence (i.e. DNA; incentivized witnesses; false confessions) and concoct extraordinary scenarios attempting to diminish the defense arguments.[2] In fact, a prosecutor is immune from prosecution in instances of prosecutorial misconduct except where they intentionally mislead the jury or committed egregious acts of misconduct (as in destroying or hiding exculpatory evidence).

A recent exception is the case of Michael Morton from Texas.[3] Mr. Morton spent over 25 years in prison for the murder of his wife. The prosecutor failed to disclose evidence of Morton's innocence. The now ex-prosecutor was found to be criminally liable and is facing charges in Texas. This is a ground-breaking case.

Some others delay the process of exoneration until years after relevant DNA testing is requested by defense counsel. A direct focus on such a case is seen in Chapter 12. Once this DNA is tested and the real perpetrator has been identified, these

---

[1] https://www.law.umich.edu/special/exoneration/Pages/about.aspx
[2] http://csidds.com/2013/08/18/another-da-in-denial-over-exonerating-dna-from-a-bitemark/
[3] http://www.innocenceproject.org/Content/Michael_Morton.php

prosecutors still deny that the original conviction is the result of a miscarriage of justice.[4]

General forensic organizations of experts, principally the American Academy of Forensic Sciences in the United States, speak platitudes about "changes occurring" to increase the reliability of some of their police science methods, but they refuse to review the cases where their own members have contributed to this problem. Forensic specialty boards are no different. The blowback to criticism of the U.S. Congress inquiry from the Executive branch of U.S. government has been extraordinary in some cases. The American Board of Forensic Odontology (aka forensic dentistry) has gone so far as to fail to publically admit there is a lack of reliability in bite mark identification (a non-DNA method using tooth pattern "matches") and professes its adherence to its pre-DNA methods of comparisons. Approximately 10% of their membership has been involved as court experts aiding in erroneous convictions and false arrests (see the Appendix: "Cases where bite mark evidence contributed to wrongful convictions and arrests").

Recent (in the last five years) University of Buffalo research[5] on the properties of skin for "matching" human teeth marks has debunked 50 years of assumed reliability of bite mark expertise. The ABFO dental group contributed funds for the initial phase of the study, but faced with results counter to their beliefs, this small forensic group now rejects the Buffalo testing results as "irrelevant." This provides a specific example of what is occurring in the interface between science, non-science, and the criminal justice system in the United States.

1.6 Post-conviction problems with forensic experts in the United States

In 2012, the New York Innocence Project summarized the problem of unreliable forensic expert testimonies' contribution to crime and conviction statistics (The innocenceproject.org).

> There have been 310 (to date) post-conviction DNA exonerations in United States history. These stories are becoming more familiar as more innocent people gain their freedom through post-conviction testing. They are not proof, however, that our system is righting itself. The common themes that run through these cases — from global problems like poverty and racial issues to criminal justice issues like eyewitness misidentification, invalid or improper forensic science, overzealous police and prosecutors, and inept defense counsel — cannot be ignored and continue to plague our criminal justice system.

- Seventeen people had been sentenced to death before DNA proved their innocence and led to their release.
- The average sentence served by DNA exonerees has been 13 years.

---

[4] http://www.innocenceproject.org/Content/Real_Perpetrator_in_Milwaukee_DNA_Exoneration_Case_Charged_with_Murder.php

[5] http://www.buffalo.edu/news/releases/2009/09/10446.html; http://www.forensic-dentistry.info/wp/?p=531

- About 70% of those exonerated by DNA testing are members of minority groups.
- In almost 40% of DNA exoneration cases, the actual perpetrator has been identified by DNA testing.
- Exonerations have been won in 35 states and Washington, D.C.

(Reproduced with permission from www.innocenceproject.org.)

1.7 Forensic experts exaggerate reliability and conclusions

The following case reports establish the context of the erroneous assumptions of forensic expertise that have damaged the criminal justice system and formed the major reason the U.S. Congress began investigations in 2007. The Ted Bundy bite mark case is also described to show how evidence was collected and presented to the court in 1978.

1.7.1 Case one: This lead's not for you

The FBI method of bullet lead analysis had its inception in 1963 and was in use since 1980, but was rejected in 2005. Also called comparative bullet lead (CBL) analysis, it studied the chemical makeup of manufactured ammunition and was promoted by the FBI as identifying specific crime scene bullets as matching bullets found later in the possession of a criminal suspect. From 1980 to 2004, it was used in about 2,500 analyses in cases submitted by law-enforcement groups.

1.7.1.1 Tipping the balance against court admissibility

The technique was not effectively challenged until a retired FBI examiner began questioning the procedure in scientific and legal journals and in the courts. These challenges coincided with a single FBI CBL expert testifying falsely in a murder case. The expert stated at a pretrial admissibility (a hearing to get the court to allow scientific testimony) that the composition of a bullet fragment removed from the victim's body was indistinguishable from bullets found at the home of the defendant's parents. The court found this testimony to be deceptive and not scientifically true. The expert later admitted to lying, and on June 17, 2003, pleaded guilty to testifying falsely and was sentenced to a suspended ninety-day jail sentence and a $250 fine (Giannelli, 2010).

In response to this case, the FBI requested that the National Academy of Sciences study the theories and the courtroom uses of this forensic method.

In 2004, the NAS stated the chemical testing (using a FBI nuclear reactor and gamma rays) and identity of the bullet lead material was scientifically competent, but statistics of frequency of the material composition generated by the FBI could cause confusion and misinterpretation when transmitted to prosecutors or when explained to a trial jury.

Nearly five years after the FBI abandoned its comparative bullet lead analysis, the FBI had yet to complete its review of nearly 2,500 cases where law enforcement used such evidence to investigate a case. The FBI did find 187 cases where bullet lead analysis evidence was not only used in the investigation, but came into play at trial where FBI experts provided testimony. It had notified prosecutors and the Innocence Project in those cases where testimony of its experts exceeded the limits of the science and would not be supported by the FBI. The FBI review did not include defendants who had either confessed or pled guilty to crimes (Giannelli, 2010).

The following 2005 FBI letter to 300 crime labs admits to CBL unreliability, but tries to minimize their in-house research problems and instead place responsibility onto other parties.

FBI Laboratory Announces Discontinuation of Bullet Lead Examinations

2005, Washington, DC FBI National Press Office

"The FBI Laboratory today announced that, after extensive study and consideration, it will no longer conduct the examination of bullet lead. Bullet lead examinations have historically been performed in limited circumstances, typically when a firearm has not been recovered or when a fired bullet is too mutilated for comparison of physical markings. Bullet lead examinations use analytical chemistry to determine the amounts of trace elements (such as copper, arsenic, antimony, tin, etc.) found within bullets. The result of that analysis allows crime-scene bullets to be compared to bullets associated with a suspect. Since the early 1980's the FBI Laboratory has conducted bullet lead examinations in approximately 2,500 cases submitted by federal, state, local, and foreign law enforcement agencies. In less than 20% of those cases was the result introduced into evidence at trial.

In 2002, the FBI asked the National Research Council (NRC) of the National Academy of Science to have an independent committee of experts evaluate the scientific basis of comparative bullet lead analysis. Specifically, the FBI divided the bullet lead examination into three parts (the scientific method, the data analysis, and the interpretation of the results) and asked the NRC for an impartial review of each area. The technology reviewed by the NRC had been used by the FBI Laboratory since 1996. The NRC's recommendations, following the study, were set forth in a report entitled 'Forensic Analysis: Weighing Bullet Lead Evidence.'

The NRC found that the FBI Laboratory's analytical instrumentation is appropriate and the best available technology with respect to precision and accuracy for the elements analyzed. It also found that the elements selected by the FBI for this analysis are appropriate. The NRC expressed concerns, however, relating to the interpretation of the results of bullet lead examinations.

Following the issuance of the report the FBI Laboratory embarked on an exhaustive 14-month review to study the recommendations, offered by the NRC, including an evaluation of statistical methodologies. Although the NRC stated that the FBI Laboratory did not need to suspend bullet lead examinations while undertaking this review, the FBI elected to do so while the review was pending.

One factor significantly influenced the Laboratory's decision to no longer conduct the examination of bullet lead: neither scientists nor bullet manufacturers are able to definitively attest to the significance of an association made between bullets in

Continued

FBI Laboratory Announces Discontinuation of Bullet Lead Examinations—Cont'd

the course of a bullet lead examination. While the FBI Laboratory still firmly supports the scientific foundation of bullet lead analysis, given the costs of maintaining the equipment, the resources necessary to do the examination, and its relative probative value, the FBI Laboratory has decided that it will no longer conduct this exam.

Letters outlining the FBI Laboratory's decision to discontinue these examinations are being sent to approximately 300 agencies that received laboratory reports indicating positive results since 1996. The letters are being sent so that these agencies may take whatever steps they deem appropriate, if any, given the facts of their particular case. It is important to note that the FBI Laboratory has not determined that previously issued bullet lead reports were in "… error"[1].

[1]http://www.fbi.gov/news/pressrel/press-releases/fbi-laboratory-announces-discontinuation-of-bullet-lead-examinations

---

1.7.1.2 Is this lead from you?

The advance of scientific research has resulted in the rejection of forensic methods after years of acceptance. Examples include bullet lead comparisons, and human hair comparison which were long used and promoted by the FBI. Forensic disciplines not recognized by the U.S. government such as bite mark comparisons are immune from such governmental oversight.

FBI Laboratory to Increase Outreach in Bullet Lead Cases

2007, Washington, DC FBI National Press Office

"Expanding on a series of efforts that were first initiated in 2002, the FBI Laboratory announced today that it has undertaken an additional round of outreach, analysis, and review efforts concerning a discontinued forensic test known as Bullet Lead Analysis, or BLA. Previously, in September 2005, the FBI Laboratory announced that, after extensive study and consideration, it would permanently discontinue the examination of bullet lead.

'Recently, joint reporting by *The Washington Post* and CBS News brought to our attention concerns that our messages on the discontinuation of bullet lead analysis were not clear enough and getting to the right people,' said John Miller, FBI Assistant Director for Public Affairs.

'In addition, working with the Innocence Project, the reporters brought to our attention some cases that may require closer examination of the scientific findings and testimony by FBI experts, and we are committed to go forward with that,' Miller said.

Those additional steps being taken by the FBI and the Department of Justice include the following:

- The FBI has offered to work jointly with the Innocence Project, which has done legal research to identify criminal cases where bullet lead analysis has been introduced at trial.
- An additional round of letters is being transmitted to the original recipients of the FBI notices in 2005, updating those state and local crime laboratories and other agencies on the additional developments noted above and requesting that they again notify state and local prosecutors that may have introduced bullet lead analysis during trial.

- In particular, in BLA cases in which an examiner testified and which resulted in a conviction state, local, and other prosecutors are being asked to obtain and provide transcripts to the FBI and the DOJ of BLA testimony by FBI Laboratory examiners.
- These transcripts will undergo a multi-step review conducted by scientific and legal experts at the FBI and DOJ to determine whether the testimony was consistent with the findings of the FBI Laboratory in 2005, particularly concerning the inability of scientists and manufacturers to definitively evaluate the significance of an association between bullets made in the course of a bullet lead examination.
- If the reviews identify questions about the testimony, the prosecuting offices responsible for any such cases will be specifically and individually notified.
- An enhanced system for monitoring testimony to ensure it comports with the findings contained in lab reports is being implemented by the FBI Laboratory.

Bullet lead examinations have historically been performed when a firearm has not been recovered or when a fired bullet is too mutilated for comparison of physical markings. BLA uses analytical chemistry to determine the amounts of trace elements (such as copper, arsenic, antimony, tin, etc.) found within bullets. As a result of that analysis, crime-scene bullets were compared to bullets associated with a suspect. From the early 1980s through 2004, the FBI Laboratory conducted bullet lead examinations in approximately 2,500 cases submitted by federal, state, local, and foreign law enforcement agencies. The results were introduced into evidence at trial in less than 20 percent of those cases.

In 2002, the FBI asked the National Research Council (NRC) of the National Academy of Science to have an independent committee of experts evaluate the scientific basis of comparative BLA. Specifically, the FBI divided the bullet lead examination into three parts – the scientific method, the data analysis, and the interpretation of the results – and asked the NRC for an impartial review of each area. The technology reviewed by the NRC had been used by the FBI Laboratory since 1996. Following the study, the NRC's recommendations were set forth in a 2004 report entitled "Forensic Analysis: Weighing Bullet Lead Evidence."

The NRC (National Research Council), of the National Academy of Sciences 2004 report titled "Forensic Analysis: Weighing bullet lead evidence" (2004) had a significant effect in the FBI later discontinuing its use.

The NRC found that the FBI Laboratory's analytical instrumentation was appropriate and the best available technology with respect to precision and accuracy for the elements analyzed. It also found that the elements selected by the FBI for this analysis are appropriate. The NRC expressed concerns, however, on the interpretation of the results of bullet lead examinations.

Following the issuance of the report, the FBI Laboratory voluntarily discontinued bullet lead analysis while it embarked on an exhaustive 14-month review to study the recommendations offered by the NRC, including an evaluation of numerous statistical methodologies. That review resulted in the FBI announcement in 2005 that the temporary discontinuation of BLA would be made permanent. Several factors played a role in the decision, but it was primarily based on the inability of scientists and manufacturers to definitively evaluate the significance of an association between bullets made in the course of a bullet lead examination. The announcement received prominent media attention at the time.

At the time, Congress was briefed and letters outlining the FBI Laboratory's decision to discontinue BLA were sent to approximately 300 state and local crime

Continued

FBI Laboratory to Increase Outreach in Bullet Lead Cases—Cont'd

laboratories and other agencies that received laboratory reports indicating positive results, as well as the National District Attorney's Association, the National
Association of Criminal Defense Lawyers, and the Innocence Project, a litigation
and public policy organization. Recipients were provided with a link to the NRC
report and asked to provide a copy of the letter to all prosecutors working on any
case to which the BLA may relate. The FBI offered to assist recipients, including
assistance with regard to any discovery obligations, and provided name and contact
information for experts at the Department of Justice and the FBI Laboratory. State
prosecutors were asked to consult with discovery experts or appellate specialists
within their office of the State Attorney General's Office to determine the effect
of the announcement on their prosecutions. In addition, for all federal cases, the
FBI notified its field offices and the Executive Office for United States Attorneys
advised those U.S. Attorneys offices where cases had been brought utilizing BLA
testimony.

Recently, in response to the 2005 notification, two news organizations working
with the Innocence Project initiated an effort to obtain selected trial transcripts from
state and local court cases and to undertake additional assessment. The Innocence
Project analysis of some of the transcripts that were identified raised a question
concerning the BLA testimony of FBI examiners, particularly concerning the inability of
scientists and manufacturers to definitively evaluate the significance of an association
between bullets made in the course of a bullet lead examination.

Assistant Director Miller acknowledged the efforts of both the legal organization
and the news media.

"The digging into individual cases done by the Innocence Project, *The Washington
Post*, and CBS News brought some serious concerns to our attention. The FBI is
committed to addressing those concerns. It's the right thing to do," Miller said.

"These additional and ongoing efforts further demonstrate the commitment
of the FBI to advancing the cause of forensic science and to the utilization of the
highest scientific and evidentiary standards – and to protect innocent Americans from
erroneous accusations," Miller said[2].

[2]http://www.fbi.gov/news/pressrel/press-releases/fbi-laboratory-to-increase-outreach-in-bullet-lead-cases

---

1.7.2 Case two: The tale of the hair experts

In its continuing saga of systemic forensic identification failures, the FBI promises
to join forces with the Innocence Project and the National Association of Criminal
Defense Lawyers to uncover criminal convictions that used the FBI's brand of hair
analysis which they promoted for decades as another "smoking gun" in identifying
criminals.[6] The Report on "Strengthening Forensic Science in the United States: A
Path Forward" (NAS, 2009), had admonished the FBI and labeled hair comparison
"science" as faulty in its untested use, misleading, and overstated by its prosecution
experts. This same type of case scrutiny may be utilized for other police forensic
methods. It's only a matter of a little more time.

---

[6]http://www.nap.edu/catalog.php?record_id=12589

1.7.2.1 Washington

The FBI will review thousands of old cases, including some involving the death penalty, in which hair samples helped secure convictions, under an ambitious plan made public Thursday.

More than 2,000 cases the FBI processed from 1985 to 2000 will be re-examined, including some in which execution dates have been set and others in which the defendants already have died in prison. In a key concession, Justice Department officials will waive usual deadlines and procedural hurdles that often block inmates from challenging their convictions.

"This will be critical to giving wrongly convicted people a fair chance at a fair review," said Steven D. Benjamin, a Virginia attorney who's the president of the National Association of Criminal Defense Lawyers.

The defense lawyers' association joined with The Innocence Project, based at New York City's Cardozo School of Law at Yeshiva University, as well as pro bono attorneys to press for the review.[7]

The Flawed FBI Dictum on Hair Investigation: Circa 2000

Hair Evidence

Hairs, which are composed primarily of the protein keratin, can be defined as slender outgrowths of the skin of mammals. Each species of animal possesses hair with characteristic length, color, shape, root appearance, and internal microscopic features that distinguish one animal from another. Considerable variability also exists in the types of hairs that are found on the body of an animal. In humans, hairs found on the head, pubic region, arms, legs, and other body areas have characteristics that can determine their origin. On animals, hair types include coarse outer hairs or guard hairs, the finer fur hairs, tactile hairs such as whiskers, and other hairs that originate from the tail and mane of an animal.

Because hairs can be transferred during physical contact, their presence can associate a suspect to a victim or a suspect/victim to a crime scene. The types of hair recovered and the condition and number of hairs found all impact on their value as evidence in a criminal investigation. Comparison of the microscopic characteristics of questioned hairs to known hair samples helps determine whether a transfer may have occurred (Deedrick, 2000).

1.7.2.2 The problem of unreliability and another failure to make public disclosures by the justice department

The overreaching of hair examiners was established in a nine-year study of misconduct at the FBI crime lab. It found forensic flaws in hair analysis, but the results of the probe that ended in 2004 were revealed only to prosecutors.

---

[7] See http://www.mcclatchydc.com/2013/07/18/197069/fbi-announces-review-of-2000-cases.html#. UgLd3pLFXo4 for more information.

The Justice Department did not separately inform defendants whose cases could be affected. In one particular case, lawyers for the defendant learned of forensic hair matching problems through the media. Prosecutors disclosed problems to the defense in fewer than half of the 250 cases in which questions were raised.

Proof indicated that FBI experts exaggerated the reliability of hair comparisons and sometimes cited false statistics, indicating no chance of a false-positive match to a defendant.

The management of the FBI claimed that they had no duty to directly inform convicted defendants or their legal counsel (if they had an attorney) of the flawed evidence used against them at trial.

1.7.2.3 Post-conviction DNA evidence contradicts cases that use hair analysis to convict

Convictions against two defendants occurring in 1978 (for murder) and 1981 (sexual assault) used hair analysis to identify the perpetrators. Recently, DNA tests substantially cleared one and completely cleared the other.

The Washington Post recently wrote about Santae Tribble, who was arrested at age 17 and served 28 years in prison after his conviction (Hsu, 2012).

The Washington Post also considered an earlier case:

> *The FBI review came too late in another case. According to a prosecution memo, Benjamin Herbert Boyle would not have been eligible for the death penalty because of problems in the FBI lab work. He was executed in 1997, a year after the investigation of the lab began.*[8]

1.7.3 Case three: Who can you trust?

1.7.3.1 Gregory Wilhoit, Richard Milone and Ted Bundy: How DNA, new bite mark research, and failed cases have changed bite mark analysis

Revisiting forensic dental evidence from "old" closed cases is something that crime writers often do (Bowers, 2013). John Grisham, in his 2006 nonfiction work *The Innocent Man*, spotlighted the 1985 State v. Wilhoit murder conviction that was helped by two dentists using oral bacteria components (an untested pre-DNA theory) as well as a bite mark injury to identify the defendant as the biter. A defense-selected panel of 11 dentists helped reverse Gregory Wilhoit's conviction in 1991.

The forensic dental community seems wary of a top-to-bottom review of their more recent 20 (or more) bad bite mark expert performances in cases later overturned and determined to be wrongful convictions or incarcerations.

---

[8] http://articles.washingtonpost.com/2012-04-16/local/35453369_1_hair-and-fiber-fbi-lab-benjamin-herbert-boyle

1.7.3.2 State v. Richard Milone

In 1973, the Milone murder case dealt with a conviction heavily based on an identification of tooth marks on the thigh of the victim, 14-year-old Sally Kandel. Three dentists were for the prosecution and four were defense experts. The prosecution presented the bite mark as "excellent evidence."

Lengthy appeals ensued. Three years after the trial, one of the original defense dentists matched the Kandel bite mark to a bite mark from confessed convicted serial murderer Richard Macek. One of Milone's appeals also used the process of having a four member cohort of defense dentists. In 1986, they again argued against the three prosecution bite mark dentists' 1973 conclusions that Milone was the biter by substituting the known serial killer Macek as the actual biter.

In the same year, Milone petitioned the governor of Illinois with a claim for unconditional clemency. The governor convened a panel of three more dentists, who evaluated the bite mark evidence in Milone's case and determined Macek could not have bitten Kandel and Milone was the biter. Various efforts continued in Illinois and Milone was released from prison in 1992.

It seems that in the face of these battling dentists, the "excellent" bite mark evidence in Milone's case was a bit of forensic overstatement.

1.7.3.3 Ted Bundy

What about State v. Bundy? There is no other U.S. bite mark case that stands higher in the pantheon of the forensic odontology community than the Ted Bundy case. His trial for the murder of two sorority members in Tallahassee, Florida showcased numerous examples of bite mark expertise based on evidence from one of the victims. This case often is said to have sent Ted to his execution by "Old Sparky"—the electric chair at Florida State Prison, in Bradford County— but his 1989 execution derived from a separate death penalty trial in that state (Figure 1.1).

Nearly contemporaneous with Milone (1973 versus 1979), some of the same players once again presented themselves on opposite sides of the bite mark evidence. The case was a career-making event for those involved for the prosecution.

The prosecution experts determined the pattern was unique to Bundy. The defense also offered bite mark experts opposing this theory. This assumed concept was used in court then and even now despite the arrival of DNA. It commonly stated that every person had a dental profile of biting teeth that was individual to them, analogous to a fingerprint. There should be little argument that Bundy's lower teeth could make a pattern similar to what is seen in the autopsy picture (Figure 1.2). Are his teeth and the bite mark unique to just him? No. The scientific question of whether or not someone else's teeth could have created the same pattern is now much clearer. The probability of another's teeth duplicating the Bundy bite mark is possible. Looking at the past helps science to move on. See Figures 1.3, 1.4, and 1.5.

However, the recent U.S. exoneration cases also commonly have the dentists who made the erroneous claims still supporting their original findings despite

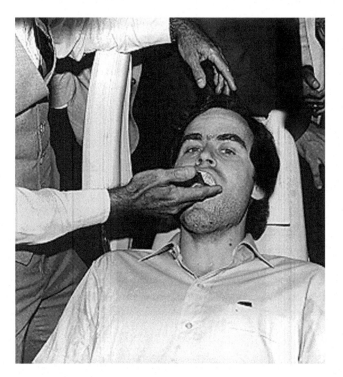

FIGURE 1.1

Ted Bundy Dental Impressions

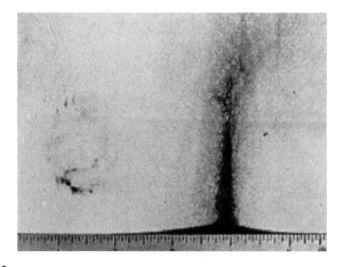

FIGURE 1.2

Bite mark on Buttocks

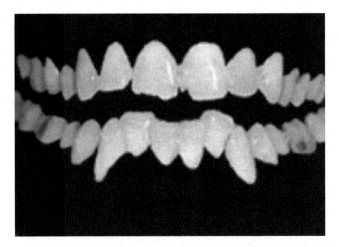

FIGURE 1.3

Bundy's Teeth

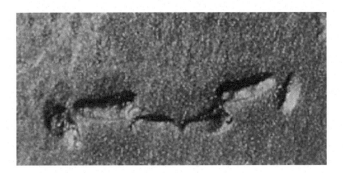

FIGURE 1.4

Wax Teeth Imprint From Ted Bundy

scientific and judicial results to the contrary. Some forensic people stick to their beliefs and don't care how they got there. See the Appendix for a list with descriptions of 14 cases of wrongful convictions and six false arrests that were aided by bite mark experts.

1.8 Conclusions

The following chapters will provide insight into the mechanisms of court procedure, the court's rules applying to expert testimony, and provide examples with explanations of good practices.

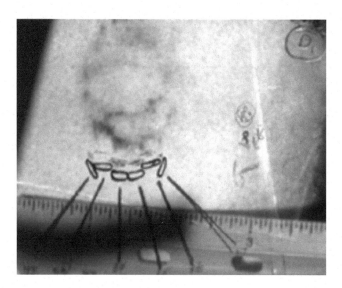

FIGURE 1.5

Bite mark Photo with Bundy Lower Teeth Outline

References

Bowers, C.M., 2013. Ted Bundy Bitemarks and Richard Milone: How DNA, bitemark research and failed cases have changed bitemark analysis. http://bitemarks.org/2011/10/2 3/ted-bundy-bitemarks-and-richard-milone-how-dna-bitemark-research-and-failed-cases-have-changed-bitemark-analysis/.

Hsu, S., 2012. D.C. man served 28 years. Then the evidence that sent him to prison fell apart. http://www.washingtonpost.com/local/crime/2012/04/16/gIQAbndgMT_story.html.

Deedrick, D.W., 2000. Part 1: Hair Evidence; Federal Bureau of Investigation Washington, DC. http://www.fbi.gov/about-us/lab/forensic-science-communications/fsc/july2000/dee dric1.htm/.

Giannelli, Paul C., 2010. Comparative Bullet Lead Analysis: A Retrospective (September 1, 2011). Criminal Law Bulletin 47, 306, Case Legal Studies Research Paper No. 2011-21.

Golan, Tal, 1999. The history of scientific testing in the English court system. Science in Context 12, 7–32.

Hand, L., 1901. Historical and practical considerations regarding expert testimony. Harvard Law Review 15, 40–58.

Rix, Keith JB., 1999. Expert evidence in the courts: 1, The history of expert science. Advances in Psychiatric Treatments 5, 71–77.

THE INNOCENCE BLOG

California Man Exonerated by DNA Evidence after 14 Years in Prison

Posted: 12 Mar 2013 02:10 PM PDT

Johnny Williams with his attorney, Melissa Dague O'Connell

A California man who was convicted of raping a nine-year-old girl in 1998 was exonerated Friday after new DNA testing secured by the <u>Northern California Innocence Project</u> and the <u>California DNA Project</u> proved his innocence.

A previously undetected DNA sample on a T-shirt the girl was wearing at the time of the assault excluded Johnny Williams who was paroled in January after serving 14 years behind bars, reported the *Oakland Tribune*. In light of the new evidence, the District Attorney's Office agreed to drop charges against Williams, and the Alameda County Superior Court Judge agreed to overturn the conviction. During the investigation, both the Oakland Police Department and the Alameda County District Attorney's Office were unable to pull DNA samples from the girl's clothing.

Williams was convicted largely based on the victim's identification which was made at the suggestion of her mother. The victim said her attacker was named Johnny and Williams was the only Johnny she knew from the neighborhood. Following his conviction, Williams wrote a letter to the Northern California Innocence Project seeking assistance, and in 2000, the project began an investigation through its sister organization, the California DNA Project.

"This little girl, just as me, too, we are both victims of this very serious crime, and we both need the person who committed this crime to be brought and placed in prison," Williams said. "If I could, I would help the Oakland Police Department find this person."

Science and Forensic Science

2

Mark Page

All who drink of this remedy recover in a short time, except those whom it does
not help, who all die. Therefore it is obvious that it fails only in incurable cases.
Galen of Pergamon, Roman philosopher, physician, and medical researcher, 129
– c.210 A.D.

2.1 Science and forensic science

The area of forensic science has come under increasing scrutiny in the last decade
through a combination of seminal court rulings and major advances in science.
Several areas of forensic science thought for many years to be of sound basis
have been criticized as being based on false assumptions, poor science, inaccurate techniques, and erroneous interpretations. Unfortunately, some of these criticisms have turned out to be well-founded. It has now become widely recognized
that bullet lead analysis was flawed science from the beginning, with irrefutable
proof that its fundamental scientific hypothesis (that the chemical composition
of lead impurities was unique to particular manufactured batches) was erroneous
(National Research Council, 2004; Ungvarsky, 2006). The FBI has now discontinued the use of bullet lead analysis due to these revelations; however, there have still
been countless convictions based on this flawed forensic "science". The science
of arson investigation, based on analysis of fire-consumed property to determine
the origin of the fire, its behavior, and whether it had been deliberately lit, has
also very recently come under severe criticism. Many of the theories underlying
this forensic area had not been tested, and when experiments were conducted in
the early 1990s, basic assumptions held for several decades about the detection
of arson were proven wrong (Russell, 2006). Unfortunately, this has only come
to light via unfavorable media exposure and, most disturbingly, events such as the
execution of a man who—after the conduct of several arson experiments attempting
to prove its validity—was revealed to be more than likely innocent (Grann, 2009).
The use of DNA to reexamine evidence in past cases via *The Innocence Project* [1]

---

[1] The Innocence Project maintains an excellent website. See www.innocenceproject.org for further
details about their cases of DNA exoneration.

Forensic Testimony. http://dx.doi.org/10.1016/B978-0-12-397005-3.00002-5

has resulted in over two hundred exonerations so far, with many of the erroneous original convictions made on the basis of evidence given by forensic scientists.

2.1.1 Forensic "science"?

In 2009, the US Congress directed the National Academy of Sciences (NAS) to prepare a report on the status of forensic science in the United States. Many witnesses called to testify before the US Senate Committee on the Judiciary provided damning evidence against the discipline of forensic science. As one witness stated, forensic science represents "a system plagued by a paucity of good research, fragmentation, inconsistent practices, and weak governance (P2)" (Edwards, 2009).

The 2009 NAS Report noted that "the law's greatest dilemma in its heavy reliance on forensic evidence concerns the question of whether and to what extent there is any *science* in any given forensic science discipline (PS-7)." This observation can be further distilled into two independent issues: first, the extent to which any forensic discipline is based on reliable science; and second, the extent to which practitioners rely on human interpretation, which itself is subject to error, bias, and variable performance standards (National Research Council, 2009). Professors Michael Saks and D. Michael Risinger have noted that forensic science differs from what most consider "science" to be, with many disciplines having never been subjected to any formal validity testing (Saks & Risinger, 2003). They have stated that there are numerous problems with the research that has already been undertaken by forensic practitioners, including placing propositions beyond empirical reach by relying on subjective means of measurement; using research designs that cannot generate clear data on individual practitioner competence; manufacturing favorable test results by giving poor practitioner performances additional help or resources to reconsider their judgments; refusing to share data with researchers who wish to reanalyze or further analyze results; encouraging over-stated interpretations of data; burying unfavorable results in reports where they are least likely to be noticed; and generating disclaimers that the data cannot be used to infer the false positive error rate it reveals.

Professor David Faigman (Faigman, 2007) has also criticized the forensic sciences, inclusive of fingerprints, firearms, tool marks and bite marks, as "failed" sciences with little or no research basis and depending largely on the subjective judgment of practitioners. Labeling these and several other areas as "anecdotal sciences," he characterizes them as areas that lead to expert testimony based primarily on inductive experience, a philosophy of science advocated by Sir Francis Bacon in the 16th century, but now disputed by most 20th century philosophers as a largely invalid mode of scientific reasoning. Additionally, Professor Faigman has stated that these sciences contain a substantive degree of subjective judgment in their application, do not test their hypotheses in any serious manner, and only look for confirmation of their practice while rationalizing or ignoring contradictory evidence. He draws a parallel between forensic science and both phrenology and bloodletting,[2] two areas of science where practices continued for decades despite no evidence they ever achieved what they claimed they could, modeled on practices of simply "what had gone before." Ultimately, both of these disciplines failed as sciences and disappeared from modern-day practice. In another publication, Professor Saks (Saks, 2002) noted that *absence* of the type of data needed to evaluate criminal case expert testimony often seemed to be the rule, rather than the exception.

Professor Robert Park has identified seven "indicators that a scientific claim lies outside the bounds of rational scientific discourse" in an article originally intended as an aid to assist federal judges to detect "scientific nonsense" (Park, 2003). More than one of these indicators can be applied to forensic sciences. One such indicator is the statement that the belief is credible because it has endured for centuries. Bullet lead analysis has benefited from this justification (Inwinkelried & William, 2003), and judges in numerous cases have deferred to the long history of use of fingerprints as evidence for their reliability.[3] Other literature clearly demonstrates that practitioners and lay people often demonstrate unwavering belief in fingerprinting simply because it has been practiced for a long time (Haber and Haber, 2008). Professor Jennifer Mnookin suggests that some people argue that the reason fingerprint analysis seems so plausible is because its claims are true, citing the vantage point of one hundred years of experience "rather than because it fit within a particular cultural paradigm of 'uniqueness' and nature's infinite variety" (Pyrek, 2007). In a rare criticism from the judiciary, the judge in *State of Maryland v. Rose* (2007) likened unquestioning confidence in fingerprint evidence to some people's stubborn long-held belief in a flat Earth.[4] Even in the most recent Senate Judiciary Committee hearing, held to discuss the findings of the NAS Report on August 31, 2009, the ranking Republican Member—Senator Jeff Sessions (R-Alabama), a former United States District Attorney—said that he did not accept the Report's finding that some areas of forensic science, including fingerprints, were not scientifically based. He stated, "I don't think that we should suggest that [these sciences] that we have been using for decades are somehow uncertain" (Senate Judiciary Committee, 2009). Faced with such blunt denial of forensic science's problems, both critics and proponents face a difficult challenge in addressing the situation in which many forensic science disciplines are finding themselves.

---

[2] Phrenology was based on the theory that personality traits and mental faculties were reflected in the size and morphology of the surface of the human skull, reflecting the size and shape of the corresponding areas of the human brain that had grown underneath. It followed that one's skull could be "read" in order to reveal personality type and intellectual capability. Criminals in particular supposedly had distinctive skull morphologies that served as proof of their propensity to commit crimes in many courts. The theory was developed in the late 1790s and practiced widely until the mid-1800s, but by 1840 it had largely been discredited. For an interesting commentary on phrenology's role in law, see Schlag (1997).

[3] See *United States v. Cline* 188 F. Supp. 2d 1287, 1294 (D. Kan. Feb 21, 2002); *United States v. Havvard* 117 F. Supp. 2d 848, 849 (S.D. Ind. 2000), aff 'd, 260 F.3d 597 (7th Cir. 2001); and *United States v. Rogers* 26 Fed. Appx. 171, 2001 WL 1635494 (4th Cir. Dec. 20, 2001).

[4] See *State of Maryland v. Bryan Rose* No. K06-0545 (Md., Baltimore Co. Cir. Oct. 19, 2007). See also the article by Sileo (2008).

Another indicator of questionable science discussed by Park is the reliance on anecdotal evidence. One does not have to look very far in the forensic sciences to discover examples where anecdote has played a large role in the development of a practice. Fingerprint examiners have often testified in court about their practices' error rate based on personal anecdotes and experience (Haber & Haber, 2003). More specific examples of anecdotal evidence come from forensic odontology, which, in support of its status as a reliable science, has supposedly been practiced since the 1st century AD, when Nero's wife was apparently identified by her stained anterior tooth (Glass, 2009). Evidence for the individuality of the dentition is often propped up by such tales as that involving King William the Conqueror, who allegedly sealed his mail by biting into wax, leaving the outline of his maligned teeth (Cottone & Standish, 1982). There remains little other than anecdotal evidence to support these stories, which may be interesting (perhaps even true), but bear no relation to the more pressing issue of establishing a reliable basis for forensic science theory and practice.

A third warning sign of pseudoscience is that of the discoverer working in isolation. Consider the example of forensic odontologist Michael West. West claimed he could use a long-wave ultraviolet light to view not only bite marks invisible to the naked eye, but also impressions of murder weapon handles, bruises, scratches, and other injuries also otherwise invisible to other observers, both with and without the ultraviolet light enhancement (Fisher, 2008). Evidence discovered with this technique also could not be documented using photographs, due to the nature of the light source. Michael West's technique represented another two of Park's warning signs: the direct pitching of the claim to a party other than the scientific community (in this case, the courts), thereby bypassing the usual filter of peer review; and the scientific "effect" being at the very limit of detection. After his subsequent resignation from the American Academy of Forensic Sciences and the International Association for Identification and a twelve-month suspension from the American Board of Forensic Odontology, Michael West accused his colleagues of professional jealousy, resenting him for "hogging all the glory" (Fisher, 2008). Professor Park cautions that his seven signs are only "warnings" of the possibility of bogus science; however, with such high stakes riding on expert testimony in courts of law, many critics maintain that we should be keen to prevent even the remotest possibility of flawed science being involved in an erroneous conviction.

2.2 Scientific reasoning: Induction, deduction, and the hypothetico-deductive model

Many of the traditional and formerly unquestioned areas of forensic science, such as fingerprints, have come under criticism for their lack of scientific underpinning.[5] One of the main issues with these areas of forensic science is that

---

[5] See Begley (2004), Benedict (2004), Cole (2003), Epstein (2001), and Giannelli (2002) for a selection of some of the more recent examples.

their theories were developed by relying on inductive reasoning, rather than the now more favorable scientific epoch of deduction and the hypothetico-deductive model.

2.2.1 Inductive reasoning

In inductive reasoning, thought processes move from specific observations to more general ones, applying the theories suggested by observation of specific circumstances to broader situations. A key feature of induction is that generally it relies on accumulation of positive instances in order to verify a theory as correct. A prime example of inductive reasoning involves the tale of the coelacanth. For many years, scientists thought that a particular ancient species of fish, the coelacanth, had been extinct since the end of the Cretaceous period, some 80 million years ago. This thinking prevailed from the year 1836, when Agassiz described and named the coelacanth from the fossil record (Thomson, 1991). For the next one hundred years, it was presumed to have been extinct, as no one had ever come across a living specimen; however, a live coelacanth was caught off the coast of South Africa in 1938. Several have since been caught since off the coasts of East Africa and Indonesia, definitively proving their existence (Erdmann, Caldwell, & Moosa, 1998), and thus reasoning that the species was extinct simply because no one had ever seen one failed spectacularly. Such are the hazards of induction.

2.2.2 Deductive reasoning

Deductive reasoning, in contrast to inductive reasoning, works the other way: by moving from more generalized observations to developing theories about very specific things. Consequently, deductive arguments tend to be much narrower in form, and are therefore more easily substantiated. For example, inductive reasoning follows the following form:

No one has ever seen two identical fingerprints belonging to different people. Therefore, all fingerprints must be unique.

Deductive reasoning follows the form:

The degree of variation between two fingerprints from the same source is very small, and there is a high degree of variation amongst fingerprints from different people.

Therefore it is likely that fingerprints from two different people are going to be distinguishably different.

As you can see, with deductive reasoning, there is ample opportunity for *testing* hypotheses at each level of premise: the high degree of variation in individual fingerprints and the particular degree of variation between two prints from the same source can easily be verified by experimentation. Furthermore, in the deductive model, if the premise proves false, it instantly calls into question the conclusion—the likelihood that the prints originated from the same source—as they are logically related. Compare this language to the inductive example: it is virtually impossible to verify the notion that no one has ever seen two fingerprints that are the same belonging to two different people. Additionally, it does not *logically* lead us to the conclusion that all fingerprints can be considered unique—Just because no one has ever seen a matching pair of prints from different people does not mean that none exist.[6]

2.2.3 The hypothetico-deductive model

Modern science tends to progress via a cyclical process whereby hypotheses are generated from observations, these hypotheses are tested, and the results of these tests feed back through deductive reasoning into the generation of modified hypotheses, which are then further tested, and so on. This process is known as the hypothetico-deductive model of science. Testing is usually carried out in order to try and falsify the theory or proposition at stake—to deliberately attempt to prove the theory *wrong* through experimentation, rather than prove it right. This concept is known as falsification, and was first described by a philosopher, Karl Popper. By making assertive attempts to prove something wrong, the inability to do so provided a more robust argument to that theory then actually being correct, rather than trying to prove a theory by simply accumulating positive instances which may simply be the result of error, bias, or opportunity. Although the concept of falsification as the main paradigm in scientific thinking as described by the Supreme Court in *Daubert v Merrell Dow Pharmaceuticals Inc.*[7] has received criticisms from many modern-day philosophers of science, it certainly remains a useful cornerstone from which to build robust scientific theory.

Philosophers of science by no means universally agree that it represents the *only* way to acquire scientific knowledge; however, it is certainly a favored theory of the current time due to its advantage over the inherent uncertainty present in inductive methods. Another advantage of the hypothetico-deductive model is that it incorporates the observable results of tests into new or modified hypotheses, and allows theories to progress as more information becomes available. It also relies on

---

[6] There is a third paradigm, known as *abductive* reasoning. In abductive reasoning, the conclusion is derived from the data as being the *most likely* given some prior knowledge, and hence the conclusion offers the most reasonable explanation for the phenomenon observed. Use of abductive reasoning therefore involves some form of "leap of faith" in order to definitively attribute some phenomenon to an explanation. Despite some reference to abductive reasoning in the forensic science literature, abduction was considered "guessing" by the proponent of the theory himself, Charles Peirce, and in 1910 he wrote that it is based on the premise that guessing and intuition often display a better than random chance of being right due to some form of human "instinct." Abductive reasoning may have a place in the legal setting as far as describing the process by which a jury arrives at a hypothesis of guilt or innocence, given their role is to make such inferences based on "leaps" of abduction as they, out of anyone in the courtroom, have the benefit of all of the a priori knowledge available regarding the particular circumstances. However, abduction is not well-accepted by most philosophers of science as a particularly robust model of scientific thinking and so is not discussed further here.

[7] See *Daubert v Merrell Dow Pharmaceuticals Inc.* 509 US 579 (1993)

observations that are accessible to anyone in order to judge the validity of the theory, thus being open to criticism while at the same time being able to demonstrate rebuttal as necessary.

2.2.4 **Validity and reliability**

Of course, science and scientific hypothesis testing is only meaningful if it is conducted in a valid and reliable way. There is much discussion about the terms "validity" and "reliability." The concept of reliability has been the source of some confusion since the Supreme Court's construction of the term in the 1993 decision *Daubert v Merrell Dow Pharmaceuticals Inc*. Justice Blackmun then used the term *reliable* to distinguish science based on supporting facts, data, and reasoning from "unreliable," "junk," or "pseudoscience." Unfortunately, Justice Blackmun and his fellow Justices' use of reliable in this manner is not consistent with definitions of the term as understood by scientists. Consider a speedometer whose needle always reads 5 miles per hour faster than the actual speed you are traveling; that speedometer is 100% reliable, because it always gives the same reading in the same circumstances. Reliability in a strictly scientific sense refers to the *consistency* of results in any given test. Many forensic areas pass muster in this respect, such as polygraphy: the results of one examiner's test generally agree with another examiner's test. But the more important question in this scenario might be "Is what the polygraph examiners agree on actually correct?" In science, this concept is known as *validity*, and it refers to the accuracy of a particular test. The speedometer described above may be 100% reliable, but because it is also 100% wrong, as it always reads 5 miles per hour faster, its validity is technically zero.

Validity in science is further distilled into two distinct concepts. *Internal validity* refers to how well experiments or theories are constructed and assesses whether they were subject to bias, whether the results were accurately measured, and whether other potentially confounding variables were taken into consideration. For example, a study that assesses a fingerprint examiner's ability to identify latent prints in a murder case can suffer from threats to its internal validity if the participants have knowledge about the suspect's identification and his or her previous criminal history, as this can unconsciously bias them towards resolving ambiguities in favor of identifying one similar print over another. Consider a hypothesis that claims that people who own semiautomatic weapons are more likely to commit murder than those who own regular handguns. A study may also show that a disproportionate number of murders were committed by owners of semiautomatic weapons, and thus you may conclude that this theory seems reasonable. However, as it turns out, semiautomatic weapons were more likely to be owned by people who had previous convictions associated with drug crimes, and so the number of murders might actually be more related to involvement in drug dealing than to ownership of weapons. Drug-related criminal history is what is known as a *confounder* in this instance, and the validity of the theory that owners of semiautomatic weapons are more likely to commit murder is reduced due to the presence of a third, influencing variable—that of drug crime history—not accounted for in the study.[8]

External validity focuses on how applicable the theory or experiment is to application in the real-world situation. In order to maximize external validity, the theory or experiment must replicate as closely as possible the circumstances of the real world. For example, one of the major studies into fingerprint variation generated "partial" latent prints by cropping whole-print images from ten-print cards. This does not realistically represent the appearance of latent prints, which are often smudged, distorted, and on less than ideal mediums, in addition to only being of partial size. Additionally, latent prints are never subsets of the same print used for comparison: they are prints taken from supposedly the same *finger*, but at a different time and in different circumstances, thus representing two different *prints*. The external validity of this study was severely compromised, as its results are not realistically generalizable to the real-world situation it attempts to replicate.[9]

Despite the fact that the terms reliability and validity are technically distinct from one another, one must be mindful of the fact that much of the critical literature in forensic science uses the term *reliability* to simultaneously encompass the meaning of validity. Similarly, most interpretations of the term "reliable" when used in legal discussions of forensic science testimony are including both concepts of reliability and validity. While a plain-meaning approach is the most obvious choice when interpreting these terms in forensic expert testimony, it is important that the forensic expert understands the difference between the two, especially in his or her day-to-day work. What the courts ultimately want is some form of evidence that the experts can do what they say they can do, but the forensic expert should be mindful that this concept consists of both validity and reliability, and that the two are distinct, non-substitutable terms when it comes to discussing the scientific underpinning of forensic techniques.

2.3 **Forensic science and the scientific method**

The emergence of DNA identification in the forensic arena, with theories and techniques developed using these fundamental principles of scientific research, has helped expose some of the shaky scientific foundations on which other forensic sciences rest (Hansen, 2005). Other disciplines external to forensic science, such as data mining, location tracking, and biometric technologies, have also contributed to

---

[8] There are research methods that can assist with controlling for confounding variables, allowing reliable conclusions to be drawn from studies where such confounders may exist, however the details are well outside the scope of this text. The important point is that the study must be designed properly in order to control for the variable: potential confounders cannot be simply ignored.

[9] This study was colloquially known as the *50-K* fingerprint study, and was commissioned by the FBI in response to a courtroom challenge to the notion that fingerprints were "unique". It was never officially published, but enough details about its methods and results were made available to enable a scathing critique of its validity by several authors. See Epstein (2001), Kaye (2003), and Wayman (2000).

the exposure of the unreliability of traditional forensic techniques (Murphy, 2007). Faigman noted at the 2005 National Academy of Sciences symposium that "there is a most notable divide between forensic science and mainstream science. I'm not sure what the cause of (this void) is. ... The greatest challenge before us is figuring out a way to bring science to forensic science (P244)" (in Pyrek, 2007).

The problem with much of forensic science theory is that it is largely inductive, and has never been subject to rigorous tests that specifically attempt to falsify it. It has been said that forensic scientists in general have failed to consistently appreciate the implications of the scientific method (Thornton, Peterson, & Legget, 2007). The progression through the stages of research, formulation of a hypothesis, testing, analyzing results, and then modifying the hypothesis where necessary has the advantages of built-in evaluators, such as the calculation of error rates, as part of the process, in addition to other benefits, including its impartiality (Gauch, 2003). Indeed, the *Daubert* indicia, while not necessarily being representative of what reliability is to all things and all disciplines, arise as being the natural products of good research. Testing allows the generation of error rates and approximations, and good quality research is generally published, thereby being subject to peer review. Standardization of techniques and theories becomes necessary so as to ensure their validity and applicability in the hands of different researchers, scientists, and practitioners. Eventually, when a theory gains overwhelming support, it may even enter the realm of "general acceptance"; however, this by itself is no substitute for these first stages of scientific endeavor.

While academics note a tension between "science" and "forensic science," there are some who disagree that the traditional "scientific method" is appropriate for forensic science to follow, due to its unique position straddling the disciplines of both science and law. These contenders exploit this relationship, and note that forensic science is required to engage in the kind of scientific inquiry that cannot be modeled after the traditional natural sciences (Pyrek, 2007). As one author has written, forensic science operates outside the carefully controlled environment that the traditional sciences endure, and thus "the law-covering model of natural science accounts for expectations of scientific certainty, which no forensic science allegedly approximates ... (P6)" (James & Nordby, 2009). While it is true that the conditions appropriate for using traditional scientific models of research, for example, those used in chemistry, biology, or physics, are not applicable to the forensic sciences, neither are they individually applicable to each other—conditions and assumptions appropriate for experiments in physics are not appropriate for experiments in chemistry or biology, and vice versa. Each of these disciplines conduct independent, valid research in order to ascertain the boundaries of external influences, which enables scientists to then measure and subsequently account for them. Claiming that forensic science does not enjoy the pristine conditions of experimental science, and thus is not directly comparable, avoids a reality that has plagued all scientific research—a reality that has already been managed by experimental scientists through careful and deliberate hypothesis testing, but dismissed by forensic scientists by simply claiming irrelevance to their own practice.

Nordby (James & Nordby, 2009) has further noted that "in the forensic sciences, we reason from a set of given results (a crime scene, for example) to their probable explanations (hopefully, a link to the perpetrator) (P8)." While the forensic scientist makes deductions from given data in order to draw conclusions, it is the theory behind these deductions that has often failed to subsequently undergo the rigorous testing, reformulation, and refining that those associated with traditional science would. There is a tendency to accept the theory without questioning its underlying basis, simply because it appears to fit one, or perhaps several, examples.

2.4 Uncertainty and error in science

One of the most distinguishing features of scientific practice is that scientists almost always attempt to describe the likelihood of their results being wrong, or they try to describe the amount of uncertainty present in any result. This feature of modern-day science helps others assign value to particular studies, acknowledging that while no study is perfect, some are clearly better than others. Forensic scientists grounded in "hard" sciences, like forensic chemistry, may have well-established thresholds for error and uncertainty, and may be used to expressing results this way. Others, such as those in the pattern-identification sciences, like fingerprint analysis and tool mark analysis, are still a long way from being able to accurately portray just how much error and uncertainty is in a given result. There has been a history of claiming infallibility, or 100% accuracy in these disciplines, rather than admitting the possibility of error or attempting to quantify it. These claims are increasingly being met with skepticism from the courts.

It appears that many forensic scientists are concerned about admitting the possibility of error, lest it potentially render their testimony obsolete; but this is not a logical consequence of being able to quantify error in forensic science. Let's use the example of the speedometer in the previous section. If we know through experimentation and assessment of its performance that the speedometer always reads 5 miles per hour faster, despite the device not being particularly valid from a theoretical standpoint, it nonetheless is still capable of providing us with very useful information about what speed we might be traveling. On the other hand, this usefulness is decreased when all we know is that it reads somewhat high—but we aren't sure by how much. Its usefulness is decreased even further when we know it might be wrong, but we don't know when or under what circumstances. The same can be said for any forensic technique. Additionally, the qualification and quantification of error allows us to then take reasonable steps to correct the problem: in this case, by mechanically adjusting the needle mechanism, thereby allowing us to systematically improve its validity. The same analogy can be applied to forensic science in that once the quantity and quality of error is determined, one can make targeted attempts at improving the practice by addressing those errors.

Results in science are often expressed as ranges in order to account for the fact that there are always flaws in any research method, including issues associated with measurement, sampling errors, bias and a host of others. These flaws introduce error into the results, and the size this error or uncertainty can be mathematically derived through some standard statistical methods. This is important to realize–reporting of uncertainty and error in science never represents an indication of how confident the researcher "feels" that they are right. Statements regarding personal certainty or confidence should have no place in forensic expert testimony.[10]

2.5 Peer review, publication, and evidence-based forensics

Critics, including the courts, have noted a somewhat lesser standard in the quality of forensic science literature compared to mainstream science. In a case from the mid-1990s the judge commented that "... the court found ... these articles [published in several forensic journals] to be significantly different from scholarly articles in such fields as medicine or physics, in their lack of critical scholarship."[11] While many critics publish in high-ranking journals, many comprehensive responses issued by members of the forensic community either fail to be published in journals of equal status, or fail to categorically disprove such criticisms. As an example, one of only two genuinely comprehensive responses to Professors Saks and Koehler's now infamous article *The Coming Paradigm Shift in Forensic Identification Science* (published in *Science,* one of the top three most cited journals in the world) appeared in the *Crime Lab Report,* the internet publication of a self-described "independent organization that analyzes media coverage, industry trends, and public-policies related to forensic science laboratory testing and its application within the criminal justice system" (Crime Lab Report, 2009). The other response appeared in the *News of the California Association of Criminalists.* Four brief replies to Saks and Koehler's article were published in an issue of *Science,* in the Letters section (Harmon et al., 2006); however, a total of twelve references were all that were cited between them in support of their rebuttals. Four of these references were by the same author, and three others were US government-sponsored reports. None of the other 21 articles by other authors that could be found published in peer-reviewed [scientific or law] journals as citing *The Coming Paradigm Shift* offered critique of Saks and Koehler's article; and in fact, other articles largely supported their position.

Edmond (2008) makes a number of valid points about the philosophy of journal publication and the peer-review process, concluding that these and other "ingredients of popular representations of science and medicine ... are unlikely to provide the kinds of discriminating criteria that might guide ... meaningful assessments of expert evidence (P12)." This may be true in terms of usefulness for a lay juror or judge; however, this is not necessarily true for the scientists and

[10] Two of the most common ways of reporting the level of certainty in science are measures known as the *confidence interval* and the *p-value*. Their derivation and applicability are beyond the scope of this text, however, any basic statistics textbook should cover these topics in more than adequate detail.
[11] See *United States v. Starzecpyzel*, 880 F.Supp. 1027 (S.D.N.Y.) 1995; See also Giannelli, 2009.

academics who form the majority population in criticizing forensic science. It is a quintessential part of scientific culture that hypotheses, theories, and methods pass through the filter of the general scientific community via publication in scientific journals. If the forensic-science community intends to address such criticisms, it needs far more scientifically valid, research-based evidence than currently exists in order to counter the growing pile of irrefutable scientific literature exposing its flaws. The process of peer-review and publication is one way to ensure that such a base can establish itself, as many other reputable areas of science and medicine have done.

In the comparison of physical evidence types, evidence may be classified as "born of" or "the same as" (Faigman, Saks, Sanders, & Cheng, 2007). Most disciplines, due to the inherent nature of the type of evidence they deal with, establish identity based on one or the other of these principles; for example, forensic chemists will identify chemicals "the same as" in analyzing whether a particular powder is heroin or not, whereas firearms investigators generally establish evidence as being "born of" a particular weapon's barrel. The latter argument is much harder to prove than the first, and represents the unique position that forensic science finds itself in—particularly the forensic identification sciences—that other sciences do not. However, the absence of a common "ultimate forensic question" should not excuse these disciplines from following perfectly rational requests to prove their long-held theories of association.

Most critics simply claim they ask for nothing more than "evidence-based forensics" (Cole, 2007; Edmond, 2008). The concept of evidence-based practice has been long accepted in other scientific disciplines, such as medicine. While evidence-based medicine (EBM) is not without controversy, it has been enormously influential in health care, and has been described as a powerful metaphor suitable for importation into other areas of technical decision making (Cole, 2007). Evidence-based practice is typified by repeated, rigorous data gathering, rather than relying on rules, singular observations, or custom. EBM has led to the development of systems to stratify evidence, and there are now several systems to choose from, with subtleties dependent on the nature of the empirical question. Fundamentally, however, they all classify evidence on a graded scale from high to low value, with anywhere from three to five main levels (one being the highest, five being the lowest). The Oxford Centre for Evidence-Based Medicine (CEBM) has developed a comprehensive schema of levels of evidence, with levels one, two, and three each being subdivided into categories a, b, and c (category a representing the highest sub-level). What is immediately apparent is that the *lowest* level of evidence, in all of the classification systems in existence, is that of "expert opinion, without specific critical appraisal, or based on bench research, or 'first principles'" (Oxford Centre for Evidence-based Medicine, 2009).[12]

---

[12] Case reports, the other favored approach of forensic scientists in reporting research data, similarly represent another example of very low-level evidence in this hierarchy.

The highest level of evidence (almost always Level 1 or A in such classification systems) is generally that obtained by a systematic review of existing experimental research that is based on randomized, controlled trials and studies validated in different populations. But just because a study is designated "randomized and controlled" does not mean that it automatically gains status in the level-of-evidence hierarchy. Studies that fail to clearly define comparison groups, fail to measure outcomes in the same objective way, fail to identify confounders, or fail to test "blind" fall into the poor-quality category, and consequently, the relative level of evidence assigned to the inferences drawn from these results falls. The advantage of the EBM model is that it has a systemized approach to look beyond the numerical results of the study in order to ascertain the true meaning of its conclusions.

Applying this evidence-hierarchy framework to forensic science highlights numerous deficiencies in its research base. Consider one discipline in forensic science that has faced a great deal of criticism over its theory in the last decade: forensic odontology. There is no question that there is an established body of literature concerning the theory and application of forensic odontology; publications such as the *Journal of Forensic Science, Forensic Science International*, and the *Journal of Forensic Odontostomatology* have published articles on bite mark analysis for many years. However, not all of this literature should be judged equal. In 2001, two researchers reviewed all of the English-language articles concerning bite marks from 1960 to 1999. From the 120 papers considered, case reports accounted for 28%, while empirical research accounted for only 15%. There were more review articles (which usually just describe the current understanding of a particular topic, and don't involve any experimental research) than the number of actual research articles published in the same period. Only 44% of all the literature published had been cited since publication, with most citation accounted for in the review articles. It would not be unreasonable to conclude that more than half of the articles published regarding bite marks are never considered seriously by other researchers in the field. This raises serious questions regarding the type and quality of the literature being produced in this discipline.

2.6 Improving the science of forensic science

Given the judiciary's own reluctance to deny long-standing forensic techniques their current status, undoubtedly due to intense political, social, and peer pressures,[13] it is clear that the law by itself has not been able to rectify the poor scientific standing of some forensic sciences. Other authors have proposed law reform in order to allow defendants wrongly convicted certain avenues of appeal (Gable & Wilkinson, 2007); however, law reform in general takes many years to evolve. Even proponents of such dramatic solutions also recognize that the shortcomings of the sciences themselves

---

[13] Among others noted by one author in an analysis of the influences on judicial decision making (Harris, 2008).

ultimately need to be addressed. This means that practitioners and professors of such "sciences" need to take responsibility to ensure the scientific basis of their own disciplines can withstand such criticism.

One of the key barriers to improving the scientific standing of much of forensic science is the lack of acknowledgement that any such improvement is necessary. Reliance on a technique simply because it has been used for many years runs the dangerous risk that the underlying theories are not as robust as once thought; comparative bullet lead analysis is a perfect example of this. Bloodletting is now a laughable proposition to most in the 21st century, yet its origins were based on similar principles of "doing what we've always done," bolstered by success in some cases, while somehow rationalizing, or even worse, ignoring those cases where it had failed. [14] Admission is the first step towards rehabilitation.

That is not to say that all, or even most, forensic science is "junk science" and of no value to the criminal justice system. To say this would be to throw not just one but many babies out with the bathwater. The problem is that many forensic science practices lack robust support for their theoretical and scientific underpinnings, which has led to various claims based on nothing more than collective opinion. These claims have been perpetuated over the years with little challenge, to the point where some claims now verge on the ridiculous, such as the ability to "identify to the exclusion of all others," or claim an error rate of "zero." Judges can attempt to limit or even exclude evidence in certain cases, but this has a very limited effect on the overall practice of the discipline due to the inherent case-, circumstance-, and jurisdiction-specific nature of judicial precedent. The only way to reign in these patently spurious claims is to actually ascertain the boundaries of what the forensic sciences can and cannot do. Fortunately, there is already a tried and tested framework available to forensic scientists on which to base this attempt: it's called *science*.

---

[14] Fingerprint examiners often cite the work of Sir Francis Galton in establishing the basis for fingerprint identification. Many of them would do well to actually read Galton's work, for it leaves much to be desired in terms of proper scientific and statistical methodology. Simon Cole's book *Suspect Identities: A history of fingerprinting and criminal identification* also provides a good historical background to and critique of Galton's work in this respect.

References

Begley, S., 2004. Despite its reputation, fingerprint evidence isn't really infallible. Wall Street Journal, 04 Jun 2004, pp. B1.

Benedict, N., 2004. Fingerprints and the Daubert Standard for Admission of Scientific Evidence: Why Fingerprints Fail and a Proposed Remedy Note. Ariz. L Rev. 46, 519.

Cole, S.A., 2003. Fingerprinting: The First Junk Science Forensics Symposium: The Use and Misuse of Forensic Evidence. Okla. City U L Rev. 28, 73.

Cole, S.A., 2007. Toward Evidence-Based Evidence: Supporting Forensic Knowledge in the Post-Daubert Era. Tulsa L Rev. 43 (2), 101.

Cole, S.A., 2001. Suspect Identities: A history of fingerprinting and criminal identification. Harvard University Press, Cambridge, MA.

Cottone, J.A., Standish, S.M., 1982. Outline of Forensic Dentistry. Yearbook Medical Publishers, Chicago.

Crime Lab Report, 2009. http://www.crimelabreport.com/library.htm, accessed on 30 Oct, 2009.

Edmond, G., 2008. Pathological Science? Demonstrable Reliability and Expert Forensic Pathology Expertise. UNSW Law Research Paper No.2008-6, 12.

Edwards, H.T., 2009. Statement before the United States Senate Committee on the Judiciary. Strengthening Forensic Science in the United States: A Path Forward, 2009, 2.

Epstein, R., 2001. Fingerprints Meet Daubert: The Myth of Fingerprint Science is Revealed. S Cal. L Rev. 75, 605.

Erdmann, M.V., Caldwell, R.L., Moosa, M.K., 1998. Indonesian 'king of the sea' discovered. Nature 395, 335.

Faigman, D.L., 2007. Anecdotal Forensics, Phrenology and Other Abject Lessons from the History of Science. Hastings L.J. 59, 979–1000.

Faigman, D.L., Saks, M.J., Sanders, J., Cheng, E.K., 2007. Modern Scientific Evidence: The Law and Science of Expert Testimony. Thomson/West, Minnesota.

Fisher, J., 2008. Forensics under fire: are bad science and dueling experts corrupting criminal justice? Rutgers University Press, New Brunswick, N.J.

Gable, J.D., Wilkinson, M.D., 2007. Good Science Gone Bad: How the Criminal Justice System Can Redress the Impact of Flawed Forensics Symposium. Hastings L.J. 59, 1001–1030.

Gauch, H.G., 2003. Scientific method in practice. Cambridge University Press, New York.

Giannelli, P.C., 2002. Fingerprints Challenged Scientific Evidence. Crim. Just. 17, 33.

Giannelli, P.C., 2009. Daubert Factors. Crim. Just. 23, 42.

Glass, R.T., 2009. Forensic Odontology. In: James, S.H., Nordby, J.J. (Eds.), Forensic Science: An Introduction to Scientific and Investigative Techniques, CRC Press, p. 757.

Grann, D., 2009. Trial by Fire - Did Texas execute an innocent man? The New Yorker, 07 Sep 2009 Reporter at Large, 42–63.

Haber, L., Haber, R.N., 2003. Error Rates for Human Latent Fingerprint Examination. In: Ratha, N.K. (Ed.), Advances in Automatic Fingerprint Recognition, Springer-Verlag, New York.

Haber, L., Haber, R.N., 2008. Scientific validation of fingerprint evidence under Daubert. Law Probablity and Risk 7 (2), 127–141.

Hansen, M., 2005. The Uncertain Science of Evidence. American Bar Association J. 91 (7), 48.

Harmon, R., Budowle, B., Langenburg, G., Houck, M., Kelly, J., 2006. Questions About Forensic Science. Science 311 (5761), 607–610.

Harris, R.C., 2008. Black robes, white coats: the puzzle of judicial policymaking and scientific evidence. Rutgers University Press, New Brunswick, N.J.

Inwinkelried, E.J.T., William, A., 2003. Comparative Bullet Lead Analysis (CBLA) Evidence: Valid Inference or Ipse Dixit Forensics Symposium: The Use and Misuse of Forensic Evidence. Okla. City U L Rev. 28, 43.

James, S.H., Nordby, J.J., 2009. Forensic science: an introduction to scientific and investigative techniques. CRC Press/Taylor & Francis Group, Boca Raton, FL, 6.

Kaye, D.H., 2003. Questioning a courtroom proof of the uniqueness of fingerprints. Int. Stat. Rev. 71 (3), 521–533.

Murphy, E., 2007. The New Forensics: Criminal Justice, False Certainty, and the Second Generation of Scientific Evidence. Cal. L Rev. 95, 721.

National Research Council, 2004. FBI Should Revise Approach to Bullet Lead Comparison And Carefully Limit Its Use in the Courtroom. Media Release, 10 Feb 2004, available at http://www8.nationalacademies.org/onpinews/newsitem.aspx?RecordID=10924.

National Research Council, 2009. Strengthening Forensic Science in the United States: A Path Forward National Academies Press. S-7.

Oxford Centre for Evidence-based Medicine, Levels of Evidence, 2009. Available at: http://www.cebm.net/index.aspx?o=1025#levels

Park, R.L., 2003. The Seven Warning Signs of Bogus Science. The Chronicle of Higher Education 49 (21), 20.

Pyrek, K., 2007. Forensic science under siege: the challenges of forensic laboratories and the medico-legal death investigation system. Elsevier Academic Press, Amsterdam; Boston, 244.

Russell, S., 2006. Down in Flames - 'Rock-solid' evidence for arson turns out to be anything but. New Scientist, 42–45, 14 Nov 2006.

Saks, M.J., 2002. The Legal and Scientific Evaluation of Forensic Science. Seton Hall L Rev. 33, 1167.

Saks, M.J., Koehler, J.J., 2005. The Coming Paradigm Shift in Forensic Identification Science. Science, 309(5739), 892.

Saks, M.J., Risinger, D.M., 2003. A House With No Foundation. Issues Sci. Tech, Fall, 35.

Schlag, P., 1997. Law and Phrenology. Harvard Law Review 97, 877.

Scientific Working Group on Friction Ridge Analysis Study and Technology, 1997. Proposed SWGFAST guidelines. J. Forensic Identification 47, 425.

Senate Judiciary Committee, 2009. Strengthening Forensic Science in the United States. Hearing before the Senate Committee on the Judiciary, 09 Sep 2009.

Sileo, C., 2008. Maryland judge rubs out fingerprint evidence. Trial 44 (2).

Thomson, K.S., 1991. Living fossil: the story of the coelacanth. W.W. Norton, New York.

Thornton, J.I., Peterson, J.L., Legget, A.S., 2007. The General Assumptions and Rationale of Forensic Identification. In: Faigman, D.L., Saks, M.J., Sanders, J., Cheng, E.K. (Eds.), Modern Scientific Evidence, Thomson West.

Ungvarsky, E.J., 2006. Remarks on the Use and Misuse of Forensic Science to Lead to False Convictions. New Eng. L Rev. 41, 609.

Wayman, J.L., 2000. When Bad Science Leads to Good Law: The disturbing irony of the Daubert hearing in the case of *U.S. v. Byron C. Mitchell*. Available at: www.engr.sjsu.edu/biometrics/publications_daubert.html

THE INNOCENCE BLOG

Compensating Colorado's Wrongfully Convicted

Posted: 11 Mar 2013 02:05 PM PDT

Legislation that would award Colorado's wrongfully convicted $70,000 for each year of incarceration was unanimously passed by the House Judiciary Committee Thursday and now moves to the House Appropriations Committee, where it faces a vote that could bring it before the House floor.

One proponent of the compensation bill, HB 1230, is Timothy Masters, whose wrongful conviction cost him nearly a decade of his life and left him broke upon his release. Masters would not personally benefit from the bill. *The Coloradoan* reports:

"To me it's a no-brainer," Masters said. "If we as a society lock somebody up for years for something they didn't do, we've got to do something for them when they get out of prison."

Masters was convicted in 1999 of the 1987 murder of a 37-year-old woman in Fort Collins, Colorado. He was 15 when the crime was committed. He was released in 2008 with only the money he earned working for minimum wage in the saddle shop at Buena Vista Correctional Facility and no state assistance. Two years later, Masters received a $10 million settlement from the city of Fort Collins and Larimer County. However, most exonerees are not able to win a lawsuit because of the challenges of proving that their wrongful conviction resulted from intentional misconduct.

The bill, proposed by Reps. Angela Williams and Dan Pabon, both Denver Democrats, would entitle death row prisoners to an additional $50,000 for each year served, and wrongfully convicted people would be eligible for $25,000 for each year they were on parole. Those wrongfully imprisoned for at least three years would be eligible for college tuition, compensation for child support they were unable to pay while incarcerated, attorney fees and fines and other costs associated with their court cases. About half of the states have a compensation law on the books, though the awards vary greatly and are often insufficient for rebuilding a life. If HB 1230 becomes law, it would rank among the nation's best.

Colorado Attorney General John Suthers testified in support of the bill. And although Masters was unable to attend the committee hearing, Innocence Project client Robert Dewey, who was exonerated of murder in Colorado last year after serving 17 years in prison, was on hand to give testimony about the challenges faced once released.

"Best job you can get is cleaning toilets," he said Thursday during testimony that left lawmakers wiping tears from their eyes.

The Admissibility of Forensic Expert Evidence

Mark Page

3.1 The admissibility of forensic expert evidence

Courts of law are governed by standards known as *rules*, sometimes referred to as *codes*. These rules articulate the procedural and legal standards by which the law is to be applied and trials are to be conducted in order to ensure consistency, transparency, and fairness across the legal system. Each state publishes its own sets of rules, to be followed in their respective state courts, and the vast majority are at least partially based on those articulated by the federal government for use in the federal court system. One of the most important series of rules that the expert forensic witness should be familiar with are the Rules of Evidence. Experts are privileged in the legal system in that they are allowed to express their opinion, a privilege that is deliberately denied from ordinary witnesses in order to ensure that only "facts" are presented to the judge and jury, and not personal opinion that may be knowingly (or unknowingly) prejudiced. The Federal Rules of Evidence outline the circumstances and standards to which material evidence is adduced in federal trials, and includes provisions that articulate expectations of forensic experts when testifying in federal courts.[1]

Yet the law is dynamic, and interpretations of statutes, rules, and codes evolve as they are applied repeatedly but in slightly different circumstances. While the rules of evidence lay down fundamental legal principles regarding procedures and standards to be followed when adducing evidence in court, the interpretation and application of these rules has been shaped by judges who have had to construe their meaning during the course of actual trials—in other words, *case law*. It is important for forensic experts to be familiar with the key case law that supports the rules in any given jurisdiction they intend to give evidence in so as to ensure that they meet the standards expected of the legal system and avoid challenges to, limitation of, or, at

---

[1] The state of Georgia represents a notable exception to the generalization that the wording of most states' rules of evidence are similar to one another and based on the federal rules. Georgia has separate codes for criminal versus civil evidence standards. While they recently adopted revised rules for expert opinion in line with Federal Rules 702 and 703 in civil trials, state prosecutors opposed any change to the existing rule in criminal trials. Consequently, in criminal cases, "the opinions of experts on any question of science, skill, trade, or like questions shall always be admissible." (See GA CODE 24-9-67 *Opinions of experts admissible in criminal cases* (2010), and Milich, 2012). This is in very different terms to that of most other states and the Federal Rules of Evidence, as discussed later in this chapter.

Forensic Testimony. http://dx.doi.org/10.1016/B978-0-12-397005-3.00003-7

worse, exclusion of their testimony. At the federal level, by far the most important cases that comment on the applicability of the Federal Rules of Evidence are the *Daubert*[2] and *Kumho*[3] cases. *Daubert* superseded the *Frye*[4] ruling on expert evidence statute interpretation in federal jurisdictions in 1993, and a majority of states have eventually followed suit; however, some states still follow *Frye*'s guidance rather than *Daubert*'s on interpretation of their respective rule's language. Discussion of these important cases will follow in this chapter. While most have explicitly adopted one of these two case law standards, other states follow different case law precedents, although usually with an over-arching *Frye* template, such as *Kelly-Frye*[5] in California, and *Frye-Reed*[6] in Maryland. Given that most statutes and case law are based on similar precedents, let us explore some cases and general legal principles regarding the admissibility of expert testimony.

3.1.1 **Frye v. United States**

A murder case, *Frye v. United States,*[7] set the standard for the admissibility of scientific expert testimony in the United States for nearly seventy years. In *Frye*, an expert for the defendant offered testimony based on the results of an early form of polygraph testing in support of his innocence. The trial judge found this evidence inadmissible, citing the fact that there was no "general acceptance" of this technique in any relevant community of experts. The appellate court upheld the trial judge's ruling, and gradually "general acceptance" became the standard to which other expert testimony was subsequently held in other US courts.[8] Initially it was claimed that the *Frye* standard promoted judicial efficiency and uniformity of decisions through the courts, as well as preventing unproven hypotheses from having a potentially prejudicial effect on the trier of fact. But the vagueness of *Frye* ultimately gave free reign to individual courts in determining fundamental issues, such as what particular scientific field should be consulted, what was meant by "general acceptance," and what exactly sufficed as proof that such acceptance had been achieved (Black, Ayala, & Saffran-Brinks, 1994). *Frye* did not appear to address the real question at hand, which was whether the testimony was derived from valid scientific knowledge; thus it led to confusion and contradictory rulings in different jurisdictions concerning the same types of evidence.

---

[2] *Daubert v. Merrell Dow Pharmaceuticals, Inc.* 509 U.S. 579 (1993)

[3] *Kumho Tire Co., Ltd v. Carmichael* 526 US 137 (1999)

[4] *Frye v. United States* 293 F. 1013 (D.C.Cir., 1923)

[5] See *People v. Kelly,* 17 Cal. 3d 24 (1976)

[6] See *Reed v. State*, 283 Md. 374 (1978)

[7] *Supra* n.4

[8] "Just when a scientific principle or discovery crosses the line between the experimental and demonstrable stages is difficult to define. Somewhere in this twilight zone the evidential force of the principle must be recognized, and while courts will go a long way in admitting expert testimony deduced from a well-recognized scientific principle or discovery, the thing from which the deduction is made must be sufficiently established to have gained general acceptance in the particular field in which it belongs." See *Frye v. United States*, 293 F. 1013, 1014 (D.C.Cir., 1923)

3.1.2 **The Federal Rules of Evidence**

In 1975, legislation pertaining to the admissibility of evidence at trial was passed in the form of the US Federal Rules of Evidence. This statute was drafted by the US Supreme Court and approved by Congress, which enacted the federal rules under public law. The rules provided a legislative framework for evidentiary standards that were intended to be applied across the federal judicial system, and therefore it was envisaged that they would provide a more standardized approach to evidence admissibility in the federal courts. Rule 702 specifically allowed anyone with scientific, technical, or other knowledge to render an opinion as an "expert," providing that opinion would assist the trier of fact. However, there was little guidance on how judges should decide whether or not evidence could be potentially helpful to a case, and this became problematic, particularly as a great many technical witnesses could now be qualified as "experts" and render opinion on any number of obscure topics. In an attempt to prevent so-called "junk science" from infiltrating criminal and civil trials, most judges still used the *Frye* notion of requiring evidence to be generally accepted by members of the scientific community in order for it to be considered relevant and therefore helpful to the trier of fact, although this was by no means a universally accepted standard, and not one that had specifically been endorsed by the Supreme Court at that time. However, in 1993, the US Supreme court agreed to hear a case that raised the very question of interpretation of Rule 702, and how judges were to go about excluding expert witnesses so as to ensure juries were not subject to spurious scientific claims.

3.1.3 **Daubert v. Merrell Dow Pharmaceuticals, Inc.**

The *Daubert* case began in 1989, when a pharmaceutical company was sued in a California court on the basis that one of their products, Bendectin, an anti-nausea drug commonly prescribed to pregnant women for morning sickness from the 1960s through the early 1980s, had caused birth defects in the plaintiff's child.[9] There was little evidence to support a link between this particular drug and birth defects; however, the plaintiff's case rested largely on the testimony of an expert who had performed his own reanalysis of much of the supporting scientific literature. He reached a conclusion *contradictory* to that suggested by most of the original research authors, who had found it unlikely to cause such injury. According to the trial judge, the plaintiff's expert did not meet the thresholds required of expert opinion; his evidence was excluded at trial, and the plaintiffs' lost the case. After the Ninth Circuit upheld this decision, the plaintiffs took their case to the US Supreme Court, and asked it to review whether the plaintiff's expert had been properly excluded as an expert witness in the original trial. The basis of the argument was that the lower courts had improperly excluded the expert from providing testimony as the trial judge had used the *Frye* principle of "general acceptance" when performing an

---

[9] Bendectin was withdrawn from the market in 1983 due to several prior lawsuits, none of which had been successful, and has not been available since. See Brody, 1983.

assessment of his expert evidence. The plaintiff argued that under the Federal Rules of Evidence there was no specific requirement for such a threshold to be met. The Supreme Court affirmed that the *Frye* standard was no longer applicable under the federal rules, which favored a much more liberal approach to assessing the validity of expert testimony; however, it went much further by then attempting to clarify several other key aspects of expert witness testimony. Trial judges were to undertake assessment of expert evidence via a two-pronged approach: assessment of the *relevancy* of the testimony, and assessment of the *reliability* of the testimony. The former was relatively easily accomplished, and had in fact already existed through the extant version of the federal rules at that time;[10] however, the specific notion of a reliability assessment was something not previously articulated by any of the extant case law.

The Supreme Court acknowledged that many considerations would bear on this reliability inquiry, including whether the theory or technique in question had been, or could be, tested, whether it had been subject to peer review and publication, what the known or potential error rate for the technique might be, whether there were particular standards upheld in order to control its operation, and, finally, in a nod to the *Frye* standard it had now displaced, whether it had attracted widespread acceptance within a relevant scientific community. The court emphasized that this list was *not* meant to serve as a definitive checklist or test that would necessarily direct a reliability enquiry—such an enquiry was to be a flexible one, and might include other factors as relevant to the evidence at hand—yet these five considerations quickly became summarized as the "*Daubert*" factors, and have been applied as pre-conditions for admissibility in some cases amid much controversy since. Furthermore, the Supreme Court in *Daubert* definitively placed the responsibility of "gatekeeping" expert witnesses on the trial judge in order to prevent spurious experts from potentially influencing juries through "junk science." The court made it very clear that it was the judge's *responsibility* to make a preliminary assessment of the evidence offered by the expert, and to decide whether or not it was admissible prior to it being heard by juries.[11]

Daubert rendered a paradigm shift in the way expert testimony was now to be considered, yet confusion initially reigned as to whether this meant a more liberal admission of expert evidence or a more restrictive one, and the answer was, essentially, both. *Daubert*, unlike *Frye*, was designed to encourage assessment of each expert discipline on its objective merits, rather than by consensus view among those who supposedly practiced what they preached. This meant that emerging areas of science with a sound basis could potentially be used in court, despite a lack of

---

[10] See Fed. R. Evid. 401 & 402 (Pub. L. 93–595, §1, Jan. 2, 1975, 88 Stat. 1931)

[11] The Supreme Court avoided a direct ruling either in favor of or against the plaintiff. Instead, they directed the Ninth Circuit to review their original decision in the plaintiff's 1991 appeal, by specifically reconsidering the question of whether the plaintiff's expert's opinion was properly excluded in light of the Supreme Court's ruling that expert testimony was not to be assessed under *Frye*, but on the basis of its reliability in addition to its relevancy. The Ninth Circuit reconsidered the case in 1995, and reached the same opinion as it did in 1991: the expert was properly excluded, and so the plaintiff ultimately lost the case. (See *Daubert v. Merrell Dow Pharmaceuticals, Inc. II* 43 F.3d 1311 [9th Cir., 1995])

"general acceptance," which is often the case in relatively new disciplines. By the same token, it meant that many areas of science that had rested on expert consensus as a basis for its foundation would find themselves in trouble in the wake of a rigorous scientific enquiry. Forensic science initially found itself in this latter category, with a startling lack of empirical data through which to verify claims of reliability in many areas considered to be mainstream forensic disciplines.[12]

3.1.4 Kumho Tire. v. Carmichael

After the *Daubert* ruling, many judges, lawyers, and witnesses still remained perplexed at the applicability of the Supreme Court's new mandate. In 1999, they ruled again on a case that addressed some of the issues left untouched by *Daubert*. Following an automotive accident in which a tire blew out, injuring three passengers and killing another, the plaintiff in *Kumho*[13] filed suit against the tire company claiming that the tire was defective and caused the accident. The plaintiff's expert's testimony was based on his visual and tactile inspection of many tires, and on his underlying theory that in the absence of at least two of four physical symptoms indicating abuse, the tire failure was due to a manufacturing or design defect. The trial court excluded this testimony, as in their opinion it did not meet the requirements set out in Rule 702 of the Federal Rules of Evidence and *Daubert*, having not been subject to peer review or testing and lacking an acceptable methodology. The appellate court disagreed with this exclusion as, in their opinion, *Daubert* only referred to *scientific* evidence; they reasoned that given the expert's testimony in *Kumho* was skill and experience based, *Daubert* did not apply. Following the reversal of the trial court's decision, the defendants appealed to the US Supreme Court, requesting a review of the Eleventh Circuit's decision. The Supreme Court, in turn, held that *Daubert* "may apply to testimony of engineers and other experts who may not be considered, strictly speaking "scientists"; and furthermore, the language of Rule 702 applied to *all* expert testimony. The court also reiterated that the factors identified for assessment of reliability in *Daubert* were not exclusive means of assessing expert testimony, and that the trial judge has broad latitude in deciding whether they were, or were not, reasonable measures of reliability. The *Kumho* court also stated that trial judges, when performing their reliability assessments, should make certain that an expert, whether basing testimony upon professional studies or personal experience, employs in the courtroom the same level of intellectual rigor that characterizes the practice of an expert in the relevant field, although this was not to be the *only* form of enquiry.

3.1.5 Expert witness testimony today

The Federal Rules of Evidence are subject to review periodically. The last major review relevant to those rules governing expert testimony occurred in the year 2000,

---

[12] See Pyrek, 2007
[13] *Kumho Tire v. Carmichael,* 526 US 137 (1997)

when several aspects of the *Daubert* and *Kumho* cases were integrated into the rules through the revision of the language of Rule 702 and 703.[14] Nonetheless, *Daubert* and *Kumho* are still the leading authorities when it comes to general interpretation of these rules, and they remain very relevant to expert witnesses today. Where clarification of the rules is sought, these and other cases continue to provide evolving guidance on application of the rules to judicial procedures. Let us now consider some of the specific aspects of the rules regarding expert testimony.

3.1.5.1 Who can give an opinion?

Rule 701 of the federal rules limits the expression of opinion from lay witnesses to one that is gained from first-hand knowledge or observation and is essential to help resolve a particular issue.[15] This limitation helps preserve the witnesses' opinion evidence as that based on fact, not potentially biased personal assertions. These witnesses can therefore essentially only testify as to what they saw or heard. Rule 701 clarifies that expert witnesses, that is, those with scientific, technical, or other specialized knowledge, are exempt from this limitation under Rule 702,[16] and therefore are entitled to give opinions that are not based on direct observation of a particular phenomenon. This is important when considering the admissibility of opinion based on the application of long-standing and well-accepted scientific theory, where the expert is able to state what a reasonable expectation would be without having to actually have observed the event itself. This is what distinguishes the privilege of expert witnesses from lay witnesses.

3.1.5.2 Who is an expert?

Rule 702 helps answer the most obvious question raised by the distinction between lay and expert witnesses: Who or what is an expert? Rule 702 establishes a very liberal approach to qualifying experts, by stating that a "witness can be qualified as an expert by knowledge, skill, experience, training or education". Therefore, experts

---

[14] The Committee on the Federal Rules denies that this represents any attempt to codify either case specifically.

[15] Fed R. Evid. 701—Opinion Testimony by Lay Witnesses

If a witness is not testifying as an expert, testimony in the form of an opinion is limited to one that is:

(a) rationally based on the witness's perception;
(b) helpful to clearly understanding the witness's testimony or to determining a fact in issue; and
(c) not based on scientific, technical, or other specialized knowledge within the scope of Rule 702.
   (Fed R. Evid. 701)

[16] Fed. R. Evid. 702—Testimony by Expert Witnesses

A witness who is qualified as an expert by knowledge, skill, experience, training, or education may testify in the form of an opinion or otherwise if:

(a) the expert's scientific, technical, or other specialized knowledge will help the trier of fact to understand the evidence or to determine a fact in issue;
(b) the testimony is based on sufficient facts or data;
(c) the testimony is the product of reliable principles and methods; and
(d) the expert has reliably applied the principles and methods to the facts of the case. (Fed. R. Evid. 702)

do not necessarily have to have formal qualifications to be considered as such by the court, as skill and experience may also count towards acceptance as an expert witness. However, in practice, this liberal approach is usually only applied to skilled professions, such as real estate agents or bankers, who can claim to be experts on the basis of skill and experience through the absence of any formalized training program or accreditation body. Courts have generally taken a dim view of scientific and forensic "experts" who claim to be such purely on the basis of skill or experience. Where a form of professional standard exists for any area of forensic practice, compliance with this professional standard in the form of membership, licensure, qualification, or other form of ratification has generally been expected in order to qualify as a forensic expert witness.[17]

3.1.5.3 What can experts say?

Rule 702 also specifies that a witness who is qualified as an expert is allowed to express their opinion as part of that testimony, providing that:

a) The expert's scientific, technical, or other specialized knowledge will help the trier of fact to understand the evidence or to determine a fact in issue.
b) The testimony is based on sufficient facts or data.
c) The testimony is the product of reliable principles and methods.
d) The expert has reliably applied the principles and methods to the facts of the case.

These four pillars appear to have been added as a direct response to the *Daubert* and *Kumho* cases during the year 2000 amendment to the rules. The language of Rule 702 also affirms the mandates employed in these seminal cases in emphasizing the fact that judges have discretion in deciding how they perform the gatekeeping function, but not whether or not to perform it (viz: "…*providing that:* …"). Assessment of the reliability of expert testimony is therefore deemed essential prior to allowing evidence that may have bearing on the case before them to be heard.

702(a), importantly, recognizes that an expert's testimony must be related to his or her area of expertise that is outside the knowledge of the layperson, in that it must be *scientific*, *technical*, or *specialized* knowledge that must assist the judge or jury in some way; he or she is not allowed to merely give opinions about matters which ordinary people could be reasonably expected to know. For example, the firearms expert in one particular case was not permitted to testify whether or not the defendant breached the standard of care in failing to properly store and secure a rifle, as this was a matter the jurors could decide on the basis of their own common knowledge.[18] Rule 702 also recognizes that the knowledge does not have to be considered purely "scientific" in order for it to be admissible, or as a reverse consequence, subject to

---

[17] See *State v. Dolan*, 1999 Minn. App. LEXIS 1197; *State v. Gainer*, 2001 Minn. App. LEXIS 1320; *Dracz v. Am Gen Life Insurance Co.*, 2006 U.S. Dist. LEXIS 15278; *Wheeler v. Olympia Sports Ctr., Inc.*, 2004 U.S. Dist. LEXIS 20462, No. 03-265-P-H, 2004 WL 2287759 (D.Me. Oct. 12, 2004), *United States v. Bourgeois*, 950 F.2d 980, 987 (5th Cir. 1992).
[18] See *Williams v. Cook,* 1999 Ohio App. LEXIS 1750.

these rules. All expert knowledge, whether it is considered "science" or not, is subject to the same standard, thus preventing the argument that certain fields—such as arson investigation or handwriting analysis—are not strictly science, and thus do not fall under these rules.[19] This is a direct outcome of the *Kumho* case, where the US Supreme Court ruled that *Daubert* was applicable to all forms of expert testimony, and not just those considered "science."

Rules 702(b) and 702(c) require that expert testimony be based on facts or data that have been derived using sound methodologies. In other words, experts cannot simply give testimony that has no basis or foundation other than their own opinion. Such testimony is often referred to as *ipse dixit*, literally translated as "he, himself, said it," and refers to the fact that such testimony is in reality an unsupported statement that rests solely on the authority of the individual who makes it. Expert testimony cannot be based upon unsupported proclamations and pronouncements, and is ideally supported with some underlying facts or data. However, recognizing that not all data might be reflective of accurate or valid processes, Rule 702 requires that the data on which expert opinion rests must also be reliable; flawed or biased data cannot be used to validate expert opinions. This issue is particularly relevant in many areas of forensic science, where experts have generated data through poorly designed studies in order to support their own particular theories.[20]

702(d) lastly requires that the testimony must be directly relevant to the facts of the case. This embodies the concept of "fit." As an example, consider a firearms identification case where an expert testified as to the reliability of identifying barrel markings on fired bullets. The court had no concern with the validity of the theory per se; however, the expert failed to then explain how this theory supported his technique of identifying bullet cartridges on the basis of magazine marks only. His testimony failed to "fit" the facts of the case, and thus was ultimately disallowed.[21]

Rule 703[22] allows the expert to base his or her opinion on forms of evidence that would otherwise be inadmissible, if they are essential to providing the judge or jury with relevant information, and if experts in the field would usually rely on such

---

[19] See *Amicus* Brief for the International Association of Arson Investigators, *Michigan Millers Mutual Insurance Corporation v. Benfield*, No. 97-2138, 140 F.3d 915 (11th Cir., 1998); *United States v. Starzecpyzel*, 880 F.Supp. 1027 (S.D.N.Y. 1995), where this argument was used in order to allow these types of testimony to escape the scrutiny required of expert testimony by *Daubert*.

[20] See *Smith v. State*, Ark. LEXIS 527 (1987) (Unreported), where the trial court deduced that the experiments conducted by the expert witness and used to support their conclusion were not conducted in a scientific manner, and therefore the evidence was not deemed admissible.

[21] See *Sexton v. State* 93 S.W.3d 96 (Tex. Crim. App., 2002)

[22] Fed R. Evid. 703—Bases of an Expert's Opinion Testimony

An expert may base an opinion on facts or data in the case that the expert has been made aware of or personally observed. If experts in the particular field would reasonably rely on those kinds of facts or data in forming an opinion on the subject, they need not be admissible for the opinion to be admitted. But if the facts or data would otherwise be inadmissible, the proponent of the opinion may disclose them to the jury only if their probative value in helping the jury evaluate the opinion substantially outweighs their prejudicial effect. (Fed R. Evid. 703)

data. For example, arson investigators generally need to rely on witness statements about where the fire began or its behavior, which is technically "hearsay" and thus not an admissible form of evidence. However, Rule 703 specifies that the basis for the expert's opinion need not be admissible in and of itself. As arson investigators usually rely on such statements in their normal practice, and it is deemed that such evidence is essential to further the understanding of some fact or issue by the jury, the expert is allowed to testify to such an opinion.

Rule 705[23] also allows experts to state their opinion and the reasons for it, without necessarily explaining the underlying facts or data prior to doing so, unless the court requires otherwise; it then states that the expert may subsequently be asked to declare those facts during cross-examination. It may sometimes be impractical for the expert to cite all the underlying facts and data regarding certain issues that arise in expert opinion; for example, a forensic chemist would not generally be expected to testify as to the underlying details of the molecular nature of chemical bonding. Similarly, a pathologist would not be expected to characterize the biological behavior of cancer cells, or the detailed cellular processes that give rise to them. However, take note that it is generally considered poor trial practice for an expert to simply state his or her opinion with *no* supporting facts or data, and this rule does not supersede that of 702, which requires a factual basis for an expert's opinion. Experts who do not reveal their underlying premises in accordance with the intent of 702 will likely face a challenge to admissibility, or heavy questioning during cross-examination in order to elucidate those facts.

3.1.5.4 *What experts can't say*

In earlier times under common law, it was considered objectionable for experts to comment on the "ultimate issue." This usually meant that experts were not allowed to comment on a person's innocence or guilt, as these were tasks for the trier of fact alone. Rule 704[24] has relaxed this attitude to some extent, now noting that such comments are not automatically objectionable, although it still expressly forbids experts to comment on whether the defendant did or did not have a mental state or condition that constituted an element of the crime or defense. The concept of the earlier rule forbidding comment on the ultimate issue was to avoid experts telling juries what to think. The absence of such an explicit rule is justified by the Committee on the Federal Rules in that trial judges have other means by which to exclude

---

[23] Fed R. Evid 705—Disclosing the Facts or Data

Underlying an Expert's Opinion Unless the court orders otherwise, an expert may state an opinion—and give the reasons for it—without first testifying to the underlying facts or data. But the expert may be required to disclose those facts or data on cross-examination. (Fed. R. Evid. 705)

[24] Fed R. Evid. 704— Opinion on an Ultimate Issue

(a) In General—Not Automatically Objectionable. An opinion is not objectionable just because it embraces an ultimate issue.

(b) Exception. In a criminal case, an expert witness must not state an opinion about whether the defendant did or did not have a mental state or condition that constitutes an element of the crime charged or of a defense. Those matters are for the trier of fact alone. (Fed. R. Evid. 704)

such statements, such as Rule 403 that permits them to exclude evidence perceived as a waste of time, and the requirement under Rule 702 that opinions must aid the trier of fact in some way.

While it is rare for comments on the ultimate issue by experts to be considered inappropriate, it raises the larger question of the role of expert witnesses in the judicial process. The expert witness is there to aid the trier of fact in reaching their own conclusions, not to reach that conclusion for them. Furthermore, the requirements under Rule 702 require that expert opinions must be supported by facts and data that have been reliably derived. There have been several high profile forensic cases where experts have opined on the "identification" of latent evidence which is not supported by adequate data to suggest that such identifications are actually possible, and so trial judges have rightfully excluded such testimony which seeks to positively "identify" individuals.[25]

Trial judges also have the ability to exclude certain testimony under Rule 403,[26] which grants them the privilege of being able to exclude testimony that is otherwise admissible, but where its value is seen as less than the danger of it being prejudicial to the defendant or the judicial process. Rule 403 gives the judge a fairly wide latitude of discretionary powers, and judges may exclude evidence on the basis that it is confusing, misleading, causing undue delay or wasting time, unfairly prejudicial to the defendant (such as the repeated showing of gory crime scene photographs), or needlessly adding to evidence that is already well established (cumulative evidence). For example, in one handwriting case the expert's testimony might have been marginally relevant to show that the defendant did not know a prescription was false or forged, but the court weighed the probative value of this testimony against the possibility that the jury would be misled into believing that the defendant was charged with forging the prescription. The court then concluded that the probative value of the proffered evidence was substantially outweighed by the danger of confusion of the issues and misleading the jury, and the expert was not permitted to testify.[27]

3.1.6 Other case law relevant to expert witness testimony

Case law is constantly evolving; however, two other cases are worth mentioning in regard to two aspects of expert witness testimony that deal with the request for appellate review of trial court decisions to exclude or admit expert testimony, and the

---

[25] See *State of Maryland v. Bryan Rose*, No. K06-0545 (Md., Baltimore Co. Cir. Oct. 19, 2007); *United States v. Diaz*, 2007 U.S. Dist. LEXIS 13152; *United States v. Green*, 405 F.Supp.2d 104 (D.Mass., 2005).

[26] Fed R. Evid. 403 – Excluding Relevant Evidence for Prejudice, Confusion, Waste of Time, or Other Reasons.

The court may exclude relevant evidence if its probative value is substantially outweighed by a danger of one or more of the following: unfair prejudice, confusing the issues, misleading the jury, undue delay, wasting time, or needlessly presenting cumulative evidence. (Fed. R. Evid. 403)

[27] See *State v. Smark,* 1999 Ohio App. LEXIS 2989.

requirement for expert witnesses to actually appear in court under the defendant's right to confront their accused.

3.1.6.1 *General Electric Co. v. Joiner*

In 1997, the Supreme Court ruled on the ability of appellate courts to overrule trial judges' decisions on admissibility. The Supreme Court affirmed in *Joiner*[28] that the trial judges' decision on the admissibility of expert evidence was not to be reversed by an appellate court carrying out their own independent assessment, except in a case where *abuse of discretion* is claimed. Abuse of discretion is a serious matter, and alleges that the trial judge erred by failing to take into proper consideration the law or facts relating to a particular issue, or has departed unreasonably from legal precedent and settled custom. By applying this high standard of review, the Supreme Court instructs appellate courts to give broad deference to trial judges' decisions on admissibility of evidence, and further cements the trial judge's role as primary gatekeeper of evidentiary standards. Reviews of trial judges' decisions to admit evidence are rarely heard given the standard of proof required for an appellate court to review a lower court's decision based on an abuse of discretion, and few appellate courts are willing to disturb an initial trial judge's finding on admissibility of an expert.

3.1.6.2 *Melendez-Diaz v. Massachusetts*

One of the most recent rulings on forensic expert testimony comes from *Melendez-Diaz,*[29] in which the Supreme Court ruled that defendants have a right to confront experts under the confrontation clause of the Sixth Amendment. The court noted that "confrontation is designed to weed out not only the fraudulent analyst, but the incompetent one as well. Serious deficiencies have been found in the forensic evidence used in criminal trials." The Supreme Court held that defendants cannot be convicted *ex-parte*, that is, purely on the basis of out-of-court documents. *Melendez-Diaz* affirms that any forensic analyst may be summoned to appear at trial to give live evidence where he or she has provided input to a written report in accordance with the defendant's right to confront the accuser. This decision is consistent with earlier Supreme Court decisions,[30] and it was clarified more recently that only the analyst who performed the work is able to satisfy this requirement for confrontation; the analyst's colleague or supervisor's appearance in court in lieu of the analyst does not meet this standard.[31] Forensic experts who write reports should do so bearing in mind that they may be called to defend and/ or explain the content of that report and its findings before a judge and jury in the future.

---

[28] *General Electric Co. v. Joiner,* 522 US 136 (1997)
[29] *Melendez-Diaz v. Massachusetts,* 557 U.S. 305 (2009)
[30] See *Crawford v. Washington*, 541 U.S. 36 (2004)
[31] See *Bullcoming v. New Mexico*, 564 U.S. ____ (2011)

3.1.7 **Court-appointed expert witnesses**

By definition, all expert witnesses are supposed to be nonpartisan. That is, they are ultimately there to assist the trier of fact in interpretation of the evidence. Nonetheless, it is not uncommon to find experts disagreeing on one fact or another, and so association with defense or prosecution teams is not unusual. However, the court retains the ability to appoint its own expert witness under Rule 706.[32] The expert appointed under this rule is technically under the employment of the court, and so may be deposed, called to testify, or cross-examined by either party. Despite the obvious advantages that a neutral court-appointed expert would bring to the process, particularly regarding the assessment of expert evidence under the *Daubert* requirement, appointment of expert witnesses by the court is a rare event, despite constant reminders by appellate courts of this authority and its potential benefits. Nonetheless, it is possible to appear as a court-retained expert witness, but being court-appointed does not absolve the expert of the requirement to adhere to the same rules as other expert witnesses regarding their testimony.

3.1.8 **The scientific burden of proof for expert testimony admissibility**

While the burden of proof of the ultimate issue always lies with the prosecution in criminal cases and the plaintiff in civil cases, the burden of proof of scientific admissibility always rests with the party tendering the expert. In other words, the proponent of the expert evidence has the burden of establishing that the admissibility requirements are met by a preponderance of the evidence. Given that the trial

---

[32] Fed. R. Evid. 706 - Court-Appointed Expert Witnesses

(a) Appointment Process. On a party's motion or on its own, the court may order the parties to show cause why expert witnesses should not be appointed and may ask the parties to submit nominations. The court may appoint any expert that the parties agree on and any of its own choosing. But the court may only appoint someone who consents to act.
(b) Expert's Role. The court must inform the expert of the expert's duties. The court may do so in writing and have a copy filed with the clerk or may do so orally at a conference in which the parties have an opportunity to participate. The expert:
   (1) must advise the parties of any findings the expert makes;
   (2) may be deposed by any party;
   (3) may be called to testify by the court or any party; and
   (4) may be cross-examined by any party, including the party that called the expert.
(c) Compensation. The expert is entitled to a reasonable compensation, as set by the court. The compensation is payable as follows:
   (1) in a criminal case or in a civil case involving just compensation under the Fifth Amendment, from any funds that are provided by law; and
   (2) in any other civil case, by the parties in the proportion and at the time that the court directs — and the compensation is then charged like other costs.
(d) Disclosing the Appointment to the Jury. The court may authorize disclosure to the jury that the court appointed the expert.
(e) Parties' Choice of Their Own Experts. This rule does not limit a party in calling its own experts.

judge is required to establish that a reliable basis for an expert's opinion exists, it can be expected that the expert witness is going to be asked to prove that his or her opinion is based on reliable facts and data. There is currently some inconsistency in application of this principle through the counter-use of *judicial notice*,[33] a principle by which judges can take certain statements to be accepted truths without relying on proof at trial, providing that the fact is generally known within the trial court's territorial jurisdiction, and that it can be accurately and readily determined from sources whose accuracy cannot reasonably be questioned. Some trial judges have controversially used the concept of judicial notice to waive the requirement for certain forensic experts to prove their claims, particularly in some of the more mainstream areas like fingerprint analysis.[34] Additionally, some judges have been known to require that the challenging party prove that the evidence is *not* reliable;[35] however, such judicial practice has been criticized by legal scholars as erroneous application of the law, and avoiding the requirement articulated through *Daubert*, *Kumho*, and Rule 702 (Kaye, 2003; Saks, 2002; Wayman, 2000). By no means are all trial judges taking these easy options, and under-prepared expert witnesses have been excluded from testifying completely where they have failed to provide trial judges with enough evidence to support their claims.[36]

Similarly, while many cases have relied upon general acceptance, or even "acceptance by the courts," as reasoning for the admissibility of forensic evidence, judges also realize that such reasoning does not sufficiently address the reliability threshold

---

[33] Fed. R. Evid. 201 – Judicial Notice of Adjudicative Facts

(a) Scope. This rule governs judicial notice of an adjudicative fact only, not a legislative fact.

(b) Kinds of Facts That May Be Judicially Noticed. The court may judicially notice a fact that is not subject to reasonable dispute because it:
  (1) is generally known within the trial court's territorial jurisdiction; or
  (2) can be accurately and readily determined from sources whose accuracy cannot reasonably be questioned.

(c) Taking Notice. The court:
  (1) may take judicial notice on its own; or
  (2) must take judicial notice if a party requests it and the court is supplied with the necessary information.

(d) Timing. The court may take judicial notice at any stage of the proceeding.

(e) Opportunity to Be Heard. On timely request, a party is entitled to be heard on the propriety of taking judicial notice and the nature of the fact to be noticed. If the court takes judicial notice before notifying a party, the party, on request, is still entitled to be heard. (Fed. R. Evid. 201)

(f) Instructing the Jury. In a civil case, the court must instruct the jury to accept the noticed fact as conclusive. In a criminal case, the court must instruct the jury that it may or may not accept the noticed fact as conclusive.

[34] See *United States v. Llera Plaza II* 188 F. Supp. 2d 549 (E.D. Pa. 2002), *United States v. Byron Mitchell*, Criminal Action No. 96-407, US District Court for the Eastern District of Pennsylvania, July 1999

[35] See *United States v. Cromer*, 2006 WL 1430210 (W.D.Mich., 2006), *People v. Partee*, 2008 WL 616249 (Cal.App. 4 Dist., Mar 07 2008)

[36] See *Austin Jacobs v. Government of the Virgin Islands*, No. 02-1135 (On Appeal from Dist. Court No. 01-cr-00065) 8 Nov 2002 (3rd Circuit); *Brown v. Primerica Life Ins. Co.*, 2006 WL 1155878 (N.D.Ill.)

as mandated by *Daubert* or the federal rules. As one trial judge noted, the reliance on long-standing use of ballistics evidence in the courts without a proper assessment of this particular testimony ran the risk of "grandfathering in irrationality."[37] Another court has held that "the historical acceptance of fingerprint evidence in courts does not qualify as general acceptance for the purposes of *Daubert* ..." and that "the reliability of ACE-V is not demonstrated by its use in prior court cases."[38] Handwriting evidence has also suffered through a reliance on past acceptance under *Frye*.[39]

3.1.9 **How judges are approaching admissibility decisions**

While *Daubert* and the federal rules articulate broad principles that expert testimony is expected to meet regarding its quality, the fact remains that exclusion is the exception rather than the rule when it comes to expert testimony. Yet the majority of empirical studies have indicated that judges are taking a more active role in scrutinizing expert evidence since the *Daubert* decision (Krafka et al., 2002). Some studies have been critical of the finding that judges appear to be referring to the *Daubert* factors, rather than technically exercising them, hypothesizing that this is perhaps due to poor comprehension or lack of skills in applying them (Groscup, 2004). While there may be some merit in these interpretations, there has been an unmistakable realization amongst the judiciary since *Kumho* that the *Daubert* "factors" themselves do not constitute a definitive checklist, should not be given undue weight, and may not be appropriate for the assessment of some disciplines. The Advisory Committee (2000) also noted that "… courts both before and after *Daubert* have found other factors relevant in determining whether expert testimony is sufficiently reliable to be considered by the trier of fact. Some of these factors have included: whether experts are testifying about matters that arose in their research independently of litigation;[40] whether the expert has unjustifiably extrapolated from an accepted premise to an unfounded conclusion;[41] whether the expert has adequately accounted for obvious alternative explanations;[42] whether the expert is being as careful as he would be in his regular professional work outside his involvement in the litigation process;[43] and whether the field of expertise claimed by the expert is known to reach reliable results for the type of opinion the expert would give.[44] All of these factors remain relevant to the determination of the reliability of expert testimony under the amended Rule 702, with no single factor supposedly being necessarily dispositive of the reliability of a particular expert's testimony." More specific reasons included in decisions to exclude forensic expert testimony on the grounds of reliability as mandated by the Federal

---

[37] See *United States v. Green*, 405 F.Supp.2d 104 (D.Mass., 2005)
[38] See *United States v. Sullivan*, 246 F.Supp.2d 702, 703 (E.D.Ky. 2003)
[39] See *United States v. Salee,* 162 F.Supp.2d 1097 (D.Alaska 2001)
[40] See *Daubert v. Merrell Dow Pharmaceuticals, Inc. II*, 43 F.3d 1311 (9th Cir. 1995)
[41] See *General Electric Co. v. Joiner*, 522 US 136 (1997)
[42] See *Claar v. Burlington NRR*, 29 F.3d 499 (9th Cir. 1994)
[43] See *Sheehan v. Daily Racing Form, Inc.*, 104 F.3d 940 (7th Cir. 1997); *Kumho*
[44] See *Kumho Tire*

Rules, *Daubert*, and *Kumho* include the use of unfounded statistics, error rates and certainties by the expert, a failure to document the analytical process or follow standardized procedures, the existence of observer bias, and an inability to clearly explain the methodology used to derive results (Page, Taylor, & Blenkin, 2010).

The term expert *opinion* is becoming less literal as the courts look for more reasoned thinking behind such opinions. The days of experts supporting themselves simply by their qualifications in the witness box are being left behind in the wake of greater judicial demand for reasoned, supported evidence from experts; the expert *ipse dixit* of the past is unlikely to hold a place in courts in the future.

References

Advisory Committee, 2000. Notes on the Federal Rules of Evidence (2000 Amendment).

Black, B., Ayala, F.J., Saffran-Brinks, C., 1994. Science and the Law in the Wake of Daubert - A New Search for Scientific Knowledge. Texas L Rev. 72, 715–784.

Brody, J.E., 1983. Shadow of Doubt Wipes Out Bendectin. New York Times, 19 June.

Federal Rules of Evidence, 2008. Federal Evidence Review. Arlington VA.

Groscup, J.L., 2004. Judicial Decision Making About Expert Testimony in the Aftermath of Daubert and Kumho. Journal of Forensic Psychology Practice 4 (2), 57–66.

Kaye, D.H., 2003. The Non-Science of Fingerprinting: United States v. Llera-Plaza. QLR 21, 1073.

Krafka, C., Dunn, M.A., Johnson, M.T., Cecil, J.S., Miletich, D., 2002. Judge and Attorney Experiences, Practices, and Concerns Regarding Expert Testimony in Federal Civil Trials. Psych. Pub. Pol. L 8 (3), 309–332.

Milich, P.S., 2012. Georgia's New Evidence Code-An Overview. Ga. St. UL Rev. 28 (2), 379.

Page, M., Taylor, J.A., Blenkin, M., 2010. Forensic Identification Evidence Since Daubert Part II - Judical Reasoning in Decisions to Exclude Forensic Identification Science Evidence on Grounds of Reliability. J. Forensic. Sci. 56 (4), 913–917.

Pyrek, K., 2007. Forensic science under siege: the challenges of forensic laboratories and the medico-legal death investigation system. Elsevier Academic Press, Amsterdam; Boston.

Saks, M.J., 2002. The Legal and Scientific Evaluation of Forensic Science. Seton Hall L Rev. 33, 1167.

Wayman, J.L., 2000. When Bad Science Leads to Good Law: The disturbing irony of the Daubert hearing in the case of *U.S. v.* Byron C. Mitchell, Available at www.engr.sjsu.edu/biometrics/publications_daubert.html.

THE INNOCENCE BLOG

Oklahoma Justice Commission Recommends Reforms to Prevent Wrongful Convictions

A new report issued on Friday by the Oklahoma Justice Commission made recommendations to improve the criminal justice system and prevent wrongful convictions.

"It's not an indictment against law enforcement," Oklahoma Police Chief and commission member Bill Citty said at a press conference. "It's just that you always want to try to do things better."

The Oklahoma Innocence Project worked closely with the 33-member Justice Commission on a two-year study of wrongful convictions. According to the Oklahoma Innocence Project, more than a dozen people were exonerated last year in the state for crimes they didn't commit, several after a decade or more of prison time.

The commission's suggestions include allowing post-conviction access to DNA testing. Oklahoma is the only state in the nation without a DNA testing law, but a bill authored by State Rep. Lee Denney (R-Cushing) has already been approved by the House and goes to the Senate to await a committee hearing. Other recommendations include videotaping interrogations, police lineup reform, training for all criminal justice professionals and post-release services for the exonerated.

Drew Edmondson, a former Oklahoma attorney general and the commission's chairman, said that although many of the recommendations could be voluntarily adopted by police departments and courts, the report pushes for legislative reform. Most of all, the report underscored the benefits the recommendations could have for both the public and law enforcement.

Professional Forensic Expert Practice

Mark Page

4.1 Documentation of evidence and investigative events

One of the cornerstones of professional scientific practice is the documentation and recording of experimental results, in order that they can be subject to both reproduction and scrutiny by peers. The concept of reproducibility ensures that the given hypothesis carries weight and is not just a random finding, while at the same time allowing others to attempt to replicate findings, further adding to the credibility of the theory. Following its supposed namesake's practice, *forensic* science likewise has a burden to ensure the reliability and validity of its results, not just in theory, but also in practice.

Documentation of the location of material evidence itself is usually required, in the form of tracking its whereabouts at any given time, in order to satisfy that the chain of custody has not been broken and that the evidence has been legitimately transferred between parties without alteration or amendment, in such a way that the opportunity for alteration or tampering, whether intentional or not, has been minimized. A large part of the successful defense argument during the O. J. Simpson trial rested on the fact that there was extremely poor handling and documentation of the physical evidence that raised serious doubts as to its integrity.

However, chain of custody requirements, which detail the physical location of evidence during its progression through all phases of collection, analysis, and storage, are still insufficient by themselves in documenting the results of forensic inquiries. Like any good scientist, forensic examiners are required to detail, in addition to the physical condition of evidence given to them, exactly what they did with the evidence, and why the results of such enquiries have led to the conclusions that they did. Documentation of the analysis of forensic samples allows the expert's data and method to be subject to, and subsequently withstand, rigorous examination.

Court cases have been lost on the basis of inadequate documentation by forensic analysts. Simple recitation of results by experts in court have been met with some skepticism by judges, who have noted that an inability to provide documented proof as to processes and procedures that forensic evidence has undergone during analysis fails to meet the reliability requirement as mandated under the Federal Rules of

Forensic Testimony. http://dx.doi.org/10.1016/B978-0-12-397005-3.00004-9

Evidence, *Daubert*,[1] and *Kumho*.[2] Consider one case involving fingerprint analysis[3] in New Hampshire, where *Daubert* was adopted as precedent in 2002.[4] The trial judge in this case found that while ACE-V was a reliable method of analyzing latent fingerprints, a failure to document this analysis and the possibility of a biased confirmation by a second examiner resulted "in an insufficient basis for the court to find that the principles were reliably applied to the facts of the case" (see Chapter 6 for more on the legal expectations of forensic expert testimony). This led the trial court to exclude the fingerprint identification until such time as it was satisfied that the New Hampshire Department of Safety's Forensic Laboratory had conducted a methodically reliable analysis on the latent print. In another case,[5] this time in Massachusetts, the judge noted that the lack of good records of the firearms analysis "pointed against admission of the testimony," even though it was ultimately allowed with limitation in this particular case.

In another firearms case,[6] the expert had failed to make any sketches or take any photographs of his comparison work, and his notes were described as "scant." He had also failed to document the verification of his results by another qualified examiner. Therefore, the judge required the government to produce documentation that proved the technique utilized in the analysis conformed to standards accepted in the forensic firearms analysis field, and that the findings had been verified by an independent second examiner. The judge granted the defendant's motion to exclude ballistics evidence, stating that the government had to ensure that its proffered firearms identification testimony comported with the established standards in the field for documentation. The judge in this case also stated that she would permit the expert to testify if the government could demonstrate that it could subsequently meet these documentation requirements.

In *Ramirez*,[7] a forensic examiner attempted to identify a knife that was allegedly used as a murder weapon in 1983 to the exclusion of all other knives. This case was decided under Florida's *Frye* rule, requiring that "the basic underlying principles of scientific evidence has [sic] been tested and accepted by the relevant scientific community, by looking to properties that traditionally inhere in scientific acceptance for the type of methodology or procedure under review."[8] The knife mark evidence in *Ramirez* was initially deemed admissible in the trial's *Frye* hearing;[9] however, the appellate court disagreed with this finding. Among the reasons given for the

---

[1] See *Daubert v. Merrell Dow Pharmaceuticals, Inc.*, 509 US 579 (1993)
[2] See *Kumho Tire v. Carmichael*, 526 US 137 (1999)
[3] *State of New Hampshire v. Richard Langill*, No. 05-5-1129 (Sup. Ct. Rockingham Jan. 19, 2007)
[4] See *Baker Valley Lumber Co. v. Ingersoll-Rand Co.*, 148 N.H. 609, 614 (2002)
[5] *United States v. Green*, 405 F.Supp.2d 104 (D.Mass., 2005)
[6] *United States v. Monteiro*, 407 F.Supp.2d 351 (D.Mass., 2006)
[7] *Ramirez v. State* 819 So.2d 836 (Fla., 2001)
[8] See *Brim v. State* 695 So.2d 268 (Fla., 1997)
[9] A hearing held separate to the trial (often during, but without the jury present) to determine the admissibility of expert evidence tendered. They are colloquially named after the case that sets the precedent for admission of expert evidence in that state. States that follow *Daubert's* precedent usually hold *Daubert* hearings.

Supreme Court's decision was the fact that the expert had not taken any photographs or prepared notes or a written report delineating the basis for identification, and the Supreme Court of Florida subsequently reversed the original verdict and vacated the defendant's sentence.

Documentation of test results by itself is often not sufficient, particularly if the forensic examiner uses a nonstandard technique. The expert needs to be prepared to defend the reliability of such a technique, and documentation of the exact processes used in analysis will be helpful to both the court and the expert in this respect. Experts, as the designation *expert* suggests, should have detailed knowledge about the tools and techniques used during the analysis phase, as it is these workings that give rise to the ultimate conclusion. Forensic experts who have not been able to describe with sufficient detail how particular analytical results have been achieved have been heavily criticized in court. In *Swinton*,[10] a challenge to the admissibility of the forensic evidence which involved images generated from a suspect's dentition being superimposed over bite mark images was successful, as the expert could offer no explanation or evidence of how the visual effect of the defendant's translucent teeth superimposed over the bite mark was produced. Because he was not familiar with Adobe Photoshop, and was using the program for the first time in this case, the expert secured the assistance of a university chemistry professor to scan these images and create the overlays by using the computer program to superimpose the defendant's dentition over the bite mark, but this professor was not made available to testify at trial. Consequently, the witness had no notes on or details of the procedures used to manipulate the images so as to achieve the superimposition.

Among the issues that this presented the appellate court were that it was now impossible to tell whether the equipment was programmed and operated correctly, or whether proper procedures were followed in connection with the input and output of information.[11] When asked how the computer actually superimposed the tracing of the biting edges of the defendant's teeth over the photograph, the odontologist was only able to manage: "[the professor]... moved them together." Importantly, the appellate court noted that the Adobe Photoshop program was capable of actually altering photographs; given the propensity for prejudice that this potentially introduced into the analysis—as the details of what had occurred during the process remained unelucidated by the witness—it ruled that the evidence was improperly admitted.

4.2 Statistics in expert testimony

The advent of DNA as the "gold standard" in forensic testimony has seen an increase in the use of statistics in court. Yet the use of statistical data is fraught with danger for the underprepared forensic expert. Most laypeople struggle with even basic concepts

---

[10] *State v. Swinton*, 2004 Conn. LEXIS 190 (Unreported)
[11] *Id.*

of probability and statistics, and there is unfortunately a trend to express likelihoods of "matches," particularly in DNA cases, with such overwhelmingly large (or small) numbers that all comprehension of magnitude is lost, and the forensic evidence is seen as conclusive when in fact it may be far from it. However, DNA analysis does provide one of the few forensic examples in which statistical probabilities are described in a mathematically accepted way,[12] and have the added bonus of being supported by large databases.

4.2.1 Statistic descriptions of likelihood of matches

Attempts have been made in fingerprints, tool marks, and firearms identifications, as well as bite mark analysis, to derive statistical likelihoods of matches; however, these methods have been met with skepticism from judges as well as statisticians (Kaye, 2003). In one case,[13] the evidentiary opinion describing the bite mark evidence came from a forensic odontologist who characterized the "match" of a mark on the victim's cheek with the petitioner's dentition in terms of overwhelming mathematical probability. The expert testified that in the Detroit metropolitan area, consisting of approximately 3.5 million people, nobody else would match. The court found that this evidence, particularly the testimony concerning the mathematical probability of an alternate random match, lacked a proper foundation as there was no particular database or record of the dentitions from this population by which to assert that this would be the case.

In another case,[14] the same expert again came under fire. The odontologist in this case concluded that there was no one in the Detroit metropolitan area of four million persons that would "even be close" to the unique pattern of the defendant's bite mark, and that "there is probably no one in the world that would have this unique dentition." He based these conclusions on his professional training and statistics concerning bite marks from a 1984 article in the *Journal of Forensic Science*, which states that if you have five unique points, the chance of another individual making that same mark is 4.1 billion to one. The expert also stated that, based on this article, if you had eight points of concordance, no other person in the world could be considered a match. This evidence was admitted by the trial court, and the appellate court agreed that it was properly admitted, as such details went to weight and not admissibility. In a further appeal, the Supreme Court of Michigan disagreed with this finding, and directed the court of appeals to conduct a *Davis-Frye* hearing on both the methodology of bite mark comparison and the expert's use of statistical probabilities.[15] The court of appeals reconsidered its earlier decision; however, it found that the bite mark testimony was still admissible, and that the statistical basis for the expert's conclusions

---

[12] Robust DNA statistics are usually derived using Bayesian statistical methods. The details are well outside the scope of this text; however, interested readers should refer to Balding (2005) for a good exploration of this topic.

[13] *Ege v. Yukins,* 2005 U.S. Dist. LEXIS 15953

[14] *People v. Wright,* 1996 Mich. App. LEXIS 2293

[15] See *People v. Wright,* 1998 Mich. LEXIS 2580

was grounded in solid scientific method. Even though the court of appeals found the testimony reliable, the Supreme Court was clearly not satisfied with this result, as it ordered a new trial following the court of appeals' submission, instructing the court to undertake its own *Davis-Frye* hearing. The problem with this testimony is two-fold: first, there cannot possibly be a mathematical foundation for statistical probabilities of a match that is based on "experience"; and second, by asserting the statement that no one in the world could be considered a match on the basis of eight points of concordance (as the probability exceeds the reciprocal of the population of the earth),[16] the expert commits a mathematical fallacy.

4.2.2 Statistical fallacies

DNA has set the benchmark for statistical modelling of likelihood matches, based on Bayesian methods of analysis that take into account prior and posterior odds. The details of these calculations is beyond the scope of this textbook; however, it is important to recognize that these calculations are not based on simple ratios of prevalence in the population. Doing so commits what is known as the *prosecutor's fallacy*. In this common error, the practitioner incorrectly assigns the probability of match to that of the probability of guilt or innocence. For example, if it is decided that the probability of a right-index fingerprint matching that of the defendant is 1 in 20,000,[17] the probability of the suspect being innocent is *not* 1 in 20,000 (and similarly, the probability they are guilty is *not* 19,999 in 20,000). If that particular town has 1 million people, then there might reasonably be at least 49 other people[18] with the same print. Therefore, the actual probability of guilt may be as low as only 1 in 50, and that of innocence as high as 49 in 50. Of course, there might be other evidence that suggests that many of these 49 other people could not reasonably have left the print; however, such knowledge should not technically be part of the analyst's opinion. This type of reasoning should be left to the judge or jury. The most conservative answer that an expert can reasonably give is that the probability of the print matching one of the current town's population is no less than 1 in 50.

4.2.3 Uniqueness fallacy

Another common error is that of the use of statistics in order to "prove" that a profile, print, or match is somehow unique, and therefore could only belong to the defendant. The reality of probability and statistic reasoning is that even denominators that are much larger than the population of the earth do not actually prove that another profile cannot exist. A well-known problem illustrates this: Ask yourself, what is

---

[16] In other words, the expert claimed that no one in the world would match the dentition as the probability of finding a match was smaller than one in 6.1 billion (as the approximate population of the *Earth* at that time). This is faulty statistical reasoning not borne out by the mathematics of probabilities, as discussed in section 4.2.3.

[17] Let's assume for the sake of example that there was a database containing 20,000 right-index prints.

[18] 1,000,000 / 20,000 = 50, and so there could be 49 people in addition to the current suspect.

the probability of having the same birthday as someone else in a room with 59 other people?[19] Most people would answer that it was unlikely, probably less than 50%, as you would need at least 364 people to safely assume that another person had the same birthday as you. The mathematics of probability and statistics proves that this is incorrect; the likelihood of having someone share a birthday with you in a room totalling 60 people is greater than 99%. The mathematics of this problem are again beyond the scope of this text, but are well described in other textbooks on probability and statistics. The "birthday problem" illustrates the fallacy of assuming that you need a probability only as large as one in 7 billion—the current approximate population of the Earth—in order to demonstrate that no one else has the same forensic feature.[20]

To assume uniqueness, the probability of finding another match should technically be *zero*. However, it is mathematically impossible to ever arrive at this number through probability calculations.[21] Lastly, it is important to note that the issue of uniqueness is separate from that of the ultimate forensic question, which seeks to simply associate samples to sources. Claiming uniqueness is simply a convenient way of conveying the verdict of guilt (or innocence) to the jury, and this is bad expert witness practice. The issue of whether there is the possibility of other matches who may have committed the crime is a question that is raised and answered by the judge or jury when considering the weight of other evidence, in addition to the forensic evidence, presented in the case. As the trial judge noted in one case,[22] "… even assuming that some of these marks *are* unique to the gun in question, the issue is their significance, how the examiner can distinguish one from another, which to discount and which to focus on, how qualified he is to do so, and how reliable his examination is." These are far more important questions that the expert needs to concern him or herself with than that of the match being "unique."[23]

---

[19] Let's ignore leap year birthdays and assume an equal likelihood of being born on any particular day of the year in order to simplify this example. There are ways to calculate this probability using more "realistic" models of the yearly birthday distribution, including accounting for leap years; however, the probabilities don't actually change all that much.

[20] The highest possible number of birthdays is 365, and yet the probability of there being another birthday the same as yours approximates near certainty with only 50 samples. Similarly, the highest number of possible fingerprints is 7 billion, but mathematically, the near certainty of a match is probable at sample sizes far less than this.

[21] This is because probability calculations necessarily involve multiplication. A product of zero means that at least one of the numbers being multiplied must be zero itself, which doesn't make sense if you are talking about population samples: measurements of incidence in the population must always be greater than one, otherwise the sample technically does not exist.

[22] *United States v. Green,* 405 F.Supp.2d 104 (D.Mass. 2005)

[23] The judge in this case wisely realized that this is because the probabilities needed to even safely assume that no other example exists on Earth would be so tiny that they end up almost being irrelevant compared to the likelihoods of other influences on the judicial outcome, such as forensic practitioner error. We already know from some studies that error rates in some disciplines are potentially as high as 1%, or one in a hundred. This pales the risk of there being a second "duplicate" case, the probability of which might be one in several trillion, into insignificance as far as its relevance to the outcome of a case reflecting ground truth.

4.2.4 **Statistical descriptions of certainty**

Descriptions of certainty, particularly those that attempt to describe this phenomenon mathematically, have little place in forensic expert testimony. While some professional organizations require that practitioners be "100% certain" in their opinions, this does not equate to being 100% right. Statistical descriptions of certainty rest entirely on opinion, *ipse dixit*, as they are impossible to measure objectively, and are, in reality, nothing more than a made-up number. In *Ballard*,[24] the appellate court found that the pronouncement of the expert that she was "99% certain" that the defendant's fingerprint was found in a stolen car "had no demonstrated basis in an established scientific discipline and rested solely upon [the expert's] personal opinion." Failure of counsel to object to this statement constituted ineffective assistance of counsel, and the appellate court ordered a new trial.

In another case,[25] the defendant challenged the conclusion of the witness that the he was the author of a signature or other writing on a document. While the court permitted him to testify, he was specifically barred from providing opinions that attempted to quantify his certainty. The court wrote: "While the evidence adduced at the *Daubert/Kumho* hearing established that [the witness] meets the minimum requirements under Rule 702 to qualify as a non-scientific witness . . . the Court shall preclude [the witness] from testifying to the degree of probability, confidence, or certainty underlying his proffered opinions." Additionally, some courts have considered restricting the testimony of forensic document examiners as to their degree of certainty in determining the genuineness of a signature, in particular restricting any reference to the nine-level ABFDE scale of association, as there has so far been little convincing statistical evidence provided to support this scale of implicit "probability" published by the American Board of Forensic Document Examiners and used to describe the likelihood of handwriting associations.[26] Not all courts have been this strict regarding the use of likelihood scales in forensic expert testimony, particularly when such a scale is generally accepted by practitioners in the field. However, these last few cases demonstrate that courts are becoming much more wary about unsupported opinion in forensic expert testimony, including that of general statements of certainty that *imply* some form of mathematical or probabilistic basis.

4.3 **Error rates in expert testimony**

In order to accurately portray the meaning of experimental results, it has become generally agreeable in modern science that practitioners should attempt to describe the likely error rate associated with their technique and the subsequent result. One author goes so far as to say he would recommend a condition of admissibility on

---

[24] *People v. Ballard*, No. 225560 Macomb Cir. Court LC No. 98-001651-FC (Mich. Feb 28, 2003)

[25] *United States v. Rutherford,* 104 F.Supp.2d 1190 (D.Neb. 2000)

[26] See *United States v. Santillan,* 1999 WL 1201765 (N.D.Cal. 1999); *United States v. Van Wyk,* 83 F.Supp.2d 515 (D.N.J. 2000); *United States v. Hines,* 55 F.Supp.2d 62 (D.Mass. 1999)

the fact finder being informed about the likelihood of error in the opinion (Saks, 2002). This does not necessarily mean a numerical figure must be assigned in order to describe the error rate, as this may not be possible for all techniques. However, an understanding of the possible sources of error associated with any particular technique, so that they may be explained to a judge or jury, is potentially just as useful to the trier of fact as a numerical figure in order for them to go about their task of assigning weight to the testimony. This type of explanation is more useful to a trier of fact than the expert "creating" figures out of thin air that are not derived from any methodological calculations relating to, nor scientific insight associated with, the forensic identification process.

Forensic authors who use judicial casework as validation for a particular forensic technique fail to ensure independent verification of the true source of any particular mark (Cole, 2005, 2007). Consequently, these "implicit tests" invariably fall into a very low-level category of evidence due to the non-independent nature of the reference standard. Many studies that have attempted to bolster the argument for forensic examiner accuracy, such as those run by the Collaborative Testing Service and the American Society of Crime Laboratory Directors, have been criticized as having many of the features of poor-quality studies, including no control over the conduction or timing of the tests, uncertain sample sizes, and varying difficulty levels (Cole, 2007). In addition, these tests often only assess a small proportion of the examiner's typical job duties, and thus do not necessarily represent accurate descriptions of examiner proficiency in court (Haber & Haber, 2003).

It is acknowledged that it is difficult to measure the true accuracy of forensic analysis. Proficiency test data obtained from crime laboratories in the late 1970s indicated very poor performances, resulting in a questioning of the general reliability of forensic laboratory work (Jonakait, 1991). This study was criticized by several authors soon after its publication, largely for using data that was already 13 years old at the time of writing and that seemingly ignored the technological advances that had eventuated in the interim, but it was also supported in its conclusion by others (Letters Forum, 1991). If error rates are indeed as high as 2%, as suggested by one author based on similar data obtained in the late 1980s,[27] up to 1400 people per year may be erroneously convicted, or erroneously exonerated, on fingerprint evidence alone (Koppl, 2005). A fingerprint study conducted in 1995 found over 30% of answer sheets containing at least one false identification, resulting in one in five of the participants potentially providing damning evidence if the proficiency test represented actual case work (Grieve, 1996). The relative rarity of errors, and under what conditions they occur at a practical level in forensic science, remains unclear; however, with proper research and subsequent systematic application, these errors could be reduced and minimized (Dror and Charlton, 2006).

Many forensic experts are reluctant to admit any existence of error, perhaps from fear that they will be seen as incompetent or even useless as witnesses in court; however, we know from past history that errors can and do occur in forensic science.

---

[27] See Peterson and Markham, 1991

Good forensic practice should involve reporting the likelihood of error associated with any technique, as it allows the judge or jury to assign proper *weight* to the expert's testimony. Additionally, it also implies that a level of intellectual and scientific rigor has been applied to the discipline through an attempt to quantify this error, with the assumption that such error rates have been properly derived, of course. Even descriptions of the potential sources of error are more useful to a jury than simply claiming that none exist a statement that will be easily disproven by any keen cross-examiner.

4.4 **Peer review**

One of the suggestions made by the *Daubert* court regarding inquiry into the reliability of any expert opinion was investigation into the existence of "peer review." This has been misinterpreted by many forensic disciplines as the necessity for peer "checks" on forensic case results, when undoubtedly the Supreme Court was referring to peer review in the context of publication of forensic research and theory. Some perspectives on peer review in the context of publication in learned journals are discussed in Chapter 2, but the alternate interpretation of "peer review" is worth some discussion here.

The notion of peer review as interpreted by some forensic scientists, perhaps more accurately described as *quality* or *results review*, is potentially advantageous in forensic practice, providing it is carried out according to strict protocols. For example, once an examiner has reached a certain conclusion regarding a particular case, there is little advantage to handing this over to a peer complete with analysis and conclusions, with the exception of checking it for procedural error in the form of quality control. This by itself is potentially useful, but nowhere near as useful as actual verification of the result of the first examiner by a truly independent assessment of his or her work. This can only realistically be achieved if the second examiner is blinded to the results and, in some cases, the methodology of the first. Numerous cases where "peer-review" has been cited to the judge in this manner have failed to bolster the admissibility of the evidence because of a lack of protocols to ensure that the reviewer has been adequately blinded, and thus not subject to the influence of the first examiner's results.

Such review is a useful adjunct to bolstering inter-examiner reliability, that is, the extent to which two independent practitioners of the discipline will agree with one another, but does not necessarily increase the overall validity or reliability of the discipline or practice by itself. Forensic experts should not confuse this process with that of peer review as meant by the Supreme Court, as they have inherently different meanings.

4.5 **Avoiding context effects and observer bias**

The 2009 National Academy of Sciences report, which called for increasing awareness of the *scientific* content of forensic science, noted that the other issue related to the reliability of forensic science concerned the extent to which practitioners rely on human interpretation, which itself is subject to error, bias, and variable performance standards (National Research Council, 2009). So-called "context effects"—contextual information surrounding a process that potentially influence human decision making—have only recently been the subject of study in forensic science. There is a growing body of literature in other disciplines suggesting that observer effects induced by extraneous or emotive information play a significant role in the outcome of decision making, and psychologists have long recognized the effects of bias introduced via the cognitive state of the subject (Risinger et al., 2002). Yet it appears that forensic scientists have not realistically progressed with solutions to these issues, aside from attempting to willingly ignore these influences (Saks et al., 2003), despite the fact that these "individualization" sciences have already been described as being top-heavy with subjectivity and ambiguity and therefore particularly susceptible to bias (Cooley, 2003). Sensitivity to the problems of observer effects is integral to the modern scientific method, where scientists have realized that observer effects can distort findings and produce misleading results in ways that are difficult to correct for (Risinger et al., 2002). A further problem associated with ignoring observer effects in forensic science reporting is that potentially erroneous conclusions reached under the influence of these effects can be remarkably resistant to disconfirmation, even in the face of compelling evidence to the contrary. Sources of these effects include common practices among forensic science practitioners, such as communication between the investigators and forensic examiner, cross-communication among examiners, and the selective reexamination of evidence. Observer bias has strengthened the case for exclusion of forensic science in a number of recent cases.[28]

The potential for decisions to be influenced by conscious or unconscious practitioner bias potentially robs the trier of fact of independent information. Forensic evidence is often taken as an independent verification of a guilty (or not guilty) hypothesis, but if forensic examiners reach a conclusion that includes consideration of factors other than the specific evidence before them, their conclusions should not carry the independent weight that the trier of fact has assumed is inherent in such testimony. For example, if a fingerprint examiner is aware that a particular latent print belongs to a person whose license plate closely matches the description given by a victim of some crime, but the print is somewhat ambiguous, psychological theory suggests he or she may unconsciously resolve the ambiguity in favor of calling a match. Despite the actual circumstances, to the jury it appears that the fingerprint examiner has reached his conclusion independent of any other information, and the presence of the fingerprint and existence of a closely matching license plate represent two independent coincidences that, together, significantly strengthen the hypothesis of guilt. In fact, these conclusions are anything but independent and the weight of the fingerprint examiner's evidence is far less than it appears. This has been described as the most corrosive aspect of cognitive bias in forensic testimony, as each piece of evidence needs to be considered independent of the other in order for the trier of fact to effectively summate them, and arrive at a realistic probability of guilt or innocence (Risinger et al., 2002).

---

[28] See *Langill*, supra n.3; *Green*, supra n.5

4.5.1 **The bias blind spot**

The ignorance of contextual effects and observer bias is a recognized psychological phenomenon in itself, and has been termed the "bias blind spot" (Pronin and Kugler, 2007). While forensic science is becoming aware of the potential for practitioner bias, the few articles that have been published by forensic scientists have potentially misunderstood several key concepts regarding the influence of contextual effects. One author, among several suggestions, recommends that the forensic practitioner "accept bias, remain objective, and limit overconfidence" (Byrd, 2006). These recommendations are admirable, but demonstrate a failure to realize that contextual effects occur at a subconscious level and cannot be avoided by simply adopting an open mind. Proficiency testing has also been recommended as a method to avoid confirmation bias (Budowle et al., 2009); however, this also fails to directly address the issue of cognitive sway at the time of actual casework analysis (Krane et al., 2004). Some forensic scientists claim that the notion that subjectivity can affect reliability is refuted via anecdotal evidence (Budowle et al., 2009), but this remains a very weak form of proof when such statements are refuted by carefully controlled, blinded studies.[29]

A more recent example of context effects in forensic science is provided by that of Brandon Mayfield in the United States, who was arrested as the suspect responsible for the Madrid bombings in 2004 on the basis of an incorrectly "matched" fingerprint that was supposedly "verified" by several experienced fingerprint examiners. The US Department of Justice report into the matter noted that one of the main contributing factors to the misidentification of the Madrid bomber was "circular reasoning," (US Department of Justice, 2006), and in their explanation of this incident, they neatly describe several incidences of unconscious practitioner bias that were directly attributable to context effects. Other authors have determined that cognitive bias has played a key role in numerous other forensic misidentifications occurring in the twentieth and twenty-first centuries (Cole, 2006).

Unquestionably, a large proportion of the forensic community do not genuinely understand the terms "cognitive bias" or "observer effects." Most often it is thought that these terms refer to bias induced by police or prosecution pressure to arrive at a particular conclusion.[30] While this certainly plays a large role in the potential for bias, this is more accurately described as motivational bias. So-called role and conformity effects introduce motivational bias by virtue of one's perceived role and the desire to conform to the belief and perceptions of others. The institutional context of forensic work and its close association with law enforcement agencies has received criticism due to the creation of motivated reasoning and a coalitional alliance towards serving a common goal (Koppl, 2005), but this is a separate (yet inter-related) phenomenon to the issue of cognitive bias.

Cognitive bias specifically refers to the psychological sway towards one opinion versus another as a result of having information extraneous to the task at hand; in

---

[29] Such as those conducted by Dror and Charlton, 2006; Dror et al., 2005
[30] See Page et al., 2012

other words, bias induced by "knowing" something. Context effects—psychological influences on decision making induced by knowledge of circumstantial information—most obviously give rise to motivational bias, which may be conscious or unconscious; however, they may also give rise to cognitive bias, particularly when there is ambiguity in the choice between two alternative hypotheses (Giannelli, 2007). This latter form of bias is easily over-ridden when the evidence presents an obvious choice between two hypotheses, but becomes problematic when evidence is "borderline," of poor quality, or ambiguous.

4.5.2 Context effects

There are a number of related phenomena that fall under the heading of "context effects." In general, context effects refer to psychological input obtained by the forensic practitioner either consciously or subconsciously, during the collection or interpretation of the primary evidence.

4.5.2.1 Emotional effects

The contextual details surrounding analysis of forensic evidence can be highly emotive, involving knowledge of death, pain, suffering, and other negative aspects of human nature. Researchers have already demonstrated that these emotive influences have a significant effect on forensic decision making (Dror et al., 2005), and to suggest that forensic experts are somehow immune to emotive influences sits at odds with other evidence, such as the higher incidence of post-traumatic stress disorder in forensic workers exposed to death and the dead (McCarroll et al., 2002; Ursano et al., 1999). It has also been suggested that even the presentation of evidence in a suggestive way, such as the labeling of evidence as "defendant" or "victim," feeds the examiner unnecessary and potentially biasing information (Jonakait, 1991).

4.5.2.2 Confirmation bias

The close relationship that forensic practitioners engender with law enforcement agencies renders them susceptible to cognitive bias through the wider problem of information sharing. Confirmation bias occurs when practitioners use selective external information, consciously or unconsciously garnered from their associates, to assist their conclusions. This is a well-studied phenomenon in eyewitness lineups, in which witnesses who are initially tentative with their identifications become positive after learning that the person they identified is the prime suspect according to the police (Giannelli, 2007).

Confirmation bias has played a role in numerous forensic scandals, and was recently acknowledged as one of the leading causes of the misidentification of the 2004 Madrid bomber (US Department of Justice, 2006). It has been claimed that experts, particularly those with experience, are less vulnerable to confirmation bias; however, Dror and colleagues (Dror et al., 2006) have provided evidence to refute this claim. In their study, five fingerprint experts were given two prints each from casework archives that they had identified approximately five years earlier as a definitive match. These pairs were also blindly verified by two independent latent print examiners as being "matches" prior to the study commencing. After being told by one of their colleagues that they were the same pair of prints that were used to erroneously identify the Madrid bomber, but to ignore this information and concentrate only on the print before them, the five subjects were asked to decide whether the two fingerprints matched. This time, only one of the five participants identified the prints as a match. Three changed their opinions to "no match" and the other decided that there was insufficient information to make a definite decision. Other studies (Dror and Charlton, 2006; Lagenburg et al., 2009), using less emotive contextual influences, verified that even low-level extraneous information affects "match" versus "non-match" decisions.

4.5.2.3 Target shifting

This phenomenon works in a similar way to information sharing and confirmation bias. Target shifting occurs when presented with *a priori* information regarding what a suspected "match" may look like; thus the forensic examiner is likely to resolve ambiguities in interpretation of the original sample towards the pattern already seen or expected from knowledge of the reference sample. The naming of this phenomenon is referenced from the notion of "painting a target around an arrow." Even DNA analysis has been the subject of criticism regarding subjective interpretation and confirmation bias, where the use of low copy number analysis, partial samples, and mixtures in order to obtain a DNA profile suggests that the incidence of ambiguity and subsequent interpretation in DNA casework probably occurs in more than a trivial fraction of cases (Whitman and Koppl, 2010). The existence of ambiguity regarding which peaks belong to which donor, in addition to the problems of allelic drop-out (and drop-in) often require the analyst to make a judgment call on the significance of electropherogram peaks. If the analyst has prior knowledge of a suspect's profile, as commonly occurs in many laboratories, then they may be more inclined to include some ambiguous readings, and dismiss others by claiming them as artifacts. This "target shifting" naturally occurs in favor of supporting the prosecution theory, as the profile used for comparison is usually that of the defendant (Thompson, 2009). Another researcher has published evidence to suggest that this effect is potentially very real in DNA casework, particularly in mixed-sample cases where potentially biasing information is known to the examiners (Dror and Hampikian, 2011).

The NAS report, discussing this issue in relation to tool marks, notes that the *a priori* stipulation of what features may or may not be considered suitable for analysis might not be possible, and hence examination of the tool in question might be warranted prior to analysis of the mark itself. This comment is also applicable to other disciplines such as bite mark analysis and fingerprint analysis. But this is now in contrast to most laboratory DNA techniques, arguably some of the most objective forensic analyses possible, which have attempted to correct for this phenomenon by initially "blinding" the examiner to the reference sample. This limiting of *a priori* knowledge represents a more scientifically justified series of steps for making conclusions regarding the source of forensic samples.

4.5.3 Other sources of cognitive bias

The main types of context effects described above are applicable across many disciplines, not just that of forensic science. In addition to these general forms, there are several other manifestations of cognitive bias that forensic experts are particularly susceptible to given the nature of their work.

4.5.3.1 Observer effects

Experimenter or observer effects involve the unintentional transfer of behavior to subjects of the experiment via the researcher's expectancy. This phenomenon results in subjects performing better or more deliberately when they know they are being studied (Holden, 2001; Wickstrom & Bendix, 2000). While obviously being applicable to research, experimenter effects can exert influence in the work environment of the forensic examiner, where the police, managers, and colleagues could be considered the "researchers," and the forensic examiner the "subject."

In conjunction with role and conformity effects, observer effects further increase the likelihood of confirmation bias. Acknowledgement of the existence of observer effects in research has given rise to research methods that have attempted to minimize them. While it is acknowledged that these "ideal" experimental conditions are difficult to achieve in forensic science, a few such studies have been attempted, and none of their results have suggested that forensic practitioners are entirely immune to observer effects. A study conducted recently on the effects of emotional information on fingerprint analysis (Hall & Player, 2008) concluded that fingerprint examiners were not *generally* susceptible to emotional bias; however, all of the participants in this study knew that the information they were given was part of a mock case. The actual emotional effect experienced by each examiner is thus difficult to assess. The design of this study has been criticized on a number of points, and it is suggested that the conclusion reached by the authors is not supported by the data they obtained (Dror, 2009). Perhaps of more concern in this study was that conclusions from 70 practitioners varied across the entire allowable spectrum: "positive identification," "some detail in agreement but not sufficient to identify," "not suitable for comparison," and "exclusion"—yet all of them were supposedly given the same two prints to compare.

4.5.3.2 The contrast effect

It is rare that forensic examiners are presented with perfectly preserved evidence. For example, forensic odontologists rarely have the opportunity to analyze the perfectly created and preserved, "ideal", bite mark. More often than not, the evidence is of poor quality, and therefore is open to interpretation via a number of alternative hypotheses. One such effect that becomes significant in this circumstance is the contrast effect. This phenomenon describes the tendency to shift the judgment standard after repeated exposure to stimuli of a certain threshold, and is particularly inherent in subjective comparison work, such as that performed by forensic odontologists (Saks et al., 2003). The susceptibility to contrast effects is demonstrated when, for example, the bite mark expert gradually begins to "see" the association between the mark and the dentition after lengthy analysis. The fact that such analysis is done in conjunction with a reference such as the suspect dentition also introduces bias via a "target-shifting" mechanism.

It is not only practitioners that can be subject to this effect: judges and juries can also be susceptible to the contrast effects when repeatedly shown images of a certain threshold and then asked to make an inferential leap to a series of images that do not meet the same standard. In an infamous Australian trial that hinged on bite mark evidence against a suspect,[31] the experts used a computer simulation to fade images of the suspect's teeth in and out over the photograph of the bite mark in order to demonstrate its similarity. Images of the teeth superimposed over the bite mark were shown to the jury on at least 40 separate occasions during the odontology evidence. Many of these occasions did not call for the superimposition to be shown; however, when counsel or the witness requested to bring up an image of the bite mark for demonstration of a particular point, it was usually presented with the superimposed cast of the dentition, or the wax "scraping" of the dentition, over the mark itself. This may not have been intentional on the part of the prosecution; however, given that as few as eight or perhaps ten occasions actually called for the superimposition to be shown,[32] the induction of the contrast effect on the jury cannot be easily dismissed. The danger with the contrast effect is that forensic analysts, witnesses, and juries become susceptible to seeing associations that simply are not there, particularly on repeated exposure to evidence where associations may be borderline similar, but not necessarily representative of "matches."

4.5.3.3 The overconfidence effect
The overconfidence effect describes the phenomenon where practitioners are generally found to be overconfident in their ability to perform, particularly when performing routine or often-repeated tasks. It has been well established in the literature that there is only a very weak link between confidence and accuracy (Krug, 2007; Risinger et al., 2002), and that one is no substitute for the other. Despite this, it has been suggested that the overconfidence effect is related primarily to tasks involving vocabulary and general knowledge, and that tasks involving perception and sensory information (such as those the forensic experts would be involved in) are subject to an *under* confidence effect. However, recent studies have refuted this notion (Pallier et al., 2002). Overconfidence of the expert carries with it the sequelae of an unconscious biasing effect on juries and judges, who, despite claims of impartiality, are still encouraged to include assessment of witness demeanor as part of the process of assessment of the expert's evidence (Porter & Parker, 2001). It is a fact of human nature that people tend to be more easily convinced by confident witnesses; however, experts should be careful not to overstate their claims, and in particular, not to confuse the concepts of confidence and accuracy.

Shynkaruk and Thompson recently affirmed that there is a striking dissociation of practitioner accuracy and confidence, particularly in deductive reasoning

---

[31] *R v. Carroll*, QSC 308 (2000)
[32] Expert witnesses during the trial usually asked for the image of the dentition or the wax scraping superimposed over the bite mark to be removed once it was projected on the screen, as they wanted the bite mark to be seen by itself; but by then, the effect had already transpired.

(Shynkaruk & Thompson, 2006), and statements regarding confidence are poor substitutes for those concerning reliability and accuracy. Unfortunately, this principle appears to be poorly understood in forensic science. A recent US Department of Justice report noted that FBI fingerprint examiners were routinely overconfident in their ability to declare matches based on latent evidence, yet examiners are required to have 100% certainty in their identification conclusions (US Department of Justice, 2006). The two statements are clearly at odds with one another, and serve as an example of the recognition, and simultaneous dismissal, of well-founded criticism in this regard.

4.5.4 Minimizing cognitive bias

Forensic science practice is littered with opportunities for the induction of motivational and cognitive bias. Practitioners need to be aware of the potential for contextual and other effects in order to develop systems that minimize their influence. Cognitive bias cannot be "willed away," as many forensic practitioners would insist is possible, because by its very nature it is not under the conscious control of the individual (Loftus & Cole, 2004).

Several organizations and academics have called for the introduction of procedures and protocols in order to minimize observer effects in forensic identification science. The Justice Project issued a report that called for the introduction of "protocols to minimize and regulate the flow of information as to reduce inadvertent bias" (The Justice Project, 2008). Budowle et al. (2009) suggest "keeping a log of inclusions, exclusions and inconclusive results to support the proposition that forensic scientists are not overly biased and do provide substantial testing that can benefit either accused individuals or the government (P799)" but this fails to address the issue of observer effects. This rather defensive approach fails to appreciate that, first, judicial casework cannot validate the error rate of any particular technique as the ground truth is never known with certainty. Second, it is assumed that establishment of a ratio of inclusions versus exclusions would provide some proof that forensic science is not biased towards the prosecution or the government, given the large number of expected "exclusions" or "inconclusives" compared to "inclusions." The ratio of exclusions to inclusions is not what concerns critics. This data would say nothing regarding the more relevant issue of how many of these conclusions are actually correct.

Budowle and colleagues have recommended that the best way to overcome bias is by "peer review," despite a lack of any literature verifying this claim. This fails to appreciate that observer effects are not necessarily individual characteristics, but are induced by environmental influences too, and thus will affect all who work in a similar environment to some degree. Aside from an erroneous use of the term "peer review" (Krane et al., 2009), the fact that Budowle et al. further articulate this process as "blind verification" demonstrates that they do not fully grasp the implications of observer effects, despite referencing the work of Saks and colleagues (Saks et al., 2003). The use of the term "verification" implies an affirmation of a result already achieved, when what is required is an independent assessment of the evidence in a context-free environment.

Role and conformity effects can be minimized by engaging as little as possible with the victim, law enforcement agencies, and lawyers. The analysis should be conducted independent of these influences. This is most practically achieved by separating the phases of *collection* and *analysis* of forensic evidence. Where possible, the practitioner who is responsible for collecting the evidence should not be actively engaged in any subsequent analysis. This is already routine practice in some areas of forensic pattern analysis; for example, the crime scene examiners who lift latent prints, collect hair and fibers, and gather bullet cartridges are rarely involved in the subsequent analysis or conclusory phases of the same evidence, but this does not hold true so much in areas like bite mark analysis.

Whitman and Koppl (2010) have also recommended a separation of *test* and *interpretation* phases in order to guard against the effects of observer bias. They are not alone in this recommendation (Cole, 2004; Koppl, 2005; Risinger et al., 2002). This lessens the likelihood of post hoc reasoning in the explanation of discrepancies. Observer bias and context effects can be minimized by limiting the amount of extraneous information available to the expert responsible for analysis of the evidence, including limitation of knowledge surrounding the case: in order to minimize emotional influences; before any viewing of the suspect reference sample in order to minimize target shifting; and before any other circumstantial evidence is revealed, such as the presence of the suspect's fingerprint or DNA.

It can be argued that context-free forensic science is impossible in most cases; context is required for the majority of forensic scientific work such as toxicology and forensic pathology in order to reach conclusions that consider all of the available medical and forensic evidence, and thus context is ultimately desirable (Forrest, 2004). In recognition that some extraneous information may be necessary in order for the forensic examiner to appropriately interpret the results, a protocol for DNA analysis known as "sequential unmasking" has recently been implemented in many DNA laboratories, where information regarding the known sample is withheld until an initial interpretation of the results has been documented. Proponents of the method claim it allows an unbiased analysis of the evidence by sequencing the laboratory workflow such that evidentiary samples are interpreted, and the interpretation is fully documented, before reference samples are compared (Krane et al., 2008). This still provides the practitioner with the necessary information in order to draw conclusions about the evidence, but does so in a way that minimizes observer effects. Such protocols should be considered best practice in all forensic expert disciplines in order to avoid the pervasive effects of unconscious bias.

4.6 Practical tips for professional expert practice

Based on a review of cases where forensic experts in the fields of fingerprints, firearms and tool marks, forensic odontology, and handwriting analysis have been excluded from trial proceedings since the advent of the *Daubert* standard for expert testimony in 1993, it was found that more than 65% of these were due to concerns with the *reliability* of the forensic evidence, with the remaining exclusions due to procedural and other legal reasoning (Page et al., 2011a, 2011b). This represents a sizeable proportion of forensic testimony being excluded mostly on the basis of fundamentally correctable professional practice. Particularly with regard to forensic experts, who are likely to face the prospect of being an expert witness in the course of their careers, the following recommendations are made.

The expert should always be able to provide sufficient references and resources in order to allow the trial judge to make an accurate assessment regarding the admissibility of the proffered evidence. This includes appropriate documentation of all stages of forensic analysis, in order that the expert's method and reasoning can be followed and, if necessary, assessed. Experts should also have a sound understanding of the methods and principles involved in conducting a forensic identification analysis, in order to be able to explain them to the court. A failure to articulate how analysis is performed, the significance of each of the stages of analysis, and the subsequent meaning of results has the potential to discredit the process by which the result has been achieved.

The expert should adhere to standard practices used within the discipline where such practices exist. Numerous cases have been lost by so-called "experts" attempting to apply their own method of analysis that is essentially untested by either their discipline or the legal system. Where such a method has been properly verified and supported with appropriate documentation it may be acceptable to proceed, but ad hoc experiments that fail to meet basic scientific standards or to replicate the conditions of the case are not useful to the court. Having said that, evidence of "general acceptance" by itself, by either the courts or the forensic community, does not act as a substitute for the demonstration of reliable methods and conclusions as applied to the case at hand.

Statistics should only be used to reinforce conclusions where they have been properly generated by recognized scientific and statistical methods. Statistics and probability are not necessarily intuitive areas of science, and many experts struggle with these concepts. While ultimately some form of statistical basis may strengthen a forensic expert's case, attempting to bolster his or her argument with inaccurately derived statistics may be their undoing in the hands of a skilled cross-examining counsel. Certainly, conclusions to degrees of "absolute certainty" and "to the exclusion of all others" are not derived scientifically and do not represent realistic inferences from the available forensic methods at the time, particularly in the forensic identification sciences.

While expression of likely error in forensic science is desirable, and most easily achieved by noting the results of proficiency testing, such testing that does not replicate day-to-day work or "real-life" situations does not carry much weight toward the overall reliability of the discipline or the expert. Having said that, any data is preferable to none at all in order to allow the judge and jury a means of assessing the weight of the forensic testimony. Forensic science, like all scientific disciplines, does not have a zero error rate, and claims of such have been met with healthy skepticism from courts and critics alike.

The notion of casework "peer review" is potentially useful for verifying forensic results, but concordance in this respect generally only speaks to the reliability of processes, and not to the underlying theories or application of these theories to casework, especially when such review is not conducted in a blinded fashion. Finally, the practice of forensic science is littered with the potential for biasing contextual effects. Forensic experts need to acknowledge the existence of these effects and take reasonable steps to control for them where possible. They cannot be "willed away," and admission of their existence does not imply that the expert is weak-minded or somehow deliberately biased. But unless experts acknowledge the existence of these concerns, they can never begin to address them adequately.

References

Balding, D.J., 2005. Weight-of-evidence for DNA profiles. John Wiley & Sons.

Budowle, B., Bottrell, M.C., Bunch, S.G., Fram, R., Harrison, D., Meagher, S., Oien, C.T., Peterson, P.E., Seiger, D.P., Smith, M.B., Smrz, M.A., Soltis, G.L., Stacey, R.B., 2009. A perspective on errors, bias, and interpretation in the forensic sciences and direction for continuing advancement. Journal of Forensic Sciences 54 (4), 799.

Byrd, J.S., 2006. Confirmation bias, ethics, and mistakes in forensics. Journal of Forensic Identification 56 (4), 511.

Cole, S.A., 2005. Implicit Testing: Can Casework Validate Forensic Techniques? Jurimetrics 46, 117.

Cole, S.A., 2006. Prevalence and Potential Causes of Wrongful Conviction by Fingerprint Evidence, The. Golden Gate University Law Review 37, 39.

Cole, S.A., 2007. Toward Evidence-Based Evidence: Supporting Forensic Knowledge in the Post-Daubert Era. Tulsa L Rev. 43 (2), 101.

Cole, S.A., 2004. More than Zero: Accounting for Error in Latent Fingerprint Identification Criminology. J. Crim. L & Criminology 95, 985.

Cooley, C.M., 2003. Psychological Influences and the State Employed Forensic Examiner: How to Elicit Evidence Concerning Observer Effect Errors through Cross-Examination and Discovery. Illinois Association of Criminal Defense Lawyers Newsletter, p. 2003.

Dror, I.E., 2009. On proper research and understanding of the interplay between bias and decision outcomes. Forensic Sci Int 191, 17–18.

Dror, I.E., Charlton, D., 2006. Why experts make errors. Journal of Forensic Identification 56 (4), 600.

Dror, I.E., Charlton, D., Peron, A.E., 2006. Contextual information renders experts vulnerable to making erroneous identifications. Forensic Sci. Int. 156 (1), 74–78.

Dror, I.E., Hampikian, G., 2011. Subjectivity and bias in forensic DNA mixture interpretation. Sci Justice 51 (4), 204–208.

Dror, I.E., Péron, A.E., Hind, S., Charlton, D., 2005. When emotions get the better of us: The effect of contextual top-down processing on matching fingerprints. Applied Cognitive Psychology 19 (6), 799–810.

Forrest, R., 2004. Context-free forensic science. Science & Justice 44 (2), 63.

Giannelli, P.C., 2007. Confirmation bias. Crim. Just. 22 (3), 60–62.

Grieve, D., 1996. Possession of Truth. J Forensic Identification 46 (5), 521–528.

Haber, L., Haber, R.N., 2003. Error Rates for Human Latent Fingerprint Examination. In: Ratha, N.K. (Ed.), Advances in Automatic Fingerprint Recognition, Springer-Verlag, New York.

Hall, L.J., Player, E., 2008. Will the introduction of an emotional context affect fingerprint analysis and decision making? Forensic Science International 181 (1), 36–39.

Holden, J.D., 2001. Hawthorne effects and research into professional practice. J. Eval. Clin. Pract. 7 (1), 65–70.

Jonakait, R.N., 1991. Forensic Science: The Need for Regulation. Harv. J. Law Tech. 4, 109–191.

Kaye, D.H., 2003. Questioning a courtroom proof of the uniqueness of fingerprints. Int. Stat. Rev. 71 (3), 521–533.

Koppl, R., 2005. How to Improve Forensic Science. Eur. J. Law and Economics 20, 255–286.

Krane, D.E., Doom, T.E., Mueller, L., Raymer, M.L., Shields, W.M., Thompson, W.C., 2004. Commentary on: Budowle B, Shea B, Niezgoda S, Chakraborty r. CODIS STR loci data from 41 sample populations. J. Forensic Sci. 2001; 46:453–489. J. Forensic Sci. 49 (6), 1388–1389, author reply 1390–3.

Krane, D.E., Ford, S., Gilder, J.R., Inman, K., Jamieson, A., Koppl, R.S., Kornfield, I.L., Risinger, D.M., Rudin, N., Taylar, M.S., Thompson, N.C., 2008. Sequential unmasking: a means of minimizing observer effects in forensic DNA interpretation. Journal of Forensic Sciences 53 (4), 1006–1007.

Krane, D.E., Ford, S., Gilder, J.R., Inman, K., Jamieson, A., Koppl, R.S., Kornfield, I.L., Risinger, D.M., Rudin, N., Taylar, M.S., Thompson, N.C., 2010. Commentary on: Budowle B, Bottrell MC, Bunch SG, Fram R, Harrison D, Meagher S, Oien CT, Peterson PE, Seiger DP, Smith MB, Smrz MA, Soltis GL, Stacey RB. A perspective on errors, bias, and interpretation in the forensic sciences and direction for continuing advancement. J. Forensic Sci. 55 (1), 273–274.

Krug, K., 2007. The Relationship Between Confidence and Accuracy: Current thoughts of the literature and a new area of research. Applied Psychology in Criminal Justice 3 (1), 7–41.

Lagenburg, G., Champod, C., Wertheim, B.A., 2009. Testing for Potential Contextual Bias Effects During the Verification Stage of the ACE-V Methodology when Conducting Fingerprint Comparisons. J. Forensic Sci. 54 (3), 571–582.

Letters Forum, 1991. Forensic Labs. Harv. J. L & Tech. 5, 1.

Loftus, E.F., Cole, S.A., 2004. Contaminated Evidence. Science 304, 959.

McCarroll, J.E., Ursano, R.J., Fullerton, C.S., Liu, X., Lundy, A., 2002. Somatic Symptoms in Gulf War Mortuary Workers. Psychosomatic Medicine 64, 29–33.

National Research Council, 2009. Strengthening Forensic Science in the United States. A Path Forward National Academies Press.

Page, M., Taylor, J.A., Blenkin, M., 2011a. Forensic Identification Evidence Since Daubert Part II - Judical Reasoning in Decisions to Exclude Forensic Identification Science Evidence on Grounds of Reliability. J. Forensic Sci. 56 (4), 913–917.

Page, M., Taylor, J.A., Blenkin, M., 2011b. Forensic Identification Evidence Since Daubert Part I - A Quantitative Analysis of the Exclusion of Forensic Identification Science Evidence. J. Forensic Sci. 56 (5), 1180–1184.

Page, M., Taylor, J.A., Blenkin, M., 2012. Context Effects and Observer Bias - Implications for Forensic Odontology. J. Forensic Sci. 57 (1), 108–111.

Pallier, G., Wilkinson, R., Danthiir, V., Kleitman, S., Knezevic, G., Stankov, L., Roberts, R.D., 2002. The role of individual differences in the accuracy of confidence judgments. Journal of General Psychology 129 (3), 257–299.

Peterson, J.L., Markham, P.N., 1991. Crime Lab Proficiency Testing Results, 1978–1991, 1:Identification and Classification of Physical Evidence. J. Forensic Sci. 40 (6), 994–1008.

Porter, C., Parker, R.W.R., 2001. The Demeanour of Expert Witnesses. Australian Journal of Forensic Sciences 33 (2), 45–50.

Pronin, E., Kugler, M.B., 2007. Valuing thoughts, ignoring behavior: The introspection illusion as a source of the bias blind spot. J. Exper. Soc. Psych. 43 (4), 565–578.

Risinger, D.M., Saks, M.J., Thompson, W.C., Rosenthal, R., 2002. The *Daubert/Kumho* Implications of Observer Effects in Forensic Science: Hidden Problems of Expectation and Suggestion. Cal. L Rev. 90 (1), 1–55.

Saks, M.J., Risinger, D.M., Rosenthal, R., Thompson, W.C., 2003. Context effects in forensic science: a review and application of the science of science to crime laboratory practice in the United States. Science & Justice 43 (2), 77–90.

Saks, M.J., 2002. The Legal and Scientific Evaluation of Forensic Science. Seton Hall L Rev. 33, 1167.

Shynkaruk, J.M., Thompson, V.A., 2006. Confidence and accuracy in deductive reasoning. Memory and Cognition 34 (4), 619–632.

The Justice Project, 2008. Improving the Practice and Use of Forensic Science: A Policy Review.

Thompson, W.C., 2009. Painting the target around the matching profile: the Texas sharpshooter fallacy in forensic DNA interpretation. Law, Probability and Risk 8 (3), 257–276.

Ursano, R.J., Fullerton, C.S., Vance, K., Kao, T.-C., 1999. Postraumatic Stress Disorder and Identification in Disaster Workers. Am. J. Psychiatry 156, 353–359.

US Department of Justice, 2006. A Review of the FBI's Handling of the Brandon Mayfield Case.

Whitman, G., Koppl, R., 2010. Rational bias in forensic science. Law, Probability and Risk 9 (1), 69–90.

Wickstrom, G., Bendix, T., 2000. The Hawthorne effect: what did the original Hawthorne studies actually show? Scand J. Work, Env. & Health 26 (4), 363–367.

THE INNOCENCE BLOG

Multiple Forensic Science Problems in Multiple Locations in the US

Possible errors of handwriting analysis are reported in Oregon, the Connecticut state lab has a new director, and attorneys argued over the quality of retested evidence from the St. Paul crime lab in Minnesota courts. Here's this week's round up of forensic news:

In Minnesota, prosecutors have attempted to introduce retested evidence from the troubled St. Paul crime lab in court. The retesting was conducted because of alleged contamination and protocol problems. Prosecutors argue the confirmed results of retesting are valid, but defense lawyers worry a fear of contamination is enough to disqualify the evidence.

Details regarding possible handwriting analysis error in an Oregon crime lab have been reported. Because laboratory protocol might not have been strictly followed, out-of-state experts are reviewing 35 cases that were analyzed by the handwriting unit.

The Connecticut Forensic Science Laboratory announced the appointment of a new director whose experience in "streamlining operations and maximizing productivity" can help address the current backlog of evidence. The director comes from the state forensic lab in Massachusetts which is separate from the Hinton State Lab associated with the current alleged misconduct.

Thousands of guns in Washington State have not been tested and entered into the Integrated Ballistics Identification System (IBIS) due to staff and funding cuts. Spokane Police prepare to confront the backlog with the help of the Washington State Patrol Crime Lab.

Managing Your Forensic Case from Beginning to End: It's All about Communication

5

C. Michael Bowers

Associate Professor of Clinical Dentistry, Ostrow School of Dentistry, University of Southern California, Los Angeles, CA USA

5.1 Communicating throughout the case—especially attorneys

From the very start, the forensic expert is constantly challenged to effectively and properly communicate in the multiple phases of casework. Communication is both written and verbal, with the attorney being central to many stages.

5.1.1 Before the attorney calls the expert about employment

Anyone starting in forensics should realize that employers within the legal community will generally inquire as to their reputation and training from legal colleagues prior to making contact with a forensic consultant. A government forensic tech or scientist would be considered or assumed to be reputable, as acknowledged by his or her employment.

The expert must be forthcoming with aspects of her professional training and activities, whether for full-time employment or as an at-will consultant hired on a case-by-case basis. The list and breadth of this biographical information is significant, and must be documented and constantly updated.

There are several categories that should be covered in the expert's curriculum vitae (C.V., or resume).

5.1.1.1 College education and degrees held

Forensic experts vary widely in the relevant education expected for their forensic subject matter. The laboratory "scientist" would show significant college or university training in the basic sciences, which is then coupled to later forensic applications. Some medical experts use their graduate programs as relevant training. Forensic sciences' advance into university-level training for specific forensic applications has been slow, as shown by "forensic degrees" being offered by third-level colleges. This trend is a slow process due to the comparative miniscule funding available for university-based forensic research that would drive undergraduate programs in those areas.

Forensic Testimony. http://dx.doi.org/10.1016/B978-0-12-397005-3.00005-0

Police science experts may have little or no college education that pertains to their forensic specialty. This large group will concentrate on detailing all in-house or police sponsored training and credentialing. Meetings for forensic investigators sponsored by regional centers are notable for offering practical training for most police crime lab methods. Independent experts involved in private forensic consulting invariably get their start working in government crime laboratories. Notable exceptions are DNA, chemical, and engineering experts, whose training origins are university based.

5.1.1.2 Work experience

This should target forensic-related employment and years of experience. Any supervisory or research responsibilities should be indicated in detail to establish the expert's professional capabilities and contributions to appropriate forensic fields. Laboratory skills and frequency of proficiency testing in methods relevant to the case in chief should also be noted, as well as an explanation of the expert's casework experience and a statement on testimonial experience in court.

5.1.1.3 Certifications

Forensic certifications vary in importance and credibility. At their best, they are issued by capable organizations that exist to promulgate effective performance expectations and protocols for forensic methods and disciplines. At their worst, they lack scientific integrity and exist for self-serving interests.

5.1.1.4 Problem areas

The "odd-man-out" expert is one who is "self-taught" or is virtually self-validated (i.e., certification by credentials based on "general experience") and falls into a suspect category. Some for profit forensic certifying businesses of this type do attract well-meaning applicants. Unfortunately, the testing requirements for acceptance are patently minimal and "entry-level" at best. However, their "certification" or implication of "expertise" can be very impressive to a jury.

Another (and fortunately rare) forensic oddity is the existence of associations who elect to call themselves a "relevant forensic scientific community" in a particular method or subject of forensic interest, but are merely motivated by financial gain and personal status. Invariably, they ignore scientific advances, refuse to admit systemic flaws of their methods, adopt a non-acceptance of qualitative analyses proving acceptable standards of reliability, and ignore common sense approaches for improvement. In court, they address their lack of scientific approach with nonsense legal gambits.[1] Some groups advocate the ridiculous excuse that "rogue" forensic examiners in their fields are the cause of erroneous opinions, which have sent innocent people to prison.

---

[1] The forensic dental board sponsored by the American Academy of Sciences is named the American Board of Forensic Odontology (www.abfo.org). This group of 100 dentists has a leadership of "pundits" that currently consider their expert role in court to be non-scientific, but nevertheless still admissible as "observational" expert testimony of a "soft science." This rebounds from their decades of claims of being a reliable method of human identification (from bite marks in skin). Approximately 10% of their current and past members have erroneously identified defendants in criminal courts and investigations, which contributed to wrongful convictions or false arrests.

5.2 **The expert talking with the attorney**

Whenever the forensic expert encounters the attorney tasked with representing a case, there are fundamental responsibilities regarding communication that immediately attach. These are some of the baseline duties the expert must provide to counsel, and her obligations regarding documentation.

5.2.1 **Information of attorney and other details**

The expert who receives an inquiry from an attorney, whether the prosecution or defense counsel, should document, at the very minimum, the following information.

- Date of first contact, the attorney's name, and contact information including address, phone numbers, fax, and email. Include information on any opposing counsel in order to identify any future inquires that may be sent directly to the expert.
- Case information regarding date(s) of criminal activity, description of evidence collected, and current location of relevant evidence.
- List of documents that will be made available to the expert or which the expert expects to need.
- Notations on the financial arrangements (if any) that the expert requires in order for employment.

5.2.2 **The attorney's theory about the case and the specific evidence**

It is best for the expert to also receive information on what the attorney's specific needs are for the case. This should be recorded at the initial time of contact. It may be altered by mutual agreement as the case develops. At the outset of employment, it is necessary for the expert to create a list of procedures that the attorney must realize have to occur. This attempts to eliminate any "surprises" for either the attorney or the expert during later stages of the case. It also is a document that may be discoverable by opposing counsel, so the expert should expressly state that no conclusions or specific results will be available until a complete analysis can be performed. It is mandatory for the expert to remain neutral regarding any expectations on the possible results of future testing.

A list of the steps necessary to render a complete review of a forensic evidence case could look like this:

1. Review of police reports and evidence collection receipts.
2. Investigation of all crime scene photographs and logs.
3. Documents related to any analyses on the evidence that have already occurred. This could involve multiple areas of forensic analysis, such as ballistics, fingerprints, and toxicology and pathology reports.
4. A statement regarding future testing that may be necessary.

It is incumbent that the expert communicates necessary additions or deletions to this task list of procedures at any point of employment or assignment to the case.

5.2.3 Inquire about the context of the evidence and the theory of the case

The expert must ask about the attorney's expectations of what the expert can accomplish. This may lead to a quick referral by the expert if her experience or training does not meet the attorney's needs. Sometimes, this will result in the suggestion of additional experts who may aid the case. Alternatively, in a more step-by-step approach, the attorney may hire the expert only for pre-trial purposes and opinions, which remain confidential until determined by counsel. Court testimony services would be decided later. In certain cases, an expert would not testify, and would instead communicate advice and information assisting the litigation. She may evaluate another expert's work to assist in cross-examination of an opposing expert, or actually attend court as a non-witness to advise the attorney on trial proceedings relevant to the evidence.

In cases where the expert is either an employee or private consultant, written confirmations between both the attorney and expert should be exchanged. This is the expert's proof that engagement has occurred, that specific services were requested, and of any financial agreement made. The financial arrangement should clearly indicate who is responsible for payment. Do not assume the attorney is responsible. In civil cases, generally the attorney's client is responsible for payment. If this is the case, the expert should take the position that a significant portion of payment should be made in advance, with the agreement allowing additional payment in stages or completed before the final report or court testimony is accomplished. In criminal matters, a defense expert is usually paid by the court system in cases of indigent clients. This must be approved by the court in writing per an "appointment order" prior to employment, as the court will specifically state an hourly rate and maximum amount to be paid. How to be paid by the court after the expert's case is completed should be clearly stated from the outset. Multiple examples of expert witness contracts are available online which principally apply to private consultations. Government employees, even though they do not receive direct payment, should take the time to create a record sufficient to detail the particulars of their case assignment.

The expert must be punctual regarding the case timeline. Many times, the case progression to trial, settlement, or dismissal depends on the expert's determination. The attorney will usually communicate his or her time demands during the initial conversation. It is important for the expert to ask if it is not mentioned. The attorney needs to know the time requirements for the expert's results. This may be undeterminable until the expert receives the evidence, but a general sense of time requirements should be discussed along with any intermediate steps which could provide progress reports.

The attorney must be informed as to the scope and limits of the expert's methods. Lawyers generally only have a conversational understanding of police science and basic biological sciences. There will be exceptions, but the expert must be the primary source of direction in regards to the evidence and how it is processed and evaluated. Notable information regarding testing limits should be communicated and well-understood by the attorney, regardless of the attorney's own knowledge. The current trend of higher scrutiny of forensic limitations, published weaknesses, and accompanying cases highlighting forensic controversies/misuse should be part of this conversation.

If all testing phases for the evidence have not been completed, the attorney needs to know about the possibility of retesting or confirmatory steps that still need to be completed before the expert can reach conclusions. The expert should counter any pressure by counsel for more rapid determinations. Requests for nonstandard tests or less determinative analyses should alert the expert to decline to cooperate, terminate the employment relationship, or transfer the case to avoid risk of promoting misconduct and unethical practice.

5.2.4 **The attorney talking with the expert**

The stereotypical attorney's style of communication has notable challenges in some cases. The most serious problem occurs when the attorney will not allow the expert to remain neutral and uncommitted to any conclusions before the completion of the analysis. Leading comments from the attorney regarding what kind of conclusions he expects are unethical. The use of hypothetical or unsupported "facts" can be used to sway the expert to an early "estimation" of results. The expert has to remain unaffected and clearly demand no further attempts by the attorney to lead the investigation.

Most lawyers are always pressed for time. Some may pay little attention to the expert until right before trial. This can be disconcerting to a less experienced expert needing some advice on the case's priorities and presentation. The expert should rely on colleagues and mentors to help in these aspects. In some cases, the lawyer is multitasking numerous cases, and delays communication until just before the expert's time "at bat."

The expert should emphasize the need for proper preparation and attorney education. For various reasons, the attorney may not be interested in the nuances of the expert's field of expertise. This may signal a lack of understanding of the terminology of the expert's field. If this persists, it will minimize any positive effect for the attorney to contribute in trial prep and later provide in-court assistance during cross-examination and redirect. A good practice tip is to have the expert prepare a short portfolio for the attorney containing documents specially written for laypersons on the expert's forensic discipline. It is not wrong to give the attorney a little homework.

Some attorneys carry their adversarial style of speech outside of the courtroom. This is probably a sign of stress. Finding sufficient time to meet face-to-face with the attorney in a neutral setting (i.e., not in the hallway before trial) can reduce this problem.

Some attorneys are unprepared and not punctual; this is a character trait that the expert will have little ability to change.

5.3 **Stages of communication in forensic casework-overview**

The phases differ in sequence, as prosecution experts generally analyze the evidence during the course of their employment in government labs before being in contact with attorneys. They may, if no safeguards are in place to prevent undo influences, be in direct contact with police investigators and lab supervisors while working the case and during trial preparation. The defense experts have no personal contact with the police, and they never see evidence until they are hired. Besides any physical evidence, they generally are given access to police reports, medical records, photographs, and other records if considered relevant by the expert or defense counsel. The typical chronology is described ahead.

5.3.1 Defense and prosecution experts

The potential defense expert will have contact from an attorney about possible employment. Prosecution experts will be "assigned" by a supervisor to the case, and come in contact with evidence provided by law enforcement to the crime lab. Experts not employed by the government may be hired via direct contact of law enforcement or district attorneys.

The government forensic expert will be paid as a course of her regular employment. The private or part-time forensic consultant for either side will need to receive assurances that hourly fees and costs will be paid. At the outset, the private expert will have to estimate time requirements after just a brief conversation with the attorney. This places the expert at a disadvantage and, where possible, a "retainer" amount or "engagement fee" should be requested by the expert to begin preliminary studies. Discussions about future payment schedules must be considered at this point. Under no circumstances should the expert rely on assurances of payment at the end of the case without first establishing the financial formalities. This should be easily done if the hiring attorney is being paid by the client, but in most, if not all, criminal forensic cases the defendants are indigent and the courts and judges rule on payment agreements with any "outside" experts. This fact makes the expert's hiring predicated on court approval. The hiring attorney will have to prepare a request for court "appointment" on a specific case, based on certain state statutes and rules, and give reasons to the judge of the necessity of employing the expert. The expert should receive an original of the court appointment, the amount of maximum costs and hours allowed, and specifics on how the court will make payment after the expert's services are completed.

5.3.2 Investigation/Analysis

Some categories of police science experts will have personally collected evidence from the crime scene or victim. In general, the fingerprints and trace-evidence technicians collect the physical evidence, and transfer it to the crime lab for others to investigate. Defense experts receive evidence from the hiring attorney via transfer originated by the prosecution to the defense counsel. Biological evidence and certain types of trace evidence may be only portions of the total collected specimens, and are intentionally set aside at the crime lab. Communication in this phase involves precise record keeping of all evidence inventories, dates, and procedures, and the equipment used must be controlled and maintained throughout the case.

5.3.3 **Preliminary report**

This applies to both types of experts, and may either be a requirement of the crime lab or done at the request of defense counsel. It is generally a snapshot of dates and descriptions of preliminary testing with any results and evidence pending further testing.

5.3.4 **Final report**

All aspects of the expert's activities should be described in relation to each piece of evidence, testing methods, testing results, data created by such testing, reference materials, and data that supports the expert's results. Mere opinion described as a result is not permitted. Experts may be allowed to amend or update a final report if significant events occur, such as collection and analysis of new evidence or a change of the expert's opinion.

Caveat: Any expert trained in a properly validated forensic method is expected not to rely on the findings of another discipline to verify her own opinion. A non-science-driven strategy has been adopted by bite mark advocates in which they wait for possible DNA analysis results before rendering a final report or, as an alternative, write a disclaimer stating that their report is subject to future DNA results. It really is merely a protective safeguard for experts of this type against later being contradicted by the scientifically reliable biological evidence. In a scientific sense, it indicates a lack of certainty in their opinions and methods.

5.3.5 **Discovery**

The prosecution has the burden to, in a timely fashion and with complete transparency, supply the defense all evidence, whether documentary or forensic in nature, that could be used at trial or substantially supports the defendant's claims of innocence. The prosecution expert seldom has any role in this step. Failure to comply with discovery is called a "Brady violation" and may be grounds for sanctions (money damages against the offending party), the exclusion of certain pro-prosecution evidence, case dismissal (before trial), or a mistrial, if the evidence is clear proof sustaining a claim of innocence.

5.3.6 **Trial**

The trial is considered the most challenging part of the expert's job, and is dependent on all steps described previously. Do not attend a judicial proceeding without sufficient preparation. In depth discussion of this phase of the expert's performance is covered later in this and other chapters of this book.

5.3.7 **Post-trial**

The expert's role in the post-trial phase generally is limited and should focus on the preservation of the work product created for the case that is not entered into trial.

Physical evidence presented in the case becomes property of the court or prosecution. After the case is completed, what happens to the evidence varies widely in the United States. In a few states, the issue of preservation after a criminal conviction is a statutory requirement for the prosecution to follow. Absent such a rule, it is determined by local law enforcement. The government expert commonly inventories all documentary evidence with his or her agency. The defense expert should relinquish to defense counsel any remaining evidence not already in custody of the court. The preservation of biological specimens has played a vital role in post-convictions that have been overturned by later DNA analysis. The expert must maintain all written records and personal documentation to access later if there is an appeal in the case of a criminal conviction.

5.4 Case preparation for the forensic expert

5.4.1 How to start an investigation

Often, the most difficult part of any task is getting started. The expert should complete four basic tasks when approaching a new assignment:

- Develop alternative hypotheses
- Survey applicable literature
- Review his or her private files
- Develop one or more action plans

"Action plan" is a catch-phrase for an organized way to break a large project into steps and sub-steps. It is an easy way to track progress and identify what needs to be done.

Many public and private experts follow some type of procedure for tracking work effort through individual assignments. Attorneys sometimes use tracking systems they have developed. Labs typically have tracking procedures in place.

Other experts use schedules, notes describing items that require follow-up, and checklists. Some experts use a standard procedure, and others do so more informally or when circumstances require it.

In situations where action plans have been used, cases are usually ready for trial on time. The chance of a successful result is significantly increased when all parties take a well-organized, pragmatic approach to the project. Because some forensic assignments are massive, the task must sometimes be broken into manageable parts.

If the action plan is prepared by the attorney, it may be a work product—the lawyer's own thought processes—and should receive very limited distribution. As such, it may be privileged and not discoverable. Without the attorney work-product blanket of protection, the action plan may be discoverable.

5.4.2 Preparation in establishing a coherent plan for your case

The foundation of an expert's presentation is the strength of its connection with the overall purpose or theory of the proceedings occurring in court. The finder of fact in court (in most cases the jury, although sometimes a judge alone) should have been given an overview of the intentions and objectives for what you will be talking about during your attorney's opening statements in court. Do not assume that this has been clearly established with the jury before you reach the stand. The expert must develop a narrative in advance of the trial that will accomplish in a clear, commonsense manner her steps taken to arrive at the conclusion presented to the court. This must also be discussed ahead of time with the attorney offering her testimony to the court and jury. The steps involved in accomplishing the narrative vary, and are a matter of style and purpose. They can range from the development of an outline for your presentation for the attorney to memorize or reference in court, to the other extreme, with the expert directing her own narrative by simply stating the conclusions at the outset and leading the jury through the steps taken to arrive at her conclusion. The "conclusions first" strategy should be left for the expert who has sufficient experience and poise in court to follow her own internal plan. Experts who frequently testify on the same subjects do well with this, as the procedures and laboratory methods they utilize are well-established and a part of their daily professional duties. In any case, it's the attorney that has to be sufficiently familiar with the methods and assumptions of the expert's analysis in order to help maintain the credibility of the expert during direct examination, cross-examination, and possible redirect examination. The basic structure of direct and cross-examination is in section 5.4.2.

5.4.2.1 *Differences between direct and cross-examination for the expert: A quick look*

Direct examination—the first questioning of a witness during a trial. The expert is presented, and must be accepted by the court as an authority on a specialized subject that has relevance and applies to the prosecutor or defense counsel theory of the case.

Cross-examination—the phase of a trial where an attorney asks questions in court of a witness who has testified in the trial on behalf of the opposing party. The subjects of the questioning are limited to the subjects covered in the direct examination of the witness, but many questions are allowed to question the credibility of the expert. This commonly extends to other case involvement, fees, prior court testimony, and the professional history of the expert. The core to the questions during "cross" is the permitting of statements to the expert that contain conclusions and opinions of the attorney. Whether they are relevant or not to the case on trial is argued by objections from the opposing attorney. Questioning of this nature is called "leading," which aptly refers to the "crossing" attorney. The questioning attempts to force the witness to agree or disagree with suppositions (called the "scope" of inquiry) that may undermine the expert's testimony provided during "direct." For example, review the following attempt to make an expert look like a one-sided, pro-prosecution expert:

> *Q: "Isn't it true, Dr. Jones, that you have mostly testified for the defense during your career as an expert witness?"*

> *A: "No, I have testified for both the defense and prosecution during my career. Many of the prosecution cases I review do not end up in court. That increases*

the number of defense cases I have testified in, but clearly I do not have favorites regarding the cases I work on."

Redirect examination—this may occur after the cross-examining of the expert has been completed. The attorney who did the questioning on "direct" has the opportunity to review subjects brought up on "cross" in order to affect a better or clearer answer, deflate arguments created by the "cross," or to re-emphasize the expert's opinion on certain subjects already narrated during the "direct" presentation.

It is important for the expert to exhibit certain qualities which are described in section 5.5. This knowledge introduces concepts of independence and scientific honesty.

5.5 **Scientific attitudes of the expert**

Professional attitude is a culmination of proper and formal education, role modeling between the expert and mentors, ethical training and intentional avoidance of bias, misrepresentation, and other dangers. Positive character traits and core values of a forensic expert should be recognizable in his or her work product and judicial performance.

- Understand the connection between the scientific method and the practice of forensic methods. This includes the acceptance that science progresses independently of past practice and current accepted practice.
- Develop a personal list of what facts and tests are necessary to render an opinion. Do not short-cut to an opinion. The common source of inconsistent or erroneous outcomes is lack of complete testing. This ignores standards which are meant to establish the minimum quantum of evidence necessary to reach an opinion. "Cherry-picking" only certain pro-prosecution evidence is biased and simply dishonest. Deferment to others regarding this decision making infers that the forensic expert is only comfortable with his or her own judicial acceptance and continued employment.
- Know, in advance, what the facts should be in relation to the level of confidence of a particular case. Extraneous facts should be recognized by the expert as dangerous to objectivity.
- The expert should attempt to keep the atmosphere of the investigation consistently neutral throughout the case. Additions, deletions, and recommendations by other parties regarding possible avenues of evidence interpretation should be ignored, regardless of who employs the expert. Some advanced forensic disciplines separate the analysis and the conclusion portions among multiple examiners as a control to these issues.
- Identify and ignore discussions that do not contain facts that are analytically relevant.
- Do not have knowledge of the primary theories of a case until after analysis and opinions are finished. This can be difficult to achieve with non-laboratory based experts. The private expert has to protect against getting involved with extraneous case information prior to finishing her analysis.

5.6 **The content of the expert's opinion**

The expert's presentation must be grounded in common sense and be focused on the task of explaining why the results are correct. The courtroom admission of expert opinions by judges is based on a checkerboard of attitudes and past case law from judicial decisions. The "truth" of the seeker of "legal truth" (i.e., that which follows the legal protocols and regulations for procedure) may be misled by adherents of outdated or personally biased methods that misrepresent facts and conclusions ("the actual truth"). The correctness of their one-sided opinions may be described by them as scientific, but they are not. The rule for experts is to speak the full truth of what they do and how they came to their opinions. It is the decision of the experts whether to admit to the limits of what they can accomplish or to ignore them in order to favor the theory of their attorney. Modern forensic methods cannot provide the ultimate answer of guilt or innocence. Regardless of the reliability of the evidence analysis, the question of guilt is left up to the jury to decide. The expert can only infer certain relationships between the evidence, the crime, and the defendant, and must avoid making statements such as, "In my opinion, the defendant attacked and murdered the victim."

5.6.1 **Caveat: Overstating the connection of certain evidence types to a crime or a suspect**

You must remember that most forensic evidence is "associative" in nature; the objects or substances under investigation do not directly identify the guilty party via use of a "smoking gun in the defendant's hand." They may instead associate objects known to be in possession of the defendant (weapons, tools, etc.) before the crime with items which were recovered from a crime scene. Or, the evidence may be trace evidence considered to have been picked up by the perpetrator during the criminal event, and subsequently recovered from her after an arrest (DNA, hair, fibers, etc.). The identifying forensic methods that place the defendant at the crime scene or as having been in contact with a victim are DNA left on a victim and, in some cases, fingerprints. Bite mark experts, bullet-lead comparison analysts, and hair analysts have tried to create similar outcomes to DNA-matching (i.e., identifying the criminal by associating probabilities of "matching" items of evidence), but the results have been shown in overturned convictions to be imperfect and unreliable "science."

5.7 **Formatting the report: The interaction of evidence and your investigation**

5.7.1 **First step: Data transfer to the expert from the lawyer, with scientific caveats**

Each of the many types of forensic subjects carry responsibilities the expert must meet to produce valid and reliable work content. The general rule that applies to all forensic methods is that the expert's case preparation and research must be meticulously performed, free of outside influences or pressures, not premeditated to achieve a particular outcome, and reliable in regards to scientific foundations.

Once an expert is retained for the case, the expert will invariably be sent documents, physical evidence, scientific reports from other parties, and generally what the attorney decides is important for the expert's future analysis. This material may be sent *in toto,* or in phases determined by the attorney or the expert. The expert must accept this information transfer as a good faith process with the attorney, but should realize that the attorney's agenda may not be the best for an independent scientific analysis. This may not be intentional deception or misdirection by the attorney, but the expert must frequently blind herself against legal theories and attitudes as much as possible. The expert may receive too much information, if not all of it at once. The expert can request the attorney outline, in advance, the list of material, and both parties then agree on what is relevant for the expert. It is in the realm of the expert's responsibility to tell the lawyer to limit the first phase of data or evidence transfer to the raw materials necessary for the expert to reach a preliminary finding before delving into extraneous information surrounding the entire case. If the attorney insists on sending everything (other experts' reports, police reports, victims' statements, defendant interrogation recordings, etc.) then the expert has to filter out those materials on her own. On the other hand, receiving little-to-no information, particularly physical evidence, should lead the expert to vigorously inquire about the same and assist the attorney to determine what evidence is expected in a particular case. The attorney may be completely unaware of the details necessary for a competent forensic exam in some cases.

Competent, experienced, and honest attorneys truly want an independent analysis from their expert, and those that attempt to argue the merits of the case during the expert's research phase should be avoided. The expert can always refuse to continue a case analysis if the attorney (prosecutor or defense counsel) becomes intrusive, suggests methods that are not validated, or otherwise tries to tell the expert what to do and not do. The relationship between the employing attorney and the forensic expert should be a beneficial one based on judicial, scientific fairness and honesty. If it is not, the expert will become involved in being complicit to misconduct or worse.

Getting past the issue of relationships, the lawyer's transfer of information may involve physical evidence and written documents. In the absence of biological physical evidence, the transfer may be digitized copies of crime scene photographs or evidence. Exemplars of physical evidence may be available. The expert must determine if the original objects of evidence should be made personally available. If such evidence exists, the lawyer should comply with the request to the custodian of those objects. Obstacles to accomplish this may occur. The opposing attorney may object, or demand the evidence be evaluated under the supervision of a crime lab in order to "protect" the authenticity of the material. Nevertheless, the analysis of poorly duplicated exemplar material will never reach an acceptable level of confidence. The essence of due process is that all parties have the same opportunity to perform independent analyses of vital evidence without impairment of the opposing party.

It is reasonable, and in most cases becoming standard, to digitize all appropriate documents in a case. The expert can then create a digital file system that allows for better organization and cross-referencing in cases where there are voluminous amounts of information and data.

5.7.2 Second step: What are the forensic issues?

Remember that forensic science is multidisciplinary, and each field has its own series of expected or possible outcomes. However, scientific-based association of items collected into evidence with specific persons is seldom possible. Opinion has it that DNA profiling possesses the only methods to reach appropriate confidence levels in concluding the common source of biologic evidence via nuclear and mitochondrial means. Experts in other forensic fields must develop theories that are balanced with more than personal opinion and inductive reasoning.

Lawyers will readily express their early theories on forensic outcomes; these should only be considered preliminary, and not irrefutable by the expert and her analysis. Experts are tasked to stay within the confines of their disciplines and their scientific support. Fingerprint analysts, footprint examiners, and so on can all contribute varying opinions and conclusions to the mix, based on the sensitivity available to each discipline. Trace evidence such as soil analysis can only determine similarities between two separate soil sample physical properties. It cannot advocate the nature or mechanism of other events outside that field. In contrast, the biologist can determine specificity of personal identification. The pathologist has the arena of mode and mechanism of death or injury. The crime scene investigation categorizes and interprets events to aid the trier of fact on actions that occur during violent crimes. All are important, but each can only tell their part of the puzzle. Expert determinations beyond their expertise or the realm of reliable possibilities of their field can expect to be considered flawed.

This process of forensic issue determination can progress throughout the preparation research phases as relationships of available evidence may expand the research into new areas. It is possible for a significant mid-research finding to reveal itself and indicate new sources of investigation from the crime scene or victim. Uncollected or unassociated evidence such as overlooked deposits of serological evidence on clothing or objects is common. The search for new evidence is of concern for both prosecution and defense throughout pretrial preparation. The search for proof of innocence or guilt drives competent examiners to modify or expand their findings and their conclusions. Those that don't accept (by word or deed) the possibility of new evidence arising that could change their opinions are failures to both society and the essence of due process.

5.7.3 Third step: Disclosure of the expert's information

The expert has additional demands on her time presented by the courts, aside from just writing a report. The federal courts have rules that are remarkably detailed. Some state courts dispense with most of these formalities except the report, but a forensic expert should be aware that keeping track of the following information throughout his or her forensic career would be wise.

5.7.3.1 Before writing the expert report: Short version of the rules

The Federal Rules of Civil Procedure mandate that the expert must make a report on the case subject to a procedural time limit. The report will be given to the opposing counsel. The report will include specific material and information:[2]

- Statement of all opinions
- Bases for all opinions
- Data or information considered
- Exhibits
- Qualifications of the expert
- Publications (for the last ten years)
- Compensation for the expert
- Prior court and deposition testimony (last four years)

In criminal proceedings, the Federal Rules of Criminal Procedure (Rule 16 *et seq.*) and certain appellate cases declare that the defense is entitled to:

1. All documents material to the defense, or which the prosecution intends to use in its case in chief.[3] It is not considered a "heavy burden" (*United States v. Caro*, 597 F.3d 608 [4th Cir. 2010]) for the prosecution, and allows for originals of evidence to be provided.
2. Defense is entitled under 16(a)(1)(F) to results or reports of tests and exams which are in the possession or control of the government, and are known to the government or by the exercise of due diligence may become known to the government, and which are material to the defense or which the government intends to introduce in its case in chief. ("Due diligence" means the government agency in possession of evidence has an obligation to thoroughly and reasonably look for additional evidence as a matter of law.)
3. Also, specifically focusing on forensic evidence, requests for results of all lab tests, results of handwriting, hair, fingernail, voice, etc. comparisons, and samples on which to conduct independent tests are allowed.[4]
4. Rule 16(a)(1)(G) requires the government to furnish, upon the defendant's request, written summary of expert testimony the government intends to use during case in chief. This is reciprocal upon request.
5. Rule 16 requires notice of the expert's qualifications, so it can be determined whether the witness actually is an expert, disclosure of the summary of expected testimony, and a list of cases in which the witness has testified (at least in some courts).

---

[2] Federal Rules of Civil Procedure. P. 26(a)(2)(B)
[3] Federal Rules of Criminal Procedure. Rule 16 (a)(1)(E)
[4] *United States v. Taylor*, 707 F. Supp. 696 (S.D.N.Y. 1989), *United States v. Noel*, 708 Supp. 177 (W.D. Tenn. 1989)

6. The rules require disclosure of the summary of the basis of the expert's opinion, whether or not the expert prepares a report. *United States v. Charley*, 189 F.3d 1251 (10th Cir. 1999). (In a child sexual abuse case, prosecution refused to disclose summaries of expert reports under old 16(a)(1)(E) because it said all of its witnesses were not experts.)

7. Under 16(b)(1)(C), defense must give a summary of the expert's testimony if defense intends to use the testimony under Fed. R. Evid. 702, 703, and 705 "as evidence at trial." The summary must include opinions of the witness, basis and underlying reasons for the opinions, and the witness's qualifications.

8. Rule 16(c), Continuing Duty to Disclose: Once a party gives some information under R. 16, the party has an obligation to apprise their opponent of any changes affecting that information. *United States v. Formanczyk*, 949 F.2d 526 (1st Cir. 1991).

9. Due process requires disclosure of evidence upon request where the evidence "is material either to guilt or to punishment, irrespective of good faith or bad faith of the prosecution." *Brady v. Maryland*, 373 U.S. 83 (1963).

   A. The evidence is material only if there is a reasonable probability that, had the evidence been disclosed to the defense, the result of the proceeding would have been different. *United States v. Bagley*, 473 U.S. 667, 682 (1985); *Pennsylvania v. Ritchie*, 480 U.S. 39 (1987).

   B. Medical examiner, *Paradis v. Ararve*, 240 F.3d 1169 (9th Cir. 2001) (the prosecution's notes regarding the medical examiner's opinion on time of death were potentially exculpatory on the issue in case and subject to disclosure); *Foster v. Delo*, 54 F.3d 463 (8th Cir. 1995); *Martinez v. Wainwright*, 621 F.2d 184 (5th Cir. 1980) (murder victim's FBI rap sheet).

5.7.4 Fourth step: Writing the expert report

Report writing should be considered a formal subject in forensic education, yet it is usually an afterthought in most educational programs. Nevertheless, if done properly, it can be a boon to the expert during trial because of its thoroughness and detailed chronology of events and steps taken in reaching findings and conclusions. A report with substantive failures to report all evidence available for analysis, an incomplete narrative on methods and lack of validation information on those methods, and a generally one-sided exposition on conclusions with little information for independent review are open for criticism and possible exclusion.

Organization of a report is not mandated by any legal statutes or case law. What is expected by the courts, however, is a document that shows the examiner's thought process and professional understanding of the events of the investigation communicated in an open, fair-minded, and organized manner.

The typical format of a forensic report should follow an outline form similar to a scientific article or oral presentation.

The introduction—All authors have the responsibility to describe who they are and why they are qualified to render an opinion on the evidence they analyzed.

Experts should list the pertinent training and proficiency testing standards they have met and any other qualifications which reflect on their expertise in the field of investigation. A current curriculum vitae can be attached as an appendix to the report, referenced in the introduction.

Results and opinion on the case—The audience for the report will consist of both experts and non-experts. As such, the early statement of results gives readers a framework to read the following sections, rather than making them guess as to the report's outcome until the end of a lengthy report. An example would be a bite mark expert who writes:

> *The evidence presented by the state in concluding that the defendant, John Smith, as the only possible individual to have made the bite mark injury on the victim's left breast is false. Due to biting dynamics of skin and trauma, the injury pattern is physically distorted and the resulting pattern detail has no dental features capable of reliable forensic pattern (dental) identification. Rather than relying on the state's bite mark expert, the determination of biter identification should be obtained from future DNA analysis of the bitten area and the clothing covering the victim in that general area.*

This is clearly a statement that describes the expert's bottom line on the evidence and goes on to suggest to the reader that there is a better method for the court to use, without needing to give background technical knowledge. In future sections of the report, the details of why and how the expert reached her opinion will be developed.

Broad description of why the expert reached her opinion—Once more, the language needs to be proper for a lay audience, as the processes used to underlie the opinion must be presented. In a brief example, the expert could say the following:

> *The scientific determination of the accuracy of a bite mark identification does not exist. A digital model of your client's dental profile was created using imaging software XYZ, and the arrangement of his teeth were scanned and analyzed for commonality to other people. The range of similarity with many other individuals is the key question of fact. This commonality was investigated, and results were achieved through use of the University of Buffalo dental database that compiles the two- and three-dimensional characteristics of human subjects. This database rendered a statistical finding that your client's dentition is capable of being matched to other individuals. This means, in terms of scientific fact, that other individuals can be randomly matched in a statistically significant group of the database. This clearly contradicts what the State's dental expert has stated to this court.*

This statement essentially attacks the baseline opinion of the opposing expert, who says that Mr. Smith's teeth are the only dentition characteristics that could "match" the injury pattern on the victim. The lack of scientific proof for "unique" dental characteristics in the human race debunks the entire theory used by the State to infer guilt on the defendant. This expert's counter-proof of random matches being possible with people unrelated to the investigation guts the State's argument of bite mark identification.

Detailed analysis—The next section entails the detailed analysis that was used to test the forensic evidence of the case in chief. The decisions of the expert as to what issues were studied are important to lead the reader through the logic and reasonablity of the investigation.

Two major issues in the example case are: the lack of proven dental uniqueness in the human population, and the scientific research that supports the occurrence of random match rates in dental patterns; and that skin patterns from biting forces are potential sources of DNA evidence, and the dynamics of skin injuries of this type prevent the biter's teeth from being accurately replicated in the bite mark. Her opinion undermines the State's reaching an opinion of a "positive match" to the defendant, and claims of this sort are scientifically impossible to prove.

The expert will have to place her investigation process step-by-step in this document to allow the court insight into how the final opinion is a culmination of scientific rigor relevant to the evidence; she will also include the report's reproducible comparison analysis.

Information and data used in the evidence analysis—This is the supporting research data that the expert utilized in reaching her opinion. This would include scientific articles from within her field of expertise, or from other disciplines which overlap and are associated with the subject matter of the case. The material often is of an academic nature, so the translation of its intended purpose and use has to be made understandable to laypersons. Large amounts of such data can be appended to the report, and merely paraphrased in this section.

THE INNOCENCE BLOG

Integrity Unit Investigates Wrongful Conviction

Three years after a Kentucky man was exonerated of a murder and robbery he did not commit, the Louisville police chief ordered an investigation to learn what led to his wrongful conviction.

Edwin Chandler spent 17 years behind bars before the Kentucky Innocence Project uncovered new evidence that led to his exoneration. When the crime occurred, Chandler was on a work release for a misdemeanor and failed to return to jail as required. He was misidentified by a neighbor and falsely confessed after a long interrogation where police threatened to arrest his sister for harboring a fugitive. Despite another witness testifying that the perpetrator was not Chandler, he was convicted and sentenced to 30 years.

Attorneys for the Kentucky Innocence Project uncovered fingerprints on crime scene evidence that excluded Chandler and implicated a known felon who has since been indicted.

On Tuesday, Louisville Police Chief Steve Conrad announced that the department's Public Integrity Unit will investigate Chandler's case before turning its results over to the commonwealth's attorney's office who will determine if charges should be filed. The investigation, which could take up to six months, will review the conduct of former detective Mark Handy who may have coerced Chandler's confession and fed him information that would have only been known to the real perpetrator. It will also review testimony from Chandler's criminal trial and his civil suit that was settled last month for $8.5 million, reported the *Courier-Journal*.

This the second time a review of Chandler's case has been announced. According to his attorney, Nick Brustin, the previous police chief ordered a review the same year Chandler was exonerated but nothing ever materialized.

Conrad also ordered an internal review of policies and training to ensure that investigations meet best practices.

Chandler served nine years in prison and seven on parole before being fully exonerated on October 13, 2009.

Character Traits of Expert Witnesses: The Good and the Bad

6

C. Michael Bowers

Associate Professor of Clinical Dentistry, Ostrow School of Dentistry,
University of Southern California, Los Angeles, CA USA

"Impressing" a jury (or a judge) is a relative term. Impressing someone may not be the same as convincing them to believe you, but the oft-referenced list of behaviors and choice of language that aid in creating a good impression are always part of the discussion about expert witnessing "success."

Witness credibility in the legal arena is a multi-factored assemblage of behaviors that the witness must possess in order to be effective. Often, the truth of statements is determined by whether the jury is comfortable with the personality traits discussed ahead.

6.1 Appearance and early mannerisms: Look friendly and professional

Overall grooming and proper choice of attire is probably the first factor readily seen by the jury. Business dress and a sensible hair style are mandatory. Standing straight during swearing in (taking the oath, "Do you promise to tell the truth, the whole truth, and nothing but the truth, so help you God?") is a must. You will be walking past the jury box in order to take the stand. Decide whether to acknowledge the jury with a smile and a nod or to ignore them on this little journey. This is your first decision regarding how to establish a relationship and rapport with them, and it is important. Declining to acknowledge that they exist will diminish your results. An alternative is to smile and say "good day" to them once you have settled into the witness stand. Take a moment to adjust the chair and microphone (this may be impossible in some courtrooms) and relax. Assess the necessary volume and range of the microphone during the initial direct questions by your representing attorney. Do not struggle with a lack of electronic amplification throughout the proceedings. In some cases, you may have to speak more loudly than normal. This can be disconcerting for some, so practice for public speaking without any public address aids.

6.2 In court materials: Plan ahead!

If your plan includes bringing materials with you onto the stand, have all materials necessary for your testimony neatly organized in one file folder. Do not encumber yourself

Forensic Testimony. http://dx.doi.org/10.1016/B978-0-12-397005-3.00006-2

with reams of loose papers. Have the materials organized in the sequence you have determined ahead of time with your representing lawyer. Most lawyers will say "bring nothing to the stand" unless you want the opposing counsel to make you read it in court.

Advance preparation for the admission of courtroom exhibits is mandatory. The use of photographs, graphs, documents, and any objects must be a major portion of the expert's pretrial conferencing with the attorney. Some lawyers are lax, and will rely on little-to-no pretrial "prep" other than to discuss any reports written by you before the trial. This is a potential danger zone, as the lawyer needs to know how you plan to communicate and the flow of exhibits you plan to enter into evidence. Defense experts must be made aware by their attorney of exhibits already admitted by the prosecution. The expert needs to inquire if "things have been added" by opposing experts that were not previously made discoverable to the defense. This is an area of potential objection by either side if "new" evidence or exhibits have not been reviewed in advance of the trial.

The use of visual aids is flourishing in contemporary US courts. The courtroom support capabilities must be known before you enter for testimony. LCD projectors for PowerPoint slides and video/audio clips may have to be brought in by counsel or the expert. Some courts only provide digital aids if the expert requests them by advance notice.

6.3 Courtroom testimony: Plan ahead!

6.3.1 Know how experts are permitted to talk in court

Discussion in court is premised on the formality of questions being presented to the expert by the attorneys (and sometimes the judge). In rare instances, a jury may be given permission to write down their questions at some point in the deliberations after both direct and cross-examination have occurred. The judge would then select from the questions those which are considered relevant to the issue at trial. Telephonic testimony can be used in some cases, with the expert witness having audio contact with the judge in the courtroom.

The court reporter is an additional participant who will be seated near the expert, in the area called "the well" below the judge's bench. These professionals are to be respected and given every consideration by the expert. This means the expert needs to remember to speak clearly and avoid machine-gun diatribes in times of witnessing stress. The trial transcript will be strongly protected and its documentation supported by the judge, so it is appropriate to consider the reporter the judge's employee. In that respect, the judge or the reporter herself may stop your testimony and direct your attention back to the microphone or to speak more clearly. Take all of this with a smile, and say "Thank you."

6.3.2 Know the expert's real audience

At this stage, you have heard a bit about the Q&A trial format, and the judge and court reporter's efforts to have a "clean" recording of the proceedings. These folks will generally sink into the background of the expert's mind as the questioning commences. The expert must never forget the third part of the audience in this milieu of listeners: the jury.

It is normal for a Q&A to be an eye-to-eye series of responses between two parties; this is not so in court. The expert cannot forget that her conversation after listening to *any* question is with the jury. The mantra is, "Question, then turn to the jury." This goes for both the prosecution and defense questions. It is only natural to feel more or less comfortable with questions depending on their source. This is where training may help. The goal is to appear equitable and unbiased regardless of who does the questioning. Do not verbally or physically react at all to uncomfortable or difficult questioning. The expert's priority should be the relationship-building aspect of testifying with the jury (or judge), rather than having eye contact with the questioner throughout answering. The answers are for the benefit of the judge and jury. Giving an appropriate response establishes that the expert is in control of the subject matter posed by the questioning.

The development of eye contact with the jury allows the expert to assess some cues available from the jury panel during the conversation. A "flowing" eye contact by the expert with each jury member, combined with slight pauses to focus on most of the panel, will prove beneficial. Benefits for the expert center on her ability to disconnect from the questioner, and answer questions in a moderate tone with positive facial responses accompanied by "open" gestures. Remember, many physical cues people assume are indicative of "truthfulness" or "deceit" have never been scientifically established; but done well, posture and arm/hand positioning do communicate a relaxed, almost familial attitude. Arm waving, pointing, and other emphatic gestures may be *de jure* for some attorneys, but the expert must abstain from adopting histrionics—no matter how you might use them in other settings.

Another benefit of this approach is that the jury can become a buffer during aggressive or overly demanding cross-examination. Caustic or uncomfortable questioning during cross-examination may have less effect if the expert has been doing well with the jury during her direct examination. The expert must remember that sincerity and enthusiasm will overrule nasty comments coming from ill-prepared opposing counsel who resort to tactics of this kind.

In the world and in life, not everyone will like you, regardless of how well you look and how pleasantly you act and communicate. Juries can bring personal bias and preconceived attitudes about the case and the evidence into the courtroom that cannot be overcome by expertise. Even jury members can show certain traits of quiet hostility or indifference during an expert's testimony. No remedy will counteract human nature, which is capable of showing up in the impaneled jury. The expert's response should be to stay calm, emphasize eye contact with more seemingly pleasant jury members, and carry on with the plan.

6.4 Credibility maintenance in court: Learn from others' gaffes

The strongest role trait for the expert to show is objectivity and do not avoid the hard questions. Act like a scientist, not an advocate for just your attorney's case. Experts can easily be considered to be too self-interested in the outcome of a trial, and to lack professional objectivity. This lawyers' trait of advocacy for their "side" is consistently praised within the legal community. The same is not said for the expert who ridicules any comments that conflict with her own, or who shows no willingness to discuss conclusions different from what the expert believes to be a fact or proven theory. This comes across when the expert will not concede to any question that even remotely could undermine his or her conclusions. This tendency shows itself when the expert frequently refuses to answer the simplest questions, demanding that the question be rephrased by opposing counsel. Another ploy is to reiterate meaningless sentences supporting his or her theory when answering a question that requires a simple "yes" or "no." The jury will quickly note when an expert is resistant to responding to fair questions. A "non" answer to probing questions generally will occur when the expert is being queried on the assumptions necessary for the expert to claim reliability of results. Many forensic experts require personal assumptions rather than a basis of empirical data. Analysts using "hard science" (physics, biochemistry, etc.) are scientifically trained, and know the extensive research and proofs behind their methods. They would have learned this in the substantive education of their college and university training. Bite mark analysts and other members of the "soft" forensic sciences (pre-forensic DNA disciplines which established themselves via court approval only) will respond to their research/data/method "gap" by relying on declarations of confidence levels (i.e., "No court has ever excluded my opinions" or "Every colleague I have shown the case to agrees with me") as a substitute for scientific facts, when they are nothing more than speculation on their forensic beliefs. These "softies" are also prone to short-stop incursions by new research into their domains. Some even publicly call researchers "inept," or not practitioners of the testifier's forensic "art and science" beliefs. Congressional investigations by the National Academies of Science (NAS) into forensic mistakes (the Innocence Project has tallied over 300 cases of incorrect convictions with later DNA exoneration, with forensic contributions to these mistakes at over 50%) have been met with the same denials of fault or weakness (i.e., " the NAS was misled by the … [contributors]"). In the NAS' 2009 "Strengthening Forensic Science in the United States: A Pathway Forward" [1] report, ballistics, bite mark identification, fingerprints, fiber analysis, and arson were disciplines reviewed and considered lacking in scientific underpinnings. The following quote is an example of what recent congressional review has said about one of these "soft" forensic sciences. What the bite mark identification community continues to say in courtrooms and in public largely discredits such "outsider" critical review as a "non-forensic opinion," and ignores the real issues of wrongful convictions aided by their "elite" membership over the past 30 years. [2]

---

[1] http://www.nap.edu/openbook.php?record_id=12589

[2] ABFO.org; This 100-member group of dentists claim to be "solving" the problem of their bad case results via new terminology and an adherence to the belief that only "rogue" dentists are to blame for the nearly 20 cases of post-conviction exonerations or dismissal of charges. They make these claims despite the fact that over 10% of current and past members, including past presidents, of this forensic certification group have participated as prosecution experts in cases accusing and/or convicting the wrong persons of serious crimes.

Bitemark Analysis Not Recommended for Funding in U.S. Senate Hearing on Forensic Science [3]

> *The United States Senate heard testimony from a distinguished panel last Wednesday on Capitol Hill. When asked by Senator Nelson which forensic discipline should not be advanced, Mr. Mearns, the Co-chair, National Academies' Committee on Identifying the Needs of the Forensic Science Community said that in his opinion, forensic odontology (bitemarks) is so far from scientific validation that it is not worthy of research funding.*

Reporting bias is the avoidance and omissions of details and data. The legal term "due process" encompasses the everyday concept of fairness. The US Constitution has incorporated the Fifth Amendment's statement against federal action as "no one shall be deprived of life, liberty, or property without due process of law." The Fourteenth Amendment, ratified in 1868 and called the Due Process Clause, prescribed this same legal obligation to all the states.

Due process failures are prejudicial acts which biases judges and the jury, impinge on the fundamental rights of a defendant at trial or during police investigation of a crime. The actions of forensic experts in criminal courts are reviewable and subject to this same tenet of fairness to avoid civil liberty damages to defendants. The first step in presenting evidence to a criminal court is to provide a written report. The report's contents generally arise in the court record in pretrial hearings that establish the threshold suspicions of a defendant's guilt. The same report (with subsequent amendments by the expert being allowed) shows itself at trial through the expert's testimony and presentation. The report's statement of methods, materials, and conclusions should be written with regard to the audience receiving it. The judge and the jury are not to be expected to understand scientific details and assumptions without

---

[3] http://bitemarks.org/tag/national-academy-of-science/. The author, Dr. David Averill, continues:

This testimony was from a hearing of the United States Senate Committee on Commerce, Science and Transportation that is investigating the science of forensics. The hearing was held on Wednesday, December 7th 2011 on Capitol Hill. Senator Jay Rockefeller is the chair of the committee which included testimony from John Grisham, Innocence Project, Charlottesville, Virginia; Constantine Gatsonis, Brown University, Providence, Rhode Island; Geoffrey S. Means, Cleveland State University, Cleveland, Ohio; and Terry W. Fenger, Marshall University Forensic Science Center, Huntington, West Virginia. Dr. Gatosonis and Mr. Means were the co-chairs of the National Academy of Science committee that produced the report in 2009 for congress called "Strengthening Forensic Science, a Pathway Forward".

The complete web archive of the video can be found at: http://commerce.senate.gov/public/index-.cfm?p=Hearings&ContentRecord_id=63e87410-acf3-45eb-a849-1b4edf6a8959&ContentType-_id=14f995b9-dfa5-407a-9d35-56cc7152a7ed&Group_id=b06c39af-e033-4cba-9221-de668ca1978a&MonthDisplay=12&YearDisplay=2011.

Senator Rockefeller in his pre-testimony opening remarks was critical of the forensic science community, not the practitioners. He feels that the problem involves the "science," partly because there are no national standards for the language used in the courtroom to report outcomes. He gave an example that says that when an expert in a fancy suit and with fancy degrees says the evidence is a "match," the next place for the defendant is a jail cell.

having them presented by the expert in a meaningful expression of what was done with the evidence obtained from a defendant, victim, or crime scene. A report with little more than an evidence list and conclusions runs the risk of being excluded due to lack of constitutional fairness.

Most forensic experts are employees of police- or government-managed crime laboratories. Some of these agencies will have report guidelines that require some modicum of explanation for protocols of evidence analysis and conclusion terminology in order to allow review by both the court and the defendant's counsel. The guidelines may not be stringently followed, or the report may not be reviewed by supervising analysts in the agency. Private or self-employed experts may have little concern for detailed documentation of data or reference materials, and may make scientific reproducibility by opposing experts impossible. This is where blatant "forensic science" unfairness occurs, in which the conclusions have no independent or discernible "testing," and are reliable only as sworn by the expert to be "in my expert opinion." This falls below the threshold of science and enters the adversarial arena once again. Brief descriptions of testing data or mere conclusions (i.e., "The fibers from underneath the victim's fingernails matched the cloth shirt worn by the husband") are insufficient. Unfortunately, this is the norm:

- reports that contain no description of the methods or procedures used,
- an absence of discussion about measurement errors of equipment, a lack of reference databases (or gaps in what they say) of similar materials (used to protect against a random match with similar fibers), and
- no quantitatively based (i.e., reproducible data available for independent review) levels of confidence or certainty.

AN EXAMPLE OF SELF-INTEREST CONFLICTING WITH SCIENTIFIC FACTS

A recent television interview contained testimony from a long time bite mark identification expert who stated that "bite mark identifications are still a valuable and meaningful contribution to forensic science." When asked if the discipline could be scientifically proved, he responded, "I don't think so." He lost credibility by claiming to be reliable, but leaving out the entire story.

Avoidance and omissions tactics give the opposing counsel more ammunition to discredit the expert. Do not fall into this trap of intentionally misleading the court, or omitting discussion of what is occurring in the scientific and forensic communities and your forensic area. The willingness to candidly discuss issues such as these makes the witness more credible, and seem above adversarial self-interest.

The end result should be a report that is transparent, and explains the strengths and limitations of what is *scientifically* possible, not just what the employing attorney (be it the prosecution or defense) wants the court to know. The 2009 NAS Report contains further guidelines:

> As a general matter, laboratory reports generated as the result of a scientific analysis should be complete and thorough. They should describe, at a minimum, methods and materials, procedures, results, and conclusions, and they should

identify, as appropriate, the sources of uncertainty in the procedures and con-clusions along with estimates of their scale (to indicate the level of confidence in the results).

Forensic science reports, and any courtroom testimony stemming from them, must include clear characterizations of the limitations of the analyses, including asso-ciated probabilities where possible. Courtroom testimony should be given in lay terms so that all trial participants can understand how to weight and interpret the testimony. In order to enable this, research must be undertaken to evaluate the reliability of the steps of the various identification methods and the confidence intervals associated with the overall conclusions. [4]

Know how to uncover the adversarial expert. The NAS inferences about fairness in report writing extend to *all* forensic experts, regardless of employment or consulting status. Additional behaviors expected of an adversarial forensic witness are:

1. Not being available for interview by opposing counsel, generally the defense attorney(s) and defense experts, in order to explain the reports' contents and the integral steps used to reach findings.
2. Withholding information because of the possible negative effect on the prosecu-tion case in chief.
3. Concealing information in a manner that makes independent review of the data and the expert's forensic laboratory examination difficult or impossible.
4. Stating findings and conclusions that are overconfident and merely disguised personal beliefs, rather than being scientifically founded.
5. Performing analytical steps that are either invalidated by other examiners or not published in the scientific literature.
6. Distorting facts or misrepresenting forensic literature as an artificial means to bolster their case. This is particularly rife in some impression evidence fields including bite mark analysis.
7. Resorting to or encouraging delaying tactics when complying with discovery orders from opposing counsel.
8. Concealing or intentionally misplacing evidence. The most egregious example in the author's experience involved a forensic dentist discarding evidence before a trial due to its "spoiling in the refrigerator."

The real proof of a forensic expert's praise of herself as a scientist or "trained analyst" only goes as far as the scientific behavior and rigor of fairness in her report and testimony.

The expert's analysis has limitations that should be acknowledged. The flow of an expert's court presentation should be evenly paced and contain a continuity of simple steps in a logical narrative. Her knowledge of a specific discipline allows for many vari-ations in presentation, but the core information must contain a commonsense approach. Less experienced or less prepared experts tend to rush wholeheartedly into the body of their conclusions without allowing the audience to absorb the preliminary basics

---

[4] National Academy of Sciences Report (Edwards and Gotsonis, 2009; pp. 186).

necessary for the conclusions to be considered reliable. A comprehensive approach from start to finish should be defined by using a categorical approach. The first phase is the expert's narrative about his or her training and experience in the lab and in court. The second would be the list of evidence analyzed and how the expert received it (collection at the scene or transferred by a third party). Management of the evidence needs to be clearly stated (known as the "chain of custody") for each phase, from the original collection through admission as evidence in court. The equipment used for evidence analysis should be simply described and presented in its most elementary form. Some evidence analysis is interpretative of computations or data received from physical analysis (i.e., blood samples for DNA typing, or chemical analysis of drugs), while other evidence may be physical comparison of impression patterns (fingerprints, foot prints, tool marks, bite marks). The limits of what each analysis can achieve regarding identifying the source of physical evidence ("Where did it come from?" or "What is it?") has to be explained. Pay close attention to avoid the "smoking gun" concept, in which any one piece of evidence "makes the case." Most, if not all, evidence presented in court merely leads the decision maker in a certain direction or to an intersection of decision making. If the experts fail to contain themselves in this respect, the point will be made by competent opposing counsel during cross-examination. It is better to accurately declare these limitations of your own volition than to have to backtrack later in the face of a substantial attack on your credibility and lack of fairness.

THE INNOCENCE BLOG

Two Innocent Men Cleared Today in Separate Murder Cases in Mississippi, 15 Years after Wrongful Convictions

Kennedy Brewer, who served time on death row, is first post-conviction DNA exoneration in Mississippi; Levon Brooks' conviction is thrown out and he is free

(NOXUBEE COUNTY, MS; February 15, 2008) – Two men who were wrongfully convicted of separate child murders in Noxubee County, Mississippi, were cleared in the crimes at a hearing this morning based on evidence proving their innocence. Kennedy Brewer and Levon Brooks, who are represented by the Innocence Project, have maintained their innocence for 15 years and were joined by more than 100 of their relatives at this morning's hearing.

New evidence, which includes DNA testing and a confession, has identified the actual perpetrator in both cases, who was arrested last week. At today's hearing, the case against Brewer was dismissed – making him the first person in Mississippi exonerated through post-conviction DNA testing. Brewer served time on death row. Brooks' conviction was vacated and he was released from custody; Brooks will be fully exonerated when the indictment against him is dismissed, which the Innocence Project expects in the next few weeks.

"It has taken 15 long years, but Kennedy Brewer and Levon Brooks are finally free. The evidence clearly shows that they are innocent – what's troubling is that their innocence has been clear for years, but they remained incarcerated while the true perpetrator was at large," Innocence Project Co-Director Peter Neufeld said. "The system wasn't just broken in these cases – different elements within the system actually conspired to convict two innocent men of heinous crimes, while the actual perpetrator remained at large. These cases should haunt Mississippi and the nation, and they should lead to a top-to-bottom review of how the state is investigating and prosecuting cases."

The same sheriff's officer investigated both crimes, the same District Attorney prosecuted both crimes, and the same discredited forensic dentist and same controversial pathologist conducted the post mortems and misled juries in both cases with false testimony implicating Brooks and Brewer. Because of concerns about whether Brewer and Brooks' cases would be handled appropriately once new evidence emerged, the Innocence Project persuaded the Mississippi Attorney General to intervene in the reinvestigation of the cases. This is the first time in the nation that a case has ended in exoneration after a state Attorney General has intervened and removed it from a local prosecutor, according to the Innocence Project.

In 1992, Brooks was convicted of the 1990 rape and murder of his ex-girlfriend's three-year-old daughter. The child was taken from her home in the middle of the night, and her body was later found in a pond near her home. Her skin had slippage and other marks consistent with a child who had been killed and then dumped in a pond – but the local forensic analysts falsely claimed that the marks on her wrists were "bite marks" from Brooks. In 1995, Brewer was convicted of an identical crime that happened just 18 months after the one for which Brooks was convicted. Brewer's girlfriend also had a three-year-old daughter who was taken from her home in the middle of the night, raped and murdered. Her body was found in a creek near her home, with cuts that the same prosecution witness said were "bite marks" from Brewer but were actually caused by insects and animals in the creek.

In 2001, while Brewer was on death row, DNA tests excluded him as the source of the semen recovered from the girl's body. His conviction was vacated, but the District Attorney (who had prosecuted the case at trial) said he was going to re-try Brewer for the crime, and again seek the death penalty. For a full five years, the prosecutor did not move the case to trial – so Brewer waited for five years in the county jail. Finally, last summer, the Innocence Project helped Andre de Gruy of the Office of Capital Defense Counsel in Mississippi secure

(Continued)

THE INNOCENCE BLOG—Cont'd

Brewer's release from jail and geared up to represent him at a new trial. Meanwhile, seeing the similarities between the two cases, the Innocence Project took Brooks' case – but quickly learned that the biological evidence from the crime was too degraded to yield results from DNA testing.

The Innocence Project was concerned that conflicts of interest in Noxubee County would hamper efforts to secure justice for Brewer, so the Innocence Project asked the Mississippi Attorney General to intervene. Ben Creekmore, the District Attorney of Oxford, was appointed Special Prosecutor of the Brewer case.

Meanwhile the Innocence Project continued its own investigation of both cases – which led to Justin Albert Johnson, a 51-year-old Noxubee County man who was an initial suspect in both cases. At the time of the Brooks case, Johnson frequently stayed in a house very close to the victim's home; at the time of the Brewer case, he lived with his parents just a couple of houses down from that victim's home. Although Johnson was the only suspect with a history of committing sexual assaults against women and young girls, local law enforcement investigating both crimes ignored him after they prematurely locked onto Brooks and Brewer as prime suspects. In recent months, the Innocence Project secured DNA testing on evidence from the Brewer case which matched Johnson's DNA profile.

Just as it had in Brewer's case, the Innocence Project feared that local conflicts and regional concerns could compromise Brooks' quest for justice. Neufeld appealed to the Attorney General to intervene and take over the arrest, interviewing and prosecution of Johnson. The Attorney General assigned its elite Integrity Unit to work on the continuing investigation of the case.

Last week, based on the DNA match, the almost identical modus operandi and his proximity to both crimes, investigators from the Attorney General's office arrested Johnson and questioned him about both cases – and he confessed to both. He also assured the investigators that he acted alone. The confession was recorded. The Innocence Project expects that he will be prosecuted for both crimes.

"If local law enforcement had properly investigated these crimes, they would have stayed focused on Albert Johnson from the beginning. In fact, if Albert Johnson had been apprehended for the first crime, the second one would never have happened – and the three-year-old victim would be approaching her 18th birthday," said Innocence Project Staff Attorney Vanessa Potkin.

The forensic analysis and testimony in both trials was deeply flawed and further illustrates the corruption that led to the two wrongful convictions, the Innocence Project said. Dr. Michael West, a Mississippi dentist who has testified for the prosecution in cases in nine states, claimed that cuts on the victims' bodies were human bite marks caused by only the two top teeth; in each case, he testified with certainty that Brewer and Brooks were the sources of the alleged bite marks. By the time of Brewer's trial, West had already been widely discredited; he was the first member ever suspended by the American Board of Forensic Odontology. Regardless, prosecutors continued to use West as an expert for years and courts allowed his testimony.

West has routinely collaborated with Steven Hayne, a medical examiner for hire who conducts nearly every autopsy for prosecutors in Mississippi. Hayne conducted the autopsies on the victims in the Brewer and Brooks cases – and called West in for both autopsies.

The innocent Brewer was sent to death row and the innocent Levon Brooks to languish in prison for the rest of his life," Neufeld said. "These cases are an urgent call for a thorough review of how crime scene evidence gets analyzed and makes it into Mississippi courtrooms and how we can make sure only the most credible, objective, reliable science is used in criminal cases."

THE INNOCENCE BLOG—Cont'd

Meanwhile, the officer who investigated both cases, Earnest Eichelberger, told Neufeld and Potkin last summer that his practice in such cases is simply to arrest everyone who had been in the house for the preceding 72 hours, then let the case sort itself out. Eichelberger worked in the Noxubee County Sheriff's office at the time of the crimes and now works for the Mississippi State Police, where he is tasked with helping solve crimes in rural communities. Last summer, Eichelberger said that he saves all of his old case files in his home, but he has since claimed that files in the Brewer and Brooks cases don't exist.

Brewer and Brooks are African-American men in rural Mississippi. They received inadequate, under-financed defenses, not that different from what many other poor black defendants received and continue to receive in Mississippi.

Including Brewer, 213 people nationwide have been exonerated with DNA testing, (at time of printing FST, the number now totals 306 DNA exonerations in the US) according to the Innocence Project, which is affiliated with Benjamin N. Cardozo School of Law at Yeshiva University. Mississippi – unlike 42 other states – does not have a law granting post-conviction DNA testing to resolve claims of innocence.

"An extraordinary number of people have helped secure justice for Kennedy Brewer, Levon Brooks, their families and the victims' families," Neufeld said. The newly established Mississippi Innocence Project is co-counsel on the Brooks case. Skadden, Arps, Slate, Meagher LLP and Affiliates provided extensive pro bono assistance on the case. Andre de Gruy of the Office of Capital Defense Counsel in Mississippi has been co-counsel on the Brewer case. Jackson attorney Robert B. McDuff is also co-counsel on the Brewer case. Lauren Kaeseberg, a Cardozo School of Law clinic student at the Innocence Project, worked on the cases for two years. Forensic Science Associates conducted DNA testing in the cases. John R. Wallace, Aquatic and Forensic Entomologist, worked on the case, along with three world-renowned experts in bite marks: Dr. David Sweet, of the University of British Columbia in Vancouver, Canada; and Dr. Iain A. Pretty of University of Manchester in the United Kingdom. Author John Grisham, who serves on the Innocence Project's Board of Directors, provided support and assistance throughout the cases.

Voir Dire and Direct Examination of the Expert

7

C. Michael Bowers

Associate Professor of Clinical Dentistry, Ostrow School of Dentistry,
University of Southern California, Los Angeles, CA USA

7.1 How the witness becomes qualified as an expert: Voir dire and beyond

This is the threshold questioning before direct examination from the expert is permitted. This occurs when any expert enters into a court to testify, regardless of prior court acceptance. The judge in every case determines the outcome. The legal rules regarding expert qualifications are encompassed in Rule 702 et seq. of the rules of evidence codes found in federal and state courts (as described in Chapter 3).

OUTLINE FOR QUALIFYING THE FORENSIC EXPERT

The lawyer offering a potential expert witness has to consider all of the following in order to establish the basis for a successful qualification:

- Educational background
- Licenses and certifications
- Experience and personal research in relevant fields
- Teaching experience
- Membership or offices held in professional organizations
- Books and articles written
- Awards won
- Number of times previously qualified as an expert

7.1.1 Considerations about voir dire

Both the expert and her attorney obviously consider the expert qualified, and she may also have a particularly impressive background. The opponent attorney may offer to stipulate to the expert's qualifications. Stipulation allows the judge to accept the expert without further discussion by either party. This eliminates questioning the witness about her qualifications in front of the jury. This should be nicely refused by the expert's attorney. *Voir dire* should be used to enhance the witness's credibility. It should not be overly verbose, as the court can limit "grandstanding." Offering the expert's resume or curriculum vitae can shorten the testimony and place this resume "in the record," but this limits what the jury can use to compare opposing expert witnesses' experience and activities. This is the jury's response when conflicting

Forensic Testimony. http://dx.doi.org/10.1016/B978-0-12-397005-3.00007-4

opinions occur. The lawyer's questioning should emphasize the training or recognition that puts his expert above others practicing in the same area. It must be understandable to the average juror, and it is the responsibility of the expert to make this point, although subtle means are necessary.

7.1.2 "Skating on thin ice," or the risk of not being qualified enough—or not qualified at all

Remember that the judge is looking for appropriate connections between what makes you a forensic expert, the evidence contained in the case, and the rules of evidence. The relationship should be a strong one. Self-education as a basis for your presence in court will not be compelling. Avoid self-published works and authorities of the expert as the only support. This should be considered suspect to the judge. A "bootstrap" testimonial on how an expert justifies her own qualifications on point with the case issues without an accompanying body of information from other independent scientific sources lacks strength and credibility. Appropriate training and experience should count if it supports a specialized knowledge in a subject that possesses relevancy to the case. Supposition without professional credibility is not relevant. Some courts might disagree, but a "scientific expert" will be expected to have formal education relevant to the subject matter of her presentation. An art historian should have little trouble discussing the aspects of an art forgery case, but should find it impossible to present opinions on aspects of crime scene interpretation of a homicide case.

7.1.3 Voir dire: The second part

When the attorney completes the qualification presentation, he will offer, or "tender," the expert to the judge in a short statement attesting to expertise appropriate to the case in chief. If opposing counsel so desires, the next step prior to judicial admission allows the opposing attorney the option to argue against the expert's admission in a myriad of questions about training, character, and, in certain circumstances, past testimony. The expert should know that her own attorney should be ready, in advance, to defend her credibility. The opposing attorney may pursue the expert with questioning that is inaccurate or intentionally misleading. This is a strategy of creating "phantom" doubts about the expert's capabilities training, certifications, and experience.

7.1.4 When objections are made about the expert in voir dire: Typical arguments

Most times, opposing counsel realizes that the qualifications of the expert are sustainable and highly likely to be accepted by the judge. Nevertheless, this is an opportunity to make the expert appear, through "leading" questioning, to be less commendable than is readily apparent. It is the first chance for this attorney to take some swings regarding the expert's training, attitudes, previous mistakes, competency, and possible bias. It has everything to do with disparaging the expert's character in the presence of the jury. Rarely will questioning of this type ever contain discussions on scientific issues. The purpose is to create "doubt" and "reasons" why the expert shouldn't even participate in presenting her analysis to the jury.

7.1.4.1 At the beginning

Even before the trial begins, a "motion *in limine*" can be requested by the opposing attorney about the expert and her particular activities in the case. It may also be made after the trial has started. This is a request that the trial judge exclude (for other purposes, it can be used to include) certain testimony regarding evidence or information a potential witness may be ready to offer to the court. This hearing is done without the presence of the jury. In criminal cases, it is a means to exclude or "shield" the jury from information about the defendant on grounds of prejudice (i.e., "unfair" information) or in violation of some rule of evidence (i.e., a rule of "discovery"). Lawyers use this technique to avoid being overruled by the judge during *voir dire* while in front of the jury.

7.1.4.2 Wait until cross

Arguing with a potential expert about the opposing expert's work can be considered better placed during the formal cross-examination period. Most lawyers stick to the practice of "Ask a few *voir dire* questions and then sit down."

7.1.4.3 The professional witness gambit

This is done to infer that the expert has a career in forensic testimony, and should be considered to have a financial interest in the case's outcome or to only be presenting in court to make money. It is obvious that when an expert is more experienced in forensics, she winds up in court more often. The properly prepared expert should be fully capable of answering such questioning with little difficulty in full context.

7.1.4.4 Questioning the expert's monetary compensation

This is a variation of the last tactic. The expert should answer compensation questions honestly and directly. Full-time law investigation and laboratory forensic personnel who testify in their own jurisdictions should not expect this question. Private forensic consultants should explain that the time taken in evidence analysis, case preparation, exhibit creation, and testimony in court costs so much per hour. Court time should include time in travel, expenses, and so forth, just like other professions and business owners. The part-time forensic expert can describe the court testimony costs in relation to earnings from their full-time profession.

7.1.4.5 Questioning if the expert advertises services

This is a holdover from the times when advertising services was poorly thought of by professional organizations. No such prohibitions exist in US forensic associations. Many forensic experts run training and educational courses throughout the country.

7.1.4.6 Questioning the expert's frequency of testimony in cases

The implication is that the expert only testifies according to personal preferences, which can imply a bias for either side. The simple fact is that most prosecution experts work for a government-owned agency, and defense experts are private consultants (some of whom may testify as defense experts in cases outside their home jurisdiction).

Remember that becoming "qualified" in a case does not mean that the court is giving the expert unlimited credibility. It means the expert is permitted to testify and is "acceptable."

A caveat: Plan to emphasize the qualifications that relate most directly to the facts of the case. This is a strengthening technique for acceptance that tells the judge and jury that you are not simply attempting to discuss your theoretical whimsy or purely academic knowledge.

- Since courts generally allow experts to testify, respond to a challenge to your expert's qualifications by saying that the quality or quantity of the witness's credentials go to the weight and not the admissibility of evidence.
- If the judge is reluctant to allow your expert to testify, suggest that the court issue a limiting instruction that the jury is free to accept or reject the witness's opinion.
- Argue that opposing counsel waived the objection if he or she failed to object to your expert immediately after you called the expert as a witness.
- Use your judgment in asking for or agreeing to a stipulation concerning qualifications. A stipulation will prevent you from questioning the witness concerning his or her qualifications, which can enhance your witness's credibility.
- Too much time spent detailing your witness's credentials can become tedious, and may come across as "showing off."
- If your expert witness has appeared as an expert in many trials, and opposing counsel characterizes the expert as a "hired gun," make it clear that many people have sought the expert's services because of the expert's excellent credentials.

7.2 The courtroom testimony: Direct examination

The culminating event in a forensic investigation has the expert attending court and presenting his or her case to the trier of fact, be it judge or judge and jury. You should consider the similarity to a dramatic public presentation. The lawyer is the director, and the expert the main character. The genre is documentary, not fictional. The critical point of direct examination success is how much preparation and communication with legal counsel has been performed prior to the court date. Inadequate discussion with counsel regarding issues to be presented on direct will lead to unwarranted surprises, weak results, and confusion in the presentation. Professional or personal credibility will also be damaged or lost. What is also important is to plan what issues are to be covered, and those to be avoided for strategic or legal reasons of the client's case. All of this planning assumes adherence to ethical standards on the subject of expert/attorney relationships.

A caveat: Lawyers may limit and direct what issues to address on direct examination, but remember that they cannot tell you *what* to say about any particular subject.

7.2.1 The strategy of direct examination: Many purposes

The core responsibility of the expert "on direct" is to tell a logical story about her theory of the evidence and her conclusions. The essence of communication is based on the good educational skills of the expert. As mentioned earlier, the lawyer offering the expert into court leads the way with questions (determined in advance) that are open-ended. The questions are simple, such as: "When did you receive the evidence you reviewed for this case?"; "What research did you perform regarding this case?"; or "How did you reach your conclusions?"; and so on. The answers are in the domain of the expert, and they are without the distraction of responding to the implied criticism that arises in most cross-examination questions.

7.2.1.1 Persona during testimony

The dynamic of the expert on direct (and on cross) should be outgoing, upbeat, and indicative of interest in telling the story. The attitude can verge on enthusiasm tempered with professional interest in describing the complete particulars of the case. This is a demanding task, as many forensic cases have challenging aspects and complicated details. The planning phase should have developed the elemental and salient categories that need to be expressed simply in court. The expert's narration must flow in statements of her opinion, the scientific basis of it, the data examined, analytical procedures used, and how all of this confirms her findings.

There are no specific organizational rules on the presentation, but there is a commonsense approach that should be followed by the counsel who hired the expert.

- First, the counsel will ask the expert to state her name.
- The next question will ask if the expert was asked to render an expert opinion in the case. The answer should be in the affirmative, and the expert has the ability to add that she was asked to analyze specific evidence of the case involving her area of expertise.
- The next question can lead directly into what her general conclusion was at the completion of her analysis. This sets up the jury for what to expect regarding the subject matter of her specialty and presentation.

This will then lead counsel to ask for a narrative from the expert on her education, training, writing, and lecturing that is associated with the forensic subject involved in her testimony. This sounds redundant, but the jury needs a fresh, sharp memory of how perfectly suited the expert is for the case. This should be considered an opportunity for the expert to be concise and direct without sounding bored, agitated, or self-conscious about giving personal information. The jury is the audience, but they will remember only a little beyond the demeanor and speaking ability of the expert if the expert does not make a conscious effort to make an impression.

7.2.1.2 Things to avoid in testimony on direct and cross-examination

The following items apply equally to all court testimony by an expert.

Do not overstate your opinion. Avoid broad spectrum statements unless it is a core issue in the case strategy.

The following is an example of an expert who made too broad of a statement during direct examination, and then had to scramble when the opposing counsel took advantage of it on cross-examination.

Q. Isn't it your opinion, Dr. Smith, that the application of bite mark analysis where teeth are compared to a bite is invalid?

A. Yes, it is my opinion.

Q. Then, as you say, a bitten piece of chewing gum would be worthless to compare to the defendant's teeth?

A. Well, not necessarily. Chewing gum is a better impression material than human skin, and it may be possible to replicate the shape of certain teeth if certain circumstances are met.

Her opinion now sounds conflicted and uncertain. The expert had earlier stated a generic opinion that tooth mark evidence and comparison to teeth should not be used in any circumstances. Then, upon reflection upon the second question by the cross-examining counsel, the expert contradicts herself. The expert must realize that the use of absolute answers are the realm of attorneys and rarely mentioned in scientific communities. They should be considered suspect questions. In this case, the expert was overzealous, emotional, or unprepared regarding the scope of her criticism of bite mark evidence in the courtroom, and agreed to something she really did not mean or which did not sufficiently describe her position. This can easily be confusing to the jury, as they do not understand the nuanced differences between forensic methods and evidence available for analysis. The expert must be confident in her opinions, speak from her accurate memory of the earlier written report (which she will have reviewed multiple times), and carefully choose statements that will not have to be later corrected. In this example, her reply must be a commonsense statement attempting to clarify or rehabilitate the overstatement. She might add:

A. Please let me clarify this for you, Mr. Jones. The best purpose for bite mark information is the recognition of a bite in any substance. This makes the investigators aware that the bitten area may be a source of DNA from saliva deposited by the biter. It is more accurate to use DNA profiling rather than perform bite mark comparison analysis, as it is proven to be too subjective and much less reliable. This applies to all bite mark evidence.

Or:

A. While I do agree with you that chewing gum marks may provide pattern details that can be compared with teeth, it is a rare find to discover such evidence. And I emphasize my use of "may" as to its forensic value for pattern comparison with teeth. However, this case is about a bite mark in the skin of the victim, and I stand by my opinion regarding the unreliability of the methods used by the state's expert.

The crossing attorney attempted to find an "exception" to the expert's general opinion on the unreliability of bite mark evidence for comparison purposes. The question of chewing gum's forensic value was a good one. The expert "opened the door" to the danger of sounding self-contradicting, as she conceded that chewing gum "may" have some pattern-matching value, though it was irrelevant to the evidence and the case at hand.

The expert made a good attempt to clarify her opinion during cross-examination. The expert should expect, however, that her attorney will make use of the upcoming "redirect" for detailed re-emphasis of her full opinion, including why the chewing gum metaphor is irrelevant to the facts of the case before the jury.

Do not hide mistakes, errors, or omissions.

Direct examination is usually where an expert will encounter the experience of having made a technical or testimonial mistake.

Mistakes or errors in computation vary from insignificant to gaffes serious enough to affect the outcome of a case. These are unintentional acts. However, they may later be used to associate the expert with unfair practice and deception. The underlying principle for the expert is to prevent such things from occurring by assiduous pretrial preparation. In complicated technical forensic subjects, computational analyses are a product of multiple stages of internal review at the forensic laboratory. Or at least, they should be. However, the error rates of methods and techniques in the forensic specialties are seldom studied (the major exception being the DNA community), almost never published, refuted or criticized right after being published, and even can be considered unnecessary by those who self-certify themselves as having a zero error rate. On the rare occasion that the expert self-corrects during direct examination, the effort should immediately be put into context regarding its effect on the ultimate opinion. This is not all bad, as long as the correction is on a minor point. It also shows that the expert is fair and honest, and not immune from the human condition.

There is no honest expert who would claim that testifying in court is stress-free. The pressure comes from many angles. One obvious source of stress is the expert verbally responding to the setting. Close scrutiny during public speaking is a venue few commonsense people would seek. The expert has to develop personal tools for public speaking and relaxation techniques. Practicing a courtroom manner in a mock trial setting is invaluable.

Overt acts relating to in-court stress can be both physical and verbal. Having a weak preparation for court can be a source of self-doubt and lack of confidence during examination. This can lead to awkward pauses during testimony and, in the worst case, it can lead to disconnected speech and wandering off the topic being discussed. When this occurs, the expert's attorney has little control. The expert on her own has to realize what is happening, stop for a moment, or ask the court for a pause, then quickly refocus, and request that the attorney restate the question. When a personality conflict occurs between the expert and a questioning attorney, the expert might mentally decide not to answer the question by repeatedly asking for clarification of the question. This is also a delaying strategy, which has a very short half-life of success. The expert's hostility is now obvious to all, which will develop into dislike by the audience. The term "jerk" is something to avoid as a forensic expert.

7.2.2 A technique for stating your opinion

The order of presentation for the expert's case is not rigidly declared by any rules. The objective is to clearly explain to the audience all the steps involved and the rationales for conclusions reached. Some thoughtful advice is to keep the goal in sight, and to present the opinion at the very beginning. The federal rules, however, are explicit in requiring the expert to express the analytical steps and investigations that compose the basis of her opinion if the court requires it.

This style of presenting is called "opinion first," and it succeeds in immediately informing the jury of the context of all subsequent data and the interpretive steps that will follow. The added clarity is a benefit that secondarily provides the leading theme before the potentially boring, protracted, and sometimes confusing technical narration. The final opinion sets the reason for all the later details.

7.2.3 Expressing the theory or theories that explain the opinion

During direct examination, an expert witness should state the basis of her opinion. The trial court has the discretion to require the reasons for any conclusion, and to allow the witness to recite the sources upon which she relied. Since different experts may have a different focus and may base their opinions on different facts, the court will allow an expert to develop her reasons based on sources and references that support her conclusions.

The actual connection between the expert's opinion and the theories necessary to prove the opinion must be part of a professional presentation. Data and reference material is the substance of science. Sadly, forensics can be something quite different. At its worst, it is akin, in some disciplines, to religious and moralistic beliefs.

Forensic experts from non-science subjects (which are usually various impression or pattern "matching" methods) attempt to substitute scientifically based theories (as are available from actual empirical research) with declarations of:

- Training (generally not in a multi-disciplinary forensic program)
- Years of judicial acceptance (which indicates the forensic method is already accepted in courts, and scientific proofs are not necessary)
- The expert's previous personal experience in court

Courts seem oddly accepting of this argument, and offer weak support to the contrary thought process. A readily apparent observation is that the courtroom and judges are ill-prepared to decide scientific merits, regardless of the growing number of erroneous convictions using these "already reviewed" methods of expert opinion.

In a scientifically based presentation, the flow of questions can be rapid.

Q1. Please tell the court your opinion.
Q2. What is the scientific basis (i.e., what are the theories) that supports your conclusions?
Q3. Please tell the courts the steps you performed to obtain your opinion.

The scientific theories enabling a conclusion vary from expert to expert and subject to subject. The more scientifically based disciplines will present multiple, and sometimes rather esoteric, biological, engineering, mathematical, and basic science determinates that are used to make their conclusions reliable. Non-science forensic experts will talk about self-published and practitioner-based theories that may not have much, if any, support of a rigorous scientific origin. In terms of scientific fact, this type of evidence is called anecdotal. This means the process of reproducibility of results from their methods does not exist, or cannot be done, or is not important to their discipline. In this absence of support, courts become confused; the case history of the use of these methods as evidence that proves the identity of people and crime scene evidence will be cloudy and inconsistent.

This is not the case for the history of forensic DNA profiling, as the extensive use of it since its inception has been based on continual testing and creation of high standards. Its protocols have led to the establishment of a consensus by diverse private industry, university and academic research groups facilitated by the National Academies of Sciences and other government sponsored research agencies. DNA has changed the face of forensics by establishing contra proof in cases where other forensic methods have been later deemed unreliable.

7.2.4 Telling the tale of forensic analysis

This is the data and supportive content of the direct presentation that is intended to prove the reliability of the expert's opinion. This may be the toughest phase of the presentation for the expert. The task must be chronologically oriented, covering how the forensic evidence was obtained, preserved, and analyzed. A step-by-step progression must be agreed upon prior to trial, during the preparation phase. The narration of data, statistics, and forensic reference materials must be organized with the audience in mind. The expert must attempt to be concise, and use common language to avoid losing the audience to indifference or overload. Voluminous recitation of data analysis must be kept to the simplest terms.

The expert has to remember that jurors often take notes. This may vary with each case, but a note-taking group of jurors can be a great indicator of how to pace the analytical presentation. If the expert allows them to keep up with the material, it means that they will be able to use this retained information during their deliberations. It is incumbent on the expert to maintain the thread of reasons for each test and each procedure and their context with the evidence and the opinion. This type of testimonial repetition is necessary for effective expert communication to the jury.

7.2.5 Be honest about evidence analysis that may rely on assumptions

Some forensic fields require certain assumptions. Assumptions are considered non-scientific as they lack proof, and are maintained by assertions of the examiner. They vary from field to field, and are not necessarily wrong or particularly important. The expert should readily admit to them in the direct presentation. It is better to address them, rather than hope the opposing attorney may miss the opportunity during cross-examination. Assumptions used in the field may be an uncomfortable topic for some experts. However, if the assumptions are the foundation of a specific field, they may certainly be expected to be a major obstacle in the expert's opinion. The best examples of this type of testimony involve attempts by experts to specifically identify objects and patterns to a single source. Certain groups have attempted to bypass scientific scrutiny by calling themselves "pattern comparison experts" who allow the jury to make their own lay interpretations of source identification (Fingerprints Can Lie, 2012).

Source attribution (i.e. linkage of evidence between a crime scene, victim, and weapons to a suspect) is an extremely powerful aspect of forensic testimony that the court system has accepted for decades. The current climate of improving scientific scrutiny in US courts is affecting its future. Shell casing and bullet "matching" (aka bullet fingerprinting) used in ballistics has recently been refined and improved with database analysis and experimental testing. The NAS report on ballistics, however, stated a cautionary opinion:

"The validity of the fundamental assumptions of uniqueness and reproducibility of firearms-related toolmarks has not yet been fully demonstrated." "Conclusions drawn in firearms identification should not be made to imply the presence of a firm statistical basis when none has been demonstrated." On the other hand, they also report that at a minimal level, "there is at least some 'signal' that may be detected" (Ballistic Imaging, 2008).

Other police science methods, such as bullet lead composition identification, have been removed from use due to the advent of reconsideration and scientifically sophisticated review (Solomon, 2007).

Other methods, such as perpetrator identification from physical hair analysis and bite mark patterns, have no established scientific support, yet the later (bite mark identification) is still admitted in each state in the US. The prosecutorial use of this long-accepted method is experiencing severe courtroom criticism due to assumptions of reliability that have continued to result in unacceptable wrongful convictions.[1]

Fingerprint matching has long been considered infallible, but a 2004 misidentification in a case involving Brandon Mayfield (erroneously considered to be a terrorist bomb maker from a partial fingerprint) has created a rethinking that error rates should be considered. The 2009 NAS report section on fingerprints raised doubt about fingerprint identification and its infallibility, stating:

"The scientific foundation of the fingerprint field has been questioned, and the suggestion has been made that latent fingerprint identifications may not be as reliable as previously assumed." (Strengthening Forensic Science in the United States, 2009).

7.2.6 When the experts battle each other: How far should criticism go?

The media opinion on the interactions of opposing experts in a criminal case emphasizes the concepts of collegiality and mutual respect. Current practice has sadly

---

[1] http://www.law.umich.edu/special/exoneration/Pages/about.aspx

changed, as biased character attacks now occur at national forensic presentations, in books, and, incredibly, in professional forensic journals and textbooks. The Internet allows similar "freedom of speech," but, invariably, the speaker exposes more of his or her own failings than the target of the diatribes. In these trying times for certain forensic methods, the adversarial nature of the legal participants has infected aspects of the forensic expert community. These unfortunate events also derive from the polarized attitudes within forensic groups which were the target of the 2009 NAS report.

There are rules regarding the appointment of experts in court cases that mandate advance notice to both parties of any pending expert witness participation. This listing allows potential contact and pretrial clarification for both parties. It seems this is becoming extinct in criminal cases for the reasons previously noted. One more aspect to this is employer bias, since most crime labs are managed and forensic experts employed by law-enforcement agencies. This is a major concern to advocates for a problem solving approach to deficits in forensic science within the United States. The current system tends to divide the experts into two separate camps, with no personal contact other than an exchange of reports that can vary in methods and resulting conclusions. Access by defense counsel to certain types of physical evidence that the prosecution plans to use at trial is commonly problematic and, at best, inconsistent. Prosecution reports can be non-existent, vague, or incomplete, which leads to judicial delays and additional arguments of lack of due process.

Trial strategy can include the expert being asked about the forensic methods and outcomes admitted by an opposing expert. In some cases, this may not be necessary. If it is necessary, a tactic can be merely to focus on the opposition's expert in the third person, such as:

Q. Dr. Jones, what is your opinion of the defense case regarding this evidence?
A. They presented a flawed analysis of the evidence, and they refuse to accept the fact that my experience in court has proven my reliability on the subject of bite mark comparisons. Their arguments that my methods are unreliable are not true. I firmly believe in my results.

The expert tries to accentuate the reliability of her results without entering into personal attitudes and attack. In reviewing this opinion, however, she thinks her belief should be sufficient to sway the jury. It doesn't address any scientific issues. An opposing lawyer and expert look forward to such weak proofs from a "scientific" expert, and should redouble their efforts to present the scientific truths backing their opinion on the evidence. In total, the answer should have contained detailed scientific reasons for the opinion, not just a restatement of the opinion. She should have given detailed and commonsense reasons for her opinion being correct.

On the opposite extreme, with much less professionalism, one can say:

A. I love it when I see the methods used by the defense expert, Dr. Brown, when he tries to convince the jury that my opinion is wrong. His methods are worthless, and his measurements unnecessary. That is why my opinion is correct.

This answer is nothing more than personal opinion, but again it is used, in this expert's belief, to state that his word is inviolate and true because he says so. This is the *ipse dixit* (i.e., I say, therefore it is) reasoning which is popular from dogmatic experts who refuse to discuss the science (if any) behind what they say in their forensic opinion. It is really just a method of attack which presses home the idea to the jury to discount everything regarding the defense case. To a knowledgeable jury, it is crude, pompous, and incredibly naïve to use.

7.2.7 **The purpose of objections during testimony**

Experts who pass *voir dire* and present their case in chief should realize that the opposing counsel may not agree to particular aspects during the trial. Non-agreement is expressed by verbal objections tendered to the judge with the jury in attendance. At the very least, it is an interruption to the presentation and may be considered annoying. Objections are commonly considered a nuisance, but they sometimes occur through the direct examination. If used as an annoyance, it can have the effect of alienating the objecting counsel from the judge and jury.

7.2.7.1 *General aspects of objections: reasoning and effects*

Unless a party makes a proper and timely objection, the grounds for objection are not preserved for appeal. While a trial court may exclude an improper or unqualified opinion on its own motion (without an objection), it is not required to act on its own.

Whether the trial court will sustain the objection depends on the circumstances of the case. Given the broad discretion of the trial judge, and the trial courts' liberal approach toward admitting expert testimony in civil and criminal cases, objections are not often sustained.

Example: A trial court properly exercised its discretion to not admit certain expert testimony, and the appellate court affirmed this ruling. But the court opined that the trial court could have allowed expert opinion, leaving its weight to the jury.

The forensic expert is not required to understand the array of possible objections concerning rules of law raised during her testimony. Most are directed at the attorney while he is questioning the expert, not at the expert herself. There are a few objections, however, worth understanding because they may result in a topic of narration being rephrased or, rarely, "struck" from the record. If an expert's comments or any accompanying exhibits are rejected by the judge (again, this rarely happens), the judge will inform the jury in varying terms to "disregard what the witness has just said," or the jury will be instructed not to take into account the contents of Exhibit XYZ in their deliberations.

Types of objections are categorized according to their target:

- The form of the attorney's questioning. This is the attorney telling the expert what to say.
- The testimony of the witness. This may involve legal restrictions to statements that describe what someone else said or described.

- The admissibility of exhibits brought by the witness to court. This best occurs before the trial begins, in the form of hearings to exclude aspects of an expert's testimony as a strategy to limit its admission during trial.
- Bad manners and aggressive nature of opposing counsel. This is a rare occurrence, but is a basis for penalties and sanctions for the misbehaving attorney.
- Anything else that the lawyer considers unfair or prejudicial to his client's rights, including the judge's actions and attitudes while in court.

Expert testimony may be grounds for an objection when:

1. The expert is speaking on a subject that is arguably outside her relevant area of expertise, or misstates or lies about her qualifications.
2. The expert does not respond to the subject matter of a question, and answers on another subject that is irrelevant or repetitive.
3. The expert did not comply with required discovery orders (i.e., exchange of expert and report information and data).
4. The expert's qualifications do not extend to the subject matter at issue. This may happen after the expert has been qualified for a particular field, but testifies at trial to opinions that could be argued as "novel" or scientifically unsubstantiated. Some experts like to "innovate" conclusions in cases where there is no scientific literature or protocols of practice. Many judges do give forensic experts free rein, and give discretion to experts with years of testifying experience, regardless of the judicial rules that should preclude extremely prejudicial experience-based testimony.

7.2.8 Quick review of redirect examination

As described earlier, redirect occurs *after* the witness has gone through cross-examination. It is covered here because the rules focus on what can be discussed by the expert's attorney on redirect.

The primary rule is that the redirect subject matter has to be on subjects raised during cross. The purpose or "scope" of redirect is to have the expert revisit criticisms and subjects presented on cross that undermine or confuse the opinion of the expert. Another term commonly used is to "rehabilitate" the witness when the cross has raised doubts to the expert's honesty, credibility, choice of methods, and other aspects of character and performance.

In that vein, the expert should understand from the outset that redirect will not revisit all of what was presented on direct. In fact, the outline used on direct won't help much, as the opposing attorney will have chosen the subjects with which to attack the expert during cross. Redirect can be a soothing part of the process for the expert after the stresses of cross. The expert may have been frequently interrupted during her attempts to answer questions, and can use redirect to reconstruct complete answers.

7.3 **Conclusion**

The courtroom experience can be a daunting and uncertain experience for everyone. The forensic expert has tremendous responsibility to render fair and demonstrative reasons for her findings, analysis and opinions. The courts demand this and have allowed experts to shape judicial outcomes because of these expectations. Significant care must be taken throughout a forensic examiner's career to ensure strict adherence to high standards and scientific proofs that match the abilities of the forensic discipline being presented.

References

Fingerprints Can Lie, Frontline: Forensic Tools: What's Reliable and What's Not-So-Scientific, Frontline: PBS; April 17, 2012.

Ballistic Imaging "Committee to Assess the Feasibility, Accuracy, and Technical Capability of a National Ballistics Database" 2008, National Academies Press.

Solomon, J., 2007. "FBI's Forensic Test Full of Holes: Lee Wayne Hunt is one of hundreds of defendants whose convictions are in question now that FBI forensic evidence has been discredited". Washington Post. http://www.washingtonpost.com/wp-dyn/content/article/2007/11/17/AR2007111701681.html

Strengthening Forensic Science in the United States: A Path Forward; The National Academy Press, 2009.

THE INNOCENCE BLOG

Bennie Starks

Contributing Causes of Conviction for Rape and Aggravated Assault: eyewitness misidentification, unvalidated for improper forensic evidence.

Bennie Starks, one of the Innocence Project's longest active clients, was fully exonerated and cleared of all charges on January 7, 2013 after a 25-year battle to clear his name of a rape and battery he didn't commit. Starks, who was convicted based in part on eyewitness misidentification and erroneous bite mark analysis, spent 20 years' in prison and six years after his release facing the threat of a retrial.

The Crime

One the evening of January 18, 1986, a 69-year-old Hispanic woman went for a walk when she was accosted by an assailant. She was grabbed from behind, beaten and dragged into a nearby ravine where she was bitten and raped. Initially, the victim denied the rape, but later told a nurse that it had occurred and a rape kit was taken.

The Investigation and Identification

The victim described her assailant as an 18-year-old, clean-shaven black male. Although initially only slippers were found in the ravine, a subsequent search of the crime scene the next day discovered a black coat, watch, scarf and gloves. Linking Starks to the crime was a dry cleaning slip that was found inside the coat. Yet Starks did not match the description. He was 26 years old and had facial hair. Furthermore, Starks stated that he had been at two bars that evening, and witnesses confirmed his presence with the exception of one 20 minute period. Starks said he had been mugged on the way home at around 11 p.m., and that his coat, watch, and gloves were stolen, which would explain their presence at the ravine.

The Trial

During the trial, a serologist testified that Starks could not be excluded as the source of semen found on the vaginal swab and the victim's underwear, disclosing that approximately 14% of the population shared his blood type. Additionally, she testified that the hairs recovered from the scarf found in the ravine could have come from Starks (although the victim did not claim that her attacker was wearing a scarf, and Starks did not claim to have lost one).

A forensic odontologist testified in court after comparing the bite marks found on the victim's shoulder with Starks' teeth. The expert concluded with a reasonable degree of dental and odontological certainty, that it was undoubtedly Starks who had bitten the victim. A second forensic odontologist, who worked with the first, testified to the same findings. Bite mark analysis has never been scientifically validated and has proven to be unreliable.

Finally, the victim identified Starks at trial as her attacker.

On September 25, 1986, a jury unanimously found Starks guilty of two counts of aggravated criminal sexual assault, one count of attempted aggravated criminal assault, one count of aggravated battery and one count of unlawful restraint. Starks was sentenced to 100 years in prison. Starks appealed his conviction, but was denied.

The Post-Conviction Appeals and Exoneration

In 1996, after Starks' appeal was denied,, he contacted the Innocence Project, which requested DNA testing. In 2000, FSA (Forensic Science Associates) issued a report stating that STR-DNA testing on the victim's underwear excluded Starks, implicating another male. Insisting that the exclusion was not probative, prosecutors maintained that Starks had been the victim's attacker and opposed entering the new DNA profile into a DNA database.

It was also discovered that the serologist's testimony at trial had been false, and that Starks should have been excluded based on his blood type alone. Starks requested a new trial, but he was denied.

(Continued)

In 2004, after finding a vaginal swab from the rape kit that was believed to no longer exist, the Innocence Project secured additional DNA testing of the vaginal swab from the victim's rape kit and discovered that the DNA came from the same person previously implicated. Starks was again excluded. In 2006, the Illinois Appellate Court for the Second District overturned Stark's conviction, and he was released on bond. Nevertheless, Lake County prosecutors refused to drop the charges, inventing increasingly outlandish theories to explain the DNA exclusion and continued to threaten to retry the case.

Finally, in May 2012, the rape charges were dropped, but not the battery charge. Though the victim had said that only one man attacked her, prosecutors now theorized that Starks beat her, even if he had not raped her, arguing that the semen could have come from an act of consensual sex even though the victim denied having sex in the two weeks prior to her attack. On January 7, 2013, the newly elected State's Attorney Mike Nerheim agreed to dismiss the remaining battery charge, and Starks was exonerated at the age 53.

Schiff Harden LLP and Lake County attorneys Lauren Kaeseberg, John Curnyn and Jed Stone provided critical legal assistance.

Cross-examination: The Expert's Challenge and the Lawyers' Strategies

8

C. Michael Bowers

Associate Professor of Clinical Dentistry, Ostrow School of Dentistry,
University of Southern California, Los Angeles, CA USA

8.1 Overview

The media presents numerous examples of the courtroom process involving cross-examination of witnesses, both layman and expert. Most of the scenes are overly dramatic and void of a basis in factual law and practice; but they are very entertaining. An expert in the real world needs to know the facts and myths regarding what can and cannot happen during cross-examination. Rules of evidence have little to do with "cross ex," as most questioning from opposing counsel is allowed with few exceptions. There is some case law that touches on some aspects of questioning, but in a courtroom phase where the expert has no control over the subject matter. This is partially why cross-examination seems so scary and stressful for some participants. The fear of the unknown may tend to explain their wariness on the matter. It actually is a result of inadequate study and practice by the expert. It is important for the forensic expert to understand the legal goals lawyers have, how they research and the finite strategies lawyers use to perform their interrogation of the expert trial witness. Experts with broader training will learn to anticipate what will usually happen before even sitting in the witness stand.

8.2 Lawyers plan ahead for cross-examination

The legal community has a culture that idealizes the role of the attorney who performs cross-examination in a "brilliant" or "devastating" manner. It is a legal concept that cross-examination is the "filter" used by the justice system to confirm or deny what real truth exists in legal controversies involving experts and criminal guilt or innocence. This is true up to a point, but is overly optimistic in the area of expert witnessing. Seasoned experts can sound extremely convincing or self-confident on the stand regardless of their flawed methods and conclusions. The extent of erroneous forensic expert testimony (over 50%) in the 310 documented exoneration cases litigated by the Innocence Project[1] is unacceptable, and is a window into cross-examination's fallibility.

---

[1] http://www.innocenceproject.org/Content/DNA_Exonerations_Nationwide.php

Forensic Testimony. http://dx.doi.org/10.1016/B978-0-12-397005-3.00008-6

Lawyers have a saying that applies to some expert witnesses: "If it quacks like a duck, walks like a duck, and smells like a duck, then it must be a duck." This is what lawyers attempt to do during cross, and if the experts start to fall apart on cross-examination, their opinions begin to make them sound like a duck. For better or worse, cross-examination is the phase in which the opposing attorney begins to exert pressure on the expert in an effort to "expose" the lawyer's own theories of the case.

8.3 The baseline goals for attorneys on cross-examination

Create opposition to the adverse expert's opinions.

There are two popular methods used to accomplish this goal.

a. Proposing theories about the case that the expert has to continually reject. At the very least, this allows the jury to hear what the attorney is presenting as alternatives to the adverse expert's opinion.

b. Personal attack or critique of the expert during cross-examination, through half-truths and hypotheticals (telling a story that does not follow the actual case or which removes facts from the story that the case does contain). *Note*: It is rare for the attorney to enter into an argument with the expert on scientific issues. They claim to study hard in scientific subjects during preparation for cases, but in reality this is not often done. When it does occur, the expert needs to be prepared to discuss the scientific technicalities and foundations for what she expressed on direct.

Both of these methods are usually carried along by the attorney trying to undermine the expert's credibility. This is done piecemeal in a step-by-step process that may (in a few cases) reach a crescendo of outcome-changing events. This is done by drawing the expert into a semantic argument that's meant to deplete, or maybe negate, what the expert said during direct examination. Getting an expert to change her mind or actually reconsider her original statements is a lawyer's "grand slam" dream.

Lines of questioning generally start innocuously with a few mundane statements that lead (i.e., by making a statement rather than asking a question) the expert into agreement with what the attorney is stating, but they end with a statement that questions the expert's attitudes, such as:

> Q. Isn't it true, Dr. Jones, that you have had extensive experience in court testifying on hair analysis?
> A. Yes sir, I have testified many times.
> Q. In fact, Dr. Jones, isn't it true that your financial gain from these cases allows you to generate quite a large income?

The expert's counsel will probably object to this question as being argumentative, but even if the judge sustains the objection (which removes it from the record transcript), the jury gets a glimpse of the expert as a person who probably makes more money than they do, and who might be suspect of testifying for only financial gain. This is the first corner of the "box" that counsel wants to create. An experienced expert could respond with:

A. I am paid for providing the services of my forensic expertise at a rate that is comparable with other experts in my field.

It is important to understand that the expert has to provide this answer without sounding defensive or insulted. If she has an emotional response, then the opposing attorney has gained control of the situation and the expert has allowed herself to be distracted, which is not a good place to be during cross-examination. The experienced expert will stay out of arguments about "red herring" questions such as these that are meant to test her patience and professional demeanor. Other themes of implying an expert's disrepute or bias are extensively focused on the expert's past cases, published treatises and articles, case outcomes, changes in the expert's testimony on her "science" over the years, and so on.

Limit and control the adverse expert.

The lawyer wants to control and dominate the expert's thought process and testimonial responses in order to raise doubts, or to confuse the jury about what the adverse expert said on direct.

The attorney may ask questions in a rapid manner, or may vary his verbal tempo and volume according to his intentions. The expert must always remember that the attorney is "performing" to the jury through the questioning. Dramatic effects in court can be a staple of an attorney's style. Most look foolish to juries, as they are a form of braggadocio and ego. It is mandatory that the expert maintain her own pace of response, regardless of what behavior the attorney is using. This is really the only control the expert has over the courtroom atmosphere and tone. The attorney leads the questioning throughout, but the expert can control her responses. It allows her to stand above any histrionics or bad manners from the opposing counsel. It also gives the expert time to think (and breathe) at a normal rate before answering, and can defuse an attorney demanding or enticing the expert into snap statements and reactions to a rather unpleasant discourse. The expert's thought process through rapid-fire demands from questioning should remain poised and calm. The court does allow the expert to pause after the opposing counsel finishes his leading questions. In a sense, it makes the attorney stand all by himself with no one to talk to for a few (or more) moments. It is imperative that the expert process the semantics of the questioning, as it is common for cross-examiners to create two stages in their leading questions. These are called "compound questions" and may be objected to on "form of the question." This means the question may be confusing to either the expert or the jury. If, however, the question is not objected to, the expert must recognize that two answers may be required.

Q. Dr. Brown, is it not true that your opinions on the DNA evidence in this case are based on many assumptions, and are therefore just speculative guesses?
A. That requires two answers. The first is yes, there are scientific assumptions that are necessary for my opinion to be considered reliable. These are the requirements that the science of DNA profiling has been verified as reliable by other

scientists, my results are reproducible or testable by others, and I have consistently followed all the accepted protocols throughout this case. My answer to your second question is that, no, my findings and opinions are not speculative or guesses because they are based on proven scientific principles.

Answering a compound question many times results in the expert giving one answer stating the affirmative (or agreeing with the attorney) and another answer which is negative. This can be very confusing to the jury and is best avoided. It is better for the expert to refuse to answer the disguised two-part question and ask the attorney to restate the two questions separately. This is another example of the expert taking control back from the cross examiner and reasserting her confidence and competence in her actions.

The attorney wants to tell his story through leading questions to the opposing expert.

This may seem impossible to most inexperienced experts, but it forms the core of a cross-examiner's repertoire. It essentially uses the expert as a chalkboard, and the crossing attorney writes his story as he sees fit. Cross takes the opposing case theories, and makes the expert have to disagree with or defend her own actions and opinions that were presented during direct examination. The attorney's questions will be accompanied by his answers (thereby "leading" the witness). The content of the questions will mostly be fact based (according to his theories only), and will show little respect, reverence, or professional demeanor towards the expert. Proficient cross-examiners will create a thread of questioning that will limit the ability of the expert to counter with alternative theories unless her preparation is extensive. The expert may commonly only be asked to agree or disagree. Most courts frown on allowing only "yes" or "no" answers, so the expert needs to supplant as many "no" answers as possible with brief and to the point explanations. This back and forth may allow the expert's countering opinions to be expressed, but usually the result will be incomplete. Because of this "shaped" line of questioning, redirect by the expert's counsel should allow a refocus on the terminative statements that need to be clarified. Still, cross-examination is the opposing attorney's chance to "lead" the witness towards agreeing with undeniable statements that, unless covered at redirect, attempt to weaken her opinions. Such is the adversarial process in the American court system.

Q. Dr. Smith, isn't it possible that the DNA evidence was contaminated during its collection at the crime scene or at any time during its transport to your crime lab for processing?

Note: Dr. Smith had testified that the blood sample containing DNA she had received in the laboratory had been from only one person (not a mixture of two or more individuals), and she had been able to isolate a full profile of 13 DNA markers that were later compared to the defendant's blood. Her final results indicated that the similarities were sufficient to allow her to say that there was a high statistical probability that the crime scene blood was left by the defendant. This places the defendant at the crime scene, having been injured sufficiently to draw blood. The opposing counsel wants to introduce his theory that this "match" occurred because of improper collection or the contamination of the crime scene sample by other unknown persons before it was given to Dr. Smith. He might later ask if it was "possible" that the defendant's blood had been placed in the evidence container by someone after the crime scene was processed and taken to the lab (i.e., attacking the "chain of custody"). In both examples, he is asking if it could have been "possible" for something like this to have happened. Quite often attorneys, and sometimes even experts, use vague statements of probabilities that are not scientifically determinable, and are nothing but a substitute for personal opinion. Later in cases these "probabilities" can be upgraded to stronger certainties in closing arguments. This is scientific and forensic ethical misconduct.

> A. I have tested the crime scene sample contained in the properly labeled protective container that was properly documented, photographed, and processed for collection at the crime scene. I found no proof of contamination or mishandling in this case.

Here the expert declined to give a "yes" or "no" answer, but instead used the cross-examination question to bolster her assurances that all procedures were followed in avoiding tampering with the evidence. Her answer is an excellent substitute for accepting the "possibility" of contamination or evidence tampering that the opposing counsel could use to his advantage.

It is best to answer questions such as these with a direct answer, and with verbal strength and conviction. You may notice the expert also tacitly disagreed with the lawyer's use of "possible" as an answer, without saying "no" to him. She understood what he was implying (i.e., cheating and dishonesty), and directly attacked it by saying there was no evidence to support his theory of evidence tampering or purposeful contamination.

Make the adverse expert seem meaningless to the jury.

The opposing attorney wants to make the forensic expert irrelevant, or at least weaken her effect on the case. The strategy of minimizing what the expert said earlier in court is another core purpose for cross-examination. When the science of the expert is solid, the attack may concentrate on how she stated her conclusions. When the science is weak, the task is considerably easier for the cross-examiner.

This is the cross-examination method of saying "So what?" to the expert. It cannot occur in some cases, but it is commonly used to discount the effect of an expert's prior statements on the cross-examiner's case theories. This is effective if the attorney knows about a forensic discipline's faults and is facing an expert who has overstated or embellished her certainty of evidence identification and association to the defendant.

> Q. Dr. Jones, you said that you collected human hair from the victim's clothing, isn't that right?
> A. Yes.
> Q. You also said that the hairs did not belong to the victim.
> A. Yes.
> Q. Then you said the hairs could not be distinguishable from hairs you collected from the defendant, Mr. Sperber.
> A. Yes.
> Q. Your use of this term "distinguishable" does not mean that the hairs are from the same person?
> A. It does not.

Q. Then, since the hairs could have come from some other person, or many other possible persons, your earlier statement that the hairs looked the same has no identification value in considering the defendant as their source? They could have been left by many people?

A. Well, yes, I don't know how many people could have left those hairs.

Q. Then with that, Dr. Brown, I am correct in saying you can't be certain that the defendant, Mr. Sperber, left them either?

A. Yes.

Q. Then do you agree with me that, since the hairs taken from the victim could have been left by an unknown number of other persons, your conclusion that a "connection" exists between the victim and Mr. Sperber is erroneous? This connection is meaningless since you cannot tell who left the hairs on the victim, or when it occured. Am I correct?

A. Yes.

Q. Thank you, Dr. Brown. No further questions for this witness, your honor.

Show what the adverse expert has said in a "new" perspective for the jury.

Another tactic on cross is to create a new "view" of the forensic expert during her cross; this is meant to show that the expert is inadequate or has misled the jury in her direct examination. It contains the opposition theories on tests not performed or assumptions that lack scientific substantiation. This is a double-tasking event for the crossing attorney in that it takes him into the role of informing the jury about scientific issues that can be quite complex while attempting to accomplish this via cross with the expert. The jury education in this regard has to be well-planned; the expert on cross will stubbornly disparage certain theories and hypotheticals which contradict her. This generally cannot all be accomplished on cross, which explains why opposing parties tend to retain their own experts to express these theories. Taken in context, the cross-examination may just be a precursor for future presentation, but it sets the stage. It's important that the cross-examination in this area be convincing, to avoid a "red herring" or lack of credibility response by the jury. The leading questions format will form most of the "conversation" with the forensic expert.

Q. Many steps in your field of bite mark analysis involve personal opinion rather than scientific results, correct?

A. Not many.

Q. You described yourself earlier as a forensic scientist. You now admit that some of your methods are opinion based. That sounds inconsistent. Can you explain that to the jury?

A. Explain what to the jury?

Q. In your opinion of this evidence, please separate what is opinion from what is scientific fact?

A. My opinions are based on my experience and training.

Q. I asked you about using assumptions in making your opinion. That means information you used in your opinion was not scientific, by your own admittance. Since you cannot base your opinion on scientific methods, I now ask you, isn't that what the National Academies of Sciences said about bite mark opinions in their 2009 review of flaws in the forensic sciences? That what you are testifying to in this case is not scientific and is unreliable?

A. I do not agree with the National Academies of Science report on bite mark analysis.

Q. Have any scientific organizations, other than the dental one you belong to, namely the American Board of Forensic Odontology, reviewed the rules and the assumptions you adhere to and publically disagreed with the National Academies' opinions about bite mark analysis?

A. None that I know of.

Going beyond leading the adverse expert with the prepared attorney approach.

The mantra for attorneys doing cross-examination is to never ask a question to an adverse expert to which he doesn't know the answer. As mentioned before, this mandates that the attorney asks questions that elicit only a yes or no response. This is accomplished with leading questioning, but that is not the only means available. A strong approach by attorneys is to not let the expert get into lengthy explanations of how and why she did things. This requires very "tight" questioning.

The subject matter of the question must not be broad, which allows the expert to take control of the narration.

Q. Dr. Jones, you took many photographs of the skin injuries on the victim, correct?

This is a leading question, but it allows the expert to expound a lengthy discourse on possibly hundreds of photographs taken at an autopsy. The questioning must be narrowed.

Q. Dr. Jones, you based your final analysis on one photograph, did you not?

Q. You described that there were eight human bite marks on the victim, correct?

Q. All those bite marks were individually photographed in dozens of pictures, correct?

Q. You have stated that multiple bite mark patterns can vary in shape and appearance, even if only one person made all the injuries?

Q. You did say that you only chose one of those bite marks to identify the defendant's teeth, did you not?

Q. Those other seven bite marks were described by you as being deficient in detail to render an identification of the defendant, correct?

Q. In other words, certain teeth of the defendant's did not match these other injuries, correct?

Q. You therefore ignored the other seven bite marks in your final analysis, did you not?

Q. Then it isn't it true, Dr. Jones, that your purpose throughout your investigation was to only find bite marks that were consistent with the defendant's teeth?

Q. You stated you ignored areas of the other bite marks because they were inconsistent with the defendant's teeth, did you not?

Q. Isn't it true, Dr. Jones, that once you found certain matching teeth of the defendant, you declined to compare any other teeth of other persons of similar ethnicity, gender, and physical makeup in order to look for similar tooth patterns?

Q. Dr. Jones, your earlier statement that bite marks are like fingerprints isn't true, correct?

Q. Fingerprint experts look at many examples, sometimes thousands of prints, before rendering an opinion, correct?

Arrangement of the leading questions should start with undeniable ones being posed first to the expert.

This has a purpose that the expert should know about. It lets the attorney settle in a bit with easy questions to the expert, and then increase the pressure with more difficult questioning at the end. It is a small dramatic tactic regarding attorney control, in that the jury hears the adverse expert agreeing with the opposing counsel. It makes the attorney sound reasonable and collegial. The attorney is actually laying the groundwork or foundation for the harder questions to come.

Q. Dr. Jones, bite mark opinions like yours have been accepted in court for many years, correct?

Q. In fact, DNA profiling wasn't being practiced until years later, correct?

Q. Isn't it true that both bite mark identification and DNA profiling can identify a single suspect?

Q. That would make your bite mark opinion just as powerful as DNA, correct?

Q. I find this part of your report, Jones, dated 1-1-11, which has already been admitted into evidence by your attorney, puzzling, then. Please read this short paragraph to the jury starting with this sentence.

'This report is considered preliminary and subject to the possibility of additional DNA evidence being brought forward and analyzed in this case.'

Q. You state in this report that you would change your final opinion on the case if DNA evidence became available which did not agree with your present opinion, correct?

Q. You are admitting in that report that bite mark analysis is not as reliable as DNA profiling, correct?

Q. In fact, Dr. Jones, your bite mark opinion could be contradicted if DNA was available in this case, correct?

In the preceding examples, the crossing attorney is bringing his attack on two levels. One is the content of the expert's report. The other is the expert's statement of confidence made in her direct examination. Both go to credibility of the expert witness, her opinions, and her methods. The "opt out for DNA clause" in her report coupled with later assurances of reliability on direct are obviously incompatible. Not asking the witness to explain or repeat her direct for a second time has been substituted for a pattern of Q&A which limits or negates her explaining.

Cross-examination of credentials can limit the ability of the expert.

Once the forensic expert has passed a *voir dire* examination before trial, there are aspects of credentialing that can continue to be examined during cross-examination. The *voir dire* standard of review establishes a legal acceptance for expert admissibility, but the "weight" (its application and the expert's opinions on issues presented to the jury) can still be contested in front of the jury or judge during the trial.

A strategy exists for when forensic issues cross into multiple areas that are related. The expert may be qualified and credible in one, but less so in another. This can be developed during cross by the attorney amplifying the argument that the lesser subject matter requires additional training and forensic certification, and therefore the expert is incompetent to testify. This may be nothing more than a weak attack, but the expert has to be cognizant of the strategy.

The attorney will often raise non-existent theories on the requirement of additional expertise, and the expert needs to calmly refute such suppositions. The attorney may sound sincerely concerned, but the jury or judge need to be educated on what common standards exist regarding the expert's abilities.

> *Q. Dr. Jones, you are certified as a crime scene analyst, are you not?*
>
> *Q. A crime scene analyst collects evidence from crime scenes, correct?*
>
> *Q. In fact, Dr. Jones, your area of training has nothing to do with digital photographic analysis in the laboratory which you are testifying about, is that so?*
>
> *A. My use of digital evidence analysis follows the training I have received while being employed by the state crime lab.*
>
> *Q. You are not certified in digital analysis, are you, Dr. Jones?*
>
> *A. There are no requirements regarding that in the forensic community. The use of digital methods to analyze crime scene photographs is a common skill many analysts use without a specific certification being necessary. The important aspect of any digital examination of photos is to avoid manipulating the image to the point that it is distorted by the introduction of extreme color changes in the process. This is what occurred to the photographic evidence in this case by your expert, Dr. Hardy.*

This response indicates to the audience that the "demand" for a special certification in the use of computer imaging software and photographs does not exist. It is a red herring offered by the attorney to discredit the expert witness. She adds her core objection to the opposing expert's digital distortion of the photos that were earlier admitted into evidence by the opposition.

Another legitimate focus of cross-examination is to openly criticize the opposing expert for having a less than impressive resume. This is par for the course regarding which expert is more credible and experienced. What this amounts to is the opportunity for the crossing attorney to brag about his expert, and to denigrate the opposition's expert as being less than capable, incomplete, and subject to suspicion regarding her findings. This may sound rancorous and distasteful, but the expert undergoing cross must be confident and prepared to clearly state why she is more than credible.

8.4 **The forensic expert's strategy on cross-examination**

The role of the expert during cross-examination is not to let the opposing attorney prevent her from reinforcing her methods, their applicability, and her opinions of her case. This must be done with a consistent air of professionalism and openness by the expert regardless of the tone the attorney chooses to use during cross. A good-natured reply to erroneously conceived theories, open hostility, and skepticism is the best bet for the expert to appear cooperative. Cooperation does not extend to having to agree to or even consider all of the opposition's attempts to discredit her. The expert should avoid trading verbal barbs or innuendos of wrongdoing or incompetency. Unfair questioning, if directed personally at the expert, should be handled with a serious reply to the contrary and with formality, regardless of the disrespect shown by the lawyer.

Educating the audience is the most important theme.

In the face of arrows and slings, the expert's activities and concepts must focus on teaching the audience rather than reacting to the attorney. Losing the jury's or judge's respect by being combative (even if justified in other social venues) has to be avoided at all costs. The expert must remember that the opposing attorney will never flinch from his decided task to undermine the expert by any means available. Do not expect the doubting cross-examiner to give up and go away with a whimper after an expert delivers a particularly brilliant reply to his query.

Reinforce your integrity without bragging.

The expert with a calm demeanor also has an opportunity to hear the questions as they come from the examiner. The astute listener will be able to more easily differentiate reasonable questions, and prepare an honest answer with much less distraction. Competing with the questioner is not rewarding. Fear sometimes drives angry responses, and the expert must develop a consistent behavior that allows for both agreements and disagreements with the examiner. Disagreements are to be expected, and the expert should tailor answers that go back to what she said earlier on direct whenever possible. That is why an excellent direct examination pays dividends when the cross-examination starts.

Be nice to the cross-examiner who asks "open" questions.

It's best for the forensic expert not to be a total cynic regarding cross-examination. There are many times when the questioning is actually meant to help clarify certain terms and statements. The expert may have launched into technical language during direct about a report that needs to be restated for the layperson. Remember who the audience is. An invitation to answer and explain details may occur during cross. Take it as an opportunity to educate the listeners and make it simple to understand.

In other cases, the attorney may just be curious. This breaks a cardinal rule of cross-examination, but use it as a chance to explain why you did nor did not accomplish or consider some aspect of evidence or testing. Just say you understand the question and would be pleased to explain. It can be a win-win situation. Do not miss it.

Good listening by the expert will discover ambiguous portions of the questioning.

Once again, the expert has to be very aware of questions that use vague phrasing or words that may not be clear and are therefore easily misinterpreted. If there is a subjective word or phrase injected into a question on cross, the witness has the privilege to ask for a definition or clarification.

> *Q. Dr. Jones, isn't it true that the injuries on the victim's body were of many color variations?*
> *A. Well, no. They all were predominately red.*
> *Q. Well, doesn't that mean they were all inflicted at the same time?*
> *A. Redness is a common biological response to skin injury, and it is called inflammation. What do you mean by "the same time?"*
> *Q. They were all inflicted one after the other, correct?*
> *A. That is impossible to positively determine. The redness of the injuries was varied from light pink to dark red. Time determination from color differences is not scientifically determinable. It is possible that they were developed over a short period of time, but not all at once, as you suggest.*

Ambiguity of language also extends to the lawyer using terms and phrases that are not in the technical language of the expert's field. He may introduce terms that are meaningless or specifically not followed by the expert. The expert is fully able to state that she is not familiar with the word or phrase, and to ask for a substitute or clarification for reasons of technical clarity and practice.

Directly answer on point to any questioning that is argumentative and ignore implied criticism from the examiner. Get to the real point of the question instead of engaging in defensive arguing.

> *Q. Dr. Jones, you didn't perform all the testing that could have possibly been accomplished, did you?*
> *A. Let me explain my decision making on this point. Testing of biological specimens presents a challenge regarding what testing should be done or not done. Many times, blood samples which are quite small, and less powerful are not done.*

The crossing attorney may interject his conclusions as a question to the expert. Better attorneys weave their cross-examination topics with facts from the case that are irrefutable. This elicits agreement from the adverse expert at the outset. If, due to some personal decision on her part, the expert tries to stonewall and not agree to the common facts of the case, the attorney wins. In the case of our forensic expert on the stand, the questioning is factual until the attorney makes a conclusive statement hidden as a question.

> *Q. Your involvement in this case began when you physically received the blood evidence from you supervisor, correct?*
> *A. Yes. Dr. Bonar is my supervisor in the DNA section.*

Q. Dr. Bonar explained to you the details of this case, did he not?
A. No, both Dr. Bonar and myself followed proper protocol, and did not discuss any circumstances of the case from the moment I received the blood sample until I completed processing and interpreting the final results.

The expert used this opportunity to educate the audience and reinforce her statements about the proper handling of the evidence. The attorney had to listen to her explain how well she adhered to proper protocols.

The expert witness may be confronted with voluminous records during cross-examination.

Trials are replete with documents which have been admitted into evidence prior to the expert taking the stand. On cross, the expert will likely be asked if she has read or "reviewed" various reports, other expert opinions, test results, and other testimony. This can become somewhat confusing and time consuming, but the expert needs to accept the fact that this will occur, and use it as a chance to look professional and detail orientated at the same time. Juries like an expert who is methodical and follows reasonable questions while on the stand (or at least, questioning that on its face seems fair to the judge or jury). She must look cooperative and friendly. The downside is that the expert will have to admit or deny reviewing certain documents. This is not of itself incorrect, as some documentation will fall outside the area of the expert's field of review. The expert has two rules in this regard.

a. Tell the truth about whether documents were reviewed or not. Expect to be questioned on why certain documents were not reviewed. The expert's preparation with her attorney should cover this subject, to ensure a recent knowledge of the details.

b. Do not rely on memory alone to answer questions about documents. The expert should sit on the stand and review each document before agreeing that she has previously reviewed them, regardless of their length. Any document said to have been reviewed can be used for cross-examination regarding inconsistencies purported to exist with what the expert has previously written or said in court.

Review the expert's strategy on "say yes or no" and other "trick questioning" used on cross-examination.

Anticipate attempts by the attorney to muzzle the expert by limiting answers and explanations. There is no rule saying the expert has to answer yes or no to *any* question. It is merely the crossing attorney's choice to assert himself and censure the expert's honest narrative about facts and opinions. The expert needs to affirmatively protect herself from this tactic.

Q. You do not perform medical autopsies, do you, Dr. Smart?
A. I perform certain aspects of medico-legal investigation during autopsy when I am requested to attend by Dr. O'Halloran, the medical examiner. I perform one aspect of medical autopsies: the dental autopsy.
Q. Please answer the question "yes" or "no." You do not perform medical autopsies, do you?

A. I cannot possibly answer "yes" or "no," due to the content of your question. It would mislead the jury.

The expert is not arguing with the lawyer at this point, and she should avoid sounding testy. She has given a responsive answer to the misleading question of what her responsibilities are ("dental autopsies"), and has side stepped the attempt to diminish her competency about what she does. This exemplifies a response to questions that cannot be answered in the manner demanded by the crossing attorney. The crossing attorney can go onto another subject, rephrase the question, or ask the judge to admonish (i.e., scold) the witness to answer the question. The judge would have no reason to object to this pleasant witness answering the question in the manner described above.

Throughout her entire testimony, the expert should practice answering with full statements, rather than using one or two words. The sentence is normal for human conversation, and the audience will see that the expert usually connects yes or no answers with explanations. When the cross-examiner attempts to grind the expert into monosyllabic answers, the expert should resist by continuing her pattern of education and normal speech, regardless of the aggressiveness of the attorney before her. Certain judges will not allow continued bullying of the expert, and the jury will soon tire of continued interruptions of a well-spoken and friendly expert. Cross usually starts with reasonable questioning, with the expert making reasonable concessions by her agreement with explanations to the opposing counsel. The lawyer will never limit the expert only to "yes or no" answers in this context. A later change to "yes or no" demands can make the attorney appear to have a multiple personality problem.

The dreaded "predicate" question positions the expert to give a lose-lose answer. This means that whether the expert agrees or disagrees, she accepts the question's underlying implication. Hence, the predicate-based question assumes something as fact that weakens the expert's testimony. The expert's rule is to not accept the assumption implied or stated in the question. This requires the expert to recognize the assumption (i.e., predicate).

Q. Dr. Jones, during a crime scene investigation, isn't it true that police personnel are a major source of contamination of evidence?
A. I do not agree that law enforcement investigators are a major source of contamination at a crime scene.

When the expert is constantly interrupted after trying to explain after saying "yes," she must change her sentence structure to place the explanation first.

Q. Your report states that you recognized eight bite marks on the victim during your dental autopsy.
A. Yes.
Q. Your earlier testimony stated that you found seven bite marks on the victim.
A. Yes, but…
Q. No more questions. You may step down.

Here's a better answer to fully explain this discrepancy:

> *Q. I testified that my final opinion is that the victim had seven bite marks on her body. My complete photographic review of the autopsy resulted in my eliminating one injury as a bite mark. So my answer is yes.*

The expert retains significant power when she understands that questioning by the attorney does not force the expert to accept his premises. The expert needs to closely follow the content of each question. There will be a series of questions based on facts that the expert has testified to or reported. All the expert's answers will be yes. Then the attorney will insert a question implying the expert missed an issue or piece of analytical testing that was important. The expert needs to respond:

> *Q. You did not consider the effects of the defendant's medical history when you considered the results of your serum blood analysis, did you?*
> *A. I need to explain the details of what the blood analysis looks for.*
> *Q. Please answer the question. You did not consider the medical history of the defendant in your analysis, is that correct?*

Here the expert has realized the attorney is interjecting his assumption or theory that the medical condition of the defendant is a serious factor that can influence the blood alcohol analysis. This inference is erroneous and misleading for the jury. The expert rule is to say:

> *A. I do not agree with you. You are incorrect.*

This statement will impact the attorney in two ways. He has to make a choice. The first choice is to attack the expert for being nonresponsive to the question. This really means she is not answering the way he desires, which is not objectionable. The second choice has the attorney responding:

> *Q. Well, then why do you not agree with me?*

Notice that the second option has the attorney requesting information with no knowledge of the answer. He may be forced to do this, as ignoring the expert's refusal will make him appear bested by the expert. He also has the option to use his closing statement as a vehicle to repeat whatever his own expert said about the issue of health effects on blood alcohol testing.

Be aware of short-stop hypothetical questions asked in less than a minute.

Cross-examination questioning that presents a hypothetical or "theoretical" query should be particularly obvious to most expert witnesses. The attorney must poise it by starting with some of the facts of the case, with later additions of facts that are not present in the investigation or the previous record of the expert's testimony. The expert actually has to answer two groups of questions at the same time. A recommended expert reply is to state his inability to answer to the group of added "facts" (which are actually assumptions) before attempting to considering the other aspects of the question that *are* present in the case. The attorney uses this bifurcation of facts and theory to lend credence to the added details that support his side of the argument or case theory.

The witness must first pause before attempting to answer. This gives her attorney time to object to the question as being inadmissible:

Attorney: I object to this line of questioning, your honor. The attorney is forcing the witness to assume facts not in evidence, and is asking this witness to speculate without a premise of fact.

The judge may overrule the objection on promise by the opposing attorney that the added evidence will come into court at a later stage. It is a means to streamline the testimony, allowing the expert to determine an opinion while being under oath. Possibly contradictory, but also effective, is the attorney arguing that the facts have already been admitted into evidence. Either way, the expert, if the objection is overruled, can express an answer which relies on the facts, and state that the additional "facts" cannot be considered since she would have to speculate and has not had a chance to evaluate a definitive answer on these new assumptions, or state that the new assumptions are vague. If this is objected to as being "nonresponsive" by the examining attorney, the witness is allowed to state a "maybe" or "maybe not" answer instead, or to ask that the question to be rephrased because she may be misinterpreting what was asked. This will allow more time for her to clarify an answer.

An expert should not try to interpret what the cross-examiner is trying to investigate or is leading toward in his questioning.

The progression of questions available during cross-examination may appear obvious regarding issues of expert credibility or other issues. The expert needs to avoid incomplete or less than total responsive answers in hope of avoiding or obstructing the line of questioning that is developing. First of all, it is distracting for the expert, and taking a proactive resistance to the question makes the expert appear biased. Answer questioning with an even tone, and attempt to not react to personal attacks.

Be aware of misdirecting questions.

The accomplished cross-examiner will continue to present his opinions and characterizations during questioning in varied ways. A popular one is to misdirect the question using exaggerations and half-truths which sound reasonable to the jury, but may tempt the expert to deny something that is actually true.

Q. Dr. Jones, what part of your report did your attorney edit before you submitted it to the court?

On this point, the witness needs to be truthful, but has to add clarifications to show that the attorney *did not* write the report for her. The crossing attorney is obviously implying that the attorney told the expert what to do and to report.

A. I wrote the entire report by myself. The attorney received a draft report which he reviewed for clarity and simplicity, considering some technical aspects might be difficult for laypersons to understand. In all aspects of the report and my analysis, I was not influenced or controlled by the attorney in any respect.

When the question is "loaded" with innuendos of mistakes and incomplete or biased results, the expert has to closely follow a truthful approach while ignoring the implied reasoning.

> *Q. Dr. Jones, you had some difficulty in analyzing the DNA evidence due to the fact that the sample was actually a mixture of two individuals, did you not?*
> *A. Any sample of DNA that contains mixtures increases demands on the analyst to follow the prescribed steps that are mandated for this type of mixed sample. I followed the rules through the analysis and interpretation phases in this case.*

Rather than denying what is true, this answer admits that some testing is more difficult because of certain circumstances, but the expert states that she was aware of the proper handling of such situations, and used mandated procedures that allowed her to reach reliable results. With a complete statement such as this, the expert fully explains herself and avoids a major pitfall.

> *Cross-examiners love to "idealize" what is expected in cases that "are the same" as the expert witness's current case.*

This gambit assumes the attorney's theory that a "complete analysis" follows a certain pattern or set of procedures. This may not always be the case. The expert must not agree to overgeneralizations that use the terms "always" and "must." If she does, she will find herself attacked for the attorney's artificial standards of care not being present in her own work.

Another possible answer to a generalized "always" question is to succinctly answer in the negative.

> *A. Considering what you are asking me regarding difficulties of mixtures, I must answer "no," as I did not experience any difficulties.*

Know the "best practice" argument on cross-examination.

This is similar to the previous overgeneralization ploy just discussed, but it also plays to the jury as an example of some analytical misstep that the examiner performed during her testing.

> *Q. Wouldn't it be more accurate to analyze your testing over a period of days, rather than just after you created your experimental bite marks on the skin of your human cadavers?*
> *A. Our experimental design was to study the shape of the experimental bite marks immediately after the bite marks were created by the biting mechanism, due our goal to observe the injuries at that baseline point. Our reasonable assumption was that if the injury patterns did not reliably replicate the biting dentition at this first stage, then the likelihood of them matching over time would be very low. Future study of the chronological changes in the patterns is certainly possible if future testing using our methods is performed. Personally, it is my opinion that it will result in proof of increasing dissimilarity as the bite mark ages.*

Be aware of the half-right and half-wrong question on cross-examination.

> *Q. You had to assume that using cadaver skin was a reliable substitute for live human skin because it is impossible to perform live human experiments in an ethical manner, correct?*

This question has three parts that must each be addressed separately, due to the mixture of correct and incorrect assumptions.

> *A1. Human cadaver skin is used for many aspects of medical research. It is an acceptable model of live human skin in most aspects. Since the few bite mark comparison studies over the decades have used wax as a substitute for human skin, it was clear that a more relevant material was needed.*
> *A2. We chose cadaver skin. Our reason was to eliminate variables in live human skin injuries that complicate observation of the bite patterns. These variables include bleeding and any bruising reaction from a live subject.*
> *A3. It is not impossible to perform experimental biting on live individuals. It is just more costly.*

8.5 Court opinions regarding scope of cross-examination

Courts allow the expert witness large latitude during civil or criminal trials in delivering information and opinion to the jury. Accompanying that powerful role, the expert is expected to be cross-examined to the full extent, the same as any other type of witness, and in addition, to be questioned on all aspects of her qualifications and the basis of the forensic science opinions she reveals to the court. Specific aspects of this questioning are expanded and modified through interpretation of individual appellate court decisions accumulated over time. The following items explain this evolving nature of expert cross-examination.

> *The expert can be questioned on the aspects of the case evidence that was unexamined or were rejected as a basis of her final opinion.*

This presses the expert to explain areas or details that were not tested or found to be insignificant for analysis. It can be presented on cross to raise suspicion that the forensic investigator was biased or intentionally narrow-minded in determining only evidence that could be used to support her final opinions. It is better form for the expert's counsel to raise the subject during direct examination to render proper explanations of the expert's rationale of evidence processing and selection of testing methods.

> *The duration of cross-examination, absent a judge's ruling, can be lengthy and repetitive.*

The cross-examining attorney has to set a foundation for an agonizingly long examination of an adverse expert, but it is given much credence when it is done to clearly bring out all the details even remotely connected to a case at trial.

Inquiry into the expert's professional papers, textbooks, and prior court testimony is allowed regarding any aspect that is considered relevant to the issue of previous written or testimonial inconsistencies of the adverse expert.

Specific excerpts of these "treatises" or "prior statements" are allowed into evidence by the court, rather than the entire contents of the documents. Treatises of a technical, professional, or scientific content, other than those created by the expert, are not generally admissible unless the expert says any of the following while on the stand. In other words, the expert does not have to admit to reading the book in order to be cross-examined about certain sections of it.

a. The witness referred to, considered, or relied on the publication.
b. The court has admitted the publication into evidence.
c. The publication has been established as a reliable authority by the witness, by other expert testimony, or by judicial notice.

If the crossing attorney has a treatise or publication that contradicts statements made by the adverse expert on the stand, the attorney essentially has an additional expert witness. The rub for the attorney is getting the publication admitted into trial. Usual questions intending to establish a "foundation" for admitting the publication as a reliable source, even if the adverse expert has not read it, include ones similar to the following:

Q1. Dr. Jones, have you heard of the author?
Q2. Dr. Jones, have you heard of the book Forensic Testimony*?*
Q3. Dr. Jones, do you consider it to be a reliable authority in the field?
Q4. Dr. Jones, do you agree with this statement?

The attorney will quote excerpts from the publication that impact her opinion. If this raises an objection, the crossing attorney can make an "offer of proof" that his expert will attest to the publication being an authority. This is a promise to later provide the information in a form offered by another expert. This can be objected to and, if sustained, the crossing attorney can reply by asking the judge to permit the expert undergoing cross-examination to be on call, in the event that the opposing expert declares the publication a reliable authority.

Legal thinking or strategy (called "work product") of the expert's attorney are protected from disclosure by the attorney-client relationship (a privilege of privacy) unless the expert has testified about it as a source or basis for her opinion.

If the expert admits to using some aspect of what her attorney theorized, then she can be cross-examined on the subject matter. This rule of procedure involves a rather unusual situation for a forensic expert. The nature of the expert as an independent reviewer should make disclosures by her of information derived solely from discussion with her attorney a non-issue for the court.

The details of the expert's opinion and materials can be criticized during cross-examination, but the attorney is disallowed from personally attacking or ridiculing the expert.

Application of this rule is a courtroom behavior variable decided through objection by the expert's counsel. The weakest form of cross presents itself when the adverse expert is scoffed at, accused of using medication during prior report writing, and otherwise presented with exclamations of incredulity and sarcasm by the opposing attorney. Objection by counsel does little to remove the theme presented by the errant attorney, so the expert has to maintain a placid and professional demeanor, while the attorney generally looks like an idiot.

Credibility is a multi-factored character trait, but the courtroom process concentrates on it or alludes to it constantly.

The expert must adhere to opinions and statements about key forensic issues and methods that show consistency in her current and previous reports, writings, and testimony. After the expert expresses an opinion, the fact she has given a contrary opinion in another case is a proper subject for impeachment on cross-examination. Radical modifications of opinion because of changes in scientific methods and research certainly are allowed, and the court expects to be properly informed of these events. Detailed explanations of such should be a major subject of direct examination, and not be left to be first heard by the jury on cross-examination.

Professional motives and biases of the adverse expert are additional grist for the attorney during cross-examination. The attorney's assertion of either should be met with calm explanations and denials of such misconduct.

The expert may have problems if her history of changing opinions appears to be dependent on who her audience is and who is paying her bill for testifying. Current controversy in the press and courts about forensic misconduct, mistakes, and failings has a few experts playing dual roles. Their courtroom attitudes can be assertive, strongly denying systemic problems in their field, and rationalizing away personal experiences of making errors in previous cases. Their "alter" role can occur in forums outside the courts, where the expert will banter to the audience with her forthright and self-righteous history of making sure the "bad apples" in the forensic community will be dealt with (this declaration is popular, in that it ignores the lack of scrutiny of the field's baseline assumptions and procedures). Courts do not appreciate being told half-truths by experts who "pose" to look like something they are not.

Cross-examination is allowed to challenge the breadth and correctness of the expert's knowledge of her field, documents reviewed and not reviewed, tests done and not done, methods of court preparation, and exhibit content and courtroom presentation.

This is where many crossing attorneys fall apart if they have not done their homework. The adverse expert's adherence to forensic performance standards underlies the reason for such in-depth preparation for the counsel for both sides. Difficulties exist in certain police sciences where standards of examination methods are unscientifically broad, inconsistent, or vague. Areas of personal decision making (i.e., subjective rather than quantitative analysis) in evidence outcomes can create a tone of underlying arbitrary opinion that the well-prepared attorney will capitalize on during cross-examination. Other personal determinates of an expert's opinion that contradict an opposing expert's analysis make for conundrums and confusion for a jury. This can undermine the credibility of the expert who has formed conclusions standing on little-to-no empirical testing. The likelihood is high that the jury will discount both experts and rely on other circumstances and evidence to reach their decision.

A challenge to the expert's presentation exists where shocking, unnecessary, or repetitive material is presented.

This objection is rather dated, as modern courtrooms seem to exert little or no effort to avoid showing juries all the graphic details of horrendous crimes against persons.

8.6 Conclusion

It should be obvious to the reader that covering all possible lines of questioning an impossible quest. The expert must gain experience, develop good listening skills and practice. The goal is to develop a confident demeanor in court and be able to understand the general principles involving how to communicate her expertise to a lay audience.

INNOCENCE BLOG

Illinois Man Declared Innocent Nearly Five Years After Being Cleared of Murder

Alan Beaman, whose conviction for a 1993 murder was overturned nearly five years ago, was finally declared innocent on Thursday when the McLean County Assistant State's Attorney confirmed that the county was dropping its three-year opposition to the innocence petition, reported the Pantagraph.

For Karen Daniel and Jeff Urdangen with the Bluhm Legal Clinic at Northwestern University School of Law, the innocence petitions ends more than a decade of legal wrangling on Beaman's behalf.

The evidence at Beaman's trial that he drove 140 miles each way from Rockford to Bloomington at high speeds to kill Lockmiller and return home before his mother could detect his absence fell far short of what was needed to convict Beaman, said Daniel.

"He was expected to prove he wasn't and couldn't have been in Normal at the time of the murder. There was simply no evidence," said Daniel, adding that the state's closing remarks at the trial comparing Beaman to Adolf Hitler were "out of control."

Alan Beaman was a college student when he was wrongfully convicted of killing his former girlfriend, Jennifer Lockmiller, and sentenced to 50 years in prison. His direct appeal was denied despite a lack of evidence linking him to the crime, and he sought assistance from the Center on Wrongful Convictions at Northwestern University School of Law. However, he was not eligible for compensation without a certificate of innocence.

Although the circuit and appellate courts continued to uphold the conviction, the Illinois Supreme Court unanimously reversed Beaman's conviction in 2008, finding that the trial prosecutor had violated Beaman's constitutional rights. Eight months later, all charges were dropped and he was released from prison after serving 13 years. In 2012, DNA tests on vaginal swabs taken from the victim revealed two unidentified male profiles and excluded Beaman and three other male suspects.

Beaman was joined in court by his wife, Gretchen and parents, Barry and Carol Beaman. He is employed as a machinist and lives with his wife, stepdaughter and nine-month-old daughter.

Uniqueness and Individualization in Forensic Science

Mark Page

Of the fundamental theories said to underpin forensic identification of individuals from latent marks (including bite marks, tool marks, fingerprints, and any other means of "pattern" identification), one of the most consistently adhered to is that of the uniqueness of the particular feature in question. Long cited as one of the cornerstones of forensic identification, the concept of "uniqueness" has received renewed scrutiny thanks to several authors who have argued that there is no scientific basis for such a claim when considering human physical characteristics (Cole, 2009; Kaye, 2009; Saks & Koehler, 2008; Saks, 2009). This chapter explores the origins of the uniqueness assumption in addition to the evidence for it, in an attempt to establish its role in forming an evidence base for forensic conclusions of identity.

9.1 The uniqueness fallacy

There appears to be widespread assumption among forensic practitioners that any given forensic trait can be considered unique to an individual. A web-based survey of 72 forensic odontologists found that 91% of respondents believed that the human dentition was unique (Pretty, 2003), and 78% of those believed that this uniqueness could be represented on human skin during the biting process.

Forensic dental experts, as well as fingerprint experts, firearms and tool mark examiners, and anthropologists have continually invoked this principle as support for their conclusions of identity. Recently, this assumption of uniqueness has come under fire from several sources, the most prominent being the 2009 National Academy of Sciences report *Strengthening Forensic Science in the United States* (National Research Council, 2009), which concluded that "in most forensic science disciplines, no studies have been conducted of large populations to establish the uniqueness of marks or features." Such criticism had previously been voiced by other academics, who question the so-called "proof" of individuality posited by forensic practitioners, and also ponder the absurdity of claiming such a notion (Cole, 2009; Kaye, 2003, 2009; Saks & Koehler, 2008). Like that of other disciplines, the notion of uniqueness in odontology often relies on tenuous proof such as anecdotal evidence and

Forensic Testimony. http://dx.doi.org/10.1016/B978-0-12-397005-3.00009-8

experience. Furthermore, literature regarding the uniqueness of the dentition that has been cited in the courts since the mid-1970s (*People v. Milone*, 1976; *People v. Smith, 1981*; and, for an Australian example, *R. v. Lewis*, 1987) all suffers major flaws when critically examined, including the application of false logic, faulty reasoning, and erroneous mathematics, which call their conclusions of support for the uniqueness proposition into question. Some of this key literature will be examined later in this chapter in order to highlight the flaws that much of the other forensic science literature on uniqueness also suffers.

9.2 The ideological origins of the uniqueness principle

The concept of "uniqueness" has more of the qualities of a cultural meme than those of scientific fact (Mnookin, 2001). "Meme" was a term first coined by Richard Dawkins in the 1970s (Dawkins, 1976) that has been refined by several others since (Wilkins, 1998); it describes a "unit of cultural transmission," a piece of "thought" transmitted from person to person. In this context, one explanation for the origin of the tenet of "nature's infinite variation" was that it provided support for the existence of God. The reasoning of the 17th century philosopher and polymath Gottfried Leibniz represented that of the time: God is infinite, and God created the Earth; therefore nature, as God's creation, reflects His infinity (Stevenson, 2005; Leibniz & Rescher, 1991). To deny nature's infinite variation was to deny God's infinity, a claim that would have been considered heresy during this time. A similar line of reasoning gave rise to the maxim "nature abhors a vacuum"; God, with his infinite power, would not have created "nothing," therefore it was thought a vacuum simply could not exist, as it would imply the absence of God.[1]

More recently, 20th century philosophers and sociologists have posited that there is a fundamental human desire to see oneself as unique, stemming from a primitive emotional need. Snyder and Fromkin suggested in their 1980 essay that humankind is most emotionally satisfied when we perceive at most only an intermediate level of similarity relative to other people. The level of personal emotional satisfaction supposedly falls dramatically when persons consider themselves too similar to others; thus, humans have a fundamentally strong desire to *want* to believe in uniqueness that is difficult to dislodge, even in the absence of definitive proof.

Moenssens (1999) has stated that the belief in the individuality of forensic traits rests on what he terms the "Snowflake Syndrome." Demonstrating another instance of the pervasiveness of the cultural meme, snowflakes are often singled out as the

---

[1] This was questioned in the 17th century after Torricelli's experiments involving the early mercury barometer, and the existence of a vacuum was definitively proven possible by Blaise Pascal in the late 1640s (Close, 2009). In the face of this irrefutable evidence, a different line of reasoning was then hastily adopted in order to explain God's role in all of this. The reasoning was now that of *course* a vacuum could exist, because to claim that it couldn't was to claim that God's powers would be somehow limited; He can create anything He sees fit, including the creation of "nothing" where "something" previously existed.

"paradigm of uniqueness" (Thornton, 1986), and are often cited by others as the archetypal analogy to the concept of individualisation in the forensic sciences (Inman & Rudin, 1997). In the late 1800s, a young farmer invented a novel way of photographing ice crystals and began documenting snowflakes. Just before his death, he declared that he had never seen any two alike, after taking 5,381 photomicrographs. This gradually morphed into the concept that no two snowflakes could *ever* be alike. Perhaps realizing that the evidence of a mere 5,400 snowflakes is somewhat meagre to stake such a claim on, society has sought other ways in which to justify this belief. Most people appear to believe that no two snowflakes are alike because of the enormously large number of possible ways to arrange the approximately 10^{15} molecules in the average snowflake (Thornton, 1986),[2] which, by contrast, dwarfs the number of snowflakes predicted to have ever existed.[3] To say, as Thornton does, that this number is "virtually" beyond human comprehension is somewhat of an understatement.

Yet the mathematics and logic behind this evaluation are deeply flawed. Just because such arrangements of molecules are mathematically possible does not imply that they are physically possible, and almost certainly some arrangements simply could never exist due to the restrictive nature of intermolecular interaction in solid crystals. A further problem with the mathematical gymnastics employed by this attempt to provide proof of uniqueness is that similar arrangements would undoubtedly be perceived as exactly the same arrangement at the observer level (Kaye, 2003). In fact, atmospheric researchers often claim that it is not impossible for two snowflakes to look the same (albeit highly unlikely), but most still hold to their tenet by explaining that on a molecular level, they would be revealed to be different (Roach, 2007). Uniqueness at a molecular level is hardly a useful foundation for the forensic scientist concerned with fingerprints, teeth, or bullets. Two snowflakes that *were* supposedly visually identical were found in 1988 by a researcher who was documenting snowflakes for the National Center for Atmospheric Research, yet this does not appear to be widely known[4] (Henson & Politovich, 1995; Kruszelnicki, 2006; Schmid, 1988).

Fingerprints have been held as a paradigm of uniqueness since the early 20th century, and have even been used as "proof" of claims of forensic uniqueness such as that of fingernails merely by anatomical association (Stone & Wilmovsky, 1984; Starrs, 1999). The high esteem of fingerprints is reflected in the modern terminology of DNA "fingerprinting." Few realize that this belief in the uniqueness of fingerprints, first suggested in the late 19th century, represents a continuation of a particular notion that fitted the appropriate cultural ideology of the time,[5] and through social and cultural forces it has come to be accepted by future generations; it is not the result of robust scientific evidence (Cole, 2001).

---

[2] The incredible figure of 10^{2250} possible arrangements.

[3] A mere 3.12×10^{31} snowflakes.

[4] Or at least, not widely accepted.

[5] Galton's work on the individuality of fingerprints originally began with an attempt to classify individuals by racial origin, using their fingerprints as a marker. This research was eventually abandoned when Galton could find no discernable link between fingerprints and race.

9.3 The evidence for uniqueness

The evidence cited for uniqueness includes the anecdotal and experiential, biological, and mathematical, yet all of these approaches suffer major disadvantages that result in little faith being able to be afforded to their conclusions. A critical discussion of the so-called "evidence" for uniqueness is necessary in order to ascertain the true standing of this supposedly fundamental tenet of forensic identification.

9.3.1 Anecdotal evidence and experience

Fingerprint examiners, odontologists, handwriting experts, and firearms and tool marks experts have all at some stage argued that uniqueness exists because as yet, in the history of their discipline, no two objects have been found to have an exact duplicate. These claims of "never observing an identical match" may be true, but they rely on the assumption that every examiner remembers the details of every object ever examined, and, even if only subconsciously, has "compared" all of the objects he has happened to examine with one another. Such a proposition is highly dubious, and relies on claims and "observations" that have neither been recorded nor compiled (Cole, 2009). More importantly, attempts to affirm the uniqueness proposition using anecdotes and experience rests on pure inductive reasoning. Several authors have cited induction as being inappropriate for application in forensic science research (Faigman, 2007; Meuwly, 2006), noting that "science" arising from pure inductive reasoning gave us the practices of bloodletting and phrenology. As an approach to scientific methodology, induction largely fell out of favor during the epoch of Sir Francis Bacon in the 16th century.

Pure inductive reasoning leads to the "induction problem," which can be simply stated as "knowledge can never exist from purely inductive reasoning." This is partly because induction necessarily invokes a positivistic approach, where the theory rests on the assumption that the future will resemble the past; yet there is no logical reason to assume this (McLachlan, 1995). The work of Hume demonstrated that there can never be any certainty in induction, even for those inductions that have never been disproved by the occurrence of a contrary (Russell, 2004). Accumulation of positive instances simply cannot lead to a conclusion of certainty.

As an illustration of the failure of inductive reasoning in the use of anecdotal and experiential evidence, consider the well-known tale of the coelacanth, as described in an earlier chapter in this text. This rare species of fish was thought to have been extinct since the end of the Cretaceous period, some 80 million years ago. This thinking prevailed from the year 1836, when Agassiz described and named the coelacanth from the fossil record (Thomson, 1991). For the next 100 years it was presumed to have been extinct, as no one had ever come across a living specimen; however, a live coelacanth was caught off the coast of South Africa in 1938. Several living coelacanths have since been caught off the coasts of East Africa and Indonesia (Erdmann et al., 1998); the reasoning that the species was extinct simply because no one had ever found a live one quickly fell apart.

Judges in the United States are becoming increasingly aware of this somewhat flawed attempt to bolster identification conclusions via the use of "experiential" evidence. Judge Albin, delivering the majority opinion of the appellate court in *State v. Fortin* (2007), noted that the original trial judge was not satisfied with the experts' conclusion that the bite marks, or even the pattern of infliction of multiple bite marks, was unique, based on their experience alone, despite the claim that they had reviewed "thousands" of cases in the course of their professional lives. The trial judge requested production of "a compilation of the sexual assault and homicide cases with human bite marks on victims, or a reasonable sampling of [such cases] from the experience"; in other words, he requested some form of data to support the reasoning. This decision was later upheld by the appellate court.

The experts in *Fortin* follow the general argument seen for "proof" of uniqueness via observational experience, which follows the lines of: "n number of samples have been observed, and none of them are the same. Therefore, one can assume that no sample will ever be the same as any other." McLachlan's, a philosopher, has directly addressed the use of this principle in fingerprint testimony, where he noted that evidence from a mere sample of human beings gives us no reason at all for doubting the existence of an identical set of fingerprints somewhere in the world. Additionally, he noted that there is no mechanism which *prevents* the occurrence of two people sharing the same fingerprint, no "check and balance" to ensure that once one fingerprint pattern has manifested itself in human friction ridge skin it will never appear again (McLachlan, 1995). This reasoning is clearly applicable to any forensic characteristic.

Using an example proposed by Saks and Koehler (2008), it can also be mathematically demonstrated that the use of experience fails to advance the uniqueness argument to any significant degree even in significantly smaller populations than that of the entire world. Suppose that there *were* 100 pairs of individuals who happen to have indistinguishable arrangements of the anterior dentition from each other. Let us say there were 100,000 people in total in a particular town. This means there are $[100,000(99,999) \div 2] = 4.99 \times 10^9$ possible ways of pairing two people's dentitions in order to compare them. Let's say that 10 forensic odontologists each compared 100 dentitions a day for 10 years, so that between them they managed 3.65×10^6 comparisons over 100 years of "collective" experience. The chance that they would miss all 100 matching pairs is approximately 93%.[6]

It is obvious to most people that the lower the incidence of a trait (i.e., the lower the probability of observing that trait—"p"), the less likely it is that it will appear in a sample. Given that sample sizes are finite, this presents a problem when p is small and N is large, as the chance of *not* observing a match within the sample then becomes very large. As the sample size is limited by human endeavor, we quickly reach the realization that proving uniqueness this way is unlikely to be successful. The problem is thus: We want to prove that something is so rare that it could be considered unique, but because

---

[6] See Saks and Koehler, 2008 for a more detailed mathematical description of how this is calculated.

it is so rare, it is more likely than not that an observance would be missed in any reasonable sample size. This can be partially addressed via the use of a probability theorem and the product rule, and its usefulness in this regard will be discussed later in this chapter.

9.3.2 Knowledge about the process of formation

Another reason for claiming that certain physical characteristics are unique stems from knowledge about how these characteristics are formed. In actual fact, such reasoning technically relies on the *lack of knowledge* about how these characteristics are formed. Fingerprint examiners often argue that because friction ridge formation is induced by the stresses and strains experienced by the fetus *in utero*, which are random and infinite, it is likely that they subsequently produce a random, infinite variety of friction ridge patterns (Budowle et al., 2006). Such reasoning begs the question rather than answering it, as it provides no better grounds for assuming that the causal process itself is infinitely variable. Additionally, McLachlan (1995) noted that there is no logical reason why the same effect cannot be caused by different processes. To make such a claim regarding the variety of forces acting upon friction ridge skin *in utero*, it would be imagined that some form of study should be conducted in order to assess the scope of variation in such variables as pressure, fluid dynamics, skin tension, temperature, and so on before concluding that such variables are infinite or even extremely large. Such a study appears yet to be conducted (Cole, 2009).

A similar argument occurs in bite mark analysis. It is well known that the spatial arrangement of the dentition is partly influenced by local environment factors, such as the natural forces exerted by the oral musculature, and other external forces such as oral habits: tongue thrusting, thumb sucking, and so on. There is no logical reason to assume that because these forces remain largely unquantified in terms of their scope and their relative influence on the position of the teeth they are infinite, and that this invariably would mean that the arrangement of the teeth is also infinite. Without studies demonstrating the magnitude and variety of forces acting on the dentition, assuming they are random and infinite is nothing more than conjecture.

9.3.3 Studies

A modern solution to the induction problem was proposed by the early 20th century philosopher of science Karl Popper, who gave renewed credence to the deductive method of reasoning (Popper, 2002). Pure deductivism involves the concept of falsification, which has also been criticized as a method of attaining knowledge (Stove, 1982); but nonetheless, refinement of Popper's work has given rise to the modern theory of attainment of scientific knowledge via the hypothetico-deductive method. This involves the use of a cyclic model incorporating hypothesis formation, testing, and reformulation (Gimbel, 2011), and it is preferable to pure inductivism because it specifically attempts to *disprove* the theory by continually attempting falsification, whereas the inductive method relies only on the tenuous accumulation of positive instances. While the hypothetico-deductive model results in more meaningful proof, the quality of this proof is still open to criticism when these studies make unrealistic assumptions regarding the model used to test the theory, or draw conclusions outside the realm of logical inference.

9.3.3.1 Observational studies

Forensic practitioners have relied on observational studies as evidence for the individuality of the frontal sinuses from data obtained as early as 1935 (Mayer, 1935).[7] Yet as McLachlan stated, evidence from a random sample of human beings does not necessarily give us reason to believe that a particular characteristic is unique. He illustrates this by inviting us to consider a random sample of, say, 400 human beings. We are likely to be able to demonstrate that none of them have the same mother, but we know that to conclude that not one person on the Earth shares the same mother defies common sense.

In studies cited as evidence for the uniqueness of the frontal sinuses, Harris examined 32 individuals (Harris et al., 1987), and Asherson (1965) studied the radiographs of 74 monozygotic and heterozygotic twins. All of these studies concluded that the frontal sinuses were *always* different. This is not disputed for the samples studied, but extrapolation to the world population from such a small sample seems to be a rather large leap of faith. Similarly, a study that concluded "that palatal rugae were unique and identification could be based on their comparison" was based on the ability of four dentists to match only 25 post-orthodontic maxillary casts with their pre-orthodontic counterparts (English et al., 1988). The study by Kieser and colleagues (2007) on the individuality of the dentition considered only 33 maxillary casts and 49 mandibular casts from a total of 50 individuals. Kieser replied to criticism of this small sample size by Bowers (2007) by stating that the study does not attempt to single-handedly "prove" the uniqueness argument, but contributes to the gradual acquisition of evidence "point[ing] towards the uniqueness of the anterior dentition" (Kieser and Bernal, 2007). This is a fair reply; however, one needs to consider the size of the sample in relation to the tens of thousands of 17–20 year olds that have post-orthodontic occlusions as a result of treatment in New Zealand alone[8] before deciding how much weight this adds to the uniqueness argument.

Rational thinking suggests that the larger the sample size n, the more faith one can have in such a conclusion. Just when n is large enough to allow extrapolation to a population N is a matter of debate, however, mathematicians and statisticians

---

[7] Mayer additionally suggests that Dr Poole's "... special study of the sinus prints of the insane [...] will also throw additional light on th[e] important problem [of insanity]"; presumably in addition to providing a means for identification.

[8] See Marriot et al., 2001. Their survey conducted in 1999 indicated that the average load of an orthodontist in New Zealand was 371 patients, based on a survey sample of 56 out of a total of 71 practicing orthodontists at that time. 77.9% of these were considered children (not defined, but let us conservatively assume that this means under 18). This means that approximately 20,500 patients under the age of 18 were receiving orthodontic treatment. Of course, not all of these would have full fixed appliances, but when considering the large number of dentists who perform similar services in New Zealand, it is easy to arrive at numbers in the tens of thousands when considering the number of 17–20 year olds who would have experienced similar orthodontic treatment in New Zealand alone.

have developed generally accepted tools to assist with this decision. The calculation of sample size is based on a statistical equation that will depend on how certain one wants to be that the induction would hold true. This level of "certainty" is often referred to as the confidence level, and it is a well-known concept in scientific studies. Most studies consider a confidence level of anything less than 0.95 unsatisfactory, although sometimes a confidence level of 0.9 is used. Studies that have used this calculation to determine sample size allowing for a confidence level of 0.95 arrive at a sample size of approximately n=385 in order to feel confident above N = 100,000.[9] However, this statistical tool was developed for determining sample sizes for surveys, and is not applicable for instances when the likelihood of observing a trait is rare as there is too great a risk that *no* positive instances would be recorded in a sample.

Of course, mathematical sampling is fraught with difficulties in applying specific theories to a large population, even for straightforward studies involving surveys. The task of adequate sampling becomes even more difficult when the traits of interest are rare, yet there are other methods that enable researchers to give more weight to the results than could otherwise be placed on simple frequency data.

9.3.3.2 Combinatorial modeling

One such method involves the use of combinatorial functions. We have already seen that small sample sizes defy extrapolation to a large population, particularly when the likelihood of a match itself is considered rare. Researchers can abrogate this issue, at least to some extent, by relying on statistical modeling of *combinations* of traits that are known to exist in a population. Observance of the trait itself (i.e., the pattern of the dentition as a whole) might be rare, but the observance of each individual characteristic that makes up the trait (i.e., the position of each individual tooth within a dentition) as a whole is probably not. By examining each individual characteristic, and applying combinatorial theorem in order to develop a probability for observing the trait as a whole (the trait being made up of different "combinations" of characteristics), modeling in this fashion reduces the mathematical error introduced by the likelihood of "missing" an observance in a simple observational sample. This is the basis for statistical analysis of DNA frequencies in the population, and has also been attempted in areas such as fingerprints and forensic odontology.[10]

One of the main concerns with the application of this technique to forensic characteristics is that the derivation of the probability that a particular characteristic will occur is often questionable. Many early studies simply assumed base-rate probabilities without attempting to verify the frequency of the trait in the population. Galton's work (Galton, 1892) is often lauded in the fingerprint community as proof of the individuality of fingerprints. He calculated that the probability of a specific ridge configuration occurring in the population was 1.45×10^{-11}. As the population was approximately 1.6 billion at the time (16 billion fingers), he concluded that the odds of finding another

---

[9]Above *N*=20,000, the sample size does not increase significantly due to the limits of the equation. The asymptote occurs when $n = 385$, theoretically allowing for *N* up to ∞. Note that these numbers also rely on an assumed confidence limit of 0.05.

[10]With arguably less believable results, as we shall see.

finger with the same ridge detail were approximately one in four. Numerous scholars criticized this crude estimation from as early as 1930, because in deriving this final probability Galton simply estimated the frequency of particular ridge details in the population, and made no attempt to experimentally verify these assumed frequencies (Cole, 2001; Pearson, 1930; Roxburgh, 1933; Stoney & Thornton, 1986; Stoney [in Lee & Gaensslen, 2001]). Galton similarly estimated that the probability of observing a particular pattern type, such as a loop or arch, was 1 in 16. Likewise, he assumed that he could predict ridge patterns, given a partial print, with a frequency of 0.5, and that the probability of the number of ridges entering a particular area of the print was 1 in 256. These were the key numbers he used to arrive at his final probability of 1.45×10^{-11}; however, *none* of these numbers were based on actual population data.

Similarly, the flawed assumption of the presence of ridge minutiae (ridge endings, bifurcations, and so on) being *equally* probable abounds in other attempts to "prove" the uniqueness of fingerprints (Stoney & Thornton, 1986). This assumption fails to realistically describe the situation, as is easily demonstrable by population frequency data. Additionally, most of these studies have also assumed that distribution of minutiae is random across the surface of the friction ridge skin, and therefore have modelled their analyses on a random probability distribution. This assumption too was proven false in the late 1980s by Stoney (Stoney, 1988), and has been recognized as contributing to significant overestimates of the likelihood of "uniqueness" for fingerprints (Chen & Moon, 2008). Several other studies (such as those by Champod & Margot, 1996; and Pankanti et al., 2002) use complicated mathematical and computer-generated models in order to calculate the possible number of combinations of fingerprint ridge minutiae. The key feature of these studies is that they calculate tiny probabilities from large numbers of possible combinations. The fact that small probabilities are predicted perhaps gives the study an aura of credibility, but the failing of all of these experiments is that the authors do not attempt to verify their model assumptions with that of data derived from the population. It is therefore impossible to ascertain to what degree their model represents the true distribution of such traits in the real world.

Two early papers in forensic odontology make similarly flawed assumptions. Rawson's attempt at proving the individuality of the human dentition initially assumed that the probability of each tooth occupying a particular position was 1/6 (Rawson et al., 1984). Keiser-Nielsen's analysis relies on the assumption that the likelihood of a tooth being missing or restored is exactly the same for each tooth (Keiser-Nielsen, 1975, 1977, 1980). It is well-established that these assumptions do not hold. For example, population studies clearly demonstrate that third molars are more likely than canines to be congenitally absent, incisors are more likely to be missing than canines due to trauma, and so on.[11]

Approaches that rely on assumed probabilities are essentially using combinatorial theorem to calculate the number of *possibilities* of combinations, and the problem arises when researchers then equate this with the *probability* of any one of these

---

[11] For some of the latest population data, see Brown & Goryakin, 2009; Lesolang et al., 2009; Starr & Hall, 2010; Upadhyaya & Humagain, 2009.

combinations appearing in the population. Keiser-Nielsen's paper is considered one of the seminal works in forensic odontology, and appeared in various forms in the late 1970s. Its earliest appearance was as a paper at the 1975 Continuing Education Course in Forensic Odontology (Keiser-Nielsen, 1975). It then appeared in the now-discontinued journal *Forensic Science* (Keiser-Nielsen, 1977), and again later in a textbook (Keiser-Nielsen, 1980). Keiser-Nielsen applied the reasoning that if the number of possible combinations of 12 or 16 "concordances" used for fingerprints are so enormous, then the presence of 32 teeth gives us a similar if not better starting point for concluding the same thing about the dentition. He calculates that the maximum number of possible combinations of 16 restored teeth is 601,080,390, using a simple combinatorial formula that assumes the remaining 16 teeth are intact.

Keiser-Nielsen stated that "whenever 16 teeth are missing in the mouth of a given person, dead or alive, then his actual and personal combination is one out of more than 600 million possible combinations." This falsely implies that the chance of observing one particular arrangement of teeth in a person with 16 teeth is greater than one in 600 million, which is fallacious in the extreme. The math is the same as that used to invoke the argument for the existence of identical snowflakes. Simply knowing that there are 600,000,000 ways to "arrange" 16 restored teeth says nothing about the probability of encountering any such combination in the population. Keiser-Nielsen has quantified the *possibilities* regarding where a tooth might be restored [or missing], but has completely failed to address the issue of *probability*. This study cannot be used to infer uniqueness in the population simply because it uses no population data whatsoever to support its claims.

Attempts at proving the uniqueness of impressed tool marks have fallen into a similar misconception, with practitioners quoting from flawed, highly theoretical analyses of the variability of tool marks as support for their claim that no two marks are identical (Nichols, 2007). As an example of this type of analysis, relying on the resolving power of the microscope and a shape characterization of the forensically significant marks that could theoretically present on the surface of a hammer, Stone (2003) calculates the number of possible positions for point, line, and curve characteristics. Arriving at astronomical figures and invoking the product rule, the implication is that no two marks could ever be the same because of the incredibly large number of possibilities. Criticizing Stone for being too *conservative*, Collins modifies these calculations (Collins & Stone, 2005) and concludes that on a practical level, tool marks are unique; but he again fails to realize that arrival at a certain number of possibilities says nothing about the relative frequency of occurrence on an actual tool face.

9.3.3.3 Combinatorial modeling from population data

Alas, the use of population data still fails to alleviate doubt regarding the conclusion that any particular characteristic is unique. Data used in any model is ideally derived from the population via some form of sampling. Therefore, a fundamental concern in any data derived from a survey is the risk that the samples are not truly random or representative of the target population. Representation of the entire world is a very difficult goal to achieve in a finite sample. MacFarlane's study on the quantification of the anterior dentition is based on figures derived from a sample of 200 emergency patients presenting at the Glasgow Dental Hospital (MacFarlane et al., 1974). Such a sample is not truly random, and would not necessarily accurately represent the population of Glasgow itself,[12] let alone that of the Earth.

Yet the fact that a study has gathered data from the population in a truly random way still does not necessarily give the study more weight. Rawson and colleagues' (1984) study, cited by many authors as proof of the individuality of the dentition (Drinnan & Melton, 1985; Pretty & Sweet, 2001)[13] and among the first to use population data, concludes that they have "demonstrate[d] … the uniqueness of the human dentition beyond any reasonable doubt." Unfortunately, the authors negate any benefit this data may have had by failing to use it in a mathematically sound way. In this study, the positions of each of the 12 anterior teeth captured in 397 wax bites were recorded. The number of positions observed was defined by the polar coordinates x, y and the angle $\emptyset$. The number of positions for each tooth ranged from 150 (for the upper right canine) to 239.9 (for the upper left lateral incisor). The authors then calculated, using the product rule, that the probability of finding two sets of dentition with six teeth in the same position for the maxillary arch was 2.2×10^{13} and for the six mandibular teeth, 6.08×10^{12}. The total number of positions for all 12 teeth was therefore deemed to be 1.36×10^{26}. Even their conservative estimate, using the minimum number of positions as 150, results in a figure of $(150)^6 \approx 1.14 \times 10^{13}$ for each arch. This might be true if the probability of encountering a tooth at any one of these positions was equal, but their own data itself proves that it is not, and so this math is fundamentally flawed.

Rawson and colleagues fail to correctly use their frequency data to calculate the probability of a tooth *actually occurring* in any given position. For example, the range of x-coordinates for the center point of tooth Participant #6 was given as $136 \leq x \leq 161$, allowing for 26 distinct possible tooth positions along the x-axis.[14] Therefore, using the reasoning applied in their concluding calculations, the "probability" that a tooth would occupy one of these x-axis positions is given as 1/26, or 0.03846.[15] However, their graphical data does not support this. At $x = 150$, the data shows a frequency of no less than 63 occurrences. Therefore, the probability of a tooth occupying the polar coordinate $x = 150$ should be more correctly calculated as 63/397, or 0.1587. Considering the probability of the tooth occupying $x = 161$, using

---

[12] Despite this flaw, a calculation of the incidence of a particular dental "signature" derived from this study arrived at the incidence of 1:10,000 and was used without objection in a Scottish court in the late 1970s (MacDonald & Laird, 1977).

[13] Although both of these sets of authors correctly conclude that it did not address the question of the uniqueness of *bite marks*, Pretty and Sweet notably state that "Rawson has proven what his article claims" regarding his proof of uniqueness of the *dentition*. Analysis of Rawson's work reveals several causes for doubt that this is the case.

[14] It is unclear in the study as to whether the digits 136…161 in the figure represent the x-axis coordinates, or simply line numbers in the computer program used to graph the frequencies. For clarity, I shall assume that it represents the x coordinate, but even if it doesn't it is irrelevant as the data clearly suggests that there were at least 26 positions observed.

[15] How they derived the number of possible positions for this tooth along the x-axis as only 5.0 remains unexplained.

the frequency data they provide (the frequency is 1) P($x=161$) = 1/397, or 0.00252. Thus the probability of a tooth occupying any given position is *not equal for all positions*, and thus the probability of observing any particular tooth in any given position depends on the total number of positions available *and* the relative distribution of frequencies. They have calculated the first variable (number of possible positions) as 1/26, and attempted to use that to calculate the overall combinatorial probability. They have completely ignored the second variable, that of the distribution of the frequency, which suggests that the likelihood of observing a tooth in one position is actually far greater than observing it in other positions. Their results are no better than Keiser-Nielsen's in that they have essentially only calculated possibilities and equated this with probability.

Of course, even if Rawson had calculated the true probabilities from his population data, he should not have made assumptions about the type of distribution of the frequencies, which determine the formula used to relate the two variables. Without conducting a proper analysis of the frequency data, one cannot assume that the distribution is a normal one. Other distribution models, such as the binomial, Gaussian, or Poisson distributions, may more adequately describe the frequency data, in which case the formula for calculating probability is different. This can only be determined by further analysis of the data.

This is one failing, among several others, in the *50-K* fingerprint study[16] (Wayman, 2000) in which it was simply assumed that the minutiae characteristics followed a binomial distribution without verifying that this was the case by analyzing the population data. This study was conducted in response to a challenge to the reliability of fingerprint evidence (*United States v. Byron Mitchell,* 1999) where the FBI commissioned Lockheed-Martin to prove that fingerprints were unique, and it has been widely cited by the fingerprint community as achieving this aim. It was the first time a large, real-print database was used in order to address the issue of uniqueness in this discipline.[17] The study essentially "scored" the relatedness of each fingerprint with every other print (including itself) using a series of computer programs, and concluded that "... the probability of a non-mate rolled fingerprint being identical to any particular fingerprint is less than 1 in 10^{97} (1 followed by 97 zeroes). [T]hus given the population of the earth, the chance of observing any two rolled fingerprints being identical is approximately 59 in 10^{88}" (cited in Kaye, 2003).

The *50-K* study has been critiqued in some detail by Kaye (2003). Even the appellate court noted this incredibly large figure with some skepticism; however, it was not merely the astronomically large number of 10^{88} that cast doubts on its validity. In the course of the matching process, three unusual scores were obtained. It turns out that these three prints were actually from the same individuals as three other prints in the database, which were inadvertently included in the sample. This presented as three scenarios where the *same finger* was rolled twice, and appeared as two separate

---

[16] This study, credited to Meagher, Budowle, and Ziesig, became known as the *50-K* study because it utilized a database of 50,000 fingerprints.
[17] The FBI's own fingerprint database.

entries in the database. The scores for these prints were clearly in the range that the researchers considered as indicating that they were from *different* fingers. The logical conclusion to be drawn from this was that the fingerprints of the same finger could be more dissimilar than prints from different fingers; therefore, one should realistically conclude that fingerprints from different fingers could *not* be unique! This finding rendered the entire study "worthless for documenting the individuality of finger-prints" (Stoney, in Lee & Gaensslen, 2001); however, this did not stop the authors from making such a claim.

Similarly, Christensen (2005) noted that no quantitative testing of the occurrence of frontal sinus features had ever been carried out, and conducted a study involv-ing 808 frontal sinus radiographs. 305 of these were actually replicates (not simply "duplicates"), enabling the inter-individual versus intra-individual variation to be compared. Using a method that involved tracing the outlines, scanning the resultant tracings, and converting the resultant closed curve to an ordered set of data points (a technique known as elliptic Fourier analysis), Euclidean distances between pairs of outlines were calculated. The results demonstrated that the mean distance between individuals was significantly larger than that of the same individuals at a p-value of less than 0.0001. However, there were instances where different individuals dis-played less Euclidean distances between them than between replicates of the same individual, and vice versa. This is demonstrated graphically in some overlap of the cumulative probability density curves. Concluding that the "frontal sinus is distinctly quantifiably different at a highly significant level" is reasonable phraseology, and the author does not make any comment on the "uniqueness" of frontal sinuses; however, the results of this study actually *disprove* any such theory that the frontal sinuses are unique, at least using this method, due to the overlap noted between inter- and intra-individual variability. Bush and colleagues have recently established the same proposition to be true for the dentition in that not only does the same dentition pro-duce variable bite marks in skin (Bush et al., 2009, 2010), but the variation between the bite marks on human skin from the same dentition can be greater than that seen between bite marks from different dentitions (Bush et al., 2011).

9.3.3.4 *Distribution models*

The most mathematically valid studies for characterizing the existence of forensic traits in the population rely on so-called "generative" distribution models. In a gen-erative model, the distribution of traits is "learned" by a computer program from a known dataset. Ideally, this should then be verified against a second dataset, in order to ensure that the modeling is applicable to other populations. Probabilities can then be calculated using derivations from this (verified) distribution model.

While this is a more sound technique than simply assuming the data fits a Bino-mial or Poisson distribution, the extrapolation to uniqueness from these results will still involve a "leap of faith" (Stoney, 1991). As Saks and Koehler (2008) point out, this is because the probability of the same series of markers (1,2...n) appearing more than once in the population should technically be zero in order for a trait to be con-sidered truly unique. Mathematically, $P(1,2...n) = 0$ is impossible to achieve using product-rule formulae, as the calculation of such a probability necessarily involves use of multiplication, based on frequencies of the individual characteristics occurring in the population. No number exists that when multiplied by another number is zero, apart from zero itself. The probability of observing such a characteristic either alone or in combination with others is always *greater* than zero, which implies that there is always the probability that a duplicate exists, no matter how small. The "leap of faith" occurs when the practitioner "rounds down" this probability to zero and then claims uniqueness.

Another more pervasive concern with probability models is that they generally rely on the assumption that each individual trait is independent of any other, thus allowing use of the product rule to calculate the likelihood that two or more of the features would occur in combination. This is also the subject of much debate. No attempts at quantifying the independence of traits has been introduced for fingerprints, bite marks, frontal sinuses, or even tool marks or firearms. Some studies simply assume independence, such as the earlier fingerprint studies, whereas others recognize the existence of the problem, but suggest inadequate or arbitrary ways of dealing with it (MacFarlane et al., 1974). Even in DNA analysis, it is accepted that complete independence of alleles is unlikely; however, DNA studies have allowed the best estimation of a constant q that is incorporated into the calculation of the random match probability for DNA samples[18] in order to compensate for this fact (National Research Council, 1996). While this is not a perfect solution, it goes at least partway to ensuring a more realistic probability estimate. At this stage, the influence of dependence remains largely unstudied (and thus unquantified) for the dentition, fingerprints, and most other forensic markers.

9.3.4 Quantifying uniqueness: The problem of numbers

Kaye (2010) criticizes Saks and Koehler for upholding the requirement to obtain a zero-probability livelihood of a match as an untenable standard that is not followed even in the most rigorous of scientific disciplines; however, even arriving at a very *low* probability of encountering a match via this form of statistical modeling does not "prove" anything. So the question arises as to how low should a probability be before we can consider something to be unique? Saks and Koehler (2008) describe the common fallacy that people assume: When the probability of sharing a characteristic is given as less than 1 in 6.7 billion, the approximate population of the Earth, it proves that no one else on the Earth could possibly have the same characteristic. In other words, uniqueness is proven when $\Pr(x|x) \leq 1.49 \times 10^{-10}$. The fallaciousness of this reasoning is given in the familiar "birthday problem." Using somewhat more fathomable numbers, the birthday problem asks "What is the probability that two people in a room share the same birthday, when there are N number of people in the

---

[18] This constant q is generally given as 0.01 for the general population, with figures anywhere from 0.001 to 0.03 used for various population sub-group calculations. This is deliberately conservative: The true value of q is estimated to be between 0.0006 and 0.001 for any population (Budowle et al., 2001).

room?" Assuming that the probability of someone having a birthday on any given day is 1 in 365,[19] most people are surprised to learn that the probability of encountering someone with the same birthday as them in a room of only 23 people is greater than 50%. For 99 people, the probability exceeds 99%, or 0.99. So even though the number of possible birthdays (365) exceeds the number of people in the room by a factor of three, there is almost a 100% chance that someone in the room will share the same birthday.

Using similar mathematics, if we consider a machine that is capable of printing tickets at random, numbered from 1 to 100, and there are only 10 tickets printed, the probability that two customers will have a ticket that has the same number is actually close to 40%, far greater than intuition would suggest. To assume that uniqueness exists simply because the number of people on Earth exceeds the total number of possible combinations of characteristics is fallacious for the same reasoning. Rawson and colleagues (1984), in addition to their poor mathematical treatment of their data, committed this error when they claimed that as few as five matching teeth would be needed to be confident of an identification, because the number of possibilities of combinations for five teeth ($150^5 = 75.9 \times 10^9$) exceeded the number of people on Earth (at that time, 4×10^9).

Using Bayesian methods, Champod (2000) calculated the probability of a person actually *being guilty* of a crime, given a "unique" trait frequency of 1 in 6 billion. However, using this very low probability of there being an identical match in the entire world, there is still only a 50% probability that this person actually committed the crime. In recognition of this fact, others have argued that it is safe to assume "uniqueness" only when the probability of encountering a duplicate characteristic exceeds the reciprocal of the population by several orders of magnitude (see Balding, 2005; Kaye, 2009; but compare with Balding, 1999). Philosophically, this makes little sense, as by its own definition, "uniqueness" implies that there will *never* be a repetition of the same arrangement of friction ridge skin, dentition, tool mark patterns, and so on. In other words, the possible number of combinations should potentially be infinite.

One should technically consider the total number of people ever to have lived on the Earth,[20] in addition to the number of people yet to be born,[21] in order to assert that a particular characteristic is truly unique (McLachlan, 1995). Implying that these former and yet to be born persons need not be considered in the equation implies that "uniqueness" only holds for a certain population size, leading to the oxymoronic notion of "observable uniqueness." The reasoning that "uniqueness is true only for numbers less than 10x, but not for greater than 10y" makes no sense. Uniqueness cannot be a spectrum; it is a binary concept by its own definition, and therefore must either exist for all numbers less than infinity or not at all. While Kaye (2010) argued

---

[19] In reality it is different for each day, due to seasonal patterns in reproductive habits, and we discount the leap years.
[20] Estimated to be approximately 1×10^{11}.
[21] An unquantifiable number.

that "uniqueness" may indeed be justified when the match probability is infinitesimally smaller than the reciprocal of the population, he is still skeptical of such claims because, as this chapter has demonstrated, it is so difficult to establish that the models used to arrive at such probabilities are realistic or accurate.

Further complicating the search for mathematical "proof" of uniqueness is the fact that the probability of a particular characteristic *existing* in a population (i.e., the figure derived by Kieser-Neilsen, Rawson, and others) does not equate to the probability of *seeing such a characteristic again* following its actual observation. It is the latter which is the all-important forensic question. What is important to realize about this semantic difference is that the probability of observing x, after it has already been seen once, is *always* greater than the probability of seeing it, had it not been seen before (Weir, 1999). This is easily demonstrated.

The probability of not observing a particular trait in a given population can be given by $P(x = 0) = (1 - p)^n$, where p is the probability of any one person having the trait and n is the size of the population. The probability of observing one instance of the trait in a population is $P(x = 1) = np(1 - p)^{n-1}$, and the probability of observing more than one instance is $P(x \geq 1) = 1 - (1 - p)^n$. We want to know what the probability of observing the trait is, given that we have already found one example of it in the population. This is represented by $P(x > 1 \mid x \geq 1)$. Conditional probability theorem gives us

$$P(A \mid B) = \frac{P(A) \cap P(B)}{P(B)}$$

where $P(A) \cap P(B)$ represents the intersection of events A and B: The probability of observing incidences occurring only *more than* once. As we do not know what this is, it must be calculated by subtracting the probability of observing *just one* instance from the probability of observing *one or more* instances, $P(x \geq 1) - P(x = 1) = P(x > 1)$, so we have

$$P(x > 1 \mid x \geq 1) = \frac{1 - (1 - P)^n - np(1 - p)^{n-1}}{1 - (1 - p)^n} = p(x \mid x)$$

Let us assume that the probability of observing a particular characteristic p is calculated to be one in 12 million, or 8.33×10^{-6}. Let us also assume that the population of interest consists of only 1 million people, and hence the probability of occurrence exceeds the reciprocal of the population by a factor of 12.[22] What is P(x)|x, the likelihood of observing another person with characteristic p out of this population, given that we know at least one exists? The answer is surprisingly high: 5% or 0.05, very much larger than one in 12 million.

---

[22] Recall earlier comments regarding those who advocate that uniqueness can be safely assumed when the probability of observing the trait is orders of magnitude greater than the reciprocal of the population. The numbers used here are smaller than the population of the Earth for ease of demonstration, but still fulfil this "requirement."

Of course, this equation would only be valid for features that follow a binomial distribution. A more accurate probability distribution for forensic purposes is the Poisson distribution, often used for modeling systems when the probability events are considered rare (although this is still not necessarily representative). Sparing the reader from the mathematical derivation of calculating the probability of observing x given that it has already been seen once, it can easily be verified that for the Poisson distribution, using the same numbers from the example above, we arrive at $P(x)|x \approx 0.041$. Again, these numbers are purely arbitrary, and the use of either the binomial or Poisson distributions for forensic traits such as fingerprints may or may not be appropriate; however, the point is made that the probability of observing a characteristic in a population, having already observed one occurrence, is always significantly *greater* than the probability of the trait actually occurring. This is in accordance with the laws of mathematics, and yet is counter-intuitive to most people. It is easy to conclude that when the probability of observing a particular characteristic is low, the likelihood that a second person would share that characteristic would be even lower; however, to do so falls into an intuitive fallacy not supported by the mathematical analysis.

9.4 The (Il)logic of the uniqueness literature

More often than not, the conclusion of uniqueness enjoyed by most studies attempting to prove the notion simply fails to follow from the data that they present. Of course, several studies often cited as "proving" the uniqueness of a forensic marker actually make no such claim. Rather, the proponents of the theory have themselves inferred a uniqueness proposition, based on misinterpretation of the study's results or conclusions. Pretty and Sweet (2001) noted that authors frequently cite the Sognnaes identical twin study (Sognnaes et al., 1982), which concludes that identical twins do not have the same anterior dental arrangements. This may be the case, but the inference from this study that the dentition is unique may represent the folly of the reader rather than the authors. Sognnaes and colleagues themselves do not make such an explicit claim, carefully limiting themselves to the conclusion that "even so-called identical twins are not identical."

Yet consider another study on the quantification of the anterior dentition by MacFarlane, MacDonald, and Sutherland (MacFarlane et al., 1974), in which the authors concluded "... that even if two individuals had similar tooth status, rotations and arch displacement of teeth, this does not mean that they would produce identical bite marks. Such factors as the length of incisal edges, exact angulation and spacing of teeth would probably combine to ensure that even apparently similar teeth produce unique bite marks." This conclusion represents an unwarranted leap from the authors' initial aim of quantifying the spatial relationship of the anterior dentition. The authors present no data on the effects of tooth angulation, incisal edge length, or spacing on the appearance of a bite mark, as these features "require more study to be evident as a distinctive feature of a bite mark," yet they conclude that these features would render bite marks unique. Furthermore, this conclusion is counterintuitive to the example they give in the introduction of the paper, where they note that an "incisor with short length might be misconstrued as a missing tooth when noting the absence of a particular feature on a bite mark." This should suggest that the possibility of more than one dentition "fitting" the bite mark is *more* likely, not less, so that bite marks are in fact *not* demonstrably unique.

Many people assume that twin studies lead us to be able to draw conclusions about uniqueness. This is a misrepresentation of the purpose of twin studies. Twin studies are useful for determining the heritability of traits by using controls where the genetic influence is supposedly the same. Any observable differences between monozygotic twins could therefore reasonably be assumed to be due to environmental factors, for if the trait were solely determined by genetics, the twins should exhibit exactly the same characteristics. Thus if twins demonstrated identical dentitions, we could say that the spatial arrangement of teeth is entirely dependent on genetic heritability.

The major premise in any twin study, although often not stated, is that "twins are genetically identical." The minor premise that would follow Sognnaes and colleagues' (1982) study, as the results demonstrate, is: "twins do not have identical dentitions." The only logical conclusion that can be drawn from this is: "Therefore, the dentition is not entirely dependent on genetic factors." A conclusion such as "therefore, the dentition is unique" bears no relation to the premises that go before it, and therefore it fails as a logical argument. According to the laws of logic, there is no syllogism that can lead to the generalization of all cases from premises based on specific observations. Such reasoning would be purely inductive, and hence we return to the familiar induction problem.

At best, we can only conclude from these studies that people who do not share 100% of their DNA with another person (i.e., non-twins) will not exhibit the same arrangement of the dentition. Unfortunately, the results of Sognnaes detract markedly from even this modest hypothesis. Sognnaes et al. proved that twins do not have identical dentitions, and therefore the (unmentioned) inference should be that the spatial arrangement of teeth is not entirely dependent on genetic heritability. The claim that Sognnaes and colleagues offer about their results is that "comparison of the bite mark pattern of monozygotic twins could offer a clue to the degree of uniqueness that can be attributed to an individual dentition." But despite their optimism, this study gives us no clues about the degree of uniqueness that could be attributed to the dentition, due to the authors' failure to quantify inter-person versus intra-twin variation, which, had it been conducted, might have actually provided us with evidence that twins may have *more similar* dentitions than non-twins. This also might have even provided clues as to the relative influence of genetics versus other factors in the position of the teeth. Yet even if this was attempted, it still does not logically lead us to the conclusion that the dentition is in any way "unique," it simply leads us to a statement regarding the amount of similarity between twins and non-twins.

Jain and colleagues (2002) conducted a twin study using a generative computer model of fingerprints that compared the index fingers of 100 pairs of identical twins.

It is worth noting that there are several robust aspects to this study; the distribution was generated by using a large random dataset, which was then compared to a second set in order to test the applicability of the model, and the dataset used two prints of the same finger in order to allow for intra- versus inter-print variation. Additionally, the threshold for a "match" was determined via a Receiver Operating Characteristic curve, which has become a widely accepted decision model for determining threshold points that minimizes the risk of false positives while maximizing the determination of true positives (Phillips et al., 2001). The study's conclusions also logically followed from its results. While the study concluded that twins did indeed have prints that were not identical, the intra-pair variation was no more than the intra-class variation seen in the general population. In other words, the variation between identical twins was similar to that seen among non-twins who had the same Level 1 classification.[23] Consequently, the "similarity" between twins was because they shared Level 1 features. Despite the fact that this was a well-designed study, it proves nothing as far as the "uniqueness" of fingerprints is concerned; it simply discusses the *similarity* between twins' and non-twins' fingerprints. This study was *not about uniqueness*, and it just tells us that twins' fingerprints are no more similar or variable to each other than they are to the rest of the population.

The most recent attempt to prove the individuality of fingerprints was a commissioned study submitted to the US Department of Justice in August of 2009 (Srihari, 2009). They first conclude that "the similarity of twin fingerprints is different to that of prints between the same finger." In other words, *twins do not have identical fingerprints.* The second conclusion is that "identical twins share the same similarity among their fingerprints as fraternal twins," that is, there is *no difference between the relative similarity of identical twin fingerprints and the relative similarity of fraternal twins' fingerprints.* The results from comparing prints from the same finger/ different print set also suggest that there is a difference in similarity observed when comparing a print image to an identical image, versus a print image to a non-identical image, but rolled from the same finger. None of these conclusions are startling; they have essentially already been surmised reasonably convincingly by prior literature, and in fact were already generally agreed upon in the field. The fact remains that just like the Sognnaes and Jain study, neither of these conclusions regarding twins advances the argument for uniqueness.

Firearms examiners claim to rely on the premise that no two gun barrels will leave the same mark on a fired bullet or cartridge case (Bonfanti & De Kinder, 1999) in order to support their identification. This proposition arises from studies of consecutively rifled barrels that demonstrate differences in either the markings transferred to a bullet (Lardizabal, 1995) or on the internal barrel surface itself (Freeman, 1986). While this may be true, the evidence for this relies on relatively few studies with very

---

[23] Level 1 features are those used to classify fingerprints, such as loops, whorls, arches, and so on. Level 2 features are the minutiae such as bifurcations and ridge endings, which are usually used to make an identification after the Level 1 detail has been assessed. Level 3 features are things like pores and ridge widths, which are rarely used in identification.

small sample sizes. In one such study, Hatcher compares only two gun barrels before concluding that *all* consecutively rifled barrels are unique (Hatcher et al., 1957). The assumption is that "barrel markings from consecutively manufactured or rifled guns are more likely to be similar than those from guns that are not." This is reasonable, but it relies on the prior assumption that the possibility of two *non-consecutively* manufactured barrels sharing the same pattern is zero. The fact that consecutively rifled or manufactured barrels do not leave identical marks on bullets or cartridges is useful for advancing the argument that "examiners can distinguish between bullets fired from two guns that were consecutively manufactured," but this does not directly address the concern that another gun could possibly have left the same pattern of marks. This latter concern has not yet been the subject of any large-scale study, and yet it is the same problem of the "random" occurrence of two fingerprints, or dental arrangements, being identical. The fact that two consecutively manufactured barrels do not share the same characteristics does not necessarily address the possibility of a random match, and represents the exact same problem of trying to prove uniqueness for any other forensic marker.

9.4.1 Study design

Many of the studies attempting to "prove" uniqueness are designed, whether intentionally or not, to favor that outcome. Studies such as Reichs' work (Reichs, 1993) on the individuality of the frontal sinuses arrive at astronomical figures simply by using a scoring model that allows a large number of combinations. Consider the alternative approach: One could design a scoring system to describe a particular forensic characteristic as being one of four possible configurations. Performing this analysis at three different locations means that the number of possible combinations is $4^3 = 64$. By the same reasoning employed by the studies above, one could conclude that it was highly likely that the characteristic was not unique, as the study "proves" there are only 64 possible combinations. It is unlikely that this would be taken seriously.[24]

As another example of how studies can be designed to demonstrate particular outcomes, consider the *50-K* experiment, supposedly proving the uniqueness of latent prints. This experiment used the now-discredited practice of using "subset" inked prints (that is, portions of existing prints that were simply cropped to provide "partials") to simulate latent images (Sparrow, 1994). No attempt at distorting the image, as might occur in a real latent print, was made, and so the fact remains that the second part of the *50-K* study continued to compare identical images when comparing "matching" prints. This results in unfairly high "match" scores that favor results toward the conclusion that no fingerprint is the same as any other.

---

[24] Indeed, no one who wanted to convincingly prove uniqueness would design such a system, because using four features does not give rise to anywhere near "enough" combinations – hence the rationale for developing more complicated methods of classification in order to ensure the study arrives at a sufficiently large number – an example of "results by design".

The *50-K* study also represents another pervasive problem in the uniqueness literature. Any experiment designed expressly for use in the courts should be carefully scrutinized for evidence of bias, and Epstein reveals some startling revelations regarding the nature of the *50-K* study, which was prepared with court presentation in mind. He has stated that as the tests proceeded, Lockheed "repeatedly provided the preliminary results to Steven Meagher, the FBI fingerprint examiner who arranged for the testing to be done, in order to make sure that the FBI was pleased with the data being produced and the manner in which it was presented" (Epstein, 2001). The *50-K* study, which has never been published, is a good example of a study prepared expressly and which higher courts had previously warned trial judges of the dangers of unreserved admission by court authorities.[25]

9.5 The irrelevance of uniqueness

In an interview with one published critic, it was stated:

> *I've written and said that the question of uniqueness is not related to the notion of scientific reliability so many times, that I don't know whether it's intentional or unintentional that fingerprint experts continue to answer 'but all fingerprints are unique.' I say '… that isn't the question I'm asking …', and they still answer '… but all fingerprints are unique …!' It's like a broken record.*

What this author has argued is that when considering the implications of uniqueness to their logical end, it can be seen that the entire notion of whether forensic markers are unique or not is, in fact, irrelevant. This irrelevance relates not only to the fundamental goal of identification, but also to the practice of forensic analysis and the subsequent question posed by the courts.

9.5.1 The irrelevance of studies to forensic practice

The very nature of the type of study used to advance the uniqueness argument often renders its results impractical to apply to real-world situations. This favors the outcome for those who believe in the uniqueness proposition, but rarely represents a realistic model of how analysis of the forensic trait is carried out. The *50-K* experiment used a model that failed to represent the situation that the fingerprint examiner would encounter, that of comparing two *identical* images to see if they match. Fingerprint examiners already agree that fingerprints taken from the same finger are never visually the same, and hence they would never end up comparing identical images in actual case work, even when encountering the strongest examples of a "match."

---

[25] "One very significant fact to be considered is whether the experts are proposing to testify about matters growing naturally and directly out of research they have conducted independent of the litigation, or whether they have developed their opinions expressly for purposes of testifying." (*Daubert v. Merrell Dow Pharmaceuticals Inc. II*, 1995, on remand).

The latter half of the most recent effort to demonstrate the uniqueness of fingerprints (Srihari, 2009) focuses on the development of a mathematical model that allows the probability of a "random match" to be calculated. Ignoring for a moment the issue of random sampling and independence, of ultimate concern in this study is that at no stage is the definition of "similarity" given, or whether it is comparable to the level of discrimination achievable by a human examiner. The study demonstrates that a computer is able to discriminate between fingerprints to a level such that the likelihood of encountering a "duplicate" is close to 1.2×10^{-23}, but whether a human being would be able to discriminate between two fingerprints at the same level as suggested in this study depends on whether the level of intra-print variation is sufficiently low such that two prints from the same finger would not be mistaken for two prints from different fingers. Without using data derived from actual human performance to model the computer comparisons, the study has little practical significance.

Returning to odontology, the study by Kieser and colleagues (2007), a geometric-morphometric analysis of 82 randomly selected post-orthodontic casts from 50 individuals ranging in age from 17–20 years, is also mathematically sound. The study concluded that there were clear differences in the anterior dentition in both shape and form, and this was demonstrated by figures depicting the two most similar and the two most dissimilar dentitions in a procrustean superimposition. However, it is unclear whether the superimposition of the two most similar dentitions would appear different without the benefit of the geometric-morphometric analysis, which is almost certainly *never* carried out in bite mark analysis.

Thomas-Johnson and colleagues (2008, 2009) demonstrated that the probability of encountering a dentition, at least in the Detroit area, with the same 36 individual parameters (as measured in their study) approaches the "one in a trillion" category. While this high number renders the possibility of witnessing a duplicate dentition to be relatively low, one of the most recent studies to consider the individuality of the dentition illustrates very well the overall irrelevance of these low probabilities in forensic practice. Miller and colleagues (2009) demonstrated that none of the 10 mandibular dentitions considered physically unique in their study actually translated these features reliably onto cadaver skin such that they could be definitively associated with only one dentition. This raises important questions about any study model that does not consider realistic parameters relevant to the practice of the discipline; that is, the individuality of the dentition does not translate to individuality of bite marks, which are the ultimate issue in bite mark analysis.

9.5.2 The irrelevance of uniqueness as a tenet of identification theory

Some forensic practitioners have avoided the uniqueness debate by utilizing the term "individualistic" to refer to the property by which each and every person has his or her own distinct physical characteristics. The process of matching these characteristics to latent marks is thus termed "individualization", and cleverly avoids the use of terms such as "unique," "identify," and "identification." Kaye (2009) has argued that "individualization" and "uniqueness" are separate phenomenon, and the two terms should not be used interchangeably. "Local individualization" refers to identification of a mark having come from a source within a defined subset, such as a particular city, town, or other geographical area. "Universal individualization" refers to the identification of a mark having come from a set that includes the entire population of the world. He also defines the term "special uniqueness," implying the quality of object Y that has left mark y from a set of objects (...., X, Y, Z, ...). He compares this with the term "general uniqueness," which implies special uniqueness for all of the object Ys in the set. This means that there is more than one object Y, and each one leaves a similar mark y, but each mark is distinguishable from the marks made by the other object Ys. This is akin to what fingerprint examiners and other pattern-matching disciplines claim, and is much more difficult to prove.

As yet, no data exists that verifies the general uniqueness proposition, but as Kaye has noted, this is not a necessary condition for individualization, at least for DNA evidence, because very rarely does the set consist of every human being on the planet. The existence of other evidence helps one to narrow down the set of people that might have committed the crime, and thus the term "individualization" may be appropriate in the context of a finite set, i.e., "local individualization". The issue then is *not* "Is this feature unique?" or even "Are all forensic features unique?" but "Is there sufficient evidence to demonstrate that this latent mark originated from this source?" Alas, this too runs into difficulties when pursuing the implication of local individualization to its logical end. Forensic practitioners are not generally aware of this other evidence, and therefore have no justification for reducing the set to a local one. This becomes important when considering the effects of bias and context effects on forensic practitioner decision making. Assessment of evidence external to that of the simple "matching" of latent marks to forensic characteristics is properly carried out by a judge or jury, and thus individualization becomes the task of the trier of fact, not the forensic practitioner. Consequently, the expert should not only avoid terms such as "unique," uniqueness being an irrelevant and unprovable notion, but also "individualization," which is an issue solely for the trier of fact (Kaye, 2009). This concept has been supported by others in the forensic identification field (Champod & Evett, 2001; Stoney, 1991).

Uniqueness is invoked as a necessary assumption for the certainty behind forensic conclusions of a "match," but this is somewhat absurd, as the very process by which a match is declared *must* result in some degree of uncertainty as a direct result of the uniqueness proposition itself that "no two objects are ever the same." According to Kwan (1977), "qualitative" identity can be established when a set of properties agrees in two objects, and hence they belong to the same set. Therefore, the stronger the match between an object and its impression, the more likely it is derived from that object. This implies that only an exact match between object and impression would definitively indicate that the object left the mark, but this too is demonstrably false. Consider how tools change over time; a tool may not match the mark it made because it might have been subject to modification, via legitimate use or otherwise, but still have made the questioned mark. Conversely, the absence of qualitative identity also does not prove that the tool did not make the questioned mark, for the same reasoning that the tool face may have changed over time.

Requiring an exact match would set an unattainable standard in forensic science, and what Kwan's example demonstrates is that conclusions regarding identity of source from the relevant "agreement" between source and object properties can only ever lead to a probabilistic conclusion: There is a point at which the number of matching characteristics can only make it *more likely than not* that the tool was the source of the mark. The concept of "uniqueness," whether it exists or not, has no bearing on the fact that absolute certainty of identification is unattainable in pattern-matching forensic analysis, and hence cannot be the basis for individualization. The uniqueness proposition is simply a justification to "round up" from an unspecified level of uncertainty to being 100% certain. Cole (2009), via a different epistemic path, considered pursuit of the implications of uniqueness to its logical end, and has also reached a similar conclusion that uniqueness is *not* the basis for individualization.

9.5.3 The irrelevance of uniqueness to the courts

Cole (2009) has argued that the condition of uniqueness also bears no relationship to the fundamental questions posed by the legal system. He has argued that the question of whether a particular forensic assay is accurate is far more important than that of whether a particular trait might be considered unique. If we consider the random match probability of a bite mark to a dentition to be 1.0×10^{-12}, under several authors' propositions, we may be justified in deciding that this particular dentition is unique. However, it also becomes apparent that the error rate for matching bite marks, due to observer effects, poor quality of the mark, and so on, might be 0.1%. In other words, this (very conservative) error rate assumes that the result is wrong about 1 out of every 1000 times.[26] The issue of "uniqueness" in the context of a remote possibility of a match becomes irrelevant, because even if the person's fingerprint *is* unique, the probability that the practitioner has falsely matched the print is a billion times larger, and thus has far more relevance to the weight that should be given to this evidence.

Some judges and lawyers have realized that uniqueness, or even proof of "high degrees of variability," takes a sideline to more important issues that result from an "identification" of a suspect by matching with a latent mark. Gertner noted in *United States v. Green* (2005) that "… even assuming that some of these marks *are* unique to the gun in question, the issue is their significance, how the examiner can distinguish one from another, which to discount and which to focus on, how qualified he is to do so, and how reliable his examination is."[27] The idea of a gun leaving marks on a bullet unique to that particular firearm was noted, but dismissed as avoiding the fundamental issues. From the prospect of ensuring admission of forensic testimony in court, studies proving the uniqueness of any particular characteristic are unlikely to prove helpful.

---

[26] It is, of course, likely to be much higher, and this demonstrates another key point: That we don't even know what it *might* be, because virtually no good-quality studies have been published that attempt to quantify examiner error rate for bite marks.
[27] Emphasis added.

9.6 **Conclusion**

Reliance on cultural memes fails as proof of the uniqueness tenet in any sense. As Thornton (1986) wisely concluded in his original article exploring the possibility of two snowflakes existing that are exactly the same: "Unlike snowflakes, gun barrels are not made in clouds, and the proof of uniqueness of other objects must be based on yet other grounds." Philosophers such as McLachlan (1995) specifically avoid arguing for the falsity of the proposition of uniqueness itself, instead restricting themselves to the argument that the theory, even if it is true, can never be known to be such, and that there is no reason to believe such a theory, as one could never exist. The dictum of philosophy tells us that uniqueness is not an establishable proposition, and belief in such represents "a highly dubious snatch of metaphysics … a philosophical assumption rather than what it is presented as being – a hard headed scientific conclusion. "

Nonetheless, forensic practitioners have tried to prove that various features are unique. Studies attempting to provide convincing evidence that any feature or combination of features is unique face insurmountable issues, most of which cannot be overcome using modern-day experimental techniques. Stoney (1991) recognized nearly twenty years ago that attempting to "prove" uniqueness using statistics was a "ridiculous notion," yet research continues to this day. For those that have attempted to prove uniqueness, analysis of their methodology fails to allow much faith in their conclusions. Even considering these efforts in combination, the evidence for the individuality of any characteristic remains minimal at best when considering their collective flaws.

These issues become secondary with the realization that "uniqueness" is not relevant to either the theory or practice of forensic identification, nor is it relevant to the fundamental forensic and legal questions asked by the courts. Identification, or "individualization" if one prefers, is the task of the judge or jury and not the odontologist. Directing odontology research resources toward proving uniqueness is therefore pointless, and diverts resources away from more useful projects (Cole, 2009). To attempt to prove uniqueness also puts the cart before the horse when more basic issues such as the meaning of the term *match*, the quantification of level of certainty, and the standard of practitioner performance—all of which will influence how we perceive uniqueness—are yet to be agreed upon. Kwan, who undertook a purely logical analysis of identification in his 1977 thesis "Inference of Identity of Source," realized that there can never be a certain conclusion regarding identity from latent marks, but there exists a threshold, or series of thresholds, at which the likelihood of identity is proportionately higher or lower. Determination of these thresholds becomes a key issue, and these need to be determined via a series of reasoned, valid experiments. Additionally, the effect of phenomena such as bias, error, variation in examination technique, standards, and other considerations will also influence the relative certainty of a conclusion, and these too should be described and quantified in order to provide the trier of fact with a reasonable estimation of the reliability of any forensic analysis. Some aspects of these phenomena will be explored in later chapters.

Uniqueness simply doesn't matter all that much; mistakes and misidentifications are not made because someone has an identical dentition or fingerprint to someone else in the world. They are made because of guesswork, poor performance, lack of standards, bias, and observer error to name but a few potential causes. While many forensic disciplines rely on such a notion as "proof" of their infallibility, the question of "uniqueness" is an entirely separate issue to one of "reliability." There are few valid reasons to continue this fruitless search for what remains a philosophical ideal. There is no valid reason to quote "uniqueness" as a tenet of forensic theory, and as nothing more than idealism, it consequently fails to advance the reliability of the discipline to any extent.

An abridged version of this chapter was published in Forensic Science International as: Page, M., Taylor, J.A. & Blenkin, M. (2011) Uniqueness in the Forensic Identification Sciences - Fact or Fiction? Forensic Science International, 206, 12-8.

References

Asherson, N., 1965. Identification by Frontal Sinus Prints: A Forensic Medical Pilot Survey. Lewis and Co, London.

Balding, D.J., 1999. When can a DNA profile be regarded as unique? Sci. & Just 39 (4), 257–260.

Balding, D.J., 2005. Weight-of-evidence for DNA profiles. John Wiley & Sons.

Bonfanti, M.S., De Kinder, J., 1999. The influence of manufacturing processes on the identification of bullets and cartridge cases-a review of the literature. Science & Justice 39 (1), 3–10.

Bowers, C.M., Commentary on: Keiser, J.A., Bernal, V., Wadell, J.N., Raju, S., 2007. The uniqueness of the human anterior dentition: a geometric and morphometric analysis. J. Forensic Sci. 2007; 52:3 J. Forensic Sci. 52 (6), 1417; discussion 1418.

Budowle, B., Buscaglia, J., Perlman, R.S., 2006. Review of the scientific basis for friction ridge comparisons as a means of identification: Committee findings and recommendations. http://www.fbi.gov/hq/lab/fsc/backissu/jan2006/research/2006_01_research02.htm, Accessed on 02 Jun 2013.

Budowle, B., Chakraborty, R., Carmody, G., Monson, K., 2001. Reply to Weir. For. Sci. Communications 3 (1).

Bush, M.A., Bush, P.J., Sheets, H.D., 2011. A study of multiple bitemarks inflicted in human skin by a single dentition using geometric morphometric analysis. Forensic Sci. Int. 211 (1), 1–8.

Bush, M.A., Cooper, H.I., Dorion, R.B., 2010. Inquiry into the scientific basis for bitemark profiling and arbitrary distortion compensation. J. Forensic Sci. 55 (4), 976–983.

Bush, M.A., Miller, R.G., Bush, P.J., Dorion, R.B., 2009. Biomechanical factors in human dermal bitemarks in a cadaver model. J. Forensic Sci. 54 (1), 167–176.

Champod, C., 2000. Identification and Individualisation - Overview and Meaning of ID. In: Siegal, J.A., Saukko, P.J., Knupfer, G.C. (Eds.), Encyclopaedia of Forensic Sciences, vol. III. Academic Press, London, pp. 1077–1084.

Champod, C., Evett, I.W., 2001. A probabilistic approach to fingerprint evidence. Journal of Forensic Identification 101–122.

Champod, C., Margot, P., 1996. Computer assisted analysis of minutiae occurences on fingerprints. In: Almog, J., Springer, E. (Eds.), Proceedings of the International Symposium for Fingerprint Detection and Identification, 305.

Chen, J., Moon, Y.-S., 2008. The statistical modelling of fingerprint minutiae distribution with implications for fingerprint individuality studies. IEEE Conference on Computer Vision and Pattern Recognition, 2008.

Christensen, A.M., 2005. Assessing the variation in individual frontal sinus outlines. Am. J. Phys. Anthropol. 127 (3), 291–295.

Close, F.E., 2009. Nothing: a very short introduction. Oxford University Press, Oxford, New York.

Cole, S.A., 2009. Forensics without uniqueness, conclusions without individualisation: the new epistemology of forensic identification. Law Probablity and Risk 8 (3), 233–255.

Cole, S.A., 2001. Suspect Identities: A history of fingerprinting and criminal identification. Harvard University Press, Cambridge, MA.

Collins, E.R., Stone, R.S., 2005. How Unique Are Impressed Toolmarks? An emprical study of 20 worn hammer faces. AFTE J. 37 (4), 252–295.

Daubert v Merrell Dow Pharmaceuticals Inc, 1995. II 43 F.3d 1311 (9th Cir)

Dawkins, R., 1976. The Selfish Gene. Oxford University Press, New York.

Drinnan, A.J., Melton, M.J., 1985. Court presentation of bite mark evidence. International dental journal 35 (4), 316.

English, W.R., Robison, S.F., Summitt, J.B., Oesterle, L.J., Brannon, R.B., Morlang, W.M., 1988. Individuality of human palatal rugae. Journal of forensic sciences 33 (3), 718.

Epstein, R., 2001. Fingerprints Meet Daubert: The Myth of Fingerprint Science Is Revealed. S. Cal. L Rev. 75, 605.

Erdmann, M.V., Caldwell, R.L., Moosa, M.K., 1998. Indonesian "king of the sea" discovered. Nature 395, 335.

Faigman, D.L., 2007. Anecdotal Forensics, Phrenology and Other Abject Lessons from the History of Science. Hastings L.J. 59, 979–1000.

Freeman, R.A., 1986. Consecutively rifled polygon barrels. AFTE J. 18 (3), 15–52.

Galton, F., 1892. Finger prints. Macmillan and Co, London, New York.

Gimbel, S., 2011. Exploring the Scientific Method. University of Chicago Press, Chicago.

Harris, A.M., Wood, R.E., Nortje, C.J., Thomas, C.J., 1987. The frontal sinus: forensic fingerprint? A pilot study. The Journal of Forensic Odonto-Stomatology 5 (1), 9.

Hatcher, J.S., Jury, F.J., Weller, J., 1957. Firearms Investigation. Identification and Evidence. The Stackpole Company, Harrisburg (Pennsylvania).

Henson, B., Politovich, M., 1995. Let it Snow, Let it Snow, Let it Snow. http://www.proquest k12.com/curr/snow/snow395/snow395.htm#snow, accessed on

Inman, K., Rudin, K., 1997. An Introduction to Forensic DNA Analysis. CRC Press, Boca Raton, Florida.

Jain, A.K., Prabhakar, S., Pankanti, S., 2002. On the similarity of identical twin fingerprints. Pattern Recognition 35 (11), 2653–2663.

Kaye, D.H., 2003. Questioning a courtroom proof of the uniqueness of fingerprints. Int. Stat. Rev. 71 (3), 521–533.

Kaye, D.H., 2009. Identification, individualization and uniqueness: What's the difference? Law Probablity and Risk 8 (1), 55–66.

Kaye, D.H., 2010. Probability, Individualisation and Uniqueness in Forensic Science Evidence: Listening to the Academies. Brooklyn. L Rev., In Press.

Keiser-Nielsen, S., 1975. Certainty v Probability in Dental Identification. Second Continuing Education Course in Forensic Odontology, November 1-2 1975.

Keiser-Nielsen, S., 1977. Dental Identification: Certainty V Probability. Forensic Science 9, 87–97.

Keiser-Nielsen, S., 1980. Personal Identification by Means of the Teeth. John Wright and Sons, Bristol.

Kieser, J.A., Bernal, V., 2007. Author's Response to Dr Bowers. J. Forensic Sci. 52 (6), 1418.

Kieser, J.A., Bernal, V., Neil Waddell, J., Raju, S., 2007. The uniqueness of the human anterior dentition: a geometric morphometric analysis. J. cole Forensic Sci. 52 (3), 671–677.

Kruszelnicki, K.S., 2006. Snowflakes Identical. http://www.abc.net.au/science/articles/2006/1 1/13/1784760.htm, accessed on 14 January, 2010.

Kwan, Q.Y., 1977. Inference of Identity of Source. Ph.D. Thesis, University of California.

Lardizabal, P.P., 1995. Cartridge case study of the Heckler & Koch USP. AFTE J. 27 (1), 49–51.

Lee, H.C., Gaensslen, R.E., 2001. Advances in fingerprint technology. CRC Press, Boca Raton, Fla.

Leibniz, G.W., Rescher, N., 1991. G.W. Leibniz's Monadology (1714): An edition for students. University of Pittsburgh Press, Pittsburgh, PA.

MacDonald, D.G., Laird, W.R.E., 1977. Bite marks in a murder case. Int. J. Forensic Dent. 3, 24–27.

MacFarlane, T.W., MacDonald, D.G., Sutherland, D.A., 1974. Statistical Problems in Dental Identification. J. Forensic Sci. Soc. 14, 247–252.

Marriot, A., Harding, W., Devlin, N., Benwell, G., 2001. The delivery of orthodontic care in New Zealand. Part 1: Analysis of a census of orthodontists. NZDJ. 97, 87–92.

Mayer, J., 1935. Identification by Sinus Prints. Virginia Med., Monthly, Dec, 517–519.

McLachlan, H., 1995. No two sets the same? Applying philosophy to the theory of fingerprints. Philosopher 83 (2), 12–18.

Meuwly, D., 2006. Forensic individualisation from biometric data. Science & Justice 46 (4), 205–213.

Miller, R.G., Bush, P.J., Dorion, R.B., Bush, M.A., 2009. Uniqueness of the dentition as impressed in human skin: a cadaver model. J. Forensic Sci. 54 (4), 909–914.

Mnookin, J.L., 2001. Fingerprint Evidence in an Age of DNA Profiling Symposium: DNA Lessons from the Past–Problems for the Future. Brook. L Rev. 67, 13–70.

Moenssens, A.A., 1999. Panel III. Junk Science, Pre-Science and Developing Science National Conference on Science and Law, 1999.

National Research Council, 1996. The Evaluation of Forensic DNA evidence National Academy Press.

National Research Council, 2009. Strengthening Forensic Science in the United States. A Path Forward National Academies Press.

Nichols, R.G., 2007. Defending the scientific foundations of the firearms and tool mark identification discipline: responding to recent challenges. J. Forensic Sci. 52 (3), 586–594.

Pankanti, S., Prabhakar, S., Jain, A.K., 2002. On the individuality of fingerprints. IEEE Transactions on Pattern Analysis and Machine Intelligence, 1010–1025.

Pearson, K., 1930. The Life and Letters of Sir Francis Galton. University Press, Cambridge.

People v. Milone 356 N.E.2d 1350, 1358 (Ill. App. Ct. 1976)

People v. Smith, 443 N.Y.S.2d 551, 556B57 (Cty. Ct. 1981)

Phillips, V.L., Saks, M.J., Peterson, J.L., 2001. The application of signal detection theory to decision-making in forensic science. J. Forensic Sci. 46 (2), 294–308.

Popper, K., 2002. The Logic of Scientific Discovery. Routledge, London.

Pretty, I.A., 2003. A web-based survey of odontologist's opinions concerning bitemark analyses. J. Forensic Sci. 48 (5), 1117–1120.

Pretty, I.A., Sweet, D., 2001. The scientific basis for human bitemark analyses - a critical review. Sci. Justice 41 (2), 85–92.

R. v. Lewis, 1987. 29 A Crim R 267.

Rawson, R.D., Ommen, R.K., Kinard, G., Johnson, J., Yfantis, A., 1984. Statistical evidence for the individuality of the human dentition. J. Forensic Sci. 29 (1), 245–253.

Reichs, K.J., 1993. Quantified comparison of frontal sinus patterns by means of computed tomography. Forensic Sci. Int. 61 (2-3), 141–168.

Roach, J., 2007. "No Two Snowflakes the Same Likely True, Research Reveals." http://news.nationalgeographic.com/news/2007/02/070213-snowflake.html, accessed on 14 January, 2010.

Roxburgh, T., 1933. Galton's work on the Evidential Value of Finger Prints. Sankhya: Indian Journal of Statistics 1, 50–62.

Russell, B., 2004. The problems of philosophy (1912). Barnes & Noble Books, New York.

Saks, M.J., 2009. Forensic Identification Science: A Summary of the Theory, the Science and the Legal History. [Updated version of Merlin and Solomon: Lessons from the Law's formative Encounters with Forensic Identification Science, 49 Hastings L J. 1069(1998)].

Saks, M.J., Koehler, J.J., 2008. The Individualization Fallacy in Forensic Science Evidence. Vand. L Rev. 61, 199–220.

Schmid, R.E., 1988. Identical Snowflakes Cause Flurry. The Boston Globe, June 15.

Snyder, C.R., Fromkin, H.L., 1980. Uniqueness, the human pursuit of difference.

Sognnaes, R.F., Rawson, R.D., Gratt, B.M., Nguyen, N.B.T., 1982. Computer comparison of bitemark patterns in identical twins. J.A.D.A 105, 449–451.

Sparrow, M.K., 1994. Measuring AFIS matcher accuracy. The Police Chief., April, 147.

Srihari, S.N., 2009. Quantitative Assessment of the Individuality of Friction Ridge Patterns: Final Report submitted to the U.S. Department of Justice.

Starrs, J.E., 1999. Judicial Control over Scientific Supermen. Fingerprint experts and others who exceed the bounds. Crim. Law Bull 35 (3), 234–276.

Fortin, State v, 2007. N.J. LEXIS 333 (Unreported).

Stevenson, J., 2005. The Complete Idiot's Guide to Philosophy. Alpha, New York.

Stone, I.C., Wilmovsky, A., 1984. Evidentiary Basis for Fingernail Striation Association. J. Pol. Sci. Admin. 12, 291–296.

Stone, R.S., 2003. How unique are impressed toolmarks? AFTE J. 35 (4), 376–383.

Stoney, D.A., 1991. What made us ever think we could individualize using statistics? Journal of the Forensic Science Society 31 (2), 197–199.

Stoney, D.A., 1988. Distribution of Epidermal Ridge Minutiae. Am. J. Phys. Anthropol. 77, 367–376.

Stoney, D.A., Thornton, J.I., 1986. A Critical Analysis of Qualitative Fingerprint Individuality Models. J. Forensic Sci. 31 (4), 1187–1216.

Stove, D.C., 1982. Popper and After: Four Modern Irrationalists. Permagon Press, Sydney.

Thomas Johnson, L., Blinka, D.D., VanScotter Asbach, P., Radner, T.W., 2008. Quantification of the Individual Characteristics of the Human Dentition: Methodology. J. Forensic Identification 58 (4), 409–509.

Thomas Johnson, L., et al., 2009. Quantification of the Individual Characteristics of the Human Dentition. J. Forensic Identification 59 (6), 609–626.

Thomson, K.S., 1991. Living fossil: the story of the coelacanth. W.W. Norton, New York.

Thornton, J.I., 1986. The Snowflake Paradigm. J. Forensic Sci. 31 (2), 399–401.

United States v. Byron Mitchell. Criminal Action No. 96–407, US District Court for the Eastern District of Pennsylvania, 1999.

United States v. Green 405 F.Supp.2d 104 (D.Mass. 2005)

Wayman, J.L., 2000. When Bad Science Leads to Good Law: The disturbing irony of the Daubert hearing in the case of U.S. v. Byron C. Mitchell. www.engr.sjsu.edu/biometrics/publications_daubert.html, accessed on 04 March, 2010.

Weir, B.S., 1999. Are DNA Profiles Unique? Proceedings of the Ninth International Symposium on Human Identification, 1999.

Wilkins, J.S., 1998. What's in a Meme? Reflections from the perspective of the history and philosophy of evolutionary biology. Journal of Memetics-Evolutionary Models of Information Transmission 2 (1), available at http://cfpm.org/jom-emit/1998/vol2/wilkins_js.html.

THE INNOCENCE BLOG

Robert Lee Stinson

Contributing Causes of Erroneous Conviction: unvalidated or improper forensic science.

Robert Lee Stinson served over 23 years in a Wisconsin prison for a brutal rape and murder DNA proves he did not commit. He was convicted based on the improper and unvalidated expert testimony of a bite-mark analyst whose conclusions were uncontested at trial.

The Crime

Early in the morning of November 3, 1984, a neighbor passing through an alley on his way to work discovered the body of 63-year-old Ione Cychosz in a vacant lot behind her home. She had been raped, stabbed and beaten to death. Her clothing was scattered around the lot. Spermatozoa cells were found in a vaginal wash, but the number of cells retrieved was too few for identification purposes. Eight bite marks, inflicted prior to death, were also identified on the victim's body.

The victim was last seen shortly after midnight, only a few hours before the murder, when a friend had dropped her off and watched her enter her building. The coroner later estimated that the time of death was between midnight and 2 a.m.

The Investigation

After examining the body, dental scientist Dr. Lowell Thomas Johnson worked with a police sketch artist and determined that the bite-marks on the body must have come from someone missing an upper front tooth.

The police questioned multiple suspects, including two men arrested for violent sexual assaults shortly after Cychosz was murdered. Both of these men had missing teeth consistent with Dr. Johnson's sketch. Police investigators also visited 21-year-old Robert Lee Stinson, whose backyard was connected to the vacant lot where Cychosz's body was discovered. While interviewing Stinson, the investigators told him a joke, and noticed both a missing front tooth and a crooked tooth when he laughed. Based on these observations, and his proximity to the crime scene, Stinson was arrested and charged with murder.

Trial

The only physical evidence against Stinson at his 1985 trial was the bite-mark testimony of two forensic odontologists. Dr. Johnson concluded that the bite marks "had to have been made by teeth identical" to Stinson's, and claimed that there was "no margin for error" in his conclusion. The State also called Dr. Raymond Rawson, the chairman of the Bite Mark Standards Committee of the American Board of Forensic Odontologists, who testified that the evidence in the case was "high quality" and "overwhelming." However, the prosecution's experts failed to note that Stinson was missing a tooth in the place where the bite marks indicated a dentition.

While Stinson's attorney moved to exclude the bite-mark testimony, he did not object to the qualifications of the State's expert witnesses, nor did he call his own expert to testify, although one had been retained. According to Stinson's attorney, he was unable to find qualified experts because Dr. Johnson had presented the results of his analysis at an odontological conference before the trial, and therefore many experts felt their analysis had already been tainted by Dr. Johnson's conclusions.

Stinson also gave inconsistent accounts of his whereabouts at the time of the murder, but as the prosecution admitted at trial, the crux of their case was based on the bite mark analysis. After a three-day trial, Stinson was convicted of first-degree murder on the strength of the forensic testimony, and sentenced to life in prison. There was no other direct evidence linking him to the murder.

THE INNOCENCE BLOG—Cont'd

On appeal, Stinson argued that the bite-mark testimony was not credible and claimed that he had been denied effective assistance of counsel. At trial, Stinson had attempted to replace his appointed counsel, since his attorney had only been on the case for two weeks and had not had time to prepare an adequate defense. Stinson also claimed to have a personality conflict with his attorney. His appeal was denied, and his conviction was upheld.

Post-Conviction

The improper bite-mark testimony would eventually provide the spark that cleared Stinson, but it took 20 years. The Wisconsin Innocence Project accepted Stinson's case in 2005, and sought DNA testing of saliva and blood-stains on the victim's sweater, which ultimately excluded Stinson. Yet this would not be enough. Working with Christopher Plourd, a California forensic science expert and attorney, the Wisconsin Innocence Project re-examined the bite-mark evidence and determined that Stinson did not match the indentations. Moreover, a panel of four nationally recognized experts independently reviewed the findings and unanimously reached the same conclusion.

Dr. Johnson now works at Marquette University with the prosecutor who tried Stinson's case. He stood by his conclusions, as did the prosecutor, who noted that, "nobody in the state of Wisconsin had done a bite-mark rape-murder case like this one before.... So we were really reinventing the wheel."

The Milwaukee County District Attorney's Office did not oppose Stinson's motion to overturn his conviction. On January 30, 2009, Circuit Judge Patricia McMahon granted the motion, and Robert Lee Stinson, then 44, was freed and his conviction was vacated. He had served more than two decades in prison for a crime DNA evidence proves he didn't commit. After his release, the District Attorney's office had six months to decide whether or not to retry him. Finally, at a hearing on July 27, 2009, prosecutors, after undertaking their own investigation, dropped all charges against Stinson.

Since his release, Stinson has moved into his sister's Milwaukee home with her children. He also plans on writing a book about his wrongful conviction.

Forensic Failures

10

Brent E. Turvey

Forensic Solutions, LLC, Sitka, Alaska

...the scientist who declines to practice his or her profession by the rules of science will soon find that he or she has earned only the derision of his or her colleagues, and eventually finds that he or she cannot continue to practice at all.

Dr. John I. Thornton, Criminalist (1994, p. 483)

The term *forensic examiner* generally refers to any professional who examines and interprets physical evidence with the expectation of courtroom testimony.[1] As this would suggest, forensic examiners are responsible for the scientific investigation that takes place within the context of a criminal investigation. They are expected to analyze evidence in a scientific manner, to interpret the results objectively, and to report their findings faithfully (Chisum & Turvey, 2011).

Despite the many misinformed fictional portrayals to the contrary, forensic examiners are not intended to be decision makers in the criminal justice system. For instance, they do not generally have the authority to make arrests or take life, they do not rule on the admissibility of evidence in court proceedings, and they do not decide whether a defendant is guilty or innocent (Crowder & Turvey, 2013). This is intentional, as the goals of the forensic examiner must remain ideologically separate from those of the police, the prosecution, and the courts to maintain scientific impartiality (Edwards & Gotsonis, 2009).

The purpose of this chapter is to discuss what happens when there is a failure with respect to forensic examinations, whether it be on the part of a single professional, among laboratory supervisors, or across an entire laboratory system. It will demonstrate that such failures cannot occur in a vacuum, and that they are often the result of influences that are external to the mandates of good science. That is to say, forensic failures are a function of both examiner shortcomings and cultural pressures (Turvey, 2013).

---

[1] Some portions of this chapter have been adapted from writing originally prepared for Crowder & Turvey (2013) and Turvey (2013).

Forensic Testimony. http://dx.doi.org/10.1016/B978-0-12-397005-3.00010-4

179

10.1 Cultural conflicts

Whether employed by the prosecution or the defense, forensic examiners are meant to serve as an objective filter within the criminal justice system. Their first onus is to dispassionately establish the objective facts of a case as determined by a scientific analysis of the evidence. They are not interested in seeking out evidence that only supports the theories of a particular institution, employer, or side. A forensic examiner must therefore work to establish the scientific facts and their contextual meaning with no investment in the outcome. Ultimately, their findings can be used to educate investigators, attorneys, courts, and juries, which ideally helps to generate more informed legal outcomes.

As described throughout this text, the forensic science enterprise is complex. It is made more difficult, however, by its suffusion with conflicted goals and expectations from different quarters of the criminal justice system. The objective and impartial creed of forensic examiners may even be at odds with the culture, code, and conduct promoted within the organizations that employ them. This remains true to varying degrees, whether they work for law enforcement, a public agency, or for a private company.[2]

10.1.1 Scientific integrity

First, consider the needs of the forensic sciences. Forensic examiners are primarily concerned with fostering and promoting a culture of scientific integrity. This ensures that the results of their examinations are reliable, valid, and generally reputable. Scientific integrity requires demonstrations of impartiality, knowledge of scientific methodology, and the employment of scientific methodology (Gardenier, 2011; Jette, 2005; NAS, 2002; and NAS, 2009). There is also a corresponding need for maintaining transparency in methodology, so that others may engage in peer review, whether this involves published research or forensic casework that may need to be evaluated by opposing counsel.

These mandates of good science require that professional incompetence and apathy must also be addressed. As explained in Faigman, Kaye, Saks, and Sanders (2004; p. 69): "The appropriate response to complexity should not be to call in the witch doctor for a magic spell, but rather to demand the best science available and remain aware of its limitations." Unfortunately, too many forensic examiners are incompletely or improperly educated and trained, the result of being drawn from non-scientist ranks or of being professionally neglected as a function of internal politics or diminished training budgets. This despite the reality that science demands a solid education in the sciences and ongoing training to keep examiners up to date.

---

[2] Police crime laboratories have traditionally employed the vast majority of forensic examiners. This is primarily because of law enforcement dominion over the crime scene, and the subsequent responsibility for physical evidence collection and testing (DeForest, 2005; Thornton & Peterson, 2007). Despite the growth of private forensic laboratories, the regular and increased outsourcing of government forensic services to the private sector (Peterson & Hickman, 2005; Durose, 2008), and the use of forensic experts by defense attorneys, this occupational dominance remains (Edwards and Gotsonis, 2009).

10.1.2 **Alternative rules and missions**

As mentioned, it is not going too far to state that these scientific requirements conflict directly with the values espoused by the majority of forensic science employers (Turvey, 2013). Generally speaking, competing cultural interests can include those of law enforcement, attorneys, and the courts. Each of these realms has their own rules and missions which distinguish them from the scientific endeavor. Law enforcement seeks to investigate and arrest criminal suspects, attorneys seek to prosecute or defend criminal suspects, and the courts are meant to referee the resulting legal proceedings (Crowder & Turvey, 2013).

Consider, for example, lawyers at trial: They are interested in only the facts and evidence that assist their case. The rest they may be content to distort or ignore. This is discussed in Ingraham (1987, p. 183):

> [O]ne often hears the following specious argument that the adversarial system
> has a built-in protection against the partial, partisan, and one-sided presentation
> of the evidence: 'Not to worry. What is left uncovered by one side of the dispute
> will surely be brought out and highlighted by the other side. Before the case is
> over, the jury will have these facts in its possession. Moreover, it will have all the
> facts critically evaluated, their having passed through a searing test of rigorous
> cross-examination.'
> ...[I]t rarely works out this way. It is not always in the best interest of the other
> side to bring out evidence that has been omitted or obfuscated by opposing coun-
> sel; that evidence may be just as damaging to the 'version' that the other side is
> pressing. Thus, quite frequently, both sides will obscure or omit facts essential for
> a just and impartial assessment of the event for tactical reasons, with the result
> that the jury never gets the full story.

In their attempts to craft the most favorable version of events for their arguments, there is often little regard from attorneys for the objective truth-seeking function of the forensic sciences. This reality often places them at cross-purposes. It is not made one bit easier by the fact that while the scientist must respect the courts and the law, the opposite is not also true. This is noted in Thornton (1994, p. 483):

> Every scientist understands that there are courts of law. By and large, they are
> accorded respect. I am not as certain that every lawyer understands that there are
> courts of science as well.

It is also necessary to confess that forensic scientists are at a terrific disadvantage when they practice within the justice system. This must be conceded at the outset of any forensic endeavor, in order to recognize the potential for abuse. A useful discussion is found in Thornton (1983, pp. 86–88):

> Basic conflicts that influence the practice of forensic science become apparent at
> the interface of law and science. Law and science on occasion have conflicting
> goals, each having developed in response to different social attitudes and intel-
> lectual needs. The goal of law is the just resolution of human conflict, while the

goal of science traditionally has been cast, although perhaps too smugly, as the search for "truth." Certainly there is nothing intrinsically dichotomous in the pursuit of these goals; the court or jury strive in good faith to determine the truth in a given situation as a way to resolve conflicts. But proof is viewed somewhat differently by law and science, as is the application of logic and the perception of societal values...

How, then, do these differences between law and science lead to abuse of forensic science? They do simply because all the players want to win and are likely to use any ethical means at their disposal to do so. The attorneys in a case are aligned with only one side, and it is entirely appropriate under the adversary system for them to advocate a particular point of view, even without full and fair disclosure of all relevant facts. Subject only to the rules of evidence, the rules of procedure, and the Code of Professional Responsibility, attorneys are free to manipulate scientific evidence to maximize the opportunity for their side to prevail. Not only is behavior of this sort countenanced by the law, it is the ethical responsibility of counsel to attempt to do so.

In all reality, the domains of science and law are so divergent and so foreign to each other's purpose that some argue forensic experts can only be abused in legal proceedings. For example, according to Ingraham (1987, p. 179):

The adversary 'game' is not a procedure whose underlying purpose is to communicate facts or determine truth but rather to communicate position statements about reality, and ultimately the expert witness is forced into the role of a coadvocate selling a partisan position to the trier-of-fact rather than an impartial source of information.

The subordination of science to attorneys, the courts, and their mercurial interpretations of the law remains a daily occurrence in the criminal justice system. It happens each time a judge makes a legal ruling about the reliability of any scientific evidence, methodology, or related testimony in such a manner as to limit or preclude its admissibility. Often this will be based on incomplete, uninformed, and erroneous argumentation from counsel with limited or no testimony from objective forensic practitioners. And often this will conflict with rulings in another courtroom, whether across the nation or just down the hallway. This does not look likely to change anytime soon.

Forensic examiners accept these realities and do their best to avoid being abused by either side of the courtroom. In doing so, they would do well to heed the following cautionary statement from Thornton and Peterson (2007, p.4):

Forensic science is science exercised on behalf of the law in the just resolution of conflict. It is therefore expected to be the handmaiden of the law, but at the same time this expectation may very well be the marina from which is launched the tension that exists between the two disciplines.

To be clear, acting as a handmaid is not necessarily a corrupted role, so long as the correct priorities are being attended. While some jurists will still seek to manipulate the findings of the ethical forensic examiner, at least there will be something scientifically competent of use to those who would defend against such manipulations. Otherwise, science abandons the courts to themselves, and this is no good solution.

10.1.3 Scientific priorities

Forensic science must do its best to avoid abuse, and there is no better way than by learning and adhering to practices that ensure scientific integrity. Therefore, regardless of their employment circumstances and the strain placed on forensic examiners by those around them, scientific integrity must be the first priority. This demands that forensic professionals be knowledgeable, competent, and ethical, that they remain impartial in their work despite their employer's needs, and that they seek to avoid cultural strain, pressure, or incentives to engage in deliberate misconduct (Chisum & Turvey, 2011; Crowder & Turvey, 2013; Edwards & Gotsonis, 2009; NAS, 2002; Turvey 2013). Failure at any of these is not acceptable, as explained in Thornton (1994; p. 483):

> The scientist who declines to practice his or her profession by the rules of science will soon find that he or she has earned only the derision of his or her colleagues, and eventually finds that he or she cannot continue to practice at all.

10.2 Scientific misconduct

The literature is clear with respect to the obligations of scientists and their institutional employers to uphold values that promote scientific integrity. This includes acknowledging that there are those operating within different scientific communities who recklessly or intentionally fail to understand, uphold, and promote these obligations (Judson, 2004; Martinson, Anderson, & de Vries, 2005; Sovacool, 2008; Titus, Wells, & Rhoades, 2008). This is in part because of human error, and the fact that "[scientific] norms represent ideal behavior, and so it is to be expected that scientists' actual behavior will fall short of perfect adherence to the norms" (Anderson, Martinson, & De Vries, 2007; p. 3). This is also, in part, owing to acts of fraud (McDowell, 2010).

The most serious violations of scientific integrity are referred to by the Office of Research Integrity (ORI) as scientific misconduct, which is defined as "fabrication, falsification, or plagiarism (FFP) in proposing, performing, or reviewing research, or in reporting research results" (NAS, 2009, p. 3). As described, scientific misconduct is a reference to fraud; it involves intentional misrepresentations by scientists designed to secure an unfair or unlawful gain. In fact, the literature treats the terms scientific fraud and scientific misconduct as essentially interchangeable. However, the term fraud is fraught with legal implications. As not all research violations involve a crime, the term misconduct has been adopted by the scientific community as the official substitute when dealing with actionable allegations in the context of internal institutional investigations (Catano & Turk, 2007; Resnick, 2003; Reynolds, 2004).

The major forms of scientific misconduct are operationalized in the ORI's "Policies on Research Misconduct" (ORI, 2009, p. 5):

(a) Fabrication is making up data or results and recording or reporting them.
(b) Falsification is manipulating research materials, equipment, or processes, or changing or omitting data or results such that the research is not accurately represented in the research record.
(c) Plagiarism is the appropriation of another person's ideas, processes, results, or words without giving appropriate credit.
(d) Research misconduct does not include honest error or differences of opinion.

These concepts are further described in Reider (2010, p. 445):

> The colloquial term for fabrication is 'dry-labbing,' making up results for experiments or trials that never occurred.... The term falsification is applied when research actually took place, but the results have been manipulated, modified, or edited so that the published work no longer accurately reflects the scientific findings.

Though not listed by the ORI in a pedantic sense, it has been demonstrated that scientific misconduct also includes ghost authorship, suppression of unfavorable results, the falsification of researcher credentials, and sexual harassment when these actions have the potential to affect the results or interpretations of scientific inquiries (Krimsky, 2007; Parrish, 1996).

10.3 Differentiating fraud and negligence

Now that we have an initial sense of what scientific failure might look like on paper, it is necessary to distinguish the concepts of fraud and error. Then we can get into the specifics of each in subsequent sections.

10.3.1 Negligence

Negligence is defined as "the failure to use such care as a reasonably prudent and careful person would use under similar circumstances" (Black, 1990, p.1032). In a professional context, it is "conduct which falls below the standard established by law for the protection of others against unreasonable risk of harm ... it is characterized chiefly by inadvertence, thoughtlessness, inattention, and the like" (Black, 1990, p.1032). Consider the following case example:

Case Example: Mark Boese, Director, Tulsa Police Department Crime Laboratory

Mark Boese was former director of the Tulsa Police Department Crime Laboratory in Oklahoma. Mr. Boese had been employed as a civilian by the Tulsa Police Department since 1999, when he was fired for negligence and incompetence, as reported in Marshall (2010):

An investigation revealed that he 'failed to perform his duties as lab director and firearms examiner and failed to properly supervise,' [Officer Jason] Willingham said.

…In a personnel order from Interim Chief Chuck Jordan, he is accused of numerous violations of both city and Tulsa Police Department rules, regulations and policies.

…Among the allegations against Boese is that he failed to comply with repeated instructions to 'properly locate and secure evidence as required by policy' beginning in March, the order states. After he was placed on administrative leave, numerous improperly handled and incomplete files were found in Boese's office, along with some evidentiary items, the personnel order states.

'Your inaction and tardiness caused inefficiency in the DNA and Firearms Sections,' Jordan wrote in the order. Boese also is accused of failing to update a firearms manual to meet international lab requirements despite having been directed to do so several times. He is accused of trying to coerce a subordinate to complete that job responsibility, the record states.

In another situation, Boese examined a firearm that was involved in a homicide in September 2008, yet 'due to negligence, inefficiency or incompetence you could not locate the case file containing your notes and did not complete a written report of your finding until October 9, 2009,' the record states.

The findings were submitted after the discovery cutoff in the homicide case following repeated pleas from the District Attorney's Office, it states. 'Your behavior as outlined in this document evinces a clear and incontrovertible pattern and practice of incompetence, inefficiency, and gross neglect of duty,' Jordan wrote in the order. 'For many years you have ignored polices and rules well-known to you.'

On suspension for about two weeks prior to his firing, Mr. Boese had been suspended by the Tulsa Police Department at least once before. In 2007, he was reprimanded for making an ethnic slur toward Hispanics and using derogatory language regarding other Tulsa Police employees. In that case, he was suspended for 10 days without pay and required to attend sensitivity training.

According to Mr. Boese's attorney, his termination was unfounded and he intended to appeal. However, those efforts proved unsuccessful. In 2012, Mr. Boese passed away at the age of 51.

Ultimately, the Tulsa Police Department Crime Laboratory received accreditation under the direction of another lab employee, Tara Valouch.

It is also negligent for an agency to retain an incompetent, unethical, or fraudulent examiner. Doing so can incur future liability and might willfully contribute to miscarriages of justice. However, the agency may not be given a choice. Consider the following case example:

Case Example: Michael Short, Criminalist, Canton-Stark County Crime Laboratory

From 2012 to early 2013, the Canton-Stark County Crime Laboratory has suffered one scandal after the next related to poor or improper management.

First, it was the crime lab director: "The city lowered the job qualifications for the director of the Canton-Stark County Crime Lab and then hand-picked a retired county sheriff's investigator for the post without advertising the vacancy" (Rink, 2013a). The retired police officer, Rick Perez, had no science or management qualifications to speak of. He was subsequently forced to resign the position under significant pressure from the Mayor's office and the city council. They had been kept in the dark by Canton Safety Director Thomas Ream and Canton Police Chief Bruce Lawver, who jointly orchestrated and initially defended the decision.

Then there is the ongoing Michael Short scandal. In May of 2012, Canton-Stark County Crime Lab criminalist Michael Short was fired for violations related to incompetence and falsifying reports. With respect to poor job performance, Mr. Short is reported to have failed to notice a bullet hole in a garment during examination. However, this was the least of it, as reported in Balint (2012a):

The falsification violation stems from Short's gunshot-related analysis in January in a felonious assault case…

In paperwork, Short used the term, 'using the firearm,' which investigators say indicated the gun had been test-fired when it had not.

Short said that the description of 'using the firearm' did not mean he test-fired the weapon, according to Ream's report. Short told a police investigator that there was not a code in the computer to specify that he didn't discharge the gun.

Short explained that his results —in determining the distance from which the gun was fired — were gained through past experience with firearms and ammunition.

An accreditation program manager told an investigator that basing lab results on experience without conducting the examination is not an acceptable practice when the items that are to be tested are available.

In addition, a crime lab employee told an investigator that he returned reports to Short to be done correctly regarding the gun-related analysis and the test-firing of a firearm. The reports, which were not corrected or administratively reviewed, were placed in a bin to be sent back to the submitting law- enforcement agency, according to police records.

However, subsequent to an appeal, Mr. Short was reinstated, as reported in Balint (2012b): "The Canton Civil Service Commission recently ruled that Michael Short should be reinstated, but he was given a 120-day suspension without pay." This because they felt that Mr. Short had not intentionally falsified the report, but rather that he had simply made an administrative error. As further reported in Balint (2012b), this decision was greatly influenced by character testimony from the prosecutor's office and the *judiciary*[3]:

---

[3] This positive character testimony should not be a surprise, as Mr. Short's expert testimony was key to securing many successful prosecutions. Keeping him employed would be in the prosecution's interests, with respect to protecting those convictions.

At the civil service hearing late last month, Assistant Stark County Prosecutor Dennis Barr and Stark County Common Pleas Court Judge Lee Sinclair were called as witnesses by Attorney Robert Tscholl representing Mr. Short at the civil service hearing, and both officials complimented the quality of Short's work, Samuel Sliman, the city's civil service director said. The testimony was influential in the commission's decision…

In March of 2013, Mr. Short was fired by the crime lab once more. The initial termination had triggered a more extensive internal review of his casework from 2007 through June of 2012. The results of that audit lead to the second firing, and new accusations reported in Rink (2013c):

Among the new accusations the city made against Short is that he never tested two pieces of clothing for gunshot residue in the murder trial of Ryan L. Hamrick of West Virginia, even though he testified to a jury that he had. Hamrick was convicted in 2011 of fatally shooting Demeris Tillman, 30, of East Cleveland, on Nov. 15, 2009, while the men were traveling from Ohio to West Virginia.

'It appears he did not do any chemical examination of the items to identify gunshot residue which would be necessary to conclude that gunshot residue existed or not due to the fact the victim was found laying in a creek for four days and the clothing was extremely soiled,' according to the Internal Affairs report. '… His testimony in Common Pleas Court … is unsatisfactory at best.'

Short also is accused of filing 147 false reports. More than 100 of the reports showed he entered ballistics information into the National Integrated Ballistic Information Network, but no evidence could be found that he actually did. He's also accused of falsely reporting 36 times that he test fired cartridges from firearms.

In other cases, Short failed to complete reports, and label and seal evidence. The Internal Affairs report found that Short did not adhere to the crime lab's analytical procedures or quality assurance standards.

The case has been reviewed by the Ohio Attorney General's Office and the Canton City Law Department.

As of this writing, Mr. Short is appealing his latest termination to the Canton Civil Service Commission.

10.3.2 Fraud

Fraud is distinguished from negligence, ignorance, and error by virtue of the fact that it is intentional, involving some level of calculation (Albrecht & Albrecht, 2003). Fraud is not accidental in nature, nor is it unplanned (Albrecht, Albrecht, Albrecht, & Zimbelman, 2011; Black, 1990; Lord, 2010). Those who commit fraud know what they are doing and are deliberate in their efforts. They are also aware that it is unethical, illegal, or otherwise improper.

In the most general terms, fraudulent intent is established by examining the documentation and behavior associated with those under suspicion. As explained in Coenen (2008, p. 8): "Manipulation of documents and evidence is often indicative of such intent. Innocent parties don't normally alter documents and conceal or destroy evidence." Other indicators can include obstructing a fraud investigation by lying or concealing pertinent information, a known history of fraudulent behavior, and being the direct recipient of benefits from suspected fraudulent acts (Coenen, 2008). Consider the following case example:

Case Example: David Kofoed, Chief Crime Scene Investigator, Douglas County Sheriff's Office Crime Laboratory

David Kofoed is the former Chief Crime Scene Investigator for the Douglas County Sheriff's Office in Omaha, Nebraska. In 2010, he was convicted of a felony (tampering with evidence) for falsifying blood evidence against two suspects in a double homicide. Mr. Kofoed spent about a year and a half in jail, failing in his appeal to the Nebraska Supreme Court for a new trial, as reported in Kelly (2012):

> ### Cass County, Neb.: The Murder of Wayne and Sharmon Stock
> *The faulty evidence in this double homicide in Murdock, Neb. landed Kofoed in prison. The Stocks were murdered in their bedroom on Easter night, 2006.*
>
> *Investigators from the Cass County Sheriff's Department and the Nebraska State Patrol succeeded in getting Matt Livers, the Stocks' nephew, to confess to the crime and implicate another man, Nick Sampson. Before the confession was discovered to be coerced and false, Kofoed claimed he found a small trace of blood in a vehicle owned by Sampson's brother.*
>
> *Suspicions about the source of that blood peaked when other evidence led police to the real killers, a pair of teenagers from Wisconsin.*
>
> *When the Nebraska Supreme Court denied Kofoed's request for a new trial, it did not end legal action related to the case. Livers and Sampson filed a civil lawsuit in U.S. District Court claiming their civil rights were denied when they were jailed without reliable evidence.*
>
> *Along with Kofoed, the case seeks damages from his former employer, the Douglas County Sheriff's Office, the Cass County Sheriff's Department, and the Nebraska State Patrol. Both the organizations and individual officers named as defendants have asked to be dropped from the suit. This spring, the Eighth District Federal Appeals Court convened in Minneapolis to hear arguments. The three-judge panel will decide if any—or all of them—should be included in the lawsuit, and if it should be allowed to proceed.*
>
> *In his argument before the court, the attorney for Livers, Locke Bowman of MacArthur Justice Center at Northwestern University in Chicago, argued that no one in the case properly shared evidence that could have cleared his client, known in law enforcement as exculpatory evidence.*

> *'This record reflects appalling, massive ignorance on the part of every employee of Douglas County CSI with respect to the obligation to disclose exculpatory evidence,' Bowman said. 'Kofoed obviously didn't get it.' In an interview after the hearing, Bowman said his client wants 'his day in court so he can show the world that he was railroaded' and he hopes for some level of compensation.*

> *Douglas County Sheriff Tim Dunning, also named in the lawsuit, told NET News last fall that he had 'expected more challenges than I have seen.' Dunning initially stood by Kofoed, but by the time the guilty verdict was declared, the sheriff came to believe he and the rest of the CSI unit had been deceived. 'He's gone. He's not coming back. We're not doing business like that ever again,' Dunning said. 'Every piece of what was here that was from him is completely gone.'*

The decision by the Nebraska Supreme Court did not equivocate regarding what it believed to be Mr. Kofoed's utter duplicity, as further reported in Kelly (2012):

> *Writing for the majority, Justice William Connolly wrote: 'Kofoed's deceit was amply demonstrated by the false statements that he made in his reports and the inconsistent statements that he made to investigators.' Connolly added later: '(Kofoed) was tangled in his own web of deceit.'*

Upon his release, Mr. Kofoed was confronted with legal challenges regarding potential falsified evidence in at least two other cases. One involves blood evidence apparently planted in relation to the disappearance of 4-year-old Brendan Gonzalez in 2003. Another involves blood evidence apparently planted in relation to the disappearance of Jessica O'Grady in 2006. In both of these cases, a body was not recovered, and Mr. Kofoed was the one who "discovered" trace amounts of evidence of victims' blood, used to associate a defendant with a murder charge. Both cases also resulted in convictions of defendants that are, as of this writing, under review.

10.4 False testimony

Part of the forensic examiner's job is to ensure that all examinations and results are wholly and effectively communicated to the intended recipients, including investigators, attorneys, and the court (Gannett, 2011). This means that the ethical forensic examiner will refrain from making any false or misleading statements. They will also refrain from false or misleading testimony. This includes statements and testimony regarding education, training, experience, and credentials. As will be discussed in the next section, it also includes testimony regarding the occurrence of examination and testing, the results of examination and testing, and the meaning of those results.

It is important to understand that the law does not always prohibit or penalize false testimony, unless it qualifies as perjury. It must therefore be prohibited by professional organizations and employers. Otherwise, false testimony can go unpunished—which it often does.

Perjury, it must be appreciated, is a strict criminal charge. It is the act of lying or making verifiably false statements on a material matter under oath or affirmation in a court of law or in any sworn statements in writing (Black, 1990). A violation of specific criminal statutes which vary from region to region, it is not sufficient for a statement to be false to meet the threshold of perjury. It must be intentionally false, and it must be regarding a *material fact*: A fact relevant to the case at hand. Consequently, not all intentional lies under oath are considered to be perjury by the court.

For example, in Title 18 of the U.S. Code of Laws, §1621 "General Perjury" provides that perjury involves a person "having taken an oath before a competent tribunal, officer, or person, in any case in which a law of the United States authorizes an oath to be administered, that he will testify, declare, depose, or certify truly, or that any written testimony, declaration, deposition, or certificate by him subscribed, is true, willfully and contrary to such oath states or subscribes any material matter which he does not believe to be true."

As a consequence of this reality, not all intentionally false statements made under oath by a forensic examiner are considered perjury, nor are all forensic examiners who give false testimony under oath charged with a crime. The decision to bring such charges is made at the discretion of the District Attorney's Office in the jurisdiction where the false testimony occurred. Consider the following case example:

Case Example: Kathleen Lundy, Forensic Scientist, FBI Crime Laboratory

Kathleen Lundy held a BS in metallurgy, and was employed as a forensic scientist by the FBI Crime Laboratory. As part of her work, she would routinely testify that bullets or bullet fragments associated with a crime were chemically and "analytically indistinguishable," or "consistent with," boxes of ammunition found in the possession of law enforcement suspects (Ragland v. Commonwealth of Kentucky, 2006). The chemical test that she used in these cases is referred to as comparative bullet lead analysis (a.k.a. CBLA). As described in Giannelli (2007, pp.199-200):

> *In* Ragland v. Commonwealth, *a Kentucky murder case, Lundy got herself in trouble while testifying at a pretrial admissibility hearing. She stated that the elemental composition of a .243 caliber bullet fragment removed from the victim's body was 'analytically indistinguishable' from bullets found at the home of the defendant's parents. Lundy further testified that the Winchester Company purchased its bullet lead in block form prior to 1996 and then remelted it at its manufacturing plant.*

> *During cross-examination at trial, however, Lundy admitted that she knew prior to the hearing that Winchester had purchased its lead in billet form in 1994. This was not a minor point. Millions more bullets could have the same "source" if they were last melted by a secondary smelter instead of by Winchester. Lundy subsequently admitted to her superiors that she had lied, and on June 17, 2003, she pleaded guilty to testifying falsely and was sentenced to a suspended ninety-day jail sentence and a $250 fine.*

Further detail regarding the circumstances of Ms. Lundy's false testimony, and the pressure she was under, was reported in Solomon (2003):

> *FBI lab scientist Kathleen Lundy, an expert witness in murder trials who performs chemical comparisons of lead bullets, was indicted by Kentucky authorities earlier this year on a charge of misdemeanor false swearing after she acknowledged she knowingly gave false testimony in a 2002 pretrial hearing for a murder suspect.*
>
> *Lundy informed her FBI superiors of the false testimony a couple of months after it occurred. By that time she had corrected her pretrial testimony at the trial and had been questioned about it by defense lawyers. Federal authorities decided not to prosecute her, but Kentucky prosecutors brought the misdemeanor charge.*
>
> *In memos and a sworn affidavit, Lundy stated she had an opportunity to correct her erroneous testimony at the hearing, but didn't. 'I had to admit it was worse than being evasive or not correcting the record. It was simply not telling the truth,' Lundy wrote in a memo to a superior. 'I cannot explain why I made the original error in my testimony … nor why, knowing that the testimony was false, I failed to correct it at the time,' Lundy wrote in a subsequent sworn affidavit. 'I was stressed out by this case and work in general.'*
>
> *Lundy also said she was increasingly concerned that a former lab colleague, retired metallurgist William Tobin, was beginning to appear as a defense witness in cases and openly questioning the FBI's science on gun lead. 'These challenges affected me a great deal, perhaps more than they should have. I also felt that there was ineffective support from the FBI to meet the challenges,' Lundy wrote.*

While Kathleen Lundy pleaded guilty to false swearing and lost her job at the FBI crime laboratory, she had already testified as a prosecution expert in CBLA in more than a hundred cases. As of this writing, those cases have all come under review, and at least three convictions secured with her testimony have been overturned.

Ultimately, subsequent to being declared junk science by the National Academies of Science in 2004 (NAS, 2004), the FBI acquiesced and put an end to all CBLA casework in their lab.

10.5 Forensic fraud

As suggested by the definitions in the prior sections, *forensic fraud* may be used to describe a scenario in which forensic examiners provide sworn testimony, opinions, or documents (e.g., affidavits, reports, or professional resumes) bound for court that contain deceptive or misleading information, findings, opinions, or conclusions, deliberately offered in order to secure an unfair or unlawful gain.

Researched and discussed at length in Turvey (2013), forensic fraud is no small problem for the justice system. It results in the conviction of innocents, destroys careers, and creates immense financial liability for law enforcement agencies, individual examiners, and the municipalities that employ them. It also creates incalculable expense for the justice system in general. Forensic fraud is therefore not something to be disregarded, minimized, or otherwise ignored. It is a serious concern that requires the close attention of any professional community intersecting with the forensic sciences.

10.5.1 The research

Much of the research into forensic fraud has come about as a consequence of the work conducted by the Innocence Project in New York. It has revealed that some forensic examiners have no concern for professional ethics whatsoever, and are content to behave in an unethical manner. Consider the following research efforts stemming from their cases.

In a study of 86 DNA exoneration cases, Saks and Koehler (2005) reported the following frequency data: forensic testing errors in 63%; police misconduct in 44%; prosecutorial misconduct in 28%; and false or misleading testimony by forensic experts in 27%.

In a broader study of 340 exonerations between 1989 and 2003, 196 of which did not involve DNA evidence, researchers Gross, Jacoby, Matheson, Montgomery, and Patil (2005) found the following: "In 5 [1.5%] of the exonerations that we have studied there are reports of perjury by police officers. In an additional 24 [7%] we have similar information on perjury by forensic scientists testifying for the government" (p. 19).

Lastly, in the first published study of scientific testimony by prosecution experts in cases where the defendant was eventually exonerated, Garrett and Neufeld (2009) reviewed the transcripts from 137 trials. They found that (pp. 1–2):

> … in the bulk of these trials of innocent defendants—82 cases or 60%—forensic analysts called by the prosecution provided invalid testimony at trial—that is, testimony with conclusions misstating empirical data or wholly unsupported by empirical data. This was not the testimony of a mere handful of analysts: this set of trials included invalid testimony by 72 forensic analysts called by the prosecution and employed by 52 laboratories, practices, or hospitals from 25 states. Unfortunately, the adversarial process largely failed to police this invalid testimony. Defense counsel rarely cross-examined analysts concerning invalid testimony and rarely obtained experts of their own. In the few cases in which invalid forensic science was challenged, judges seldom provided relief.

Examining trial testimony did not reveal the entire picture, however. Garrett and Neufeld discovered, after evaluating "post-conviction review, investigations, or civil discovery" (p. 14), that 13 (10%) of the 137 cases also involved withheld exculpatory evidence. This included three cases that did not involve invalid testimony. Consequently, 85 (63%) of the 137 cases under review involved either invalid scientific testimony or the withholding of exculpatory evidence.

10.5.2 **A fraud typology**

Adapted from, and consistent with, typologies provided in Babbage (1830), NAS (2002), ORI (2009), and Turvey (2003), forensic examiners can be cross-categorized as having used one or more of three general approaches to committing fraud, referred to as *Simulators, Dissemblers,* and *Pseudoexperts* (Turvey, 2013).

Simulators are those examiners who physically manipulate physical evidence or related forensic testing[4]. This means that they physically fabricate, tamper with, or destroy evidence. As the name suggests, they are trying to create the appearance that something happened when it didn't, or to create the appearance that nothing happened at all when in fact it did. This approach to fraud also describes those examiners engaging in evidence suppression by concealing its existence (e.g., hiding it in a desk drawer, hiding it on the evidence shelf, or removing it from the evidence log).

Dissemblers are those examiners who exaggerate, embellish, lie about, or otherwise misrepresent findings.[5] They are not tampering with the evidence; they are simply not telling the truth about it. *Dissemblers* exist on a continuum that includes those who lie outright about the significance of examination results to those who intentionally present a biased or incomplete view.

Pseudoexperts are those examiners who fabricate or misrepresent their credentials. They are also referred to as fakes, phonies, charlatans, and mountebanks.[6] Pseudoexperts exist on a continuum of severity as well, from those with valid credentials who misrepresent a credential or an affiliation, to those with no valid credentials at all.

Original research regarding forensic fraud was published in Turvey (2013); it analyzed data collected from 100 forensic examiners in the United States that had committed fraud related to the examination of physical evidence between 2000 and 2010. This research also employed the typology above, and reported the following major findings with respect to fraudulent forensic examiners:

1. 23% ($n = 23$) of the forensic examiners in this study were determined to have a history of addiction; 21% ($n = 21$), a history of fraud; and 17% ($n = 17$), a history of other criminal convictions.
2. 27% ($n = 27$) of forensic examiners in this study were found to have been lying about some or all of their education, training, and experience. They were subsequently classified as Pseudoexperts.
3. 82% ($n = 82$) of the forensic examiners in this study were determined to be involved in an ongoing pattern of fraud within their agency, often involving multiple examiners, prior to discovery. In context, this finding generally points towards the contribution of systemic and cultural factors.
4. 78% ($n = 78$) of the forensic examiners in this study were employed directly by law enforcement agencies. This finding supports the assertion that those

---

[4] Also referred to as *forging* (Babbage, 1830) or *fabrication* (ORI, 2009).
[5] Also referred to as *trimming* and *cooking* (Babbage, 1830), or *falsification* (ORI, 2009).
[6] Also referred to as *falsifying credentials* (ORI, 2009).

working on behalf of the police and the prosecution (though not necessarily the government in general) are responsible for a substantial amount, if not the majority, of the known cases of forensic fraud.

5. 37% ($n = 37$) of the fraudulent examiners in the present study were initially retained by their respective employers without severe consequences despite their misconduct; of these, the weightiest involved examiners that were reassigned or temporarily suspended.

Consider the following case examples.

Case Example: Dissembler and Pseudoexpert Annie Dookhan, Criminalist-Massachusetts Department of Public Health Drug Lab

The State Police were scheduled to take over the operation of the Massachusetts Department of Public Health (DPH) drug lab in July of 2012 as part of a new budgetary directive. A month prior, they were given information about problems and inconsistencies related to the work of criminalist Annie Dookhan. Ms. Dookhan had resigned back in March during an internal DPH investigation of her casework. Once the *State Police* were in charge, they began their own audit of the lab; based on their investigation, assembled by Assistant Attorney General John Vernor, Chief of the Criminal Bureau, on August 17, 2012, Governor Deval Patrick ordered the *State Police* to shut the lab down.

Annie Dookhan was not just an analyst, she was the most productive analyst at the lab. She was in charge of quality control, and supervisors at the lab had known about but ignored her fraud for years. During her interview with Det. Lt. Robert Irwin of the Massachusetts State Police in late August of 2012, Ms. Dookhan confessed to dry-labbing test results, forging the initials of her co-workers on reports and documentation, and intentionally mixing up drug samples to conceal her fraud (Vernor, 2012). "I messed up bad; it's my fault. I don't want the lab to get in trouble," she told him. *State Police* investigators eventually learned that just about everyone in the lab knew what was going on, and that no real action was taken by anyone to end it. In mid-October, they arrested Annie Dookhan at her home, and charged her with obstruction of justice.

As the result of the *State Police* investigation, it was also eventually confirmed that Ms. Dookhan had lied about having a master's degree in chemistry from the University of Massachusetts. As reported in Lavoie and Neidowski (2012):

> *A Massachusetts chemist accused of faking drug test results, forging paperwork and mixing samples at a state police lab was arrested Friday in a scandal that has thrown thousands of criminal cases into doubt. Annie Dookhan, 34, was led to a state police cruiser at her home in Franklin, about 40 miles southwest of Boston. Dookhan's alleged mishandling of drug samples prompted the shutdown of the Hinton State Laboratory Institute in Boston last month and resulted in the resignation of three officials, including the state's public health commissioner.*
>
> *State police say Dookhan tested more than 60,000 drug samples involving 34,000 defendants during her nine years at the lab. Defense lawyers and prosecutors are scrambling to figure out how to deal with the fallout. Since the lab closed, more*

than a dozen drug defendants are back on the street while their attorneys challenge the charges based on Dookhan's misconduct. Many more defendants are expected to be released. Authorities say more than 1,100 inmates are currently serving time in cases in which Dookhan was the primary or secondary chemist.

Dookhan could face more than 20 years in prison if convicted. She is charged with two counts of obstruction of justice, a felony count that carries up to 10 years in prison, and pretending to hold a degree for a college or university, a misdemeanor punishable by as much as a year in jail. She pleaded not guilty Friday afternoon and a judge set bail at $10,000. She was ordered to turn over her passport, submit to GPS monitoring, and not have contact with any former or current employees of the lab… The two obstruction charges accuse Dookhan of lying about drug samples she analyzed at the lab in March 2011 for a Suffolk County case, and for testifying under oath in August 2010 that she had a master's degree in chemistry from the University of Massachusetts, Attorney General Martha Coakley said at a news conference Friday.

Further detail is provided in Murphy and Lavoie (2012), including the fact that supervisors knew she had been lying about her education since 2010, but did not put a definitive stop to *it*[7]:

In 2010, supervisors did a paperwork audit of her work but didn't retest any of her samples. They didn't find problems. Dookhan had to send a resume to prosecutors whenever she testified in criminal cases. In 2010, [criminalist supervisor Elizabeth] O'Brien caught Dookhan padding her resume by claiming she had a master's degree in chemistry from the University of Massachusetts. She took it off her resume but later put it back on, O'Brien told police.

In August, another Hinton chemist told investigators her own monthly sample testing volume dropped from about 400 to 200 after Melendez-Diaz (2009)[8], but talk around the lab was that Dookhan was testing 800 a month.

Another colleague wondered in a police interview whether Dookhan had a mental breakdown. Dookhan told investigators she was in the process of a long divorce, but there is no record of any divorce complaint filed at the Norfolk Probate and Family Court. She said she wanted to get her work done and never meant to hurt anyone.

---

[7] It's worth noting that management's attitude of indifference towards phony credentials existed at the lab prior to Ms. Dookhan's hire. In 2003, it was revealed that Ralph Timperi, the Jamaica Plain lab's director for 15 years to that point, had claimed on his resume that he held "a doctorate, when the degree actually was bestowed by an online university that requires no dissertation and that grants diplomas in 72 hours for $499" (Kocian & Smith, 2003). Timperi apologized, and was not disciplined by the Department of Public Health, or by the Harvard School of Public Health where he served as adjunct faculty. Mr. Timperi stayed on as the director of the Jamaica Plain lab until 2005.

[8] The U.S. Supreme Court ruling in Melendez-Diaz (2009) reasserts that the accused have the right to confront any and all evidence and witnesses against them. This right to confrontation includes forensic scientists who have written reports to be used as evidence against them at trial.

After her March 2012 resignation, while facing an internal department probe, Dookhan told a fellow chemist she used to join for after-work drinks that she didn't want to get her in trouble, too. She told the woman not to call her anymore and to delete all her emails, text messages and records of their phone calls.

The State Police investigation also uncovered the fact that Ms. Dookhan was communicating with prosecutors via phone and text messaging to give them information outside of the regular chain of command regarding her findings, and findings on other cases. This inappropriate contact has led to the resignation of at least one prosecutor, Norfolk County Assistant District Attorney George Papachristos, as reported in Estes and Allen (2012):

The chemist at the center of the state drug lab scandal carried on an unauthorized, sometimes personal, e-mail and phone correspondence with a prosecutor whose drug evidence she analyzed, a violation of office protocol that may give defense attorneys even more ammunition to throw out drug convictions involving Annie Dookhan's work.

Though State Police have concluded that Dookhan was not romantically involved with Norfolk Assistant District Attorney George Papachristos, Dookhan's husband was suspicious. At one point, Dookhan's husband tried repeatedly to contact a startled Papachristos, according to someone involved in the investigation, apparently out of concern that the two were having an affair.

The tone in the dozens of e-mails between the two was sometimes quite familiar, according to the person who has read them. Dookhan opened up about her life, confiding in one email that she was unhappy in her marriage, though it is unclear from a printout of the e-mails whether she sent it. On another occasion, Papachristos reminded her that their relationship was strictly 'professional' in response to something Dookhan wrote.

The correspondence, which dates back to 2009, was unusual enough that State Police investigating drug lab misconduct recently interviewed Papachristos about their relationship. Lab protocol calls for prosecutors to communicate through lab supervisors to avoid any question about the integrity of drug evidence, something Dookhan has acknowledged she should have done.

The American Civil Liberties Union has asked Attorney General Martha Coakley and the district attorneys to agree to throw out all drug cases 'involving a police officer or prosecutor who, at any time, communicated directly with Annie Dookhan.'

'Chemists aren't supposed to be doing favors on a case-by-case basis for a particular police officer or prosecutor,' said Matthew R. Segal, legal director of the ACLU Foundation of Massachusetts. 'That's a good rule, no matter who the chemist is.' Dookhan wrote e-mails and spoke on the phone with other prosecutors, the person involved with the investigation said, but the correspondence with Papachristos stood out.

Papachristos declined to answer questions, but his boss, Norfolk District Attorney Michael W. Morrissey, said Papachristos told him that he and Dookhan had no personal relationship. 'George never socially met her or had a relationship with her,' said Morrissey, who took office in 2011. 'He met her once in court, and she never testified in any of his cases.' However, Morrissey admitted that he has seen only a few e-mails, and he has refused repeated efforts by investigators to provide him with copies of the rest of the correspondence, because they are 'the subject of an ongoing investigation' by Coakley and 'I don't want to interfere.' Several state officials and prosecutors expressed confusion over Morrissey's refusal to accept the emails, noting that he should know if one of his subordinates had an inappropriate relationship that could jeopardize cases in his office …

It is unclear exactly how frequently Dookhan analyzed evidence for Papachristos, but Papachristos refers to several different cases in his e-mails … In the emails, Dookhan sent Papachristos chatty messages punctuated by exclamation points, according to the person involved in the investigation who has read the messages. There is no suggestion in the correspondence that he asked her to alter results or provide other favors, but Dookhan had a reputation in the lab for being especially close to Norfolk prosecutors.

Gloria Phillips, an evidence officer, told police that Dookhan 'always wanted Norfolk County' cases to analyze. Dookhan appeared to be doing a favor for Norfolk law enforcement officials when she was caught in June 2011 taking evidence from 60 Norfolk drug cases out of a storage area without authorization. Her former supervisor, Elizabeth O'Brien, told State Police Dookhan had taken cases out of order and did not sign them out as required.

Dookhan's co-workers told State Police that she was going through a 'long divorce' from her husband, though the two still live together in Franklin. O'Brien added that Dookhan was 'going through some personal problems.'

In summer 2009, Papachristos told Dookhan with some alarm that her husband had tried to contact him repeatedly, though they did not speak. 'I have to tell my bosses,' Papachristos told Dookhan. 'Tell him not to call again.'…

Dookhan and Papachristos continued to correspond for two years after that, including for five months after June 2011 when Dookhan's supervisors say they removed her from doing drug analysis because of questions about her handling of evidence. At one point, Papachristos asks Dookhan how she likes her 'promotion,' apparently unaware that she has been removed from drug analysis because of questions about her integrity. Later in the year, Dookhan asked Papachristos about his Thanksgiving celebration. Dookhan stressed that she worked alone and that no prosecutors urged her to break the rules.

Nonetheless, Segal said Dookhan's direct contact with prosecutors, without following proper protocol, should be grounds for dismissal of cases, suggesting the prosecutors knew that she would do what they wanted—give them the evidence they needed for drug convictions—without even asking.

The fallout from the scandal is, as of this writing, as follows: Annie Dookhan has been arrested and criminally charged with two counts of obstruction of justice (no trial date set); Linda Han, the Director of Bureau of Lab Sciences, has resigned; Julie Nassif, the Director of the Analytic Chemistry Division, was fired; Department of Public Health Commissioner John Auerbach has resigned; and Norfolk County ADA George Papachristos has resigned. In terms of cases, tens of thousands of Dookhan's results are under *review*[9]; hundreds have been set aside or overturned; and numerous criminals have been released, at least one of whom has already been rearrested (Randall, 2013).

What is known for certain is that the problems in this lab were systemic, they arose from negligent leadership and management, they could have been avoided with a resume check that resulted in termination or a zero-tolerance policy towards fraud, and they were exacerbated by an inappropriate relationship between Annie Dookhan, a forensic scientist, and George Papachristos, a prosecutor. These facts and circumstances comport with the findings and recommendations of the present research.

Case Example: Simulator, Deborah Madden, Criminalist SFPD Crime Lab

In early 2010, the San Francisco Police Department's crime lab suspended all drug testing and was forced to submit to an external audit due to revelations that one of its veteran criminalists, Deborah Madden, had been stealing cocaine for personal use. Apparently, she had been abusing her position at the crime lab for a number of years, in order to feed her substance abuse problem. As reported in Burack (2012):

> In 2010, revelations that a department criminalist was pilfering drug evidence led to the dismissal of hundreds of drug cases. And in 2011, more than 100 more drug cases were dismissed after [Public Defender Jeff] Adachi's office discovered videos allegedly depicting officers illegally entering residences and falsifying police reports and stealing suspects' valuables.

Ms. Madden was not arrested for any crimes by local government. Instead she was given immunity, allowed to resign, and also allowed to collect a pension while she continued to serve as an expert witness for the state in multiple criminal trials. As reported in Eskenazi (2011):

> Disgraced former crime lab technician Deborah Madden will not face any criminal charges, despite triggering a scandal that led to millions of dollars in city costs and a literal Get Out of Jail Free card for thousands of accused drug criminals. Madden is now free to begin drawing her city pension; with 29 years on the job, she's entitled to somewhere in the neighborhood of 75 percent of her $63,000 yearly salary.

This author experienced the hypocrisy of the prosecutor's office first hand when testifying as an expert for the defense in California v. Culton against Deborah Madden.

---

[9]Approximately 60,000 cases, for which Governor Patrick has requested 30 million dollars to cover initial investigative and retesting costs (Salsberg, 2012).

For instance, the district attorney became furious when this author explained, under oath, that he did not seek out information about the homicide scene directly from Ms. Madden, who processed it for evidence. This, the author explained, was because she was in fact a known fraud and therefore unreliable. When the district attorney objected, the trial told him to stop asking questions that he did not want the answers to. As reported in Burack (2011):

> The former San Francisco Police department criminalist whose alleged theft of drugs from the crime lab scandalized the department will be called soon to testify in a nearly 30-year-old murder case. Debbie Madden appeared at a pretrial court hearing Wednesday in the case of Dwight Culton, 61, accused of killing 43-year-old Joan Baldwin at a former auto body shop near the Hall of Justice on April 6, 1984.
>
> Madden, 61, will testify at Culton's trial, with immunity from prosecution for any statements she might make about her recently scrutinized activities at the lab, her attorney Paul DeMeester said Thursday. He said this was the first nondrug case in which she had been called to testify since leaving the department in 2009. Madden's alleged admission that she took small amounts of cocaine from evidence at the lab in late 2009 could potentially be used by defense attorneys to impeach her credibility as a witness, even in a decades-old murder case.
>
> DeMeester said the relatively recent accusations of Madden's misconduct at the drug lab 'have nothing to do with what she did on the case in 1984.' Madden was called to the scene of Baldwin's murder to collect blood evidence and later did some of the testing. 'She is a material witness in this case, and her testimony is necessary for us to establish chain of custody,' District Attorney's Office spokeswoman Erica Derryck said.

When proffering her as a witness for the state the prosecution routinely attempted to hide Ms. Madden's identity and, by extension, her duplicitous character. For instance, they placed her on the witness list under a misleading name, they did not initially disclose her criminal history, and they did not disclose her termination for laboratory drug theft. Despite the requirements of discovery set forth in Brady v. Maryland (1963), the prosecution argued that these were lawful tactics. As reported in Begin (2010):

> The District Attorney's Office had no formal policy regarding releasing the criminal history of its expert witnesses to the defense, prosecutors told a judge Thursday. That information will be used to challenge evidence in a trial. The admission came as Superior Court Judge Anne-Christine Massullo is creating a framework for hundreds of future drug cases that could be revisited after a debacle at the San Francisco Police Department's crime lab that became public March 9.
>
> Documents released this week show top narcotics prosecutor Sharon Woo complained to her superiors in November of 'disturbing' problems with the attendance of longtime lab technician Deborah Madden. While the chief attorney in the office, Russ Giuntini, relayed a message of concern to police, it did not include Madden's name.

> On Thursday, Massullo ordered the release of more documents to defense attorneys related to the Police Department's investigation into Madden, who is suspected of taking cocaine from evidence samples at the crime lab. Massullo also pressed Woo for District Attorney Kamala Harris' policy on notifying defense attorneys of the criminal history of a witness.
>
> In 2008, Madden was convicted in San Mateo County on a count of misdemeanor domestic violence for throwing a cordless phone at her domestic partner's head. Despite the conviction and a subsequent internal investigation, the Police Department never informed the District Attorney's Office, which it's required to do under California law.
>
> 'I don't believe there is a written policy,' Woo said. 'There is no written procedure. Our policy is to follow the law.' The District Attorney's Office relies on the Police Department to provide information about one of its employees, Woo said.
>
> 'Saying we rely on the police to tell us really isn't [sufficient] under this court's eyes,' Massullo said.

When it became clear that local authorities had lost perspective regarding Ms. Madden's conduct, allowing her to essentially skate on one of the biggest lab scandals in the country at the time, the US Government stepped in and charged her with criminal violations of relevant federal statutes. As reported in Drumwright (2011):

> Felony drug charges were filed in federal court Thursday against Deborah Madden, the disgraced former technician at the San Francisco Police Department's crime lab. In a one-sentence indictment, federal prosecutors allege that Madden did 'knowingly and intentionally acquire and obtain possession of, by misrepresentation, fraud, forgery, deception and subterfuge' cocaine from the lab.
>
> Madden, who has admitted to taking small amounts of drugs from the lab in 2009, is due to make an initial appearance before U.S. Northern District Court Judge Elizabeth D. Laporte on Wednesday. The drug scandal rocked the crime lab, which was temporarily shut down in March 2010. The incident led to the outsourcing of drug testing to other labs in the Bay Area.
>
> Madden, 61, who has not been jailed on the charge, has never been prosecuted by The City. She did plead no contest in San Mateo County to charges that stemmed from San Mateo police finding 0.09 grams of cocaine during a search of Madden's home there.

In October of 2012, the *federal* case against Deborah Madden ended with a mistrial. During a retrial for the same felony charges, she was allowed to plead guilty to a misdemeanor count of cocaine possession in March of 2103, confessing, "I knowingly possessed cocaine outside the scope of my employment" (Griffin, 2013). It is believed that this plea, and the language involved, was crafted by the defense with an eye to preserving Ms. Madden's government pension.

This case serves to demonstrate that there are those within law enforcement culture willing to tolerate criminality, and also willing to actively conceal it in order to get what they want. Had the police department and the district attorney's office adopted a zero-tolerance policy for criminal conduct by police department employees, Ms. Madden's domestic violence conviction in 2008 would have removed her from the department and from active casework. This would have prevented at least two years of misconduct.

10.6 Conclusion

The forensic science enterprise is complex, and those working to serve it suffer from an array of conflicting expectations and pressures. In addition, the alignment of the forensic sciences with law enforcement brings its own perils. Apart from examiner pressure to conform with norms and missions that are contrary to scientific integrity, an association with the prosecutor's office can ultimately work against examiner accountability. As the research and case examples provided in this chapter demonstrate, this is because the prosecution may seek to protect and retain those witnesses key to securing and maintaining criminal convictions, despite evidence of negligence or misconduct.

Failures in the forensic sciences occur for a variety of reasons. However, the majority relate to an employment culture that rejects the mandates of good science out of ignorance, neglect, bias, or compromise (Turvey, 2013). By raising awareness of the requirements for scientific integrity, and by illuminating cases where non-scientific agendas have been protected and even promoted, it is hoped that ethical forensic examiners will take note. By doing so, they can better understand and secure their scientific values. They will also be more capable of helping their colleagues to nurture and safeguard the objective mission of the forensic sciences.

References

Albrecht, W.S., Albrecht, C.O., 2003. Fraud Examination and Prevention. South-Western Educational Publishing, Mason, Ohio.

Albrecht, W.S., Albrecht, C.O., Albrecht, C.C., Zimbelman, M.F., 2011. Fraud Examination, fourth ed. South-Western, Cengage Learning, Mason, Ohio.

Anderson, M., Martinson, B., De Vries, R., 2007. Normative Dissonance in Science: Results from a National Survey of U.S. Scientists. Journal of Empirical Research in Human Research Ethics 2 (4), 3–14.

Babbage, C., 1830. Reflections on the Decline of Science in England, and on Some of Its Causes. B. Fellowes Publisher, London.

Balint, E., 2012a. Crime lab worker fired over reports. Canton Repository, May 23.

Balint, E., 2012b. Crime-lab Worker Reinstated. Canton Repository, October 31.

Begin, B., 2010. Policy on expert witnesses lacking. San Francisco Examiner, April 15.

Black, H.C., 1990. Black's Law Dictionary, sixth ed. West Publishing Co, St. Paul, MN.

Brady, v., Maryland, 1963. U.S. Supreme Court (373 U.S. 83).

Burack, A., 2011. DUI convictions at risk following SFPD revelations. San Francisco Examiner, March 5.

Burack, A., 2012. Former SF crime lab technician Debbie Madden to testify in murder trial. San Francisco Examiner, April 1.

Catano, V., Turk, J., 2007. Fraud and Misconduct in Scientific Research: A Definition and Procedures for Investigation. Medicine and Law 26, 465–476.

Chisum, W.J., Turvey, B., 2011. Crime Reconstruction, second ed. Elsevier Science, San Diego.

Coenen, T., 2008. Essentials of Corporate Fraud. John Wiley & Sons, Inc, Hoboken, NJ.

Crowder, S., Turvey, B., 2013. Ethical Justice: Applied Issues for Criminal Justice Students and Professionals. Elsevier Science, San Diego.

DeForest, P., 2005. Crime Scene Investigation. In: Sullivan, L.E., Rosen, M.S. (Eds.), Encyclopedia of Law Enforcement, vol. 1. Sage, Thousand Oaks, CA, pp. 111–116.

Drumwright, S., 2011. Feds dish out drug charges to former San Francisco crime lab tech. San Francisco Examiner, December 1.

Durose, M., 2008. Census of Publicly Funded Forensic Crime Laboratories, 2005. Office of Justice Programs, Bureau of Justice Statistics, NCJ 222181, July.

Edwards, H., Gotsonis, C., 2009. Strengthening Forensic Science in the United States: A Path Forward. National Academies Press, Washington, DC.

Eskenazi, J., 2011. Can San Francisco Tap into Deborah Madden's Pension? San Francisco Weekly, January 4.

Estes, A., Allen, S., 2012. Chemist often called, wrote to prosecutor. Boston Globe, October 17.

Faigman, D.L., Kaye, D.H., Saks, M.J., Sanders, J., 2004. Annotated Scientific Evidence Reference Manual. West Publishing Co., St. Paul, MN.

Gardenier, J., 2011. Data Integrity Is Earned, Not Given. Office of Research Integrity Newsletter 19 (3), 3.

Gannett, C., 2011. Ethical Dilemmas. CAC News, 25–32, First Quarter.

Garrett, B., Neufeld, P., 2009. Invalid Forensic Science Testimony and Wrongful Convictions. Virginia Law Review 95 (1), 1–97.

Giannelli, P., 2007. Wrongful Convictions and Forensic Science: The Need to Regulate Crime Labs. North Carolina Law Review 86, 163–236.

Griffin, M., 2013. Was Deborah Madden's confession a move to keep her city pension? San Francisco Examiner, March 20.

Gross, S., Jacoby, K., Matheson, D., Montgomery, N., Patil, S., 2005. Exonerations in the United States, 1989 through 2003. Journal of Criminal Law and Criminology 95, 523–559, Winter.

Ingraham, B., 1987. The Ethics of Testimony: Conflicting Views on the Role of the Criminologist as Expert Witness. In: Anderson, P., Winfree, L. (Eds.), Expert Witnesses: Criminologists in the Courtroom, State University on New York Press, Albany, NY.

Jette, A., 2005. Without Scientific Integrity, There Can Be No Evidence Base. Physical Therapy 85 (1), 1122–1123.

Judson, H., 2004. The Great Betrayal: Fraud in Science. Harcourt, Inc, New York.

Kelly, B., 2012. Former CSI Kofoed Dogged By Legal Challenges As Jailtime Ends. NET News–NPR, May 29; url: http://netnebraska.org/article/news/former-csi-kofoed-dogged-legal-challenges-jailtime-ends.

Kocian, L., Smith, S., 2003. Lab chief apologizes over online doctorate. Boston Globe, November 13.

Krimsky, S., 2007. Defining Scientific Misconduct: When Conflict-of-Interest Is a Factor in Scientific Misconduct. Medicine and Law 26, 447–463.

Lavoie, D., Niedowski, E., 2012. Mass. chemist in drug test flap is arrested. Associated Press September 28.

Lord, A., 2010. The Prevalence of Fraud: What should we, as academics, be doing to address the problem? Accounting and Management Information Systems 9 (1), 4–21.

Marshall, N., 2010. Tulsa police forensic laboratory director fired. Tulsa World, June 21; url: http://www.tulsaworld.com/article.aspx/Tulsa_police_forensic_laboratory_director_fired/20100621_11_0_thetul193309.

Martinson, B., Anderson, M., de Vries, R., 2005. Scientists behaving badly. Nature 435 (9), 737–738.

McDowell, R., 2010. Fat Finger, Falsification, or Fraud? Spectroscopy 25 (12), 15–18.

Melendez-Diaz v. Massachusetts, 2009. U.S. Supreme Court, Case No. 07-591, June 25.

NAS, 2002. Integrity in Scientific Research: Creating an Environment That Promotes Responsible Conduct. National Academy of Science Committee on Assessing Integrity in Research Environments National Academies Press, Washington, D.C.

NAS, 2004. Forensic Analysis Weighing Bullet Lead Evidence. National Academy of Science Committee on Scientific Assessment of Bullet Lead Elemental Composition Comparison National Academies Press, Washington, D.C.

NAS, 2009. On Being a Scientist: A Guide to Responsible Conduct in Research, National Academy of Science Committee on Science, Engineering, and Public Policy, third ed. National Academies Press, Washington, DC.

ORI, 2009. The Office of Research Integrity Annual Report 2009. Office of Research Integrity, Washington D.C.: U.S. Department of Health and Human Services; http://ori.hhs.gov/documents/annual_reports/ori_annual_report_2009.pdf.

Parrish, D., 1996. The scientific misconduct definition and falsification of credentials. Professional Ethics Report 9 (4), 1–5.

Peterson, J., Hickman, M., 2005. Census of Publicly Funded Forensic Crime Laboratories, 2002. Washington DC: U.S. Department of Justice, Office of Justice Programs, Bureau of Justice Statistics Bulletin, NCJ 207205, February.

Ragland, v., Commonwealth of Kentucky, 2006. Supreme Court of Kentucky. No. 2002-SC-0388-MR, 2003-SC-0084-TG, 191 S.W.3d 569, March 23.

Randall, E., 2012. Man released from prison thanks to Dookhan re-arrested thanks to cocaine. Boston Daily, November 13.

Reider, B., 2010. Fabrication, Falsification et al. American Journal of Sports Medicine 38 (3), 445–447.

Resnick, D., 2003. From Baltimore to Bell Labs: Reflections on Two Decades of Debate about Scientific Misconduct. Accountability in Research 10 (2), 123–135.

Reynolds, S., 2004. ORI Findings of Scientific Misconduct in Clinical Trials and Publicly Funded Research, 1992–2002. Clinical Trials 1 (6), 509–516.

Ridolphi, K., Possley, M., 2010. Preventable Error: A Report on Prosecutorial Misconduct in California 1997–2009. Northern California Innocence Project at Santa Clara University School of Law, Santa Clara, CA.

Rink, M., 2013a. Rick Perez will be new crime lab director. Canton Repository, February 7.

Rink, M., 2013b. Rick Perez out as crime lab director. Canton Repository, February 11.

Rink, M., 2013c. Crime lab worker fired again. Canton Repository, March 30.

Solomon, J., 2003. New allegations target two FBI crime-lab scientists. Seattle Times, April 16; url: http://community.seattletimes.nwsource.com/archive/?date=20030416&slug=fbilab16.

Sovacool, B., 2008. Exploring Scientific Misconduct: Isolated Individuals, Impure Institutions, or an Inevitable Idiom of Modern Science? Bioethical Inquiry 5 (4), 271–282.

Thornton, J.I., 1983. Uses and abuses of forensic science. In: Thomas, W. (Ed.), Science and Law: An Essential Alliance, Westview Press, Boulder, CO.

Thornton, J.I., 1994. Courts of Law v. Courts of Science: A Forensic Scientist's Reaction to Daubert. Shepard's Expert Scientific Evidence Quarterly 1 (3), 475–485.

Thornton, J., Peterson, J., 2007. The General Assumptions and Rationale of Forensic Identification. In: Faigman, D., Kaye, D., Saks, M., Sanders, J. (Eds.), *Modern Scientific Evidence: The Law and Science of Expert Testimony*, vol. 1. West Publishing Group, St. Paul, MN.

Titus, S., Wells, J., Rhoades, L., 2008. Repairing Research Integrity. Nature 453 (19), 980–982.

Turvey, B., 2013. Forensic Fraud: Evaluating Law Enforcement and Forensic Science Cultures in the Context of Examiner Misconduct. Elsevier Science, San Diego.

Vernor, J., 2012. Memo and State Police interviews compiled by Assistant Attorney General John Vernor. Chief of the Criminal Bureau, to District Attorney C. Samuel Sutter, Bristol County District Attorney's Office, September 17.

THE INNOCENCE BLOG

Calvin Washington

Contributing Causes for Erroneous Conviction: unvalidated or improper forensic science

Calvin E. Washington was convicted of capital murder in 1987.

On the night of March 1, 1986, the victim, who resided in Waco, Texas, returned home from work. The next morning her body was discovered—she had been beaten, raped, and murdered. It was alleged that Washington, either acting alone or with Joe Sidney Williams, intentionally murdered the victim in the course of committing burglary and sexually assaulting the victim.

The state determined the cause of death to be from blunt force injuries and asphyxia by smothering or strangulation. The prosecution also produced evidence that the defendants were in possession of the victim's car on the morning of March 2, 1986 and had sold items belonging to the victim on the night of the crime. Witnesses testified that Washington had admitted to the burglary and a forensic testified that a bite mark found on the victim was "consistent" with Washington's co-defendant. While the analyst excluded Washington as the source of the bite mark, his bite mark testimony about the codefendant (which was given at Washington's trial) tied Washington to the crime. Because there is not adequate empirical data on bite mark analysis, the analyst's assertion that the bite mark was consistent with Washington's co-defendant was inherently prejudicial and lacked probative value.

A jury convicted Washington of capital murder and sentenced him to life in prison.

After serving more than 13 years of this sentence, Calvin E. Washington was exonerated after post-conviction DNA testing showed that blood on a shirt found in Washington's home did not come from the victim, as previously asserted. Testing also showed that fluids taken from the victim did not come from Washington, but rather from another man, Bennie Carrol, now deceased. Bennie Carrol committed suicide three years after admitting that he had raped an elderly woman who happened to be a neighbor of the victim.

Forensic Expert Ethics

Cases and Concepts about Ethical Forensic Practice and Testimony in Court

11

C. Michael Bowers

*Associate Professor of Clinical Dentistry, Ostrow School of Dentistry,
University of Southern California, Los Angeles, CA USA*

Where there is smoke, there is fire.
Anon

Nothing seems more logical to the general public than to assume a forensic scientist or examiner has properly performed and maintains high standards of ethical, moral, and technical conduct. This assumption is predominately true, giving everyone the benefit of the doubt, but human nature being what it is, there can be occasional slips, bumps, and ethical disasters which occur. The forensic community as experts in any trial must swear under oath to "tell the truth, the whole truth, so help you God." They also must sign affidavits swearing under the penalty of perjury (see Chapter 10) that procedures and protocols have been met. We see these oaths given in real life and in the fictional crime shows which overpopulate the entertainment world. But, as an empirical source of ethical data, the problems that have occurred are prime evidence of the misadventures that continue to happen. What is telling, however, is that most transgressions are revealed via "special review" of external investigations published or generated by media involvement. What goes on within specific fields or disciplines of forensics is not sufficiently transparent to review available data, or at least inhibits a view on what occurs across the entire scope of what is considered "forensic."

11.1 The expected review of ethical tenets

Any publication on professionalism has the obligatory list of rules and principles to adhere to. In an effort not to sound redundant, most of those will not be discussed herein; but the legal area of expert testimony does have salient aspects that are appropriate to mention.

Forensic Testimony. http://dx.doi.org/10.1016/B978-0-12-397005-3.00011-6

11.1.1 Undue influence in forensic environments

This subject has many analogies such as personal biases, peer pressure, and contextual and institutional bias. The institutional version is said to exist based on the mere fact that most crime labs are directly associated with and financially supported by law enforcement agencies, and due to the culture within their associated systems. Critics of such arrangements are clear in their concerns, and include the well documented missteps within the FBI crime lab that have led to their recent self-debunking of decades long promulgations and training programs supporting bullet lead comparisons and physical hair matching.

Personal bias is hard to detect by observers, absent outright testimony in which the expert states: "I only work on cases for the prosecution." This is a bit ambiguous as to his reasoning, but possible meanings are:

a. His employment with a law enforcement-owned laboratory may prohibit being an expert for a defense case.
b. He may make this statement when he testifies that the defendant is guilty or "highly suspect." This lies in the area of pro-prosecution bias adhering to the belief that a defendant is "probably" always guilty.

"I always testify for the defense" can be explained as:

a. "There is a need for defendants to have their own, independent expert to review all the steps in the prosecution's case. I have that skill set and the credentials to accomplish this task."

Peer pressure comes within many different social groups and events, but the forensic aspect is particularly related to government job security, past practices within the lab, coworker influences, or memberships in fraternal forensic organizations that express strong traditions which lack scientific approaches to support their opinions. Some closed-minded forensic cultures object to or put pressure on individual examiners who speak out about weaknesses or omissions present in their particular fields of investigation. The current effects of the 2009 NAS Report on forensic science vary within these groups, which range from arrogant dismissal of this congressionally requested review (which noted a serious lack of empirical testing within major forensic or "police science" fields) to acceptance of the report's rationale, and proactive research progressing toward better outcomes and practices.

11.1.2 Lawyers and experts must remain independent entities

The best attorney for a forensic expert is one who states at the outset of inquiry with the potential expert that: "The universe of your inquiry will be limited just to the aspects of whether this injury pattern was caused by human teeth," or, "You will be limited to evaluating the state expert's report regarding his compliance to standards published by the IAI Photography Section on the enhancement of digital evidence."

These are limiting requests that are specific tasks, and that carry no expectations of the expert rendering any subjective opinions or probabilities. Quantitative measurements in other more scientific areas still demand interpretative opinions, but the position of this type of attorney clearly sets the request in a neutral, non-assumptive or leading manner.

A police lab environment could produce a tasking statement such as this: "The extent of your inquiry will be limited to the ballistics evidence obtained from the victim and the murder weapon." This is a direct request that also gives the examiner much unnecessary information, which can develop a contextual bias:

a. The examiner has knowledge that the weapon is suspected of being used in a murder case.
b. There was only one weapon available for analysis.

This last scenario is obviously troubling. Procedures in laboratories can be developed to shield examiners from knowledge of details, and the importance or context of certain physical evidence. Experts that are in private practice have the same obligation to avoid and demand *not* to hear information beyond what is absolutely necessary to perform the tasks asked of them.

11.1.3 Presenting data analysis, or just personal opinion

There are ethical considerations regarding what an expert says or doesn't say regarding the basis of certainty of opinion. A science-based expert in biochemistry can describe her proper handling and processing of biological specimens in a way that's very different than that of the bite mark expert who only "observes" results from comparing plaster tooth models to bite marks on skin. In the first instance, the biological research and reliability testing in the uses of DNA are the foundation of conclusions, along with appropriate proficiency testing of the examiner. The latter has to rely on substitutes for scientific reliability via statements of years of experience and court acceptance. Courts and juries have had problems discerning these experts' differences for decades because they can be made to sound very similar. Such is the power of the forensic expert performing as an assumed neutral determinant of the truth. The jury will ask (only if these issues are brought up in court by a properly prepared attorney) which method is more reliable to base their decision on. What data did the expert rely on? Was there any data even available? Is it just the examiner making an observation of the available evidence (i.e., "the bite mark pattern shows the same arrangement of teeth as possessed by the defendant")? Are there indicators of reliability other than the examiner's certainty that her opinion is correct? Ultimately, the expert has to give a clear and convincing story, with supporting evidence, as to why her conclusions are acceptable.

11.1.4 Identifying with the victim: Losing objectivity

Victims of crime certainly deserve advocates for their cause and help from the criminal justice system. However, this should stay in the realm of the advocates, not the forensic experts involved as evidence examiners. A common statement seen in the media is that the police and prosecutors "speak" for the victim, whether alive or dead. This dedication is admirable and necessary. The expert must create a mental firewall to avoid similar influences. Certainly contact with victims or their families should be avoided at all costs. If information is needed, persons other than the analyst should obtain this information. This runs counter to the typical death investigation involving crime scene analysts, medical examiners, and law enforcement, but they too must advance statements regarding fact and not mere opinions when testifying in court. Arriving at opinions too soon (either at the scene or in the lab) can make outcomes less than dispassionate, and produce dependent rather than independent expressions of results.

11.2 Social science research on improper forensic science in the courts

Nothing is more effective than case review in problem analysis regarding forensic ethics issues. It is the bedrock of legal research to review methods, practices, and forensic failures in relation to legal outcomes. Medical and engineering sciences use risk management and failure analysis as a matter of due course. This is a newly recognized forensic concept, and in regards to many prosecutors' opinions, a very dubious one with few rewards. A popular opinion from DAs and judges faced with post-conviction physical evidence of compelling claims of innocence is that the initial conviction is a sacrosanct event. This releases the previous judgment from review on scientific and forensic issues presented at later proceedings of exoneration or habeas corpus (e.g., petitions for a new trial). Chapter 12 is a compelling story of a case where new forensic evidence should have resulted in freedom for the defendant after 20 years in jail. The history of this case poses as an example of why wrongful convictons occur.

11.2.1 The road to wrongful convictions

Case profiling allows social science researchers to recognize indicators and events which lead to wrongful convictions. A forensic expert should be knowledgeable of this information. These factors should be called "risk factors" because their appearance in trials creates a dangerous nexus for unreliable legal outcomes. A recent study outlined 10 factors that led to the wrongful conviction of defendants who were factually innocent:

- Weak evidence by the prosecution
- Weak defense
- Prosecution withholding exculpatory evidence
- Forensic error
- Inadvertent misidentification by an eyewitness
- Lying by a non-witness
- Youth of a defendant

- Punitiveness of the state
- Any criminal history by the defendant
- *Brady* violations[1]

The study also identified the effect of "tunnel vision" in erroneous convictions:

> *In instances of tunnel vision, one small fact gets all the attention. Prosecutors or police become too attached to a particular fact, and thus are unable to see the weaknesses present in the case.*[1]

In Chapter 12, the prosecutorial missteps in the William Richards case clearly outline a number of these risk factors.

11.2.2 More ethical conundrums: A detailed review of experts' effects in wrongful convictions

The Innocence Project has published a forensic outcome evaluation based on empirical statistics from over 300 cases of exonerations by DNA.[2]

11.2.2.1 Unreliable or improper forensic science

Since the late 1980s, DNA analysis has helped identify the guilty and exonerate the innocent nationwide. While DNA testing was developed through extensive scientific research at top academic centers, many other forensic techniques—such as hair microscopy, bite mark comparisons, firearm tool mark analysis and shoe print comparisons—have never been subjected to rigorous scientific evaluation. Meanwhile, forensics techniques that have been properly validated—such as serology, commonly known as blood typing—are sometimes improperly conducted or inaccurately conveyed in trial testimony. In some cases, forensic analysts have fabricated results or engaged in other misconduct.

All of these problems constitute unvalidated or improper forensic science, which is the second-greatest contributor to wrongful convictions that have been overturned with DNA testing. In more than 50% of DNA exonerations, unvalidated or improper forensic science contributed to the wrongful conviction.

While DNA exonerations are a window into the effect of unvalidated or improper forensic science contributing to wrongful convictions, DNA does not solve the problem. In fact, experts estimate that only 5–10% of all criminal cases involve biological evidence that could be subjected to DNA testing. In the other 90–95% of crimes, DNA testing is not an option – so the criminal justice system relies on other kinds of evidence, including forensic disciplines that may not be scientifically sound or properly conducted.

The Absence of Scientific Standards

Unlike DNA testing, many forensic disciplines – particularly those that deal with comparing impression marks and objects like hair and fiber – were developed solely to solve crime. These disciplines have evolved primarily through their use in individual cases. Without the benefit of basic research or adequate financial resources, applied research has also been minimal. In fact, many forensic testing methods have been

---

[1] http://nij.gov/topics/courts/sentencing/wrongful-convictions/predicting-preventing.htm.
[2] http://www.innocenceproject.org.

applied with little or no scientific validation and with inadequate assessments of their robustness or reliability. Furthermore, they lacked scientifically acceptable standards for quality assurance and quality control before their implementation in cases.

As a result, forensic analysts sometimes testify in cases without a proper scientific basis for their findings. Testimony about more dubious forensic disciplines, such as efforts to match a defendant's teeth to marks on a victim or attempts to compare a defendant's voice to a voicemail recording, are cloaked in science but lack even the most basic scientific standards. Even within forensic disciplines that are more firmly grounded in science, evidence is often made to sound more precise than it should. For example, analysts will testify that hairs from a crime scene "match" or "are consistent with" defendants' hair – but because scientific research on validity and reliability of hair analysis is lacking, they have no way of knowing how rare these similarities are, so there is no way to know how meaningful this evidence is.

Improper Forensic Testimony

Too often, forensic analysts' testimony goes further than the science allows. Many forensic techniques that have been practiced for years – but not subjected to the rigors of scientific research – are accepted and repeated as fact. Juries are left with the impression that the evidence is more scientific than it is, and the potential for wrongful convictions increases. Improper forensic testimony is not limited to unvalidated disciplines, however. Among the DNA exoneration cases, scores of people were wrongfully convicted after forensic testimony misrepresented serology results. Serology is still used, but before DNA testing it was the only way to help identify the source of blood, semen or other bodily fluids at a crime scene. Using serology, forensic analysts could determine what blood type was present in fluids collected in a rape kit, for example. In many cases, analysts testify properly about what the serology can tell and what percentage of the population shares the perpetrator's blood type. But in other cases, analysts fail to recognize that the biological sample could be a mixture of fluids from the victim and perpetrator, and the victim's blood type could mask the perpetrator's – making it impossible to know the blood type of the perpetrator. In other cases, analysts provide inaccurate statistics for the percentage of the population who share the perpetrator's blood type.

Forensic Misconduct

The vast majority of forensic employees are hardworking, ethical and responsible. They use the best scientific techniques available to deliver objective, solid information – regardless of whether the science favors the defendant, supports the prosecution or is inconclusive. In many cases, the science – rather than the scientist – is inadequate. In other cases, forensic analysts make mistakes that could result from lack of training, poor support or insufficient resources to meet an ever-growing demand. But in some cases, forensic analysts have engaged in misconduct. While these "bad apples" don't reflect the entire forensic field, one fraudulent forensic analyst can taint countless cases. For example, in some wrongful convictions later overturned with DNA testing, forensic analysts fabricated test results, reported results when no tests were conducted or concealed parts of test results that were favorable to defendants. In virtually all of these cases, analysts had engaged in misconduct that led to multiple separate wrongful convictions, sometimes in multiple states.[3]

11.3 Specific forensic acts contributing to wrongful convictions

A deconstruction of the first 74 Innocence Project-litigated DNA exonerations produced a sharper focus on forensic issues by categories.[4] The 74 reviewed cases revealed the types and frequencies of forensic mistakes and intentional acts.

- Misinterpretation (11)
- Statistical Exaggeration (10)
- Suppression of Exculpatory Evidence (7)
- Expert Lied About Credentials (5)
- Falsified Results (7)
- Contamination (5)
- Experts Testified To Tests Never Conducted (4)
- Other (2)

Although not a comprehensive study and subject to future analyses, the apparent focus weakness of every case is the moral and subjective attitudes of the examiner. As suggested by the Innocence Project, proper supervision and supportive education with mandated standardization is the only answer. To date, the only recourse for defendants in criminal cases is an average of 13 years of post-conviction litigation in order to overcome such systemic problems that are unmitigated.

A more recent 2009 study of 180 exonerations (Brandon and Peter, 2009) increases the focus on systemic ethical forensic problems.

> *Trial transcripts were sought for all 156 exonerees identified as having trial testimony by forensic analysts, of which 137 were located and reviewed. These trials most commonly included serological analysis and microscopic hair comparison, but some included bite mark, shoe print, soil, fiber, and fingerprint comparisons, and several included DNA testing. This study found that in the bulk of these trials of innocent defendants—82 cases or 60 percent—forensic analysts called by the prosecution provided invalid testimony at trial—that is, testimony with conclusions misstating empirical data or wholly unsupported by empirical data.*

The six types of invalid testimony that were identified include:

- Presentation of non-probative evidence as probative
- Discounting exculpatory evidence
- Inaccurate presentation of statistics or frequency

---

[3] http://www.innocenceproject.org/understand/Unreliable-Limited-Science.php.
[4] http://www.innocenceproject.org/understand/Forensic-Science-Misconduct.php.

- Providing statistics without supporting empirical data
- Making non-statistical statements without supporting empirical data
- Concluding that evidence originated from the defendant without supporting empirical data

The trials reviewed included invalid testimony from 72 forensic experts employed by 52 different agencies in 25 different states. Defense counsel was revealed to have had no objections or have received little relief from judges hearing such protests.

11.4 Do forensic experts have a duty to critically balance telling the truth with their own discipline's standards?

Forensic experts' foundation for admittance (determined by the trial judge who "gate-keeps" the acceptance or exclusion of expert trial testimony) is the expert's adherence to scientific principles, and his use of validated methods to reach conclusions. These conclusions often are not completely certain, but are instead opinions couched in probabilities of fact. The stronger the methods used, the more weight may be given to their court opinion. The weaker the scientific basis, the more that the "expert help" provided to the court and jury may be minimal, subject to exclusion by the judge, or actually counterproductive to the outcome desired by the party hiring the expert. In no circumstance should the expert try to magnify his or her own work or opinions (or that of another colleague) based on external or personal expectations. The scientific method is based on objective observation. Unfortunately, legal summaries of prior trials are rife with such ethical departures. Experts or forensic disciplines most likely to be guilty of this are those without relevant standards and SOPs (standard operating procedures) that have been thoroughly tested and proven capable of achieving repetitive testing with consistent results by multiple examiners.

One means to avoid influence from outside the scientific process is to use well-tested methods and standards for the evaluation of evidence brought to the forensic expert for analysis. This is harder than one might think, due to the two-tiered characteristics in forensic disciplines mentioned in Chapter 1.

11.5 Is there a forensic SOP the court may rely on? Do forensic organizations have a duty to conform to scientific methods?

The SOP is the first level for the expert to consider at the beginning of any case. The training and job performance of most forensic examiners starts in the law enforcement environment of the United States police sciences. DNA- and biology-based laboratory examiners have university training. Both groups have SOPs. But they may not all be equal. The legal traditions of forensic acceptability of police science (the forensic experts within fingerprints, firearms, ballistics, hair and fiber, pattern or tool marks, and bite marks) in the United States and abroad has, until very recently, avoided the "heat" of serious scrutiny. However, years of being given carte blanche in court is no guarantee of accuracy of either the methods or the opinions attached to them. The scrutiny of these and similar police sciences has multiplied for two reasons: 1) The introduction of new judicial standards for expert expertise (*US v. Daubert*, 1993); 2) Criminal trial convictions which have been overturned by DNA evidence that determined that the wrong person was "proven" guilty.

11.5.1 One U.S. forensic group in particular

Some forensic organizations have examined exoneration cases involving mistakes or flawed forensic methods and learned from them. The FBI recently agreed to co-investigate with the Innocence Project in over 2000 FBI and prosecution cases which used the now refuted methods of physical hair analysis.[5] As is to be expected, some forensic groups ignore or blame "rogue" examiners for the increasing numbers of flawed cases involving their members.[6] The best example of forensic philandering is the American Board of Forensic Odontology (ABFO), a self-serving organization recognized by the American Academy of Forensic Sciences. Fully 10% of the small ABFO group (N=100) have helped incarcerate or convict innocent persons by using their flawed methods of bite mark comparison. It is a prime example of ignoring the systemic weaknesses in certain methods and assumptions of validity. See the Appendix for the current description of these cases. Its legacy of non-researched SOPs (their bite mark practices are merely theory and assumptions rather than proven scientific results) and refutation of recent relevant research raises irrefutable evidence of a systemic failure of methods. This new research has quashed their traditional bite mark theories of the individuality of teeth and the accuracy of human skin in reliably reflecting the patterns of those teeth. This poses as a reminder to all the forensic community that some of its experts rely only on furtherance of their own agendas (JADA, 2011).

Speaking of validity, the discerning expert should understand the importance of validity testing. The current reviews and media publication of forensic misadventures in courts demand that the expert have knowledge of the details of each police science proof. These proofs must be supportable beyond the mere personal beliefs of those who practice a forensic technique.

The best outline of SOPs and their validity testing lies in the field of DNA comparison, or "DNA profiling." Here is an example of the US government's expectations regarding validity testing for public DNA laboratories.

11.6 Ethical foundations of forensic validation

Validation refers to the process of demonstrating that a laboratory procedure is robust, reliable, and reproducible in the hands of the personnel performing the test in that laboratory. A robust method is one in which successful results are obtained a

---

[5] http://www.mcclatchydc.com/2013/07/18/197069/fbi-announces-review-of-2000-cases.html#.UfagQHjn-00.

[6] http://www.innocenceproject.org/Content/DNA_Exonerations_Nationwide.php.

high percentage of the time and few, if any, samples need to be repeated. A reliable method refers to one in which the obtained results are accurate and correctly reflect the sample being tested. A reproducible method means that the same or very similar results are obtained each time a sample is tested. All three types of methods are important for techniques performed in forensic laboratories.

In layman's terms, the validation process of the expert analyst's techniques requires more than statements that they have been previously accepted in courts. Assuming that testifying in the past renders these questions moot is wishful thinking, whether the expert is employed by a governmental agency or a private concern. Previous knowledge of the steps rendered within the subject discipline's scientific community to assure validity is mandatory. This is easily accessible by the DNA community, in this specific case, but is significantly more difficult for other police sciences. DNA in its forensic context is a direct result of significant university research in the multinational community of biochemistry and related sciences, where the scientific methods and data have been exchanged and retested since the late 1950s. Fingerprint examiners have been admissible since the 1920s but only recently have the chances of multiple people having similar print characteristics been considered. The bite mark comparison advocates, in the extreme case again, use only their years of courtroom acceptance as a substitute for testing data and experimentation.[7]

11.6.1 What happens when forensic validation is faulty or incomplete?

Seldom in the history of American jurisprudence has an identification or analytical method used in criminal prosecutions been determined faulty and inadmissible in court. In fact, there are only three instances. This first opinion came from a court ruling; the other two came from the FBI crime lab.

It is striking that the first case occurred in 1923 and involved lie detection methods (i.e., polygraph tests). The testing at the time was amazingly crude, as the opinion of truth telling was based on a stethoscope and a blood pressure gauge. The court of appeals case that ruled out these methods in 1923 is named *United States v. Frye,* and it stands as the first legal interpretation in the United States regarding courtroom review of expert testimony and its use of "novel" associated means of analysis. The defense counsel in *Frye* presented the lie detection expert, who claimed that his "testing" indicated innocence, contradicting the defendant's earlier confession to murder. The prosecutor objected, and the judge ruled the methods to be inadmissible. Current polygraph methods are much more sophisticated, and are extensively used by governmental agencies and private companies, with each agency comporting their own means of interpretation. The *Frye* decision still stands regarding its inadmissibility in court.

The FBI laboratory's activities involve the agency, during two separate decades, ruling that their decades-long practices in composite bullet lead analysis (CBL) and hair analysis should no longer be considered reliable. The first was CBL in 2008.

---

[7] For more information, see *The Real CSI: How Reliable is the Science Behind Forensics*, http://www.pbs.org/wgbh/pages/frontline/real-csi/.

...a six-month investigation by 60 Minutes *and* The Washington Post *last November showed that there are hundreds of defendants imprisoned around the country who were convicted with the help of a now discredited forensic tool, and that the FBI never notified them, their lawyers, or the courts, that the their cases may have been affected by faulty testimony. The science, called bullet lead analysis, was used by the FBI for 40 years in thousands of cases, and some of the people it helped put in jail may be innocent (Evidence of Injustice, 2009).*

11.6.1.1 Hair and fiber

The second instance of the FBI rescinding previously accepted forensic methods was focused on human hair and fiber "matching," and it was revealed by another *Washington Post* investigation.

Justice Department officials have known for years that flawed forensic work might have led to the convictions of potentially innocent people, but prosecutors failed to notify defendants or their attorneys even in many cases they knew were troubled.

Officials started reviewing the cases in the 1990s after reports that sloppy work by examiners at the FBI lab was producing unreliable forensic evidence in court trials.

...The Post worked with the nonprofit National Whistleblowers Center, which had obtained dozens of boxes of task force documents through a years-long Freedom of Information Act fight (Washington Post, 2012).

11.6.1.2 Can you reliably perform the SOP?

In simple terms, can the examiner provide accurate results in analysis? Proficiency is a well-developed concept in analytical laboratories. Some forensic labs certified by outside reviewing companies in the United States are mandated to periodically test their examiners for proficiency. Testing may be internal within the lab's SOPs and/or performed by standards of the certification boards or similar companies. However, the adherence to regular proficiency testing is actually a bit nebulous in the larger forensic community. The American Academy of Forensic Sciences created a Forensic Science Accreditation Board to set standards for its ten subsections of various disciplines. Critical thinking regarding the form and format of proficiency testing is left up to each of them. There is concern from numerous critics outside this 6,200 member group that leaving proficiency testing to the practitioners is an equation for stagnation with little substantive progress. It is obvious that the cases of wrongful convictions aided by forensic opinion will never be directly reviewed by the AAFS.

11.6.1.3 The outside review and oversight of the forensic science community: Debated since 2009

The National Academies of Science was mandated by Congress in 2007 to investigate and address major problematic aspects of forensic disciplines. Judge Harry

T. Edwards was the co-chair and the primary author of the 2009 NAS Report. It stated, in part, that there should be governmental oversight at the Executive branch level to establish objective standards and the application of these standards to the forensic community. Waves of debate have occurred since its publication, with issues typical of political and turf wars between the "stakeholders" comprised of the judicial, prosecutorial, defense counsel, and forensic practitioners. Validation of methods and proficiency of practitioners is hotly considered an intrusion by the US crime lab system, which is controlled by law enforcement funding and management in affiliation with in-domain certification "boards."

The Executive branch has also agreed to review forensic disciplines via the aegis of a White House Subcommittee on Forensic Science. This group has also been concerned with the same issues as the NAS.

11.6.1.4 The purpose and methods of proficiency testing for forensic examiners, summed up by Koehler

Professor Koehler (2013) argues that the incumbent need of the forensic community is to recognize errors that occur in forensic analysis and to pursue measures to standardize proficiency protocols.

Forensic science evidence is widely believed to be the most powerful form of evidence in existence. Like eyewitness evidence, some types of forensic science evidence can tie a particular person to a crime scene or a criminal act. Unlike eyewitness evidence, the testimonial infirmities associated with forensic match testimony seem slight. Whereas legal decision makers readily understand that eyewitnesses may misperceive, misremember, mis describe, or lie, they are less likely to worry about these infirmities when evaluating forensic science testimony. But how accurate are forensic match reports? How can we provide legal decision makers with an empirically-based sense of the frequency with which various types of forensic testimony are wrong or misleading?

Adding to the confusion, a 1996 National Academy of Sciences (NAS) report on DNA evidence flatly contradicted the recommendation made in a 1992 NAS report on DNA evidence about the need to identify error rates. Whereas the 1992 report indicated that blind proficiency tests that estimate error rates should be required for all new DNA methods (National Academy of Sciences, 1992, p. 55), the 1996 report countered that error rate estimates from proficiency tests are 'almost certain to yield wrongs values' because '[w]hen errors are discovered, they are investigated thoroughly so that corrections can be made' (National Academy of Sciences, 1996, p. 86).

According to this logic, error rate estimates based on proficiency test data provide no insight into the risk of an error in a given case. These and other arguments that the 1996 NAS report offered up against the value of error rate data were rebutted in a Symposium issue of Jurimetrics (see Balding, 1997; Koehler, 1997; Lempert, 1997; Thompson, 1997). Those rebuttal arguments will not be repeated here. But

the reality is that, following the 1996 NAS report, DNA error rate data from profi-
ciency testing became scarce and rarely found its way into the courtroom. Likewise,
the non-DNA forensic sciences, which had little tradition of using proficiency tests
to estimate error rates in the first place, continued to be promoted as reliable and
even error-free.

The mere need for these arguments may seem incredible to some readers. These are
true statements based on fact, and they reflect the inconsistent results and poor judicial interpretation regarding what is and is not reliable forensic science. The progress
towards relevant forensic reliability testing has also been very slow to nonexistent.
Judge Harry Edwards succinctly describes what the esteemed reviewers for the NAS
2009 Report on Forensic Science saw as the weaknesses in courtroom science and
the prosecutorial process:

In an adversarial system, once you decide to go to trial, your interest is in prevail-
ing. So you're not looking to make it easier for the other side. You're not going to
find scientific truth in the adversarial process. That work has got to be done by
the scientists.
'We assumed there might be mistakes,' says Judge Edwards, 'but I don't think that
we had been forewarned in any way that there were the serious problems that the
committee uncovered.'

Judge Harry T. Edwards, 2012[8]

11.7 Conclusion

This chapter covered the multiple issues involved in how court presented expert opinion testimony can lead to erroneous convictions.

The following chapter details the real case scenario where an innocent man is
subjected to a myriad of forensic missteps and prosecutorial excess that have put
him in prison for 20 years. The defendant, William Richards and one of his appellate
attorneys, Wendy Koen presents the case from beginning to the present status.

References

Brandon, L.G., Peter, J.N., 2009. Invalid Forensic Science Testimony and Wrongful
    Convictions: 95 Va. L Rev. 1 2009
Koehler, J., 2013. Proficiency tests to estimate error rates in the forensic sciences. Law,
    Probability and Risk 12, 89–98. doi:10.1093/lpr/mgs013.
JADA 2011. JADA leads with bitemark editorial, 142(9) p.997. http://jada.ada.org. http://
    www.forensicdentistry.info/wp/?p=531.
http://www.innocenceproject.org/understand/Unreliable-Limited-Science.php.

---

[8] From an edited 2012 interview: http://www.pbs.org/wgbh/pages/frontline/criminal-justice/real-
csi/judge-harry-t-edwards-how-reliable-is-forensic-evidence-in-court/.

Evidence of Injustice, 2009. 60 Minutes, February 11, http://www.cbsnews.com/2100-18560_162-3512453.html.

Washington Post, 2012. "Convicted defendants left uninformed of forensic flaws found by justice department". http://www.washingtonpost.com/local/crime/convicted-defendants-left-uninformed-of-forensic-flaws-found-by-justice-dept/2012/04/16/gIQAWTcgMT_story.html).

The Unparalleled Power of Expert Testimony

12

Wendy J. Koen

Post-Conviction Attorney, formerly with the California Innocence Project; Panel Attorney with Appellate Defender's Inc., San Diego, CA USA; Associate of Applications of Psychology to Law, San Diego, CA USA

12.1 Introduction

In the competitive arena we call our justice system, when the desire to win and ensure that the "bad guy" rots in prison becomes the driving force, it is easy to forget that the defendant is not always the "bad guy." The police and the prosecutor mostly get it right, and charge the actual perpetrator. But because the state is fallible, we have created a system that presumes that the defendant is innocent until proven otherwise. A quick survey of public defenders reveals that this presumption is illusory. After a year toiling as public defenders, most stop believing that any of the people they represent are actually innocent. In fact, in most criminal courtrooms, most people present believe that the police got it right and that the trial will simply confirm the defendant's guilt.

An expert enters this arena with a powerful arsenal. Naturally, the prosecutor will strive to use that arsenal to the state's fullest advantage. The expert possesses an aura of infallibility. Almost invariably, the jurors will adopt the expert's opinion as their own. The expert must be a steadfast guardian of the truth. This is most difficult in cases involving senseless brutal murders, the death of an infant, or other crimes that shock us and make us hope to exact swift blind justice upon whoever is at the defendant's table, truth be damned. Nothing illustrates our tendency to take up a witch-hunt mentality more than the epidemic of ritual satanic child abuse cases that led to scores of wrongful convictions in the 1980s and 1990s (Nathan & Snedeker, 2001). This witch hunt was so successful because it played on the fears of us all. The witch hunt resulted in many wrongful convictions because expert witnesses, like most everyone in the United States, were swept away in the frenzy. Indeed, they virtually armed themselves with pitchforks and led the charge. When experts get swept up in a witch-hunt mentality, there is no hope that truth will prevail in the courtroom.

As an attorney with the California Innocence Project (CIP), I became all too familiar with the root causes of wrongful convictions. According to the Innocence Project's research, the main causes of wrongful convictions are: Eyewitness misidentification,

Forensic Testimony. http://dx.doi.org/10.1016/B978-0-12-397005-3.00012-8

unvalidated or improper forensic science, false confessions or admissions, government misconduct, informants or snitches, and bad lawyering.[1]

Expert testimony can lead to wrongful convictions because in certain cases expert testimony based on unvalidated or improper forensic science is the only evidence that implicates the defendant. Experts are used to establish every element of some crimes. In shaken baby cases, expert testimony is used to establish when an infant was injured, that the injury was not accidental and was therefore criminal, who injured the infant, and that person's malicious intent. In this way, the state has been able to convict such unlikely suspects as Suzanne Johnson (all information regarding Suzanne Johnson's case was taken from the trial record in *People v. Johnson*, SCD129703, 1999, and post-conviction filings).

When Suzanne was charged with causing injury leading to the death of a child, she was an elderly woman who had no criminal record. What she did have was a two-decade long record of lovingly caring for infants and children in her home. In 1997, an infant fell from a highchair while in her care; later that day, the infant began to vomit, stopped breathing, became unresponsive, and died. Suzanne was charged with the infant's death. There was no real evidence of motive or anything in Suzanne's history that would lead anyone to believe that she would purposefully hurt a child.

The only evidence against Suzanne was offered by experts who agreed that the infant's injury had to have been inflicted by Suzanne because the child would not have been lucid after the injury; thus, they argued, Suzanne's version of events was false. Further, because Suzanne was the last adult with the infant when she became ill, they argued that Suzanne must have intentionally and viciously inflicted the injury. The injury could not have resulted from a fall from a bed the infant sustained two months before, or from a fall from a highchair the day she died; the experts agreed that infants do not sustain severe injury from these types of accidents. The injury must have been viciously inflicted because it was tantamount to an injury sustained from a fall from a third story window or from a car accident. As the judge in Suzanne's case concluded, although Suzanne's character and history defied the charge against her, the expert evidence was powerful, conclusive, and virtually unrefuted.

As the science of infant head injury has advanced, it is now clear that the experts in Suzanne's case were wrong. Experts no longer determine that the last person with the infant necessarily inflicted that infant's injury. Experts acknowledge that an infant's skull can be injured severely, and the effects of that injury sometimes do not make themselves known for days, weeks, or even months. Experts agree that relatively short falls, such as from a bed or a highchair, can and do cause serious injury and death. There was *never* any basis for the experts' claims that the injury was tantamount to an injury sustained from a fall from a third story window or from a car accident.

In fact, all of the expert testimony that led to Suzanne's conviction and lengthy prison sentence has been refuted in the scientific community. Regardless, a conviction founded on what is now known to be faulty expert evidence still stands. So an elderly lady sits in prison, waiting for justice to catch up with science.

---

[1] Innocence Project, Understand the Causes, http://www.innocenceproject.org/understand/.

Similarly, arson cases often rely heavily or exclusively on expert testimony. Experts are relied upon to establish whether a fire was purposefully set, and thus whether a crime occurred at all, as well as who set it and the degree of their malicious intent.

The tragic Texas case of Cameron Todd Willingham is an example of an arson case that never should have been prosecuted.[2] Willingham was convicted of murdering his three young children by arson at their home in Corsicana, Texas on December 23, 1991. In spite of advances in the science of fire and arson investigation that showed that the Corsicana fire was not intentionally set, Willingham was executed for the triple murder in 2004. The prosecutor relied on what the experts described as an incendiary pour pattern under one of the infant's beds to prove that Willingham maliciously intended to kill his own children. This claim, as well as the other claims upon which Willingham's conviction was founded, are proven to be false (Beyler, 2009). In fact, if these charges were brought today, a prosecutor relying on what is now known about fire and arson would not seek to prosecute Willingham. Although Willingham's family is seeking a pardon for Willingham, he suffered the ultimate punishment, and justice is no longer possible for him (New York Times, 2012).

Regardless of these and other horrific instances when justice has been butchered by unvalidated or improper scientific expert testimony, and the innocent have been sacrificed, the courts are slow to recognize scientific advances that could undo some of the damage inflicted. While justice catches up with science, these cases should make us mindful of the power of the expert to create a wrongful conviction.

One CIP case in particular epitomizes the power of forensic expert testimony to both create and sustain a wrongful conviction. The case of William (Bill) Richards reveals the chasm that still exists between the American justice system and science. It also emphasizes the relative difficulty of undoing a wrongful conviction that was based on expert evidence as opposed to other types of false testimony.

I first met Bill after the exoneration of Timothy Atkins (all facts about the *Atkins* case come from the trial record in *People v. Atkins*, Superior Court No. A090938, 1987, and post-conviction filings and opinions). Atkins was exonerated after a witness against him recanted her testimony. At Atkins's preliminary hearing, Denise Powell testified that Atkins admitted to her that he had killed the victim. Although Powell did not testify at trial, the prosecutor persuaded the court that Powell was missing and unavailable, so her preliminary hearing testimony was read into evidence. Decades after Atkins was convicted, the CIP found Powell, and she recanted her testimony. Powell was tough to locate; she had been living on the streets for decades, sustaining her addiction to crack cocaine by prostitution. Powell testified in post-conviction proceedings that she had lied in her previous testimony because she felt pressured by the police. In spite of the witness's obvious character issues, the judge believed her recantation, and Atkins was subsequently released. It was on the heels of this victory that I first visited Bill in prison.

I knew immediately that Bill's case faced different challenges than did Atkins's. It was not a homeless woman's testimony that led to Bill's conviction. It was the testimony of the founding father of forensic odontology himself, Dr. Norman "Skip"

---

[2] www.pbs.org/wgbh/pages/frontline/death-by-fire/.

Sperber, along with a constellation of errors common in wrongful conviction cases. As CIP investigated the case, the deeper they looked the more the case reeked of sloppy, unsubstantiated, and unreliable forensic and expert evidence. In fact, no real evidence pointed to Bill at all, and his conviction rested firmly on the shoulders of bad "science." Today, unlike Timothy Atkins, Bill remains incarcerated, although his conviction was based on expert testimony now known to be false. The discussion of Bill that follows should impress upon us the staying power of forensic expert evidence (all facts about Bill's case come from the trial record in *People v. Richards*, FVI00826, 1998, and post-conviction filings and opinions).

12.2 **William (Bill) Richards**

On August 10, 1993, Bill's wife, Pamela Richards, was severely beaten with fist-sized rocks, manually strangled, and a cinder block and paving stone were used to crush her skull. This created blood spatter for a radius of fifteen feet. This beating took place on her property outside of her home. Strangulation was most probably the cause of death, and Pamela was moved to the final resting area perimortem.

Bill has always maintained that he arrived home from work that night and found Pamela's battered body. Indeed, even according to the prosecution's timeline, there was at the most an eight-minute window in which Bill could have killed Pamela. Evidence against Bill was weak and circumstantial, and Bill was not convicted until his fourth trial.

During the first three trials, the prosecutor's case was based on three foundational tenets. First, there was discord in the Richards' marriage. Second, they argued that a tuft of fibers caught in a deep crack in Pamela's fingernail was indistinguishable from the fabric of the shirt Bill was wearing the night of the murder. Third, the prosecutor repeatedly elicited testimony and argued that no one other than Bill could have committed the murder because there was no evidence of anyone other than Bill and Pamela at the murder scene. This evidence was presented in three complete trials that resulted in hung juries. After initial failure to convince three juries that Bill was guilty, bite mark evidence was introduced against Bill in the fourth and final trial. After the five-week trial, the jury deliberated for two days and then reached a deadlock. The jury asked for further clarification on the definition of "reasonable doubt." The court refused to clarify; the jury was instructed to continue deliberations. The following day, the jury found Bill guilty of the first-degree murder of his wife, and he was sentenced to twenty-five years to life.

12.2.1 **Tunnel vision**

The initial responding officer determined that Bill killed his wife. He made this determination because of Bill's demeanor, the remote location of the crime, and based on other faulty assumptions.

Bill is a talker. He is also a logical thinker. When he arrived at home and found Pamela dead, his instinct was to figure out what had happened and then to tell the responding officer what he thought. Initially, Bill thought Pamela had fallen off of the porch and hit her head on a cinderblock. He used his Maglite—a high powered flashlight that was essential to life out in the country when relying on a generator for power—and found a blood-splattered steppingstone and cinderblock near Pamela's crushed skull. It is not surprising that Bill determined that someone had bludgeoned Pamela with these instruments.

Bill did not remain silent, and he told the first responding officer just how he thought Pamela was killed. He was also in shock and stricken with grief. He would fall to the ground and weep at times and wanted desperately to simply hold Pamela's battered body. The officer found this odd and thought Bill's actions were rehearsed. The officer did not think this was the way a husband in Bill's circumstance should act. He found it suspicious that Bill knew where the murder weapons were and, when testifying, did not remember that Bill had a Maglite (the high-powered flashlight was clearly captured by crime scene photos). Thus, he reasoned, Bill must have been the killer because not only did his grief seem rehearsed, but Bill also knew things only the killer would know.

12.2.2 Failure to investigate

Because of initial faulty assumptions, law enforcement conducted their investigation as if Bill was the only suspect. They did not fingerprint the inside of the home where the victim and assailant struggled. They did not retain or fingerprint the fist-sized rocks the assailant used to bludgeon the victim. They did not conduct tests that are normally conducted to pinpoint time of death, even though Bill was at work the evening of the murder, and evidence that Pamela had died earlier would have conclusively cleared Bill. They determined that all hairs found on Pamela's body and clothes and all blood found at the scene belonged to Pamela. Given that tunnel vision caused investigators to pass over tests that may have led to another suspect, it is disconcerting that one main theme that was argued by the prosecutor repeatedly at trial was that they could find "neither hide nor hair" of any evidence that another person was at the Richards' home.

12.2.3 Blood spatter evidence

Forensic experts testified that blood on clothing Bill wore the night of the murder was not consistent with Bill cradling his wife after finding her body. The expert identified what he believed was a small amount of medium-energy blood spatter on Bill's shoe. The experts conducted experiments with a papier-mâché dummy (Figure 12.1), which by most standards would be considered absolutely ridiculous. The experts filled the dummy's head with blood, and crushed it with a cinderblock. Then one of the experts donned clothing similar to the clothing Bill was wearing the night of the murder and cradled the dummy how Bill indicated he cradled his wife when he found her body. It is puzzling why no photos were taken of the protective clothing worn by the expert who did the crushing.

FIGURE 12.1

Papier-mâché dummy

FIGURE 12.2

Bill's clothing the night of the murder

According to the expert, this experiment established that Bill's story was false, and the blood on his clothing was consistent with Bill bludgeoning his wife. Although experts for the defense refuted the state's blood spatter evidence, the prosecution experts' explanations were obviously enough to convince the jury that it was at least possible for Bill to have engaged in a violent struggle with Pamela that created blood spatter in a radius of fifteen feet and walk away with a relatively miniscule amount of blood on his clothing (Figure 12.2).

12.2.4 Post-conviction DNA evidence

One foundational tenet upon which the state based Bill's prosecution was the notion that there was no evidence of another person on the Richards property the night of the murder. This contention was somewhat surprising because, for the most part, the investigators did not look for signs of another person on the property. They hung their hat on the fact that they could not find any shoeprints other than Bill's and Pamela's. However, the ground was not conducive to shoeprints. Although Bill admitted he walked near Pamela's body and in other areas where the struggle took place after he found Pamela, the investigators could not even find Bill's shoeprints in those areas. The shoeprints the officers did find were in a few sandier areas not involved in the scene of the struggle.

At trial, the experts agreed that all blood, hair, and tissue found on the scene were consistent with Pamela. While investigating Bill's case after his conviction, the CIP submitted one of the murder weapons—the stepping stone—and Pamela's finger-nail scrapings for DNA testing. The stepping stone analysis yielded DNA from an unknown male. This DNA was more important because it was taken from two areas of the steppingstone the criminalist had identified as the areas the suspect's DNA would be found. It was also in a quantity expected to be left by one using the stone as a weapon.

In the fingernail scrapings, the criminalist found a two-centimeter-long hair. At trial, it was attributed to Pamela. Mitochondrial DNA testing revealed that the hair did not belong to Pamela or Bill, but was from an unknown person. Because it was nearly an inch long and deep under the fingernail, it was a likely product of the struggle.

12.2.5 Suspicious fiber evidence

The tuft of fibers the expert reported that he found in a crack in Pamela's fingernail was a substantial part of the prosecutor's case against Bill. The state's expert showed the jury a videotape of the tuft being removed from Pamela's fingertip, emphasizing that the tuft was lodged in a crack in Pamela's fingernail with great force. The expert's contention was that the fibers could not be distinguished from the fibers in the shirt Bill was wearing the night of the murder. This was established through expert testimony that stated that the tuft was analyzed microscopically, under a fluorescent microscope, and with microspectometry. Thus, it was determined that the tuft of fibers was from Bill's shirt, and it was forcibly lodged deep in a crack in Pamela's fingernail while she struggled with Bill.

A careful review of crime scene photographs leads to another conclusion. Pamela's fingertips were severed after autopsy and sent to the crime lab, along with Bill's shirt. In all of the autopsy photos, taken before Pamela's fingertips were severed, there is no tuft of fibers present. The tuft of fibers does not appear until after the fingertips were severed (Figure 12.3). Although other experts examined the body and took scrapings of Pamela's fingernails, none mentioned the tuft of fibers until after the fingers were severed.

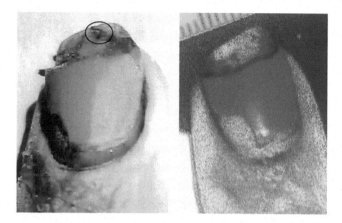

FIGURE 12.3

Left: The blue fiber. Right: Enlarged autopsy photo (blue color saturation).

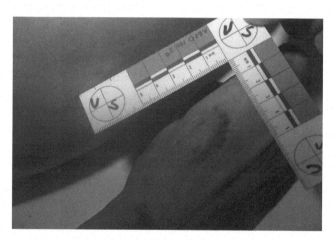

FIGURE 12.4

Original bite mark photograph

12.2.6 Bite mark evidence

After three trials that culminated in hung juries, Bill persuaded his defense attorney to hire a forensic odontologist to examine a photo of an injury (Figure 12.4) that was on the victim's hand. Bill always believed that the injury was a bite mark and that an examination of the injury would prove that someone other than he had attacked and killed his wife. Dr. Golden looked at the photo and determined that Bill could not be excluded as a possible biter. He also determined the photo was taken off-angle, and the individual marks were diffuse. Although Dr. Golden could not eliminate Bill as the biter, he also could not eliminate several of the dental models he had in his office.

In response to Dr. Golden's testimony, the prosecutor hired Dr. Norman Sperber to analyze the bite mark photo. Dr. Sperber agreed with Dr. Golden's analysis and added that Bill had an abnormal tooth. Tooth number 27 was under-erupted and lower than his other teeth. If tooth number 27 had left a mark, Bill would be ruled out. Although the picture was taken off-angle, and the marks were diffuse, Sperber concluded that Bill's abnormal tooth matched a blank spot in the injury pattern. Dr. Sperber testified that Bill's abnormal tooth was present in "one or two or less" out of every 100 people.

The jury heard from both Dr. Sperber and Dr. Golden that Sperber was internationally known as the father of forensic odontology. Dr. Golden praised Dr. Sperber's work from the witness stand and admitted that his analysis of the bite mark injury resulted in the same conclusion as Dr. Sperber's analysis; Bill's dentition was consistent with the bite mark injury in the photo.

In closing arguments the prosecutor used Dr. Sperber's testimony to its fullest advantage. He argued that it would be preposterous for the jury to conclude that someone with Bill's exact rare dental abnormality just happened to bite and kill Pamela that night. In was in this way that a diffuse, off-angled photograph of an injury on the victim's hand was used to identify Bill as his wife's killer.

At the conclusion of the presentation of evidence, the jury deliberated for a few days and came back deadlocked. The judge refused the jury request for a clarification on the definition of "reasonable doubt" and sent the jury back for further deliberations. Hours later, the jury announced its guilty verdict.

12.2.7 Post-conviction bite mark analyses

Bill made a motion for a new trial after his conviction, based in part on the work of C. Michael Bowers. The motion was denied, and Dr. Bowers was not given the opportunity to present his analysis. What his analysis would have revealed to the judge was that Bill's dentition was excluded as a possible match. Bowers made a model of Bill's teeth, and made an impression in Styrofoam (Figure 12.5). Contrary to Dr. Sperber's testimony that Bill's tooth 27 would not leave a mark, tooth 27 left a distinct mark. According to Dr. Sperber himself, if tooth 27 left a mark, Bill would be excluded as a possible match. As Dr. Bowers waited in the wings holding information that should have set Bill free, Bill remained incarcerated, hoping for another way for the truth to be heard.

As Bill languished in prison, advances in Photoshop allowed forensic specialists to rectify photographs that were taken off-angle. Dr. Bowers used this technology to rectify the bite mark injury image on Pamela's hand. Once the image was rectified, Drs. Sperber and Golden agreed with Dr. Bowers. Dr. Golden testified in post-conviction proceedings that, based on his analysis of the rectified image, Bill's "dental signature [did] not line up with the injury." Therefore, he excluded Bill as the suspected biter.

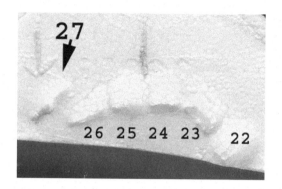

FIGURE 12.5

An impression in Styrofoam from the model of Bill's teeth

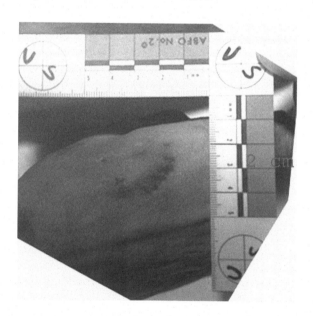

FIGURE 12.6

Rectified photograph

During post-conviction proceedings Dr. Sperber admitted that he made his determinations about the "bite mark" and testified at the 1997 trial based on a single distorted picture. After further analysis of the rectified bite mark image (Figure 12.6), Dr. Sperber has now "ruled out" Bill as the person who caused the injury.

The state's case against Bill was completely undermined. DNA from the murder weapon and from under Pamela's fingernails belonged to an unknown male. The bite mark injury on Pamela's hand did not match Bill's dentition. The tuft of fibers linking him to his wife's brutal attack appeared in her fingernail *after* autopsy. After a judge heard this new evidence, he found that Bill was not guilty of murder, and he overturned Bill's conviction.

The California Supreme Court, however, determined that false expert testimony is different than other false testimony. It would, from that day forth, be held to an even higher standard than general false evidence. The finding gutted the law that once offered relief whenever a convict established that false evidence was relied upon to obtain his or her conviction. Using arguments that strain logic, the court held that, if a person was convicted based on false evidence provided by an expert witness, there can now be no relief under the false evidence statute.[3] The court reasoned that expert testimony is simply opinion, and opinion cannot be true or false.

To an appellate attorney, this result was staggering. It not only meant that Bill, although innocent, would spend the rest of his days in prison, it also meant that Suzanne and others like her, convicted based on antiquated science, had no real avenue of relief. California is not alone in this result. All over the country, courts are loath to overturn convictions that are based on outdated science.

Most Americans would be surprised to hear that it is constitutional to uphold a conviction that we know was based on false testimony. Such a conviction is only unconstitutional if the witness who testified falsely did so purposefully and with the knowledge of the state. What this means, and what every expert witness should know, is that the expert witness's testimony, even if it is false, almost always stands eternally.

12.3 The human toll

It would be eye-opening if every expert, before venturing into the field of forensics, could sit for an afternoon and talk to Bill or Suzanne Johnson. While the statistics on wrongful convictions are staggering, it is difficult for most people to understand the devastating human toll. Bill was 42 when he came home to find his wife's battered body. In the shock and agony of that horrible night, he was thrown into a second nightmare. The American justice system, a monstrous and exacting blind machine, had focused on him and decided he would pay for the horrendous murder of his wife. The weapon the system would use to keep Bill in its clutches was the testimony of experts. The experts appeared to be caught up in a witch-hunt mentality. Bill saw the truth ignored. He saw his words twisted. He saw the witch-hunt mentality blossom even as his acquaintances and neighbors rewrote his history. He saw the reality of what he experienced on that horrible night perverted into a story, crafted, manipulated, and perfected in three complete trials by a prosecutor who was determined that Bill would pay for Pamela's death. Fight as he would against the machine, he could not prevail. He was voiceless, powerless, and hopeless.

Bill's introduction to the CIP gave him hope. That hope was dashed when the standard for relief was changed. In a stunning break with reality, the California

---

[3] http://law.justia.com/cases/california/supreme-court/2012/s189275.html.

Supreme Court eviscerated a California law that provides relief for inmates who were convicted based on false evidence.[4]

A lawyer's words cannot convey Bill's feelings as he sits in prison, realizing that all hopes for freedom are gone. This chapter concludes with Bill's words.

12.4 In Bill's words

I doubt that my words can convey the emotional roller coaster ride caused by a wrongful conviction. Frustration, hopelessness, depression, loneliness, alienation, and a broken heart. You deal with injustice, sadism, deprivation, and persecution all the time, but memories are the worst. All memories are painful—memories of a life with loved ones who are gone and friends who have forgotten you and moved on— memories of a life you were torn out of—a life so different from the life inside you might as well be on a hostile alien planet. Actually, you are.

Try to imagine the loneliness of being locked up away from everyone you've ever loved. After awhile, everyone dies or moves on. Everyone. There was a period of time where I was afraid to get my mail because almost every letter informed me of another death. Your mother is dead. Your brother died. Never good news. You don't go to funerals. You can't blame the friends who don't write anymore.

The world changes and people move on but the living dead in here don't move forward—they just grow old trapped in a time warp. My time warp is 1993. I've never been on the internet, used a cell phone, or tasted pizza with cheese in the crust. God, how I used to love pizza.

Writing about the life and emotions of an innocent man in prison is a daunting task. How do you describe hell when it comes on every level, from all directions? It encompasses all things, even your dreams. It makes you question your faith in everything, from God to humanity, government, to the very concept of justice.

Doing life in prison is bad enough on the guilty who often "fit in," let alone an innocent outsider. One lifer, who was guilty, once told me that he was not suicidal, but that he prayed every night before going to sleep that he would not wake up in the morning. Few men in here are as honest about their emotional distress but the hopelessness shows up anyway.

Think about never having anything to look forward to...for the rest of your life. All you have is an excruciating existence behind the walls. You wear what they give you, eat what they feed you, live where they put you. They treat you like dirt. Forget everything you've ever enjoyed doing. Simply, there is no reason to live. Try and imagine what this would be like and not be guilty. The hopelessness is only increased when added to the anger and frustration.

It is the ultimate betrayal of American ideals for the government to steal a person's property, life, and liberty. Your freedom can be taken by someone pointing

---

[4] www.leginfo.ca.gov/cgi-bin/displaycode?section=pen&group=01001-02000&file=1473-1508.

a finger at you. The whole power of the state comes down on you…all the state's resources focused and used against you. When the state finds it has used its resources to convict and imprison an innocent man, should not the power of the state come down to help that man back up? Should the resources of the state not be focused and used to make that man whole? Instead, the state fights to maintain the injustice, and the resources of the state are focused on concealing its inadequacy.

I used to dream about being outside, being free. But now, even when I dream, I have handcuffs on. I am always wearing handcuffs. You can't win your life back. Carl Sandburg said, "Time is the coin of your life. It's the only coin you have…be careful lest other people spend it for you." After the "good guys" have stolen and spent your coin, there is no getting it back. It is gone. Period. No one gets through years of physical, mental, and emotional torture intact. Koontz said, "Splints, casts, miracle drugs, and time can't mend fractured hearts, wounded minds, or torn spirits." Guaranteed to have suffered all of the above, damaged and broken, the innocent person deserves all of the help, compassion, and compensation society can give.

12.5 Conclusion

As faulty expert testimony is one of the leading causes of wrongful convictions, it is incumbent on every expert venturing into the legal arena to hold sacred the search for truth, and disdain any attempt to bolster an opinion or suppress or conceal unhelpful information. A witch-hunt mentality is deeply ingrained in human nature. We naturally band together to eradicate the monster from among us. Too often, the witch hunt sweeps up the innocent, and the hunters become the monsters. The expert does not have the luxury of joining the fray, but must only offer the truth.

References

Beyler, Craig, L, August 17, 2009. Analysis of the Fire Investigation Methods and Procedures Used in the Criminal Arson Cases Against Ernest Ray Willis and Cameron Todd Willingham. Hughes Associates, Inc.

Nathan, D., Snedeker, M., 2001. Satan's Silence: Ritual Abuse and the Making of a Modern American Witch Hunt. Authors Choice Press.

New York Times, 2012. Ethan Bronner: Executed Texan's Family Seeks Pardon, October 2012, at http://www.nytimes.com/2012/10/25/us/willingham-family-seeks-posthumous-pardon-in-texas.html?_r=0 as of 07/19/13.

THE INNOCENCE BLOG

Michael Morton

After spending nearly 25 years in prison for the murder of his wife, Michael Morton was released on October 4, 2011, and officially exonerated in December. DNA evidence implicated another man, who has also been tied to a similar Texas murder that occurred two years after the murder of Morton's wife.

The Crime

After celebrating his birthday at a restaurant with his wife, Christine, and their three-year-old son, on August 12, 1986, Michael Morton and his family returned home. The next morning, Morton left a note on the bathroom vanity expressing disappointment that his wife had declined to have sex the night before, but ending with the words, "I love you." He then left for work at about 5:30 a.m., arriving half an hour later; his co-workers would later testify that he did not act unusually.

That morning, Christine's body was found. She appeared to have been bludgeoned to death in her bed with a weapon made of wood. A wicker basket and suitcase were piled on top of her. The sheets upon which she lay were stained with what was later determined to be semen.

The Investigation

The day after Christine's body was found, August 14, police recovered a bloody bandana found at a construction site located about 100 yards from the Morton home.

Later that month, Christine's mother told police that the Mortons' three-year-old son, Eric, had been present during the murder. According to Eric, the murderer was not Michael, but a "monster." Eric described the crime scene and murder in great detail, and specifically said that his "Daddy" was "not home" when it happened. Upon questioning the Mortons' neighbors, police were told that a man had repeatedly parked a green van on the street behind the Mortons' house and walked off into a nearby wooded area. Police records also indicated that Christine Morton's missing Visa card may have been recovered in a San Antonio jewelry store, and that a San Antonio officer stated that he could identify the woman who had attempted to use the card. According to Morton's defense lawyers, none of this evidence was turned over to them at the trial.

Morton maintained his innocence. He believed that his wife had been killed by an intruder sometime after he left for work on the morning of August 13.

The Trial

When the defense learned that the prosecution did not plan to call the chief investigator in the case, Sgt. Don Wood, to the stand, they suspected that the prosecution might be concealing potentially exculpatory evidence. After the defense raised this issue with the judge, the prosecution assured the court that all favorable evidence had been given to the defense as required. They also presented a sealed file for the judge to review which was to contain all of Sgt. Wood's reports and notes. Evidence concerning Eric's eyewitness account, the green van, the Visa card, and the forged check were all absent.

At the trial, the Travis County medical examiner testified that Christine had been killed no later than 1:15 am, based on the contents of her stomach. He did, however, admit that this estimate was "not a scientific statement." A state serologist gave testimony supporting the prosecution's argument that the semen stain found on the sheets was consistent with ejaculation, rather than marital intercourse. The prosecution claimed that, after beating his wife to death, Morton masturbated on her corpse.

The prosecution presented no witnesses or physical evidence that tied Morton to the crime. They hypothesized that he had beaten Christine to death because she refused to

THE INNOCENCE BLOG—Cont'd

have sex with him on his birthday. At the time, Morton had no arrests, convictions, or history of violence against anyone.

On February 17, 1987, Michael Morton was convicted of murder and given a life sentence.

Post-Conviction

Morton immediately appealed his conviction, but this appeal was denied. He first requested post-conviction DNA testing in 1990 on the semen stain from the bedsheet. The stain matched his own DNA profile; however, this result was not surprising since the crime occurred in his bed.

In 2005, the Innocence Project and the law firm of Raley & Bowick in Houston filed a motion requesting additional DNA testing on other items of evidence from the crime scene. The District Attorney of Williamson County opposed the motion. The court granted permission to test some of the items in evidence, but not others. Once again, tests could not exclude Morton as the source of the DNA collected from the bed, and other tests did not yield any DNA for comparison.

On January 8, 2010, Morton successfully appealed the denial of testing on the bandana and hair from the bandana in the Third Circuit Court of Appeals.

On June 30, 2011, Orchid Cellmark reported that DNA testing on the bandana had revealed that it contained Christine Morton's blood and hair. It also contained the DNA of another, unknown male. The unknown male DNA profile was run through the CODIS databank and matched a convicted felon from California, who also had a criminal record in Texas and who lived in Texas at the time of Christine Morton's murder. Further investigation by Morton's lawyers and the Travis County District Attorney revealed that a pubic hair from Norwood was also found at the scene of the murder of Debra Masters Baker in Travis County. Mrs. Baker was, like Christine Morton, bludgeoned to death in her bed; her murder occurred two years after Christine's death, while Michael Morton was in prison.

During the course of the DNA litigation, Morton's attorneys filed a Public Information Act request, and finally obtained the other documents showing Morton's innocence in the State's file that had apparently been withheld at trial. At the request of Morton's attorneys, the Texas Supreme Court has ordered a Court of Inquiry into possible misconduct by the former Williamson County District Attorney who prosecuted the Morton case, Ken Anderson, who is now a Judge in Williamson County.

Michael Morton was released on October 4, 2011, after spending nearly 25 years in prison. He was officially exonerated on December 19, 2011.

Appendix

BITE MARK EXONERATIONS AND ERRONEOUS INCARCERATIONS

The common thread of all the following cases is that prosecutors introduced bite mark experts during police investigations and in courts. This evidence helped achieve convictions of defendants who were later released or exonerated after conviction. These bite mark opinions are prime examples of the misapplication of forensic science.

The majority of defendants listed in the following cases were clients of the Innocence Project Network. These cases have been used in legal arguments supporting the exclusion of bite mark evidence in U.S. courts at both the trial and appellate levels. The editor of this book has assisted in eight of the 24 cases. Thanks and credit for this legal compilation must be given to the IP Strategic Litigation Unit staff, and its Director Chris Fabricant for this legal research compilation.

There is no denying that in the future, other cases will be added to this list.

1. **Robert Lee Stinson:** Robert Lee Stinson served over 23 years in a Wisconsin prison for the brutal rape and murder of 63-year-old victim Ione Cychosz. The only physical evidence against Stinson at his 1985 trial was the bite mark testimony of two board-certified ABFO Diplomates, Drs. Lowell Thomas Johnson and Raymond Rawson. Dr. Johnson concluded that the bite marks "had to have been made by teeth identical" to Stinson's, and claimed that there was "no margin for error" in his conclusion. Dr. Rawson, the chairman of the Bite Mark Standards Committee of the ABFO testified that the bite mark evidence was "high quality" and "overwhelming." Both experts testified "to a reasonable degree of scientific certainty," that the bite marks on the victim had been inflicted at or near the time of death, and that Stinson was the only person who could have inflicted the wounds. After examining Dr. Johnson's workup, Dr. Rawson stated that the methods Dr. Johnson used in gathering the evidence complied with the "standards of the American Board of Forensic Odontology."

    The Wisconsin Innocence Project accepted Stinson's case in 2005, and sought DNA testing of saliva and bloodstains on the victim's sweater, which ultimately excluded Stinson. On January 30, 2009, Stinson, then 44, was freed and his conviction was vacated.[1]

2. **Willie Jackson:** On May 26, 2006, Willie Jackson was exonerated after post-conviction DNA testing proved his innocence in a 1986 sexual assault case. He

---

[1]The Innocence Project – Know the Cases: Browse Profiles: Robert Lee Stinson, http:// www.innocence project.org/ Content/Robert_Lee_Stinson.php; *State v. Stinson*, 134 Wis. 2d 224, 228, 231, 397 N.W.2d 136, 137–38 (Ct. App. 1986).

had spent 17 years in prison for a crime he did not commit. At Jackson's trial, Dr. Robert Barsley, past president of the American Board of Forensic Odontology (ABFO) and the American Academy of Forensic Sciences (AAFS), told the jury that the bite marks on the victim matched Jackson, testifying: "My conclusion is that Mr. Jackson is the person who bit this lady." Ultimately, DNA evidence showed that it was Willie Jackson's brother, Milton Jackson, who attacked and raped the victim.[2]

3. **Roy Brown:** In January 2007, Roy Brown was exonerated of stabbing and strangling Sabina Kulakowski. He was convicted of her murder in January 1992 based on bite mark evidence which was the centerpiece of the prosecution's case against Brown. Kulakowski's body had been discovered with multiple bite marks on her back, arm and thigh, all of which board-certified ABFO Diplomate Dr. Edward Mofson[3] claimed matched Brown's teeth. Mofson testified to a "reasonable degree of dental certainty" that Brown's dentition was "entirely consistent" and "completely consistent" with all of the bite marks, noting that the bite marks depicted the absence of the same two teeth Brown was missing.

   15 years after the conviction, however, DNA testing performed on saliva stains left by the perpetrator excluded Brown and matched another suspect, Barry Bench. Nevertheless, citing the prosecution's bite mark evidence at the original trial, which the jury asked to review during deliberations, the judge in the case initially refused to release Brown. Ultimately, in January 2007, the district attorney acknowledged Brown's innocence and he was exonerated after spending 15 years in prison for a murder he did not commit.[4]

4. **Ray Krone:** On December 31, 1991, Ray Krone was arrested and charged with the murder, kidnapping, and sexual assault of a woman who worked at a bar he frequented. Police had a styrofoam impression made of Krone's teeth for comparison to bite marks found on the victim's body and, thereafter, he became known in the media as the "Snaggle Tooth Killer" due to his crooked teeth.

[2]The Innocence Project – Know the Cases: Browse Profiles: Willie Jackson, http://www.innocenceproject.org/ Content/Willie_Jackson.php; *Jackson v. Day*, No. Civ. A. 95–1224, 1996 WL 225021, at *1 (E.D. La. May 2, 1996), rev'd, 121 F.3d 705 (5th Cir. 1997); Barsley 1989 trial court testimony, transcript available at http://www.law. virginia.edu/pdf/faculty/garrett/innocence/jackson.pdf.
[3]All representations that the dentists at issue in this appendix were "board-certified ABFO Diplomates" are based on the American Board of Forensic Odontology Diplomate Information, available at http://www.abfo.org/wp-content/ uploads/2012/08/ABFO-Diplomate-Information-revised-November-2012.pdf.
[4]Fernando Santos, "In Quest for a Killer, an Inmate Finds Vindication," *New York Times* (Dec. 21, 2006), http://www. nytimes.com/2006/12/21/nyregion/21brown.html?pagewanted=all&_r=0; The Innocence Project – Know the Cases: Browse Profiles: Roy Brown, http://www.innocenceproject.org/Content/ Proven_Innocent_by_DNA_Roy_Brown_ Is_Fully_Exonerated.php; Brandon L. Garrett, Convicting the Innocent: Where Criminal Prosecutions Go Wrong 108–09 (Harvard University Press 2011); Mofson 1992 trial court testimony, transcript available at http://www.law.virginia.edu/pdf/faculty/ garrett/innocence/brown1.pdf; David Lohr, "Quest for Freedom: The True Story of Roy Brown," http:// www.trutv.com/library/crime/criminal_mind/forensics/ff311_roy_brown/5.html.

Dr. Raymond Rawson, a board-certified ABFO Diplomate, testified that the bite marks found on the victim's body matched Krone's teeth. Based on this, Krone was convicted of murder and kidnapping, and sentenced to death.

In 1996, Krone won a new trial on appeal, but was convicted again based mainly on the state's supposed expert bite mark testimony. This time, however, the judge sentenced him to life in prison, citing doubts about whether or not Krone was the true killer. It was not until 2002, after Krone had served more than ten years in prison, that DNA testing proved his innocence.[5]

5. **Calvin Washington & Joe Sidney Williams:** Calvin Washington was convicted of capital murder in 1987 after a woman was found beaten, raped, and murdered in Waco, Texas. It was alleged that Washington and Williams murdered and sexually assaulted the victim in the course of committing a burglary. Forensic dentist and former president of the American Academy of Forensic Sciences, and board-certified ABFO Diplomate Dr. Homer Campbell, testified that a bite mark found on the victim was "consistent with" Williams's dentition. While Campbell excluded Washington as the source of the bite mark, his bite mark testimony about Williams (which was given at Washington's trial) tied Washington to the crime.

After serving more than 13 years of this sentence, Washington was finally exonerated in 2000 when DNA testing showed that blood on a shirt found in Washington's home did not come from the victim, as previously asserted; testing conducted a year later pointed to another man as the perpetrator.[6] Prior to Washington's exoneration, the Texas Court of Criminal Appeals had set aside Williams's conviction in 1992 and charges against him were dismissed on June 30, 1993.

6. **James O'Donnell:** James O'Donnell was convicted in 1998 of attempted sodomy and second-degree assault. Board-certified ABFO Diplomate Dr. Harvey Silverstein opined that a bite mark on the victim's hand was consistent with O'Donnell's dentition. Based on the eyewitness identification and the bite mark evidence, and despite testimony from his wife and son that he had been at home with them when the crime occurred, the jury convicted O'Donnell. He was sentenced to three and a half to seven years in prison.

In 2000, after DNA samples from a rape kit excluded O'Donnell as the source of the semen found on the victim, his conviction was formally vacated.[7]

---

[5]The Innocence Project – Know the Cases: Browse Profiles: Ray Krone, http://www.innocenceproject.org/Content/ Ray_Krone.php.

[6]The Innocence Project – Know the Cases: Browse Profiles: Calvin Washington, http://www.innocenceproject.org/ Content/Calvin_Washington.php; Michael Hall, "The Exonerated," *Texas Monthly* (Nov. 2008), available at http:// www.texasmonthly.com/story/exonerated.

[7]The Innocence Project – Know the Cases: Cases Where DNA Revealed That Bite Mark Analysis Led to Wrongful Arrests and Convictions, http://www.innocenceproject.org/Content/Cases_Where_DNA_Revealed_that_Bite_Mark_*Analysis_Led_to_Wrongful_Arrests_and_Convictions.php*; Silverstein 1998 trial court testimony, *transcript available at* http://www.*law.virginia.edu/pdf/faculty/garrett/innocence/odonnell.pdf.*

7. **Levon Brooks:** Levon Brooks spent 16 years in prison for the rape and murder of a three-year-old girl that he did not commit. Board-certified ABFO Diplomate Dr. Michael West claimed that the marks on the victim's body were human bite marks and he testified at Brooks's trial that of 13 suspects whose bite marks he had compared to the ones on the victim's body, Brooks's teeth "matched" the marks on the victim. As he explained, "it could be no one but Levon Brooks that bit this girl's arm." Based on this, Brooks was convicted of capital murder and sentenced to life in prison.

In 2001, DNA testing and a subsequent confession revealed that Justin Albert Johnson committed the murder. Johnson had been one of the 12 other suspects whose dental impressions Dr. West had determined did not match the bite marks on the victim's body. Following Johnson's confession, Brooks was freed on February 15, 2008.[8]

8. **Kennedy Brewer:** In 1992, Kennedy Brewer was arrested in Mississippi and accused of killing his girlfriend's three-year-old daughter. The medical examiner who conducted the autopsy, Steven Hayne, testified that he had found several marks on the victim's body that he believed to be bite marks. Hayne called in board-certified ABFO Diplomate Dr. West to analyze the marks and Dr. West concluded that 19 marks found on the victim's body were "indeed and without a doubt" inflicted by Brewer. Brewer was convicted of capital murder and sexual battery on March 24, 1995, and sentenced to death. His conviction was based almost entirely on the bite mark evidence.

In 2001, DNA tests proved that Justin Albert Johnson, not Kennedy Brewer, committed the crime. Johnson was the same perpetrator responsible for murdering the child in the Levon Brooks case. In 2002, the prosecution intended to retry Brewer for capital murder, but for a full five years the case was not moved to trial. Brewer eventually spent five years in Noxumbee County jail. Due to conflicts of interest in the Noxubee County District Attorney's office, in 2007 Ben Creekmore, the District Attorney of Oxford, Mississippi, was appointed Special Prosecutor in the Brewer case. Creekmore decided not to seek the death penalty and agreed not to oppose bail. Brewer was released in August 2007 while a new trial was pending as Noxumbee County District Attorney Forrest Allgood still supported the bite mark evdence as proof of guilt. On February 15, 2008, charges against Kennedy Brewer were dropped and he was exonerated.[9]

9. **Bennie Starks:** Bennie Starks was convicted of raping and assaulting a 69-year-old woman in 1986, based in part on testimony by two forensic dentists, Drs. Russell Schneider and Carl Hagstrom. Both dentists, members of the AAFS, testified that a bite mark on the victim's shoulder matched Starks's dentition. Starks spent 20 years in prison before an appeals court ordered a new

[8]The Innocence Project – Know the Cases: Browse Profiles: Levon Brooks, http://www.innocence project.org/ Content/Levon_Brooks.php.
[9]The Innocence Project – Know the Cases: Browse Profiles: Kennedy Brewer, http://www.innocence project.org/ Content/Kennedy_Brewer.php.

trial, after DNA testing on semen recovered from the victim excluded Starks. On January 7, 2013, the district attorney dismissed all charges against Starks.[10]

10. **Douglas Prade:** Douglas Prade, a former Akron police captain, was convicted in 1998 of the murder of his ex-wife, Dr. Margo Prade, and sentenced to life in prison. The victim's body was discovered slumped behind the wheel of her car in her office parking lot. She had been shot six times and there was a bite mark on her arm. Dr. Thomas Marshall, a forensic dentist from Akron, Ohio, testified that the bite mark was an exact match to Mr. Prade's dentition. Another dentist, Dr. Lowell Levine, a board-certified ABFO Diplomate and past ABFO president, said that although he could not say with certainty that Prade had caused the bite mark, Prade's dentition was "consistent with" the bite mark on the victim.

   After DNA taken from the bite mark excluded him as a possible source, Prade was cleared of murder charges in January 2013. He had spent nearly 15 years in prison for the crime. Jurors in his original trial said they relied heavily on the bite mark evidence to convict Mr. Prade. One juror said, "[Prade] had crooked teeth and they fit right in, like a little puzzle. And it was just so exact."[11]

11. **Michael Cristini & Jeffrey Moldowan:** In 1991, Michael Cristini and Jeffrey Moldowan were convicted of the rape, kidnapping, and attempted murder of Moldowan's ex-girlfriend, Maureen Fournier. At trial, two board-certified ABFO Diplomates, Drs. Allan Warnick and Pamela Hammel, testified that bite marks on the victim's body had to have come from both defendants, to the exclusion of all others. Both men were convicted. Cristini was sentenced to 44 to 60 years, and Moldowan to 60 to 90 years.

---

[10]The Innocence Project – Innocence Blog: Bennie Starks Exonerated After 25 Year Struggle to Clear His Name, http://www.innocenceproject.org/Content/Bennie_Starks_Exonerated_After_25_Year_Str uggle_to_Clear_His_Nam e.php; Lisa Black, "Exonerated Man's Ordeal Ends: 'I Am Overwhelmed with Joy,'" *Chicago Tribune* (Jan. 7, 2013), http://articles.chicagotribune.com/2013-01-07/news/chi-bennie-starks-lake-county-charges-dropped_1_bennie- starks-mike-nerheim-ordeal-ends; Steve Mills, Chicago Trib, http://articles.chicagotribune.com/2011-12-25/news/ct-met-bitemark-lawsuit-20111225_ 1_bite-mark-evidence-wrongful-convictions-dna-evidence.

[11]Staff, Crimesider, "Douglas Prade, Former Ohio Police Captain, Exonerated in Ex-wife's Murder after Nearly 15 Years in Prison," CBSNews (Jan. 30, 2013), http://www.cbsnews.com/8301-504083_162-57566533-504083/douglas- prade-former-ohio-police-captain-exonerated-in-ex-wifes-murder-after-nearly-15-years-in-prison/; Rick Armon, Ed Meyer & Phil Trexler, "Former Akron Police Captain Douglas Prade Cleared in Murder, Released from Prison," *Akron Beacon Journal Online* (Jan. 30,2013),http://www.ohio.com/news/break-news/former-akron-police-captain-douglas-prade-cleared-in-murder-released-from-prison-1.368825; Ed Myer, "Former Prade Jurors Speak About Evidence Leading to 1998 Conviction," *Akron Beacon Journal Online* (Feb. 28, 2003), http://www.ohio.com/news/ local/former-prade-jurors-speak-about-evidence-leading-to-1998-conviction-1.377105; Dennis McEaneney, "Bite Evidence Lines Up: Forensic Dental Expert Testifies That Wound on Slain Doctor's Arm Matches Ex Husband's Lower Front Teeth," *Akron Beacon Journal Online* (Sept. 15, 1998), http://www. ohio.com/news/1998-trial-coverage-bite-evidence-lines-up-forensic-dental-expert-testifies-that-wound-on-slain-doctor-s-arm-matches-ex-husband-s-lower-front-teeth-every-mark-lined-up-akron-dentist-says-1.368882.

After the conviction, an investigator hired by the Moldowan family found a witness who said he had seen four black men standing around a naked woman at the scene of the crime. The witness's story contradicted Fournier's, as Cristini and Moldowan are both white. Dr. Hammel then recanted her testimony, saying that she had been uncertain that either defendant had in fact been responsible for the bite marks. According to Dr. Hammel, she had agreed to testify only when Dr. Warnick had assured her that a third odontologist had also confirmed that the bite marks could be matched to Cristini and Moldowan to the exclusion of all others.

On October 20, 2003, the Macomb County Circuit Court granted Cristini a new trial, citing the new eyewitness evidence, Dr. Hammel's recantation, and stronger alibi evidence. Cristini was acquitted by a jury on April 8, 2004, after having served 13 years in prison. Later, Cristini filed wrongful conviction lawsuits against the city of Warren, Macomb County, and Dr. Warnick. The suit against Dr. Warnick was settled quickly for an undisclosed amount.

In 2002, the Michigan Supreme Court reversed Moldowan's conviction. On retrial, in February 2003, Moldowan was acquitted of all charges and released, having served nearly 12 years in prison. Moldowan's lawsuit was settled for $2.8 million in 2011.[12]

12. **Anthony Keko:** Anthony Keko was convicted in 1994 for the 1991 murder of his estranged wife Louise Keko. Dr. Michael West, a board-certified ABFO Diplomate (at the time under a one-year suspension by the ABFO) testified that a bite mark on the victim's shoulder matched Anthony Keko's dentition. Dr. West's testimony was the only direct evidence linking Keko to the crime, and prosecutors conceded that without the bite mark evidence there was no case. Keko was found guilty and sentenced to life in prison. In December 1994, however, the trial judge became aware of previously undisclosed disciplinary proceedings against Dr. West. The judge began to express doubts regarding West's forensic abilities and ultimately reversed Keko's conviction.[13]

---

[12]*People v. Moldowan*, 466 Mich. 862, 643 N.W.2d 570 (2002); *Moldowan v. City of Warren*, 578 F.3d 351 (6th Cir. 2009); Ed White, "Warren Settles Rape Case Lawsuit for $2.8 Million – Falsely Imprisoned Man Sued for Violation of His Civil Rights," *Detroit Legal News* (Oct. 19, 2011). http://www.leg alnews.com/detroit/1109085; Jameson Cook, "Michael Cristini Wants Bigger Settlement than Jeffrey Moldowan," *Macomb Daily* (Dec. 25, 2012), http://www.macombdaily.com/article/20121225/NE-WS01/121229769/michael-cristini-wants-bigger-settlement- than-jeffrey-moldowan#full_story; Michael S. Perry, Exoneration Case Detail: Michael Cristini, Nat'l Registry of Exonerations, http://www.law.umich.edu/special/exoneration/Pages/casedetail.aspx?caseid=3133 (last visited Apr. 12, 2013); Hans Sherrer, "Prosecutor Indicted For Bribery After Two Men Exonerated of Kidnapping and Rape," *Justice: Denied*, no. 27, 2005, at 10, available at http://www.justicedenied.org/issue/issue_27/Moldow an_cristini_exonerated.html.

[13] "A Dentist Takes The Stand," The Daily Beast, (Aug. 19, 2001, 8:00 P.M.), http://www.thedailybea-st.com/newsweek/2001/08/20/a-dentist-takes-the-stand.html; Mark Hansen, "Out of the Blue," *ABA Journal* Feb. 1996, available at http://www.abajournal.com/magazine/article/out_of_the_blue/print/.

13. **Harold Hill & Dan Young Jr.:** Harold Hill was 16 when he and his codefendant, Dan Young, Jr., were convicted of the rape and murder of 39-year-old Kathy Morgan in 1990. Both men would end up spending 15 years in prison for a crime they did not commit. At trial, board-certified ABFO Diplomate and past ABFO president Dr. John Kenney linked a bruise and a bite mark on the victim's body to Hill and Young. Both were found guilty and sentenced to life in prison without parole. It wasn't until 2004 that DNA tests excluded both Hill and Young as the source of DNA evidence found on the victim. In 2005 prosecutors finally dismissed the charges against both men. Dr. Kenney later said that the prosecution pushed him to exaggerate his results.[14]

14. **Greg Wilhoit:** Greg Wilhoit's wife, Kathy, was murdered in Tulsa, Oklahoma in June 1985. Wilhoit was left to raise his two daughters—a 4 month old and a 1 year old. A year later, he was arrested and charged with the murder based on the opinions of two forensic odontologists that his dentition matched a bite mark on his wife's body. Wilhoit was found guilty and sentenced to death.

   During his appeal, other forensic odontologists examined the bite mark evidence and independently concluded that the bite mark could not be matched to Wilhoit. He was released on bail for two years and when a retrial was finally held in 1993 the judge issued a directed innocence verdict. In total, Wilhoit dealt with this tragedy for eight years, fighting a case built entirely on bite mark analysis. Wilhoit's story was documented by John Grisham in *The Innocent Man*.[15]

WRONGFUL ARRESTS BASED ON BITE MARK EVIDENCE

1. **Dale Morris, Jr.:** In 1997, Dale Morris, Jr. was arrested based on bite mark analysis matching his dentition to a mark found on a nine-year-old murder victim, Sharra Ferger. Morris was a neighbor to the little girl, who had been found stabbed, sexually assaulted, and bitten in a field near her Florida home. Board-certified ABFO Diplomates Dr. Richard Souviron and Dr. Kenneth Martin agreed that the bite marks on the girl were a probable match to Morris. Morris spent four months in jail until DNA tests proved his innocence. Highlighting the importance of the bite mark evidence to the police's decision to arrest Morris, Detective John Corbin said that Morris "was probably one of our least likely

---

[14]Ctr. on Wrongful Convictions, *Exoneration Case Detail: Harold Hill*, Nat'l Registry of Exonerations, http://www.law.umich.edu/special/exoneration/Pages/casedetail.aspx?caseid=3296 (last visited Apr. 12, 2013).

[15]Journey of Hope, Greg Wilhoit, CA, available at http://journeyofhope.org/who-we-are/exonerated-from-death-row/greg-wilhoit/; Witness to Innocence, Exonerees: Greg Wilhoit, available at http://www.witnesstoinnocence.org/exonerees/greg-wilhoit.html.

suspects in the neighborhood, but through the forensics that we conducted in the investigation he was linked to the crime."[16]

2. **Edmund Burke**: In 1998, Edmund Burke was arrested for raping and murdering a 75- year-old woman. The victim had bite marks on her breasts and board-certified ABFO Diplomate Dr. Lowell Levine, the same expert involved in Douglas Prade's case (discussed above), "formed an initial opinion that Burke could not be excluded as the source of the bite marks," but asked to see enhanced photos before rendering a final opinion. After examining the enhanced photos, Dr. Levine concluded that Burke's teeth matched the bite mark on the victim's left breast to a "reasonable degree of scientific certainty." DNA testing on saliva taken from the bite mark site excluded Burke as the source of the DNA, however, and prosecutors dropped the case against him. The true killer was later identified when DNA from the bite mark was matched to a profile in the national DNA database. Dr. Levine remains one of the few full-time forensic odontologists in the nation, and is regarded as one of the field's top practitioners.[17]

3. **Anthony Otero:** In 1994, Anthony Otero was charged with larceny and the first-degree murder and rape of a 60-year-old woman, Virginia Airasolo, in Detroit, Michigan. A warrant for Otero's arrest was issued after ABFO Diplomate Dr. Allan Warnick claimed to have matched the bite marks on the victim's body to Otero's dentition. At the preliminary hearing on December 13, 1994, Dr. Warnick testified that Otero was "the only person in the world" who could have caused the bite marks on Airasolo's body.

In January 1995, DNA testing excluded Otero as the source of the DNA found on the victim and he was released in April, after spending five months in jail. Following Otero's release, a second forensic odontologist, ABFO Diplomate Dr. Richard Souviron, concluded that the marks on the victim were consistent with human bite marks, but were too indistinct to be used to identify a suspect. Ultimately, the charges against Otero were dismissed.[18]

4. **Johnny Bourn:** In 1992, Johnny Bourn was arrested for the rape and murder of an elderly Mississippi man after board-certified ABFO Diplomate Dr. Michael West matched a bite mark on the victim to Bourn. Bourn was imprisoned for 18 months, despite hair and fingerprint evidence pointing to another suspect. Ultimately, Bourn was released when he was excluded as a suspect by DNA testing

---

[16]Ian James & Geoff Dougherty, "Suspect in Girl's Murder Freed after Four Months," *St. Petersburg Times*, Feb. 28, 1998, at 1.A, available at http://www.wearethehope.org/pdf/times_02_28_1998.pdf; Cases Where DNA Revealed That Bite Mark Analysis Led to Wrongful Arrests and Convictions, Innocence Project, supra note 7; Flynn McRoberts & Steve Mills, "From the Start, a Faulty Science," *Chicago Tribune* (Oct. 19, 2004), http://www.chicagotribune. com/news/watchdog/chi-041019forensics,0,7597688.story.

[17]*Burke v. Town of Walpole*, 405 F.3d 66, 73 (1st Cir. 2005).

[18]Cases Where DNA Revealed That Bite Mark Analysis Led to Wrongful Arrests and Convictions, Innocence, http://www.innocenceproject.org/Content/Cases_Where_DNA_Revealed_that_Bite_Mark_Analysis_Led_to_Wrongful_Arrests_and_Convictions.php

performed on fingernail scrapings from the victim, but not before he had spent about one and a half years in jail awaiting trial.[19]

5. **Dane Collins:** In 1989, Dane Collins was arrested and charged with the rape and murder of his 22-year-old stepdaughter, based largely on bite mark comparison evidence. The Sante Fe, New Mexico District Attorney declared his intent to seek the death penalty. Despite evidence that Collins could not produce sperm and therefore could not have been the perpetrator, the DA gave several public interviews stating that while there was not enough evidence to try the case, he believed Collins was guilty of the crime. Fifteen years later, Chris McClendon was matched to DNA found on the victim. He pled "no contest" to the crime in exchange for describing how he had committed the rape and murder. (McClendon was already serving life in prison after he was convicted of kidnapping and raping a 24-year-old woman).[20]

6. **Ricky Amolsch:** Ricky Amolsch's girlfriend, Jane Marie Fray, was found dead on August 23, 1994. She had been stabbed 22 times and had an electrical cord wrapped around her neck. The arrest warrant for Amolsch was based on a finding by board-certified ABFO Diplomate Dr. Allan Warnick that a bite mark that had been found on the victim's left ear was "highly consistent" with Amolsch's dentition. Charges were not dropped until 10 months later when the eyewitness who had identified Amolsch's van at the crime scene was himself arrested for raping another woman in the same trailer park. Amolsch was jailed for 10 months until his trial. During that time, he lost his home, savings, and children.[21]

---

[19]Hansen, *supra* note 13; "Michael West Responds," Part 167, *The Agitator* (March 1, 2009), http://www. theagitator. *com/page/167/*; Paul C. Giannelli & Kevin C. McMunigal, "Prosecutors, Ethics, and Expert Witnesses," 76 *Fordham Law Review* 1493 (2007).

[20]Jeremy Pawloski, "Suspect in '89 Slaying to Plead Guilty," *Albuquerque Journal* (Aug. 11, 2005), http://www.abqjournal. com/north/379728north_news08-11-05.htm.

[21]Bite Mark Evidence, Forensics Under Fire, Jim Fisher, The Official Website, http://jimfisher. edinboro.edu/ forensics/fire/mark.html (last updated Jan. 16, 2008); Katherine Ramsland, "Bite Marks as Evidence to Convict – Whose Bite Mark is it, Anyway?" Crime Library, TruTV.com, http://www. trutv.com/library/crime/criminal_mind/ forensics/bitemarks/5.html (last visited Apr. 12, 2013).

Legal Terminology

A

Abet Encouraging or inciting another to do a certain thing, such as commit a crime.

Absolute discharge The sentence of a person guilty of a crime in which the accused is deemed to have not been convicted.

Accomplice Person that aids, abets, advises, or encourages the commission of the crime.

Accusation The formal criminal charge against a person which specifies the essential ingredients in regards to the alleged offense such as time and place and the relevant reference to the criminal law allegedly breached.

Acquittal A verdict by a judge or jury that a criminal defendant is not guilty of a crime. In other words, the evidence is insufficient to support a conviction.

Administration of justice The personnel, activity, and structure of the justice system—courts and police—in the detection, investigation, apprehension, interviewing, and trial of persons suspected of a crime.

Admissible A term used to describe evidence that may be considered by a jury or judge in criminal cases.

Adversarial proceeding The format of U.S. courts where two disputing parties provide evidence to support each side of a controversy before a judge or magistrate.

Affiant The person who swears under oath to a notary public that his or her statements or documents are true.

Affidavit A written or printed statement made under oath.

Affirmed A court of appeals procedure that means that the higher court has concluded that the lower court decision is correct and considered approved.

Alibi A defense to a criminal charge that argues the accused was elsewhere than at the scene of the crime at the time the crime was committed.

Amicus curiae Latin for "friend of the court." It is most often unsolicited advice given to a trial judge in appeals court or Supreme Court by a person or organization interested in, but not involved in, a dispute.

Amnesty A general pardon extended by the government to those persons facing prosecution for or convicted of the specified criminal offenses.

Answer The defendant's response to a plaintiff's complaint. The answer admits or denies the claims contained in the plaintiff's complaint.

Appeal A request made after a trial by a party that has lost one or more issues for a higher court to review the decision and determine if it was correct. To make such a request is to "appeal" or "to take and appeal." One who appeals is called the "appellant," the other party is the "appellee."

Appellant The side that lost in trial court and has filed an appeal. Sometimes called the petitioner.

Appellee The side in a trial that won in the court decision, and whose victory is being appealed by the losing side. Also called the respondent.

Arraignment A proceeding in which a criminal defendant is brought into court, told of the charges in an indictment, and asked to plead guilty or not guilty.

B

Bail The release, prior to trial, of a person accused of a crime under specified conditions designed to assure that person's appearance in court when required. Also can refer to the amount of bond money posted as a financial condition of pretrial release.

Bar General term referring to a membership of licensed attorneys.

Battery Offensive and intentional contact, direct or indirect, which causes injury.

Bench A term used to refer to judges or the court; for example, "please approach the bench" refers to approaching the judge.

Bench trial A trial without a jury in which the judge serves as the fact finder.

Beyond a reasonable doubt The standard in a criminal case that must be met by the prosecution in order to convict the defendant. It means the evidence is fully satisfied, all the facts are proven, and guilt is established.

Brady rule The suppression by the prosecution upon request of evidence favorable to the accused violates due process where the evidence is material either to guilt or punishment.

Brief A written statement submitted in a trial or appellate proceeding that explains one side's legal and factual arguments.

Burden of proof The duty to prove disputed facts. In civil cases, a plaintiff generally has the burden of proving his or her case. In criminal cases, the government has the burden of proving the defendant's guilt. If the proof is insufficient, the contrary will be assumed by the court.

C

Capital crime A criminal offense for which the punishment, or one of the punishments, is death (capital punishment).

Case law The law as established in previous court decisions. A synonym for legal precedent. A series of legal decisions that determine court rules and judicial opinion.

Causation The cause and effect relationship between an act or omission and damages alleged in a tort or personal injury action.

Character evidence Information regarding past acts and legal record of a defendant or witness asked to testify about a person involved in the litigation. The weight of this evidence of a person's character may be positive or negative.

Circumstantial evidence Evidence which may allow a judge or jury to deduce a certain fact from other facts which have been proven.

Common law Judge-declared law; the legal system that originated in England and is now in use in the United States, which uses legal decisions based on precedence. Common law decisions can be altered or vacated by legislation.

Commutation The reduction of a sentence by the government.

Complicity Accountable for a criminal offense committed by another due to previous knowledge of the crime.

Concurrent sentence Prison terms for two or more offenses to be served at the same time, rather than one after the other. For example, multiple concurrent sentences of 2, 3, and 4 years results in a total time of incarceration of 4 years.

Confrontation clause The constitutional guarantee in the Sixth Amendment to the United States Constitution which requires that an accused person have the right to be confronted with the witnesses against him.

Consecutive sentence Prison terms for two or more offenses to be served one after the other. For example, multiple consecutive convictions of 2, 3, and 4 years results in 9 years of incarceration.

Contempt of court Conduct that is disobedient, obstructive, or contemptuous to the court.

Counsel Legal advice, a term also used to refer to the lawyers in a case.

Count When a criminal defendant is charged with multiple crimes, each alleged crime is called a count.

Crime Conduct that is prohibited and has a specific punishment (such as incarceration or a fine) prescribed by public law.

Criminal code A statute which sets out all prohibited or criminal offenses and their various punishments.

Criminal law Public law that deals with crimes, their prosecution, and their defenses.

D

Deceit Willful or reckless misrepresentation or concealment of material facts with an intent to mislead.

Defendant The person or business against whom a lawsuit is filed.

De jure Latin, meaning "in law." Something that exists by operation of law.

De novo Latin, meaning "new." Refers to trials *de novo*, which are new trials that have no relation to any previous judicial proceedings.

Deposition An oral statement made under oath for the purposes of questioning the witness in order to obtain information about and answers to matters relating to litigation.

Directed verdict This is when the court stops a trial upon determining that an essential fact has not been proven.

Discharge The sentence of a person found guilty of a crime in which that person does not receive a criminal record of conviction, either absolutely or conditionally.

Discovery Procedures used to obtain disclosure of evidence before trial.

Dismissal with prejudice Court action that prevents an identical lawsuit from being filed later.

Dismissal without prejudice Court action that allows later filing of the same complaint, be it criminal or civil.

Docket A log containing the complete history of each case in the form of brief chronological entries summarizing the court proceedings.

Double-blind photographic presentation The presentation of an array of photos to a crime victim by an officer neither involved in the investigation nor aware of who the suspect is for the purposes of identifying the perpetrator.

Double jeopardy A prohibition against being tried or sentenced twice for the same offense.

Due process clauses The Fourth and Fourteenth Amendments in the U.S. Constitution assure a fair and impartial trial, and prohibit the government from depriving a person of life, liberty, or property without due process of law.

Dying declaration Exception to the hearsay rule: A statement of fact made by a dying victim relating to the cause and circumstances of a homicide.

E

Eighth Amendment A U.S. Constitution amendment that prohibits "excessive bail (or) fines (and) cruel and unusual punishment … "

Empanel Also "impanel"; the official call to duty of a jury, usually as called by the clerk of the court in which the jury is to act, just before the jurors are sworn in.

En banc French, meaning "on the bench." All judges of an appellate court sitting together to hear a case, as opposed to the routine complement of three judges.

Evidence Something (such as testimony, writings, or objects) presented at a judicial or administrative proceeding for the purpose of establishing the truth or falsity of an alleged matter of fact.

Exclusionary rule Rules of evidence that exclude or suppress evidence one party wishes to admit into the court record; a rule of evidence that excludes or suppresses evidence obtained in violation of a defendant's constitutional rights.

Exculpate That which excuses from fault or justifies a wrong action.

Ex parte A proceeding brought before a court by one party only, without notice to or challenge by the other side.

Expert testimony Testimony given regarding some scientific, technical, or professional matter by experts; i.e., persons qualified to speak authoritatively by reason of their special training, skill, or knowledge.

Expunge To remove permanently; to cancel.

F

Federal public defender An attorney employed by the federal courts on a full-time basis to provide legal defense to defendants who are unable to afford counsel. The judiciary administers the federal defender program pursuant to the Criminal Justice Act.

Federal Rules of Evidence Rules which govern the admissibility of evidence at trials in the Federal District Courts and before Federal Magistrates. Most U.S. states have adopted evidence rules patterned on these federal rules.

Federal question jurisdiction Jurisdiction given to federal courts in cases involving the interpretation and application of the U.S. Constitution, acts of congress, interstate commerce, and foreign treaties.

Felony Crimes that have a greater punishment imposed by statute than that imposed for a misdemeanor.

Fifth Amendment A U.S. Constitution article which provides fundamental rights in regards to legal process such as immunity to self-incrimination.

File To place a paper in the official custody of the clerk of court to enter into the files or records of a case.

Fruit of the poisonous tree doctrine Bars the admission of physical evidence and live testimony obtained directly or indirectly through the exploitation of unconstitutional police conduct.

G

Grand jury An American criminal justice procedure whereby, in each court district, a group of 16-23 citizens hold an inquiry on criminal complaints brought by the prosecutor and decide if a trial is warranted, in which case an indictment is issued. Also see: **Indictment**.

Guilty verdict A verdict convicting a criminal defendant of a charge or charges. When a verdict of guilty is returned, the court orders a separate hearing in order to determine punishment.

H

Habeas corpus Latin, meaning "you have the body." A writ of habeas corpus generally is a judicial order forcing law enforcement authorities to produce a prisoner they are holding, and to justify the prisoner's continued confinement. Federal judges receive petitions for a writ of *habeas corpus* from state prison inmates who say their state prosecutions violated federally protected rights in some way.

Hearsay A statement made by a witness who did not see or hear the incident in question, but heard about it from someone else. It is also called hearsay evidence, and is generally inadmissible and excluded from the court record. There are exceptions to excluding this type of evidence.

Hung Jury A jury which is unable to arrive at a required unanimous or near unanimous verdict.

I

Immunity An exemption that a person enjoys from the normal operation of the law such as a legal duty or liability, either criminal or civil.

Impeachment 1. The process of calling a witness's testimony into doubt. For example, if the attorney can show that the witness may have fabricated portions of his testimony, the witness is said to be "impeached"; 2. The constitutional process whereby the U.S. House of Representatives may "impeach" (accuse of misconduct) high officers of the federal government, who are then tried by the U.S. Senate.

In absentia In Latin, meaning "in the absence." When a defendant is not present for a hearing or trial. The proceedings continue to conclusion despite this abscence.

In camera Latin, meaning "in a judge's chambers." Often means outside the presence of a jury and the public, i.e., in private.

Inculpatory evidence Evidence indicating that a defendant did commit the crime.

Indictment The formal charge issued by a grand jury that states that there is enough evidence that the defendant committed the crime to justify having a trial; it is used primarily for felonies.

Ineffective assistance In U.S. constitutional law, grounds for reversing a criminal law judicial determination where relevant legal advice was deficient and prejudicial.

Insanity A defendant's lack of ability to understand the nature, circumstances, and facts of the case against him. It is used in criminal court as a defense. It prevents the defendant from having the mental capacity required by law to be competent to stand trial. This must be determined by psychological evaluations and a special hearing.

Interrogatories A form of discovery consisting of written questions to be answered in writing and under oath.

Involuntary manslaughter A criminal offense contingent on language in any given jurisdiction; but, generally, the unlawful killing of a human being without malice in the commission of an unlawful act or in the commission of an act which might produce death in an unlawful manner or without due caution and circumspection.

Issue 1. The disputed point between parties in a lawsuit; 2. To send out officially, as in a court issuing an order.

J

Judicial misconduct Conduct on the part of a judge that is prohibited and which could lead to a form of discipline.

Jurisdiction The legal authority of a court to hear and decide a certain type of case. It also is used as a synonym for venue, meaning the geographic area over which the court has territorial jurisdiction to decide cases. Local and federal courts have specific statutes determining which court has authority over criminal and civil issues.

Jury A group of citizens randomly selected from the general population and brought together to assist justice by deciding what, in their opinion, constitutes "the truth" when given different evidence by opposing parties.

Jury instructions A judge's directions to the jury before it begins deliberations regarding the factual questions it must answer and the legal rules that it must apply.

Jury nullification The extraordinary power of a jury to issue a verdict contrary to the law as applied to the proven facts of a trial.

Justifiable homicide An answer or defense to an allegation of wrongful conduct that the act or omission, though admittedly committed, was not wrongful in the circumstances.

L

Litigation A case, controversy, or lawsuit. Participants (plaintiffs and defendants) in lawsuits are called litigants. In criminal trials, the state represents the "people" of the state against the criminal defendant.

M

Magistrate judge A judicial officer of a district court who conducts initial proceedings in criminal cases, decides criminal misdemeanor cases, conducts many pretrial civil and criminal matters on behalf of district judges, and decides civil cases with the consent of the parties.

Mens rea Latin, meaning "mental state or mental awareness." A mental state or capability defined as someone showing intent or knowledge of the nature of the criminal act they are accused of committing.

Miranda admonishment A requirement that police officers in the United States, before any questioning begins, must warn suspects upon arrest that they have the right to remain silent, that any statement that they make could be used against them in a court of law, that they have the right to contact a lawyer, and that if they cannot afford a lawyer, one will be provided.

Miscarriage of justice A substantial wrong that occurs during a trial which so infects the proceedings as to merit quashing the result on appeal.

Misdemeanor A crime that carries less punishment than a felony. By definition, it is a crime punishable by a fine and a term of imprisonment not to be served in a penitentiary and not to exceed one year.

Mistrial An invalid trial, caused by fundamental error. When a mistrial is declared, the trial must start again with the selection of a new jury.

Mitigating circumstances Facts that, while not negating a wrongful action, tend to show that the defendant may have had some grounds for acting the way he or she did.

Modus operandi Latin, meaning "method of operation"; often used to address the manner in which a crime was committed.

Moot Not subject to a court ruling because the controversy either has not actually arisen or has ended.

Motion A request by a litigant to a judge for a decision on an issue relating to the case.

Motion in limine A pretrial motion requesting that the court prohibit the other side from presenting, or even referring to, evidence on matters said to be so highly prejudicial that no steps taken by the judge can prevent the jury from being unduly influenced. "In limine" is Latin, meaning "at the start."

Motion to strike A motion put to the court to strike (aka not allow into the court record or allow judge to consider during their deliberations) the plea or evidence of a witness.

Motive The intent or purpose behind an act that is considered a crime.

Murder The crime of unlawfully and unjustifiably killing a human being.

N

Nolo contendere Latin, meaning "I will not defend." No contest. A plea of *nolo contendere* has the same effect as a plea of guilty as far as the criminal sentence is concerned, but may not be considered an admission of guilt for any other purpose.

O

Opening statement A lawyer or litigant's initial remarks at trial to the finder of fact, either a judge or jury, setting out their road-map or case theory.

Opinion A judge's written explanation of the decision of the court. Because a case may be heard by three or more judges in the court of appeals, the opinion in appellate decisions can take several forms. If all the judges completely agree on the result, one judge will write the opinion for all. If all the judges do not agree, the formal decision will be based upon the view of the majority, and one member of the majority will write the opinion. The judges who did not agree with the majority may write separately in dissenting or concurring opinions to present their views. A dissenting opinion disagrees with the majority opinion because of the reasoning and/or the principles of law the majority used to decide the case. A concurring opinion agrees with the decision of the majority opinion, but offers further comment or clarification or even an entirely different reason for reaching the same result. Only the majority opinion can serve as binding precedent in future cases.

P

Panel 1. In appellate cases, a group of judges (usually three) assigned to decide the case; 2. In the jury selection process, the group of potential jurors; 3. The list of attorneys who are both available and qualified to serve as court-appointed counsel for criminal defendants who cannot afford their own counsel.

Pardon A government decision to free a person who has been convicted of a crime and absolve him or her of that conviction, as if never convicted.

Plea In a criminal case, the defendant's statement that pleads "guilty" or "not guilty" in answer to the charges. See also *nolo contendere*.

Plea bargaining Negotiations during a criminal trial in which the accused agrees to admit to a smaller crime in exchange for the prosecutor asking for a more lenient sentence than would have been recommended if the original charge had been proceeded with.

Pleadings Written statements filed with the court that describe a party's legal or factual assertions about the case.

Police interrogation Questioning put to an accused person by the police with the purpose of eliciting a statement.

Precedent A court decision in an earlier case with facts and legal issues similar to a dispute currently before a court. Judges will generally "follow precedent," meaning that they use the principles established in earlier cases to decide new cases that have similar facts and which raise similar legal issues. A judge will disregard precedent if a party can show that the earlier case was wrongly decided or that it differed in some significant way from the current case.

Preemptory challenge A party's challenge of a prospective juror for which no reason or justification need be given.

Premeditation The defendant intended to commit an illegal act for some time before it occurred. It is often described as "planning ahead."

Preponderance of the evidence A measure of proof of evidence or culpability that is defined by a certainty of 51%. The evidence meeting this standard is commonly used in civil court.

Presumption of innocence A legal presumption that benefits a defendant in a criminal case, and which results in acquittal in the event that the prosecutor does not prove guilt beyond a reasonable doubt.

Procedure The rules for conducting a lawsuit; there are rules of civil procedure, criminal procedure, evidence, bankruptcy, and appellate procedure.

Pro se Latin, meaning "for himself." Representing oneself; serving as one's own lawyer.

Prosecute To charge someone with a crime. A prosecutor tries a criminal case on behalf of the government.

Prosecutorial discretion Discretionary powers exercised by the government's prosecution service such as whether to prosecute a charge recommended by police, stay an ongoing proceeding, plea bargain, or take over a private prosecution.

Public defender A lawyer who usually holds a governmental position, or is appointed by a court to represent criminal defendants unable to pay for legal assistance.

R

Record A written account of the proceedings in a case, including all pleadings, evidence, and exhibits submitted in the course of the case.

Reasonable doubt A legal conclusion required for all proof or evidence used to convict a defendant. After fair and thorough consideration of the evidence, there is no doubt that either the evidence or the guilt is faulty or incorrect. The criminal defense focuses on presenting evidence or opinions that indicate that the prosecution's case fails to reach this level of certainty.

Remand Send back.

Reverse The act of a court setting aside the decision of a lower court. A reversal is often accompanied by a remand to the lower court for further proceedings.

S

Sanction A penalty or other type of enforcement used to bring about compliance with the law or with rules and regulations.

Search and seizure Law enforcement recovering property or evidence from an individual must follow rules that are established by the U.S. Constitution, statutes, and case law to protect against illegal searches and seizures.

Search warrant A court order that gives police the permission to enter private property and search for evidence of the commission of a crime, for the proceeds of crime, or for property that the police suspect may be used to commit a crime.

Sentence The punishment ordered by a court for a defendant convicted of a crime.

Sequester To separate. Sometimes juries are sequestered from outside influences during their deliberations.

Standard of proof Degree of proof required. In criminal cases, prosecutors must prove a defendant's guilt "beyond a reasonable doubt." The majority of civil lawsuits require proof "by a preponderance of the evidence" (50% certainty or more), but in some the standard is higher and requires "clear and convincing" proof.

Statute of limitations The time within which a lawsuit must be filed or a criminal prosecution begun. The deadline can vary, depending on the type of civil case or the crime charged.

Speedy trial A trial must be conducted according to prevailing rules and procedures, and take place without unreasonable or undue delay as determined by statute. This right can be waived by the defendant.

Subpoena A command, issued under a court's authority, to a witness to appear and give testimony.

Subpoena duces tecum A command to a witness to appear and produce documents.

Suppressed evidence The intentional nondisclosure by the prosecution of evidence favorable to the accused and asked for by the accused, where that evidence is material either to guilt or punishment.

T

Testimony Verbal evidence furnished by a witness under oath at trial via written affidavit or transcribed deposition.

Transcript A written, word-for-word record of what was said, either in a proceeding such as a trial, or during some other formal conversation, such as a hearing or oral deposition.

Toll The time limit for a crime to be charged can be extendend (tolled) in certain legal circumstances. See **Statute of limitations**.

W

Witness a person possessing information of judicial interest who testifies under oath at the proceedings.

Index

Note: Page numbers with "f" denote figures; "t" tables; "b" boxes.